SPEAK CANTONESE
BOOK I

Parker Po-fei Huang

Gerard P. Kok

Revised Edition

D1601635

FAR EASTERN PUBLICATIONS

YALE UNIVERSITY

NEW HAVEN, CONNECTICUT

Reprinted, August, 1978

PREFACE

For almost twenty years, Speak Cantonese Book I has been used
by men and women in the armed forces and the foreign service, by
missionaries serving as doctors, nurses, or evangelists, and more
recently by students and scholars. Its every use brings it a new
significance, and I have always deeply felt that I am vicariously
with them in their work while they are using Cantonese learned
through this and the other books of the series. This has been a
source of great pleasure to me.

I have had the idea of revising Book I ever since I went to
Hong Kong in 1963-64, but I have not been able to do it until this
summer. It is a tough job, but I think this is the only way for
me to show my appreciation for its acceptance by so many readers
over such a long period.

I would like to mention a few people who have helped me to go
through the revising job more easily: Mr. Gerald P. Kok, the co-
author of the original edition gave me his full consent to revise
as I felt neccessary, Mr. Toshio Kono arranged the publication, and
Mr. Peter Sargent assisted in the editing and did the proofreading.

It's a great relief to see the book safely through what has
been a rather major operation. With all the energy, help, and
good will that have been put into it, I hope it will last for a
while.

                                        Parker Po-fei Huang

INTRODUCTION

This book is a beginning text in spoken Cantonese. It covers the basic sentence patterns of the spoken language within a vocabulary of 700 items. The book parallels Speak Chinese, a Mandarin text by Mr. M. Gardner Tewksbury; its use can facilitate the transition from one dialect to the other in either direction.

The lessons comprise the following study material for the students:

1. Dialogue or Narrative
2. Vocabulary
3. Pattern sentences
4. Additional sentences
5. Translation exercises

Each lesson calls for eight to ten contact hours with an instructor plus an equal amount of individual study. In learning to speak a language, as much time as possible should be spent with the native speaker and with recordings when available. If the demand for this text justifies, a set of tape recordings will be prepared to accompany it.

Each teacher will have his own plan as to how to present the lesson. The following outline is suggested from the experience of teaching Cantonese at the Institute of Far Eastern Languages at Yale University.

Dialogue or Narrative. These are live situations placed in as natural a setting as possible. The instructor reads the dialogue or narrative to the class in a normal conversational manner and at normal speed, watching for signs of comprehension or of failure to understand. This may be followed by drawing the story out of the class in English and piecing it together. The teacher may read it through a second time with occasional stops to ask a student to translate as a check on comprehension. This method of introduction is most effective after completing the first unit of six lessons.

Vocabulary. Each new term introduced, except nouns, will be illustrated by a phrase or a sentence for drill purposes. The instructor should avoid merely asking the meaning of a given vocabulary item. Additional examples may be made up by the instructor but he should be careful to avoid meanings and uses for words not already covered.

Pattern Sentences. This is the most important section of the lesson. The sentences under each heading should be practiced until they become not only correct in pronunciation and rhythm, but automatic. These patterns and at least two or three of the illustrative sentences which follow should be memorized. In drilling the pattern sentence the teacher should first make certain that the student can repeat the sentences after him with ease. This can be followed with a question/answer drill. A variation to this drill is for the teacher to make a statement to which the student forms a question. If the pattern involves an activity, ask the student to do something, before he carries out the action ask him what he is going to do, after he has completed his action ask him what he did. This type of drill can only be used after Lesson 12.

Additional Sentences. This part of the lesson gives further illustrations of the patterns and the vocabulary introduced, it also reviews some of the patterns learned in earlier lessons. The teacher should add to this section and make it a point to work out a systematic review. For instance when studying Lesson 15, the teacher in reviewing may emphasize materials studied in Lessons 5 and 10; when studying Lesson 16, Review 6 and 11, etc.

Translation Exercises. A few sentences in English are given at the end of each lesson which the student should translate and bring to class. The teacher, in going over the sentences, should make certain the student understands the mistakes he has made so he can forestall repetition of the error. To gain additional practice translating from English to Cantonese the student should turn to the Pattern Section, cover up the Cantonese and translate the English sentences. After completing a page he can check his results immediately by referring to the Cantonese.

We assume that a spoken language should be learned from a native speaker rather than from a text alone. In the practice of the Institute of Far Eastern Languages at Yale University, sound recordings are used to supplement the teacher but never to displace him. Below are some suggested Do's and Don'ts in classroom procedures.

Teacher

1. Don't read the sentences. Get the sentence in mind first; then say it naturally and at normal speed. Don't slow down.

2. Have the student imitate you as closely as possible, then repeat after the student so that he will hear the correct pronunciation both before and after he has said a sentence. This is particularly important at the beginning.

3. Avoid introducing new words. To do this you must familiarize yourself thoroughly with the vocabulary range and patterns introduced.

4. Keep reviewing vocabulary and patterns from earlier lessons.

5. Use as little English in class as possible.

Student

1. Hear it, repeat it. It is best to approach new expressions by hearing them spoken before attempting to say them.

2. Mimic the teacher. Keep your eyes on him. Use your text only to jog your memory.

3. Don't learn words in isolation, memorize the sample sentence given with the word.

4. Be sure to memorize at least two sentences for each pattern presented. Memory work is essential to language study. The speech habits of a foreign language must be made

habit of the student, just as his native
speech habits are. Do your memory work in
short stretches, with other types of work
between. The easiest way to remember is with
time-spaced repetition.

5. Avoid English. Say it in Cantonese if at all
possible.

Description of Sounds of Cantonese

Cantonese refers to the dialects as spoken in Canton
City but includes also a whole group of similar dialects
spoken in the area of the Western half of Kwangtung province and Southern half of Kwangsi province. This text
uses the dialect spoken in Canton City as its standard.
However, even in Canton City there are certain variants.
The primary variants are non-distinction of the initial
l and *n*, and the dropping of the initial *ng*. In this
text, we shall follow the majority of speakers who distinguish these sounds.

1. <u>Initials</u> A syllable in Chinese is made up of three
elements: (1) an initial, or the beginning
sound, (2) a final, the ending of a syllable, (3) a tone,
which may be regarded as characterizing the whole syllable.
Below is a list of initials with examples in English when
feasible. Notice particularly the distinction between
the aspirated and unaspirated groups. The aspirated group
is similar to the aspirates in English, such as *p*ill, *t*ill,
*k*ill, *ch*ill and *qu*ill, except there is a stronger puff of
breath as you pronounce the initials. In contrast to
these are the unaspirated initials which are similar to *p*,
t, *k* in such English words as s*p*ill, s*t*ill and s*k*ill.
These sounds do not have a puff of air, and are not voiced
such as the *b*, *d*, *g* sounds in *b*ill, *d*ill and *g*ill in English. The initials *j*, *ch*, *s* should be pronounced without
protruding the lips.

Aspirated Stops

Symbol	As In	IPA
p	u*p*hill	p'
t	an*t*hill	t'
k	roc*k*hill	k'
ch	between it's *h*igh and reac*h*high	tʃ'
kw	as*kw*hy	k'w

Unaspirated Stops

Symbol	As In	IPA
b	s*p*ill	p
d	s*t*ill	t
g	s*k*īll	k
j	between *j*udge and a*dd*s	tʃ
gw	s*qu*ill	kw

Nasals

Symbol	As In	IPA
m	*m*a	m
n	*n*o	n
ng	si*ng*	ŋ

x

Fricative and Continuants

Symbol	As In	IPA
f	*f*ar	f
l	*l*ay	l
h	*h*oe	h
s	between *s*he and *s*ee	ʃ

Semi-vowels

Symbol	As In	IPA
y	*y*et	j
w	*w*et	w

2. **Finals** A final is composed of a main vowel with or without a consonant or semi-vowel as an ending. The vowels in Cantonese may be either long or short and the ending may be pronounced weakly or strongly according to whether the vowel is long or short. Thus *aai* has a long *a* and a weak *i*, while *ai* has a short *a* and a strong *i*. Endings *p*, *t*, *k*, whether they follow a strong or a weak vowel, are pronounced without any puff of breath, such as the *p* in the English word *stop* when pronounced without opening the lips. Below is a Table of Finals.

FINALS

	a long	a short	e long	e short	eu long	eu short	i long	i short	o long	o short	u long	u short	yu long	yu short
	a		e		eu		i		o		u		yu	
	aai	ai		ei		eui	iu		oi	ou	ui			
	aau	au												
	aam	am					im							
	aan	an				eun	in		on		un		yun	
	aang	ang	eng		eung			ing	ong			ung		
	aap	ap					ip							
	aat	at				eut	it		ot		ut		yut	
	aak	ak	ek		.euk			ik	ok			uk		

3. <u>Tones</u> The pronunciation of every Chinese syllable involves in conjunction with the vowel and consonant elements, a pitch contour of a definite character called the tone. Cantonese has three main contours with two levels of pitch. The pitch will vary relatively to the range of the speaker's voice. The qualities of the three main contours are falling, rising and level. Each has an upper and a lower register, making six tones altogether. In addition there is a high level tone which occurs less frequently. The following diacritics are used to distinguish the tones: falling *à*, rising *á*, high-level *ā*, and level *a* with no diacritical mark. For distinction between upper and lower registers the letter *h* is used after the vowel when it occurs. Thus, *dou, faan, bong, hai* are in the upper register, while *dough, faahn, bohng, haih* are in the lower register. Most words beginning with *m, n,* and *ng,* are in the lower register group and the *h* will not be used as an indicator. In the rare instance when a word beginning with *m, n, ng* is in the upper range it will be underlined, such as *néui* is low rising, while *néui* is high rising

In Cantonese every syllable retains practically the same tone values whether it stands alone or is pronounced in conjunction with another syllable. The only exception is when two high falling tones follow each other, the first becomes high level. For example, *sìnsàang* 'gentleman' is actually pronounced *sīnsàang.*

The following is a diagram of the tones in Cantonese.

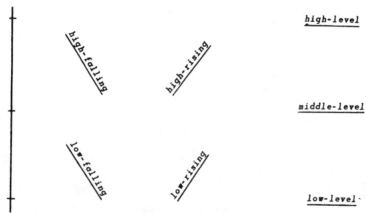

Verticle line indicates the range of the speaker's voice which may total about six musical notes of the scale.

The comparative chart of sounds and tones below is given to facilitate the use of ·the Student's Cantonese-English Dictionary in characters by Bernard F. Meyer and Theodore F. Wempe, Field Afar Press, 1947, Maryknoll, New York.

COMPARATIVE CHART - Initials

Yale	Meyer-Wempe	IPA
p	p'	p'
b	p	p̣
t	t'	ṭ'
d	t	t
k	k'	k'
g	k	k
ch	ch', ts'	tʃ'
j	ch, ts	tʃ
kw	k'w	k'w
gw	kw	kw
m	m	m
n	n	n
ng	ng	ŋ
f	f	f
l	l	l
h	h	h
s	s, sh	ʃ
y	i, y	j
w	oo, w	w

COMPARATIVE CHART - Finals

Yale	Meyer-Wempe	IPA
a	a	a:
aai	aai	a:i
aau	aau	a:u
aam	aam	a:m
aap	aap	a:p
aan	aan	a:n
aat	aat	a:t
aang	aang	a:ŋ
aak	aak	a:k

COMPARATIVE CHART - Finals (Cont'd.)

Yale	Meyer-Wempe	IPA
ai	ai	ai
au	au	au
am	am, om	am
ap	ap, op	ap
an	an	an
at	at	at
ang	ang	aŋ
ak	ak	ak
e	e	ɛ:
eng	eng	ɛ:ŋ
ek	ek	ɛ:k
ei	ei	ei
eu	oeh	oe:
eung	eung	oe:ŋ
euk	euk	oe:k
eui	ui	oei
eun	un	oen
eut	ut	oet
i	i	i:
iu	iu	i:u
im	im	i:m
ip	ip	i:p
in	in	i:ŋ
it	it	i:t
ing	ing	iŋ
ik	ik	ik
o	oh	o
oi	oi	o:i
on	on	o:n
ot	ot	o:t
ong	ong	o:ŋ
ok	ok	o:k
ou	o	ou

COMPARATIVE CHART - Finals (Cont'd.)

Yale	Meyer-Wempe	IPA
u	oo	u
ui	ooi	u:i
un	oon	u:n
ut	oot	u:t
ung	ung	u:ŋ
uk	uk	u:k
yu	ue	y:
yun	uen	y:n
yut	uet	y:t

COMPARATIVE CHART - Tones

Yale			Meyer-Wempe
high falling	à	a	upper even
high rising	á	á	upper rising
middle level	a, at	à àt	upper going middle entering
high level	ā, āt	a at	upper even upper entering
low falling	àh	ā	lower even
low rising	áh	ǎ	lower rising
low level	ah, aht	â ât	lower going lower entering

In Cantonese there is a variation between the reading tones of certain characters and the spoken tone. The Meyer-Wempe system of tones does not show this variation and therefore it will be noted above that the Yale system has one additional tone listed. This is the high-level tone, (ā, āt). Most of these variations involve words listed by Meyer-Wempe under the upper even and upper entering groups. For example:

	Yale	Meyer-Wempe
watch	bīu	piu
gun	chēung	ts'eung
north	bāk	pak
one	yāt	yat

April, 1960   Gerard P. Kok

CONTENTS

xviii

GRAMMATICAL NOTATIONS

A	adverb	Ph	phrase
Att	attributive	PN	pronoun
AV	auxiliary verb	PV	postverb
BF	boundform	PW	placeword
CV	coverb	QW	question word
EV	equative verb	RV	resultative verb
IE	idiomatic expression	RVE	resultative ending
M	measure	SP	specifier
MA	movable adverb	SV	stative
N	noun	TW	timeword
NU	number	V	verb (functive verb)
P	particle	VO	verb-object compound
Patt	pattern		

DESCRIPTIVE SENTENCES - - QUESTIONS AND ANSWERS

Conversation

1. A: Néi hóu ma?   How are you?
   B: Ngó hóu. Néi hóu ma?   I'm fine. How are you?
   A: Ngó hóu hóu!   I am very well.

2. A: Ngó gòu ma?   Am I tall?
   B: Néi m̀gòu.   You're not tall.
   A: Kéuih gòu ma?   Is he tall?
   B: Kéuih hóu gòu.   He's very tall.
   A: Néi gòu ma?   Are you tall?
   B: Ngó taai gòu.   I'm too tall.

3. A: Kéuih hóu guih àh?   He's very tired!?
   B: Kéuih m̀haih hóu guih.   He's not very tired.
   A: Néi guih ma?   Are you tired?
   B: Ngó m̀guih.   I'm not tired.

4. A: Kéuih leng m̀leng a?   Is she pretty?
   B: Kéuih leng.   She is pretty.
   A: Hóu leng àh!?   Very pretty!?
   B: Hóu leng.   Very pretty.

Vocabulary

ngó   PN: I, me

néi   PN: you (sing.)

kéuih   PN: he, she, him, her

ngódeih   PN: we, us

néideih   PN: you (pl.)

kéuihdeih	PN: they, them
gòu	SV: be tall, high
leng	SV: be pretty, handsome, good looking
hóu	SV: be good, well, OK, fine
guih	SV: be tired
taai	A: too
hóu	A: very, quite
géi	A: fairly, quite, rather
m̀	P: negative prefix to unmodified verbs
m̀haih	Ph: negative used instead of 'm̀' when verb i preceded by an adverb, e.g. m̀haih géi ..., is not very...
ma?	P: sentence particle; makes a statement int a yes-no question (see note 7)
a?	P: sentence particle to choice type question and questions made with interrogative wor (see note 9)
àh? (!?)	P: sentence particle making statement into yes-no question; expresses surprise or disbelief, asks for confirmation of surprising statement.

Pattern Sentences

I. Simple Descriptive Sentences.

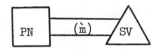

1. Ngó guih.   I'm tired.

2. Néi gòu.   You're tall.

3. Kéuih hóu.   He is well.

4. Ngó m̀gòu.   I'm not tall.

5. Néi leng.   You are pretty.

6. Kéuih m̀guih.   She isn't tired.

7. Kéuihdeih leng.   They are handsome.

8. Ngódeih m̀guih.   We are not tired.

9. Néideih m̀gòu.   You (pl) are not tall.

10. Ngódeih m̀leng.   We are not good looking.

1. <u>Descriptive</u> <u>Statements</u> are statements based on the Stative **verb**.

2. PN A <u>pronoun</u> is a personalized noun, but differs from a noun in not being so readily modified by other nouns (N) and stative verbs (SV).

3. <u>Verbs</u> in Chinese are not inflected. One verb form suffices for all three persons, singular and plural.

4. SV A <u>stative verb</u> expresses a quality or condition: It describes rather than predicates action. Besides its verbal function, it may also function as modifier of a noun ---thus behaving like the English adjective.

II. Descriptive Sentences with Adverbial Modifiers.

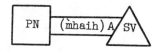

1. Ngó taai gòu.   I'm too tall.

2. Néi hóu leng   You are very pretty.

3. Kéuih hóu guih.   She is very tired.

4. Kéuih géi leng.   He is fairly good looking.

5. Ngó m̀haih géi gòu.   I'm not very tall.

6. Ngódeih taai guih.   We're too tired.

7. Kéuihdeih géi leng.   They are quite pretty.

8. Kéuihdeih m̀haih géi leng.   They are not very pretty.

9. Néihdeih taai gòu.   You (pl) are too tall.

10. Kéuihdeih m̀haih hóu hóu.   They are not very well.

5. <u>Adverbs</u> (A) modify verbs or other adverbs and always precede the verbs they modify.

6. When verbs are modified by adverbs 'm̀haih' is used for negation instead of the simple 'm̀'.

III. Questions and Answers.

  A. Simple-type questions.

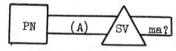

1. Néi hóu ma?   Ngó hóu.
   How are you?   I'm fine.

2. Néideih géi hóu ma?   Ngódeih géi hóu.
   How are you (pl)?   We are quite well.

3. Kéuih géi hóu ma?   Kéuih géi hóu.
   Is he quite well?   He is quite well.

4. Kéuih leng ma?   M̀leng.
   Is he handsome?   No.

5. Kéuih géi leng ma?   Kéuih m̀haih géi leng.
   Is she quite pretty?   She is not very pretty.

6. Kéuihdeih guih ma?   Kéuihdeih m̀haih géi guih.
   Are they tired?   They aren't very tired.

7. Ngó gòu ma?   Néi hóu gòu.
   Am I tall?   You are very tall.

8. Néideih guih ma?   Ngódeih hóu guih.
   Are you (pl) tired?   We are very tired.

7. Questions of the simple type, whose answer in English is either
   yes or no, are formed by adding the particle 'ma' to the statement. The word order is not altered. It should be noted that
   'ma' is usually pronounced with a middle-level tone ma; however
   the line under the 'm' will be omitted due to the frequent
   occurrence of the particle.

   Statement: Kéuih hóu.   He is well. (Literally)

   Question: Kéuih hóu ma?   Is he well? (Idiomatically: How is he?)

8. Answers to questions asking for 'yes' or 'no' are formed by
   repeating the verb of the question in its positive or negative
   form. The inclusion of elements other than the verb (i.e. subject,
   adverb, object) in the answer is optional.

   Question: Néi guih ma?   Are you tired?

   Answer: Guih.   Yes, (I am).

                Ṁguih.   No, (I'm not).

                Ṁhaih hóu guih.   No, not very.

                Ngó hóu guih.   I'm very tired.

B. Choice-yype questions.

1. Kéuih gòu ṁgòu a?   Kéuih gòu.
   Is he tall or not?   Yes, He is.

2. Néideih guih ṁguih a?   Ngódeih ṁguih.
   Are you (pl) tired?   We are not tired.

3. Kéuih leng ṁleng a?   Kéuih géi leng.
   Is she pretty?   She's quite pretty.

4. Néi gòu m̀gòu a?   Ngó m̀haih géi gòu, kéuih gòu.
   Are you tall?   I'm not very tall, he is tall.

5. Ngó gòu m̀gòu a?   Néi hóu gòu.
   Am I tall?   You are very tall.

6. Néi guih m̀guih a?   Ngó hóu guih.
   Are you tired?   I am tired.

7. Kéuihdeih guih m̀guih a?   Kéuihdeih m̀haih géi guih.
   Are they tired?   They aren't very tired.

8. Kéuihdeih gòu m̀gòu a?   Kéuiheih hóu gòu.
   Are they tall?   They are very tall.

9. Choice-type questions are formed by coupling the positive and
   negative forms of the verb and are usually followed by the
   sentence particle 'a'.

   Question: Kéuih gòu m̀gòu a? (He is tall not tall?)
                        Is he tall (or not)?

   Answers: Kéuih gòu.   He is (tall).

               Kéuih m̀gòu.   He isn't (tall).

C. 'Àh'-type questions.

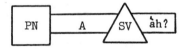

1. Néi guih ma?   Guih.   Néi hóu guih àh!?   Ngó hóu guih.
   Are you tired?   Yes.   You're very tired?   I am very tired.

2. Néideih hóu ma?   Ngódeih hóu.   Hóu hóu àh!?   Hóu hóu.
   How are you (pl)?   We're O.K.   Very well?   Very well.

3. Kéuih leng m̀leng a?   Kéuih hóu leng.   Kéuih hóu leng àh!?
   Hóu leng.
   Is she pretty?   She's very pretty.   She's very pretty?
   Very pretty.

4. Kéuih gòu ma?   M̀gòu.   Kéuih m̀gòu àh!?   Kéuih m̀gòu.
   Is he tall?   No.   He's not tall?   He isn't tall.

5. Kéuih guih ma?   Guih.   Kéuih hóu guih àh!?   Mhaih hóu guih.
   Is he tired?   Yes.   He is very tired?   He isn't very tired.

10. When a previous statement is repeated in the form of a question
    expecting agreement or indicating a bit of surprise the final
    particle 'ah' is used.

    Ngó guih   I am tired.

    Néi guih àh!?   You're tired!?

DIRECT OBJECT * * ADVERB 'DŌU'

Conversation

A: Néi máai boují àh?	You are buying a newspaper, are you
B: Ngó m̀máai boují.	I'm not buying a newspaper.
A: Néi tái m̀tái boují a?	Do you read newspapers?
B: Ngó m̀tái boují ngó tái syù.	I don't read newspaper; I read book
A: Néi máai m̀máai syù a?	Will you buy a book?
B: Syù gwai m̀gwai a?	Are the books expensive?
A: Syù m̀gwai.	The books are not expensive.
B: Méigwok syù gwai ma?	Are American books expensive?
A: Méigwok syù gwai.	American books are expensive.
B: Jùnggwok syù gwai m̀gwai a?	Are Chinese books expensive?
A: Jùnggwok syù m̀gwai. Néi yiu (Jùnggwok syù) ma?	Chinese books are not expensive. Do you want one?
B: Ngó yiu.	I do.
A: Mr. G dōu yiu syù àh!?	Mr. G want a book, too, huh?
B: Syù, boují, kéuih dōu yiu.	He wants both a book and a newspape

Vocabulary

syù (M: bún)	N:	book
boují (M: fahn 'copy')	N:	newspaper
Jùnggwok	N:	China
Méigwok	N:	America (USA)
gwai	SV:	be expensive
máai	V:	buy
tái	V:	look, look at, read
yiu (or ngoi)	V:	want

8

dōu   A: also; too, likewise; in all cases;
                             in either case; both.

Jóusàhn   Good morning

Gwaising a?   What is your surname ? (Lit. What is your
                             honorable name?)

Joigin   Goodbye

Ngó sing Wòhng   My surname is Huang

Pattern Sentences

I. Subject-Verb-Object sentence.

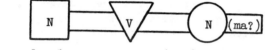

1. Néi máai syù ma?   Ngó m̀máai syù.
   Do you (want to) buy a book?   I don't (want to) buy a book.

2. Néi m̀tái syù àh?   Ngó m̀tái syù, ngó tái boují.
   You don't read books?   I don't read books, I read newspapers.

3. Néi máai boují ma?   Ngó máai.
   Do you (want to) buy a newspaper?   I do.

4. Néi máai Jùnggwok boují àh?
   You (want to) buy a Chinese newspaper?

5. Ngó m̀máai Jùnggwok boují, ngó máai Méigwok boují.
   No, I don't (want to) buy a Chinese newspaper, I (want to)
   buy an American newspaper.

6. Kéuih yiu boují ma?
   Does she want a newspaper?

7. Kéuih m̀yiu boují, kéuih yiu syù.
   She doesn't want a newspaper; she wants a book.

8. Néideih m̀tái Jùnggwok boují àh?   Ngódeih m̀tái Jùnggwok boují
   ngódeih tái Méigwok boují.
   You(pl) don't read Chinese newspapers?   We don't read Chinese
   newspapers; we read American newspaper.

9. Kéuihdeih m̄máai Méigwok syù àh?   Kéuihdeih m̄máai Méigwok syù
   kéuihdeih máai Jùnggwok syù.
   They don't buy American books?   They don't buy American book
   they buy Chinese books.

10. Néideih máai syù ma?   Ngó máai syù, kéuih máai boují.
    Do you (pl) (want to) buy books?   I (want to) buy a book, he
    want to buy a newspaper.

11. (V) Functive verbs constitute the majority of Chinese verbs.
    They indicate action or function; most of them take an object.

12. Chinese verbs are not inflected for tense. Time distinctions
    are made by the addition of other elements to the sentence, or
    by the context itself. Hence the simple statement 'ngó máai syù
    (Lit. I buy book) means different things in different contexts
    e.g. 'I buy books' (customarily or continuously), 'I am going
    to buy a book' (later), 'I bought a book' (yesterday), etc.
    In other words 'ngó máai syù' indicates either a single act or
    a customary action, with no reference to time.

13. A Noun may function as the subject or object of the action of
    a verb; it may also modify another noun, by standing immediatel
    before it. When desirable the subject and object may be dis-
    tinguished by ☐ or subject and ◯ for object.

II. Choice-type questions involving Verb and Object.

    1. Néi máai m̄máai syù a?
       Do you (want to) buy a book?

    2. Kéuih yiu m̄yiu boují a?
       Does she want a newspaper, or not?

    3. Néi tái m̄tái Jùnggwok syù a?
       Do you read Chinese books?

    4. Kéuih máai m̄máai Méigwok boují a?
       Does he (want to) buy an American newspaper?

    5. Néi yiu m̄yiu Jùnggwok boují a?
       Do you want a Chinese newspaper?

6. Kéuih tái m̀tái Méigwok syù a?
   Does he read American books?

7. Néideih yiu m̀yiu Méigwok syù a?
   Do you (pl) want American books?

8. Kéuihdeih máai m̀máai Jùnggwok boují a?
   Do they (want to) buy a Chinese newspaper?

9. Néideih tái m̀tái Jùnggwok boují a?
   Do you (pl) read Chinese newspapers?

10. Kéuihdeih yiu m̀yiu Jùnggwok syù a?
    Do they want Chinese books?

14. In choice-type questions the object may follow the positive-
    negative form of the verb, or a positive statement is made
    followed by the negative form of the verb. In the following
    sentences emphasis is placed upon the object.

   Néi máai syù m̀máai a?   Do you (want to) buy a book?

   Néi tái boují m̀tái a?   Do you read newspapers or not?

III. Use of the Adverb 'dōu'.

1. Ngó hóu, kéuih dōu hóu.
   I am well, she is also well.

2. Néi leng, kéuih dōu leng.
   You are pretty, and she is also pretty.

3. Jùnggwok syù gwai, Méigwok syù dōu gwai.
   Chinese books are expensive, American books are expensive
   too.

4. Néi máai syù, ngó dōu máai syù.
   You are buying a book, I am also buying a book.

5. Ngó m̀yiu boují, néideih dōu m̀yiu boují àh?
   I don't want a newpaper, you (pl) don't want a newspaper
   either?

6. Kéuihdeih m̀tái boují, néideih dōu m̀tái boují àh?
   They don't read newspapers, don't you read newspapers either?

7. Ngó hóu guih, kéuih dōu hóu guih.
   I am very tired, she is also very tired.

8. Néi dōu hóu guih àh?
   You are also very tired?

9. Boují mhaih géi gwai, syù dōu mhaih géi gwai.
   Newspapers are not very expensive, neither are books very
   expensive.

10. Néi géi hóu ma?   Kéuih dōu géi hóu ma?
    Are you quite well?   Is he also quite well?

15. The adverb 'dōu' not only modifies the verb it immediately
    precedes, but also refers back to plural items which precede
    it.

    Méigwok syù, Jùnggwok syù ngó dōu yiu.
    I want both American books and Chinese books.

NUMBER AND MEASURE

Conversation

A: Néi yáuh móu bāt a?   Do you have any pens?
B: Ngó yáuh.   I do have.
A: Néi yáuh géidòjì a?   How many do you have?
B: Ngó yáuh léuhngjì.   I have two.
A: (Néi yáuh) léuhngjì Jùnggwok   (You have) two Chinese pens?
   bāt àh?
B: Yātjì Jùnggwok bāt, yātjì   One Chinese pen and one American
   Méigwok bāt.   pen.
A: Néi máai jūng ma?   Do you want to buy a clock?[1]
B: M̀máai jūng, ngó máai bīu.   I don't want to buy a clock, I want
                                                 to buy a watch.
A: Néi yiu géidògo bīu a?   How many watches do you want?
B: Yātgo.   One.
A: Néi yiu tói m̀yiu a?   Do you want a table?
B: Ngó yáuh sàamjèung tói,   I have three tables, I don't want
   ngó m̀yiu tói.   a table.
A: Néi yáuh yí móu a?   Do you have chairs?
B: Móu.   No.
A: Néi máai m̀máai yí a?   Do you want to buy a chair?
B: Máai.   Yes.
A: Néi yiu géidòjèung yí a?   How many chairs do you want?
B: Léuhngjèung.   Two.
A: Néi yáuh Jùnggwok syù ma?   Do you have Chinese books?
B: Ngó yáuh.   Yes, I have.
A: Néi yáuh géidòbún a?   How many do you have?
B: Luhkbún.   Six.

---

1. Note that the Cantonese sentence need not include a word specifi-
   cally meaning "want to."

Vocabulary

yāt	NU: one
yih	NU: two
sàam	NU: **three**
sei	NU: four
nǵ	NU: five
luhk	NU: six
chāt	NU: seven
baat	NU: eight
gáu	NU: nine
sahp	NU: ten
yihsahp or yah	NU: twenty (abbreviated form)
sàamsahp or sà'ah[1]	NU: thirty (abbreviated form)
léuhng	NU: two <u>or</u> a couple
géi(dò)	NU: how many, how much
jūng[2]	N: clock, bell
bīu	N: watch
bāt (M: jì)	N: pen, pencil, writing brush
tói (M: jèung)	N: table, desk

1. The apostrophe is used to indicate two separate syllables.

2. If no measure word is given with a noun in the vocabulary, it is understood that the noun takes the general measure 'go.'

yí (M: jèung)   N: chair

-go   M: (for persons or things)

-bún   M: (for books)

-jèung   M: (for tables, chairs, paper)

-jì   M: (for writing instruments)

yáuh   V: have

móu   V: have not

daihgéifo a?   which lesson?

daihsàamfo   the third lesson

Pattern Sentences

I. Numbered Nouns.

1. géidògo jūng a?   2. géidògo bīu a?
   yātgo jūng   luhkgo bīu
   léuhnggo jūng   chātgo bīu
   sàamgo jūng   baatgo bīu
   seigo jūng   gáugo bīu
   nggo jūng   sahpgo bīu

3. géidòjèung yí a?   4. géidòjèung tói a?
   yātjèung yí   luhkjèung tói
   léuhngjèung yí   chātjèung tói
   sàamjèung yí   baatjèung tói
   seijèung yí   gáujèung tói
   ngjèung yí   sahpjèung tói

5. géidòjèung jí a? 6.géidòjì bāt a? 7. géidòbún syù a?
   yātjèung jí   léuhngjì bāt   yāt-léuhngbún syù
   sàamjèung jí   seijì bāt   sàam-seibún syù
   ngjèung jí   luhkjì bāt   ng-luhkbún syù
   chātjèung jí   baatjì bāt   chāt-baatbún syù
   gáujèung jí   sahpjì bāt

16. A question word occupies in the sentence the same position as
    the word or phrase which replaces it in the answer. The
    sentence particle 'a' is always used in forming the question.

    1. Néi yáuh géidòjì bāt a? How many pens do you have?

    2. Ngó yáuh sàamjì bāt.   I have three pens.

    3. Néi yiu géidòjèung jí a? How many chairs do you want?

    4. Ngó yiu sàamjèung.   I want three.

17. In Chinese, nouns are usually not inflected for number; when it
    is desired to indicate these aspects, a noun is preceded by
    both a number and a measure. The number-measure combination
    can stand alone.

    In English we say 'an ounce of gold,' 'a pair of shoes,' 'a
    drop of water,' etc.: there is a similar counterpart in Chinese
    except that in Chinese every ordinary Chinese noun has its own
    measure. Measures are usually bound to numbers or specifiers
    (Note 21) to form qualifying nouns. In most cases the measures
    need not be translated into English.

    1. Ngó yáuh yātgo jūng.   I have a clock.

    2. Kéuih dōu yáuh yātgo.   He also has one.

    3. Kéuih yiu léuhngbún syù. He wants two books.

    4. Néi dōu yiu léuhngbún àh?Do you also want a couple?

18. Numbers (NU) include cardinal numbers and a few other words
    which function like numbers. Numbers are usually bound to
    measures to form a noun.

    1. Ngó yiu n̄ggo.   I want five.

II. Duplication of Measures and 'dōu.'

    1. Gogo bīu dōu hóu gwai.
       All the watches are very expensive.

    2. Jèungjèung tói dōu móu yí.
       None of the tables has chairs.

3. Jìjì bāt dōu m̀hóu.
   None of the pens is good.

4. Jèungjèung boují ngó dōu tái.
   I read all the papers.

5. Búnbún syù dōu m̀haih hóu hóu.
   None of the books are very good.

6. Gogo (yàhn) dōu máai syù.
   Everyone buys books.

7. Gogo dōu hóu gòu, hóu leng.
   All of them are very tall and very pretty.

8. Gogo dōu m̀haih taai guih.
   No one is too tired.

9. Gogo dōu yiu léuhngbún syù.
   Everybody wants two books.

10. Gogo dōu máai yàtjèung boují.
    Everybody buys one newspaper.

19. Duplicated measures plus 'dōu' are translated as 'all,' 'everyone;'
    when followed by móu or m̄, the meaning is 'no...,' 'nobody,' etc.

III. Exercise using question word 'géidò.'

   A. Translate and answer the following questions:

   1. Kéuih yáuh géidògo bīu a?
   2. Néi yiu géidòbún syù a?
   3. Kéuih máai géidòjèung boují a?
   4. Néideih yáuh géidòjì Méigwok bāt a?
   5. Kéihdeih yiu géidòjèung tói a?
   6. Néideih yáuh géidòjì bāt a?
   7. Kéuih yáuh géidò-jèung Jùnggwok yí a?
   8. Néi tái géidòjèung boují a?
   9. Kéuihdeih yáuh géidòbún Jùnggwok syù a?
   10. Néideih yiu géidòjèung Méigwok boují a?

B. Translate and make up questions to fit the answers:

1. Kéuih yiu chātjèung yí.
2. Ngó máai luhkbún syù.
3. Kéuih yáuh léuhngjèung boují.
4. Ngódeih yáuh sàamgo jūng.
5. Kéuihdeih yiu sahpjì bāt.
6. Ngódeih máai seijèung tói.
7. Kéuih móu bīu.
8. Ngódeih yáuh yātgo jūng, léuhnggo bīu.
9. Kéuihdeih yiu sàamjèung Méigwok boují.
10. Ngódeih móu Jùnggwok syù.

IV. Counting to 99.

1 - 10	11 - 20	21 - 30
yāt	sahpyāt	yah-yāt (yihsahp-yāt)
yih	sahpyih	yah-yih (yihsahp-yih)
sàam	sahpsàam	yah-sàam (yihsahp-sàam)
sei	sahpsei	yah-sei (yihsahp-sei)
ng	sahpng	yah-ng (yihsahp-ng)
luhk	sahpluhk	yah-luhk (yihsahp-luhk)
chāt	sahpchāt	yah-chāt (yihsahp-chāt)
baat	sahpbaat	yah-baat (yihsahp-baat)
gáu	sahpgáu	yah-gáu (yihsahp-gáu)
sahp	yihsahp	sàamsahp

31 - 40	41 - 50
sà'ah-yāt (sàamsahp-yāt)	sei'ah-yāt (seisahp-yāt)
sà'ah-yih (sàamsahp-yih)	sei'ah-yih (seisahp-yih)
. .	. .
. .	. .
.	.
seisahp	ngsahp

51 - 60

ng'ah-yāt (ngsahp-yāt)
ng'ah-yih (ngsahp-yih)
    .   .
    .   .
    .   .
luhksahp

61 - 70   luhk'ah-yāt (luhksahp-yāt) . . . . chātsahp

71 - 80   chāt'ah-yāt (chātsahp-yāt) . . . . baatsahp

81 - 90   baat'ah-yāt (baatsahp-yāt) . . . . gáusahp

90 - 99   gáu'ah-yāt (gáusahp-yāt) . . . . gáu'ah-gáu
                                            (gáusahp-gáu)

20. Numbers from 1 to 99 are counted as above. When there is a
    measure(M), 'léuhng' is used for 'two' instead of 'yih', as
    in léuhnggo' (see note 17, page 16). However, when there is
    another number preceding 'yih' is used instead 'léuhng' i.e.
    'sahp-yihgo', 'yahyihgo', 'sà'ahyihgo' etc.

Exercise

Fill in the blanks with correct forms:

1. Ngó yáuh sàam ____ bāt.

2. Kéuih yiu ____ -jèung yí.

3. Néi tái ___ tái syù a?

4. Jūng, bīu, ____ gwai.

5. Néi yáuh _____ -jì bāt a?

6. Kéuih m̀haih hóu _____.

7. Ngó tái boují, kéuih ____ tái boují.

8. Néi yáuh léuhng ____ syù ma?

9. Tói gwai, yí dōu gwai ____ ?

10. Ngó yáuh yāt ____ Jùnggwok syù, _____ -jì bāt, sàam _____
    tói, sei ___ jūng, ng ____ bīu.

LESSON 4

SPECFIED, NUMBERED AND MEASURED NOUNS

Conversation

A: Bīngo a?
B: Ngó. Ngó yiu máai jūng.
A: Néi yiu máai géidògo a?
B: Ngó yiu máai léuhnggo.
A: Léuhnggo daaih jūng àh?
B: Daaih jūng gwai m̀gwai a?
A: Daaih jūng hóu gwai, daahnhaih nīgo (daaih jūng)
   m̀haih hóu gwai.
B: Sai jūng nē?
A: Sai jūng m̀gwai.
B: Chéng néi béi yātgo daaih jūng, yātgo sai jūng ngó.

****

B: Ngó yiu máai yātjì Jùnggwok bāt néi yáuh móu a?
A: Ngó móu bāt, daahnhaih ngó yáuh tói, yáuh yí. Néi yiu ma?
B: Nījèung tói gwai m̀gwai a?
A: Nījèung hóu gwai, gójèung m̀gwai.
B: Daahnhaih gójèung tói taai sai. Nījèung nē?
A: Nījèung m̀haih hóu gwai. Néi yiu bīnjèung a?
B: Ngó yiu nī léuhngjèung, daahnhaih m̀yiu gójèung.
A: Néi m̀jùngyi gójèung àh?
B: Ngó jùngyi gójèung, daahnhaih gójèung taai gwai.

- - Translation appears at end of lesson - -

Vocabulary

yàhn	N: man, person
pàhngyáuh	N: friend

20

bīn-	SP: which, who, whom
nī-	SP: this (here)
gó-	SP: that (there)
daaih	SV: be large, big
sai	SV: be small, little
béi	'V: to give
jùngyi	'V: to like, be fond of
chéng	'V/CV: invite/please, ask (invitational sense), request
m̀gòi	Ph: please
nē	P: a question particle
daahnhaih	MA: but, however
géi	NU: several, some, a few (see lesson 13 vocabulary)

Useful Expressions

m̀gòi	thank you (for a favor); sorry; excuse me
m̀gòisaai	thank you for everything; thank you very much
m̀sái m̀gòi	don't mention it; you are welcome
hóuwah	you are welcome; kind of you to say so
dòjeh (néi)	thank you (for a gift)
dòjehsaai	thanks for everything; thank you very much
m̀sáihaakhei	don't mention it: please don't bother

yáuhsàm   thank you for inquiring

...hóu ma?   ...all right? Would you...?

Pattern Sentences

I. Specified nouns.

A. 1. Bīnbún syù a?   Góbún syù.
      Which book?   That book.

   2. Bīnjèung tói a? Níjèung.
      Which table?   This one.

   3. Bīngo pàhngyáuh a?   Gógo pàhngyáuh.
      Which friend?   That friend.

   4. Bīngo a?   Ngó.
      Who is it?   I.

   5. Bīnjì bāt a?   Níjì.
      Which pen?   This one.

   6. Bīnbún syù gwai a?   Níbún gwai.

   7. Bīngo yàhn hóu leng a?   Gógo

   8. Bīngo pàhngyáuh guih a?   Gógo.

   9. Bīngo gòu a?   Nígo gòu.

  10. Bīngo bīu gwai a?   Gógo bīu gwai.

  11. Néi yiu bīnbún syù a?   Ngó yiu níbún.

  12. Kéuih tái bīnjèung boují a?   Kéuih tái gójèung.

  13. Néi máai bīnjì bāt a?   Níjì.

  14. Néi yiu m̀yiu gógo jūng a?   Ngó m̀yiu.

  15. Néi yiu gójì bāt m̀yiu a?   Yiu.

21. Specifiers (SP) serve to mark a particular thing or things
pointed to or otherwise referred to. When a noun or noun
understood is specified, the correct measure will be attached
to the specifier, as in the case of numbered nouns (cf. Note 17)

      bīngo yàhn (a)?   which person?

      nīgo (yàhn)   this one

      gógo (yàhn)   that one

If the noun specified is also numbered, the specifier precedes
the numbered noun as a free noun.

      Bīn léuhngbún syù a?   Which two books?

      Nī léuhngbún (syù).   These two.

      Gó léuhngbún (syù).   Those two.

In answering a question involving a stative verb,

      Bīnbún syù gwai a?   Bīnjì bāt leng a?

the answer should be:

      Nībún.   Nījì.

      Nībún gwai.   Nījì leng.

      Nībún syù gwai.   Nījì bāt leng.

But not   Nībún syù   but not Nījì bāt.

B. 1. Bīn sàamjèung boují a? Nī sàamjèung.
     Which three newspapers? These three.

  2. Bīn seibún syù a? Nī seibún.
     Which four books? These four books.

  3. Bīn léuhnggo yàhn a? Nī léuhnggo.
     Which two persons? These two persons.

  4. Bīn géibún syù a? Nī géibún.
     Which several books? These (several).

    5. Bīn ńgjèung tói a?   Gó ńgjèung.
       Which five tables?   Those five.

    6. Bīn géibún syù gwai a?   Nī sàambún syù gwai, (daahnhaih)
       gó seibún m̀gwai.

    7. Bīn géijì bāt gwai a?   Nī sahpjì gwai, (daahnhaih) gó
       sahpjì m̀gwai.

    8. Bīn géijèung yí daaih a?   Nī léuhngjèung yí daaih,
       (daahnhaih) gó léuhngjèung sai.

    9. Bīn géigo jūng daaih a?   Nī seigo jūng daaih, (daahnhaih)
       gó léuhnggo jūng sai.

   10. Néi máai bīn géijì bāt a?   Ngó máai gó léuhngjì, m̀máai nī
        léuhngjì.

22. The question word 'géi' is commonly used as an indefinite to
     mean 'some' or 'several' or 'a few.'

    1. Ngó yiu géibún syù.
       I want some books.

    2. Bīn géibún syù gwai a?   Gó géibún syù gwai.
       Which books are expensive?   Those (several) books are
       expensive.

23. When question words such as 'bīn,' 'géi,' 'mātyéh,' etc. are
     used in forming a question, the final particle of the question
     is 'a.'

C. 1. Néi góbún syù gwai m̀gwai a?   Ngó góbún syù hóu gwai.
       Is that book of yours expensive?   That book of mine is
       very expensive.

    2. Néi gó géibún syù gwai m̀gwai a?   Ngó gó géibún syù m̀haih
       hou gwai.
       Are those books of yours expensive?   Those books of mine
       are not very expensive.

    3. Néi bún syù gwai m̀gwai a?   Ngó bún syù hóu gwai.
       Is your book expensive?   My book is very expensive.

    4. Néi gógo pàhngyáuh gòu m̀gòu a?   Ngó gógo pàhngyáuh hóu gòu
       Is that friend of yours tall?   That friend of mine is
       very tall.

5. Néi go pàhngyáuh yáuh móu bīu a?   Ngó nī(yāt)go[1] pàhngyáuh
yáuh.
Does your friend have a watch?   This friend of mine has
(one).

6. Néi go pàhngyáuh guih ma?   Ngó go pàhngyàuh m̀haih hóu guih.

7. Néi go pàhngyáuh leng m̀leng a?   Ngó go pàhngyáuh hóu leng.

8. Kéuih jì bāt gwai m̀gwai a?   Kéuih jì Méigwok bāt m̀haih hóu
gwai.

9. Kéuih bīngo bīu gwai a?   Kéuih gógo Méigwok bīu gwai.

10. Kéuih bīn yātgo jūng gwai a?   Gó yātgo gwai.

24. If a numbered or specified noun is further modified by a pronoun, the pronoun comes first:

1. ngó léuhngjì bāt   my two pens

2. kéuih nīgo bīu   this watch of his

3. kéuih gó léuhnggo jūng   those two clocks of his

II. Indirect object with 'béi.'

1. Kéuih béi bún syù bīngo a?   Kéuih béi bún syù ngó.
To whom did he give the book?   He gave the book to me.

2. Kéuih béi bún syù néi àh?   Kéuih béi bún syù ngó.
He gave the book to you?   Yes, he gave the book to me.

3. Kéuih béi (yāt) go bīu néi àh?   Kéuih béi go bīu ngó.
He gave you a watch?   He gave me a watch.

4. Kéuih m̀béi go bīu néi àh?   Kéuih m̀béi go bīu ngó.
He isn't giving you a watch?   He isn't giving me a watch.

1. 'yāt' 'gó' or 'nī' may be omitted before measures. If a
measure stands alone before a noun 'yāt' or 'gó' is understood,
the measure used alone has about the same meaning as 'a' or 'the'
in English.

5. Bīngo béi go jūng néi a?   Kéuih béi go jūng ngó.
   Who gave you the clock?   He gave me the clock.

6. Bīngo béi jèung tói kéuih a?   Ngó béi jèung tói kéuih.

7. Néi béi jèung yí bīngo a?   Ngó béi jèung yí kéuih.

8. M̀gòi néi béi jèung boují ngó.   Hóu, ngó béi jèung boují
   néi.

9. Chéng néi béi gójì bāt kéuih.   Ngó béi gójì bāt kéuih.

10. M̀gòi néi béi léuhngjèung yí kéuih.

11. Chéng néi béi géibún syù ngó.

12. M̀gòi néi béi yātjèung tói gógo yàhn.

13. Ngó béi léuhngjì bāt kéuih go (or gógo) pàhngyáuh.

14. M̀gòi néi béi sàambún syù ngó gógo pàhngyáuh.

15. Néi béi m̀béi go jūng ngó go (or gógo) pàhngyáuh a?

25. An indirect object follows the direct object as in the
    English sentence, 'I give a book to you.' 'Ngó béi yātbún
    syù néi.'

III. Use of sentence suffix 'nē.'

1. Nībún syù hóu ma?   M̀hóu.   Góbún nē?   Góbún hóu.
   Is this book good?   No, it isn't. How about that one?
   That one is good.

2. Néi hóu ma?   Ngó géi hóu.   Néi nē?   Ngó dōu hóu.
   How are you?   I'm fairly well.   How about you?
   I'm well, too.

3. Nījì bāt m̀hóu, gójì nē?   Gójì hóu.
   This pen is no good, how about that one?   That one is good.

4. Ngó m̀tái boují, néi nē?   Ngó dōu m̀tái.
   I don't read newspapers, how about you?   Neither do I.

5. Ngó móu bīu, néi nē? Ngó   móu, kéuih yáuh.
   I have no watch. How about you? I haven't one either,
   (but) he has.

26. Nē is a final particle used in the following patterns:

1. 'Ne' directly following a noun has the force of 'how about
   ...?' or 'and ...?'

   Néi guih m̀guih a?   Are you tired?

   Ngó m̀guih, néi nē?   I'm not tired, how about you?

   Ngó máai syù, néi nē?   I'm buying books; and you?

2. 'nē' may replace the question particle 'a' to place emphasis
   on the subject in question.

   Syù gwai m̀gwai nē?   And are <u>books</u> expensive?

IV. Use of polite expressions.

A: Wòhng sìnsàang (<u>Mr.</u> Wòhng) néi géi hóu ma?
B: Hóu, yáuhsàm.
A: Néi tái Jùnggwok syù ma?
B: Ngó tái.
A: Ngó béi nībún syù néi, néi yiu ma?
B: Dòjeh néi!
A: M̀sái haakhei!
B: Néi tái boují ma?
A: Ngó tái, m̀gòi néi béi (yāt) jèung ngó hóu ma?
B: Ngó béi jèung Jùnggwok boují néi, hóu ma?
A: Hóu, m̀gòi!
B: Hòuwah!
A: M̀gòi néi béi (yāt) bún Jùnggwok syù ngó, hóu ma?
B: Ngó móu Jùnggwok syù. Néi yiu nībún Méigwok syù ma?
A: M̀gòi! Méigwok syù dōu hóu, ngó dōu jùngyi tái Méigwok syù.
B: Néi tái Méigwok boují ma? Ngó béi nījèung néi, néi yiu ma?
A: Dòjeh! Dòjeh!
B: M̀sái haakhei!

Translate the following sentences:

1. Chéng néi béi yātbún syù ngó. Bīnbún a? Góbún.
2. Néi yáuh géidògo Jùnggwok pàhngyáuh a? Sàamgo.
3. Gógo yàhn máai léuhngjèung daaih tói.
4. Ngó nīgo pàhngyáuh tái Méigwok boují.
5. Néi bīngo pàhngyáuh béi bīu ngó a?
6. Kéuih bīn léuhnggo pàhngyáuh máai gó léuhngbún syù a?
7. Néi máai bīngo bīu a? Ngó máai nīgo.
8. Nījèung yí m̀haih taai daaih, gójèung dōu m̀haih taai daaih.
9. Néi gógo pàhngyáuh gòu m̀gòu a?
10. Kéuih béi nījì bāt bīngo a?
11. Kéuih béi nījì bāt gógo pàhngyáuh.
12. Nījì bāt gwai ma? Nījì bāt m̀gwai, gójì gwai.
13. Néi nī léuhnggo pàhngyáuh, bīngo gòu a? Nīgo gòu.
14. Néi jùngyi nījèung yí ma? Ngó m̀jùngyi nījèung, ngó jùngyi gójèung.
15. Ngó béi nījèung yí néi gógo pàhngyáuh.
16. Néi guih ma? Ngó m̀guih, daahnhaih ngó go pàhngyáuh guih.
17. Jùnggwok yàhn yáuh Méigwok bāt, daahnhaih Méigwok yàhn móu Jùnggwok bāt.
18. Néi tái boují ma? M̀tái. Kéuih dōu m̀tái.
19. Néi máai syù ma? M̀máai. Néi go pàhngyáuh nē? Kéuih dōu m̀máai.
20. Ngódeih jùngyi nīgo yàhn, daahnhaih kéuih m̀jùngyi.

Translation of Dialogue

Use this as an exercise in translating back to Chinese and see how close you can come to the Chinese version printed at the beginning of the lesson.

A: Who is it?
B: I. I want to buy a clock.
A: How many do you want to buy?
B: I want to buy two.
A: Two large ones, I suppose.
B: Are large clocks expensive?
A: Large clocks are expensive, however this one isn't very expensive.
B: How about small clocks?
A: Small clocks are inexpensive.
B: Please give me a large clock and a small clock.

****

B: I want to buy a Chinese writing brush, do you have any?
A: I don't have; however, I have tables and chairs. Do you want any?
B: Is this table expensive?
A: This one is very expensive; that one isn't expensive.
B: But that table is too small. How about this one?
A: This one isn't very expensive. Which one do you want?
B: I want these two, but (I) don't want that one.
A: You don't like that one?
B: I like that one, however, that one is too expensive.

LESSON 5

EQUATIONAL SENTENCES

Conversation

A: Sìnsàang, néi gwaising a?
B: ngó sing Jèung. Néi nē?
A: Ngó sing Wòhng. Jèung sìnsàang,[1] gógo yàhn haih bīngo a?
B: Gógo haih ngó yātgo pàhngyáuh.
A: Néi gógo pàhngyáuh sing mātyéh a?
B: Kéuih sing Léih. Wòhng sìnsàang, néi hai mhaih Jùnggwok
   yàhn a?
A: Haih, ngó haih Jùnggwok yàhn. Jèung sìnsàang, néi nē?
B: Ngó haih Méigwok yàhn.
A: Léih sìnsàang nē, Kéuih dōu haih Méigwok yàhn àh?
B: Háih, ngódeih léuhnggo dōu haih Méigwok yàhn. Wòhng sìnsàang,
   néi yáuh saimānjái ma?
A: Yáuh, ngó yáuh sàamgo saimānjái.
B: Wòhng taaitáai hóu ma?
A: Kéuih hóu hóu, yáuhsàm. Néi taaitáai nē? Kéuih hóu ma?
B: Yáuhsàm, kéuih dōu hóu hóu.
A: Néi jì gógo haih bīngo ma?
B: Mjì. Léih sìnsàang, néi jì mjì a?
C: Ngó jì. Kéuih haih Chàhn síujé. Kéuih yiu gó géibún syù.
A: Kéuih yiu bīn géibún syù a?
B: Kéuih yiu gó géibún Jùnggwok syù.

- - Translation appears at end of lesson - -

1. 'sìnsàang' and 'taaitáai' are often contracted when used
   with a surname to 'sàang,' as 'Wòhng sàang;' 'táai' as
   'Chàhn táai.'

30

Vocabulary

sìnsàang (M: wái, go)[1]	N: Mr., sir, gentleman; teacher; husband (polite)
taaitáai (M: wái, go)	N: Mrs., Madam; wife (polite); lady (married)
síujé (M: wái, go)	N: Miss, daughter (polite); lady (unmarried)
saimānjái	N: child, children
yéh (M: gihn)	N: thing
Chàhn	N: Chen (surname)
daih-	P: prefix to make cardinal numbers ordinal (see note 30)
daihyih (plus measure)	SP: other, another
daihyih (plus dī)	SP: other, others
Léih	N: surname: Li, Lee
Jèung	N: surname: Cheung, Chang
Wòhng	N: surname: Wong, Huang, Wang
haih	EV: to be: equal; it is
sing	EV/N: be surnamed/ surname

1. The polite form of the measure for 'sìnsàang,' 'taaitáai,' and síujé' is wái,' i.e. 'gówái sìnsàang (or taaitáai, síujé). The general measure 'go' can always be used in certain circumstances, such as: 'gó sàamgo sìnsàang,' those three teachers.)

mãt(yéh)   N: what (mãtyéh is sometime contracted
                               to mē'éh or <u>mè</u>)

jì(dou)   V: know about, know

Useful Expressions

Chéng néi joi góng yātchi   Please say it again.

Ngāam ma?   Is this correct?

Ngāam. Ngāam la. M̀ngāam.   Yes. That's right. No, it is
                                   not correct

Pattern Sentences

I. Use of 'haih' and m̀haih' to show emphasis.

   1. A. Kéuih gòu m̀gòu a?
      .   Is he tall?

      B. Kéuih hóu gòu.
         Yes, he is.

      A. Kéuih <u>haih m̀haih</u> hóu gòu a?
         Is he very tall, or isn't he?

      B. Kéuih haih hóu gòu.
         Yes, he <u>is</u>.

   2. A. Kéuih haih m̀haih hóu gòu a?
         <u>Is</u> he very tall?

      B. Haih, kéuih hóu gòu.
         Yes, he is very tall.

      A. Kéuih haih hóu gòu àh?
         He <u>is</u> very tall?

      B. Kéuih haih hóu gòu.
         Yes, he <u>is</u>.

3. A. Kéuih yiu m̀yiu bāt a?
      Does he want a pen?

   B. Kéuih m̀yiu bāt.
      He doesn't.

   A. Kéuih <u>haih</u> m̀yiu bāt <u>àh</u>?
      He rea<u>lly</u> <u>doesn't</u> want a pen?

   B. Kéuih <u>haih</u> m̀yiu bāt.
      He does <u>not</u>.

4. A. Wòhng sìnsàang yáuh móu saimānjái a?
      Does Mr. Wohng have children?

   B. Wòhng sìnsàang yáuh saimānjái.
      Yes, he has.

   A. Wòhng sìnsàang yáuh géidògo saimānjái a?
      How many children does Mr. Wohng have?

   B. ....
      ....

   A. Wòhng sìnsàang <u>haih m̀haih</u> yáuh léuhnggo saimānjái a?
      Mr. Wohng has two children, doesn't he?

   B. Wòhng sìnsàang haih yáuh léuhnggo saimānjái.
      Yes, Mr. Wohng does have two children.

27. When 'haih' is used before a verb, it shows emphasis. But when
    'haih m̀haih' is used in a question, it doesn't necessarily carry
    special emphasis. Whether emphasis is intended or not will be
    made apparent by the context in which the sentence appears. The
    'haih m̀haih' underlined in sect. 1 and 4, indicates that emphasis
    is intended. The answer form for 'haih m̀haih' type of question
    is alway 'haih' or 'm̀haih.'

II. Equational sentences.

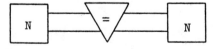

1. Néi haih bīngo a?   Ngó haih Wòhng sìnsàang.
   Who are you?   I am Mr. Huang.

2. Nīgo haih mātyéh a?   Nīgo haih bīu.
   What is this?   This is a watch.

3. Kéuih sing māt(yéh) a?   Kéuih sing Chàhn.
   What is her name?   Her name is Chen.

4. Bīnwái haih Jèung taaitáai a?   Gówái haih Jèung taaitáai.
   Which one is Mrs. Chang?   That one is Mrs. Chang.

5. Néi haih m̀haih sing Léih a?   Ngó m̀haih sing Léih, ngó sing
   Wòhng.
   Is your name Lee?   My name is not Lee. My name is Huang.

6. Góbún haih m̀haih Méigwok syù a?   Góbún m̀haih Méigwok syù.
   góbún haih Jùnggwok syù.

7. Bīngo sing Jèung a?   Gógo sing Jèung.

8. Néi haih m̀haih Chàhn sìnsàang a?   M̀haih, ngó sing Wòhng.

9. Gógo (yàhn) haih bīngo a?   Gógo haih Wòhng sìnsàang. Nīgo
   nē? Nīgo haih Chàhn síujé.

10. Nīgo haih m̀haih jūng a?   M̀haih, nīgo m̀haih jūng, nīgo haih
    bīu.

11. Bīnjì haih Jùnggwok bāt a?   Gójì haih Jùnggwok bāt.

12. Bīnjèung haih Méigwok boují a?   Nījèung.

13. Néideih bīngo haih Méigwok yàhn a?   Ngódeih gogo dōu m̀haih.

14. Néideih m̀haih Méigwok yàhn, néideih haih m̀haih Jùnggwok yàhn
    a?

15. Nī léuhngbún haih m̀haih Jùnggwok syù a?   Nī léuhngbún dōu
    m̀haih Jùnggwok syù.

28. Equational verb (EV) are verbs which equate two nouns or nominal
    expressions on either side of the verb.

Kéuih haih Méigwok yàhn.
He is an American.

Gójì haih Jùnggwok bāt.
That is a Chinese brush.

Néi sing mātyéh?
What is your surname?

29. To form a question with the verb 'sing' either use the question
word 'mātyéh' (as it used in note 28) or use the 'àh' -type
question form, or precede the verb 'sing' with 'haih mhaih'.
There is no 'ma' -type question form.

   Néi sing Wòhng àh?   Haih.
   Is your name Huang?   Yes.

   Néi haih mhaih sing Wòhng a?   Mhaih.
   Is your name Huang?   No.

III. 'Daih-' as a prefix.

  A. Ordinalizer

    1. Gó sàambún syù daihyātbún daihyihbún dōu haih Jùnggwok syù,
      daihsàambún haih Méigwok syù.
      Of those three books, the first and the second both are
      Chinese books, the third is an American book.

    2. Daihyātgo haih Méigwok yàhn; daihyihgo mhaih Méigwok yàhn;
      daihsàamgo haih Jùnggwok yàhn; daihseigo...; daihnggo...
      The first one is an American; the second is not an American;
      the third one is a Chinese; the fourth..,;the fifth...

    3. Nī chātjèung tói, ngó jùngyi daihluhkjèung (or daihluhkgó-
      jèung).
      Of these seven tables, I like the sixth one.

    4. Ngó mhaih daihyātgo, ngó haih daihyihgo.
      I am not the first one, I am the second one.

    5. Daihyātjèung yí taai daaih, daihyihjèung (yí) taai sai,
      daihsàamjèung ngó hóu jùngyi, daahnhaih...
      The first chair is too large, the second one is too small,
      the third one I like very much, but...

30. 'Daih-' when prefixed to cardinal numbers makes them ordinals.

daihyātgo pàhngyáuh
The first friend

daihyihjèung tói
The second table

daihseijì bāt
the fourth pen

B. 'Daihyih-' meaning 'another' or 'other.'

1. Ngó m̀jùngyi nībún syù, chéng néi béi daihyihbún ngó.
   I don't like this book, please give me another one.

2. Néi m̀jùngyi nījì bāt, ngó béi daihyihjì néi.
   If you don't like this pen I'll give you another one.

3. Néi yáuh móu daihyihgo pàhngyáuh a?
   Do you have another friend?

4. Nījèung tói taai daaih, néi yáuh móu daiyihjèung a?
   This table is too big, do you have another one?

5. Ngó jì kéuih haih Wòhng sìnsàang, ngó m̀jì daihyihgo haih bīngo.
   I know he is Mr. Huang, but I don't know who the other one is.

Drill on the Sentence Finals

1. Néi guih ma?   Ngó guih.
   Néi hóu guih àh?   Ngó m̀haih hóu guih.
   Kéuih nē?   Kéuih dōu guih.

2. Tói gwai ma?   Jèungjèung tói dōu gwai.
   Yí nē?   Yí m̀haih géi gwai.

3. Néi gwaising a?   Ngó sing Wòhng.
   Kéuih nē?   Kéuih dōu sing Wòhng.

4. Néi máai syù àh?   Ngó m̀máai syù, ngó máai boují.
   Kéuih dōu máai boují àh?   Kéuih m̀máai boují, kéuih máai bāt.
   Kéuih yiu géidòjì a?   Sàamjì àh?
   Néi nē, néi yiu géidòjèung boují a?   Léuhngjèung àh?

5. Néi yáuh syù ma?   Yáuh.
   Bāt nē?   Bāt, ngó dōu yáuh.
   Néi yáuh géidòbún syù, géidòjì bāt a?   Luhkbún syù, luhkjì bāt.
   Luhkbún syù, luhkjìbāt àh?   Haih, luhkbún syù, luhkjì bāt.

6. Gógo haih bīngo a?   Gógo haih Chàhn taaitáai.
   Kéuih m̀haih Jèung taaitáai àh?   M̀haih.
   Gógo nē?   Gógo dōu m̀haih Jèung taaitáai, kéuih haih Léih
   taaitáai.

7. Néi haih m̀haih Léih sìnsàang a?   M̀haih, ngó sing Wòhng.
   Néi sing Wòhng àh?   Gógo nē?   Kéuih dōu sing Wòhng.
   Kéuih dōu m̀haih sing Léih àh?   Bīngo haih Léih sìnsàang a?
   Gógo haih Léih sìnsàang.

Translate the following sentences:

1. Nīgo haih mātyéh a?   Nīgo haih daaih jūng.
2. Néi yáuh géidògo Jùnggwok pàhngyáuh a?   Baatgo.
3. Néi gó géigo pàhngyáuh jùngyi tái Méigwok syù ma?
4. Kéuihdeih m̀jùngyi tái Méigwok syù.   Kéuihdeih jùngyi tái
   Jùnggok syù.
5. Nīgo síujé sing mātyéh a?   Nīgo síujé sing Chàhn.
6. Chéng néi béi nījì bāt Léih taaitáai.
7. Nīgo haih mātyéh a?   Ngó m̀jì, néi nē, néi jì m̀jì a?   Ngó
   dōu m̀jì.
8. Ngó hóu jùngyi nīgo saimānjái.
9. Nīgo saimānjái haih m̀haih yiu Jùnggwok bāt a?   M̀haih, kéuih
   yiu Méigwok bāt.
10. Néi yiu m̀yiu ngó nībún syù a?   Ngó yiu.
11. Kéuih haih m̀haih béi yéh ngó a?   Kéuih m̀haih béi yéh néi.
12. Kéuih haih m̀haih m̀jìdou ngó sing māt a?   Kéuih haih m̀jì.
13. Néi jì m̀jì bīngo haih Wòhng sìnsàang a?   Ngó m̀jì.
14. Ngó jìdou daihyātgo haih Jèung sìnsàang, daihyihgo haih Léih
    sìnsàang, daihsàamgo haih Wòhng sìnsàang.
15. Chàhn sìnsàang yáuh seigo saimānjái, gogo dōu hóu jùngyi góbún
    syù.

Translation of Dialogue

Use this as an exercise in translating back to Chinese and see how close you can come to the Chinese version printed at the beginning of the lesson.

A: What is your name, sir?
B: My name is Chang, and yours?
A: My name is Huang, Mr. Chang, who is that person?
B: He's a friend of mine.
A: What is the name of that friend of yours?
B: His name is Lee. Mr. Huang, are you a Chinese?
A: Yes, I am. How about you, Mr. Chang?
B: I am an American.
A: And Mr. Lee, is he also an American?
B: Yes, both of us are Americans, Do you have any children, Mr. Huang?
A: Yes, I have three children.
B: Is Mrs. Huang well?
A: She's very well, thanks. How about your wife? Is she well?
B: Thank you, she's also very well.
A: Do you know who that person is?
B: No; Mr. Lee, do you know?
C: I know. She is Miss Chen. She wants those few books.
A: Which few books does she want?
B: She wants those several Chinese books.

LESSON 6

QUALIFIED NOUNS -- NUMBERS AND MONEY

Conversation

Chàhn: Wòhng sìnsàang, néi yáuh chín ma?
Wòhng: Yáuh, néi yiu géidò a? Léuhnggo ngànchín gau m̀gau a?
Chàhn: Néi yáuh ngmān ma? Ngó séung máai yātbún Jùnggwok syù.
Wòhng: Ngó béi sahpmān néi. Chéng néi máai léuhngbún. Ngó dōu
yiu yātbún.

****

Chàhn: Léih sìnsàang, néi maai syù ma?
Léih: Maai, néi séung máai mātyéh syù a?
Chàhn: Néi yáuh mātyéh syù a?
Léih: Jùnggwok syù, Méigwok syù, ngó dōu yáuh.
Chàhn: Jùnggwok syù gwai m̀gwai a?
Léih: Yáuhdī gwai, yáuhdī m̀haih géi gwai.
Chàhn: Bīndī gwai, bīndī m̀gwai a?
Léih: Sàange gwai, gauge m̀gwai.
Chàhn: Nībun geido chin a?
Léih: Luhkgo ngànchín yātbún.
Chàhn: Luhkgo ngànchín yātbún, gam gwai àh? Gáumān léuhngbún, hóu
ma?
Léih: Sahpmān léuhngbún, néi yiu m̀yiu a?
Chàhn: Hóu, ngó máai léuhngbún.
Léih: Dòjeh, dòjeh, Joigin.
Chàhn: Jogin.

- - Translation appears at end of lesson - -

Vocabulary

chín   N: money

yáuhchín   SV: be rich, wealthy

39

ngán   N: money (vernacular)

ngànchín (M: go)   N: dollar

mān   M: dollar unit (used for whole dollars)

hòuhjí (M: go)   N: dime, ten-cent piece

hòuhjí, hòuh   M: ten-cent unit

sīn   N: cent

gwok   N: country

dò   SV: be much, many; more

siu   SV: be little, few, less

dī   M: (indicates that the noun following is plural)

(yāt)dī   N: a little, a few

yáuh(yāt)dī   N: some, a little (Lit. there are some; there is a little)

nīdī   N: these

gódī   N: those

bīndī   N: which (plural)

bun   NU: half

yātbun   N: a half

-lìhng (lèhng)   NU: zero (where one or more digits in the middle of a number are zeros, 'lìhng' is inserted. see p.46)

baak   NU/M: hundred

séung   AV: consider (doing something): plan to, want to, wish to, would like to

     séung   V: think of, think about

maai	V: sell, sell for, for sale (maai géi chìn a? how much does cost?)
gam	A: so, such
-ge	P: (particle indicating modification --see note 31-34)
chìn	NU/M: thousand
maan	NU/M: ten thousand
gau	SV: be enough, sufficient
gau chìn	Ph: have enough money
gauh	SV: be old (opposite of new)
sàn	SV: be new
yāt (plus M)	N: each (e.g., 'Sàammān yātgo.' Three dollars each. 'yāt' may also be omitted.)

bungo	1/2	(yāt)gobun	1 1/2
sàamgobun	3 1/2	sàamgo bungo	three halves

Pattern Sentences

I. Nouns qualifying nouns.

□□ or □ ge □

1. ngóge syù
   my book

2. bīngoge syù a?
   whose book?

3. néideih pàhngyáuhge
   belonging to your friends'

4. Wòhng sìnsàangge saimānjái
   Mr. Huang's children

5. Gógo yàhnge jūng
   that person's clock

6. Nībún syù haih ngóge.

7. Gógo haih ngó pàhngyáuhge.

8. Ngódeihge pàhngyáuh dōu haih Jùnggwok yàhn.

9. Nīgo saimānjái haih m̀haih Wòhng sìnsàang ga?

10. Gógo jūng haih Chàhn síujége, m̀haih ngóge.

11. Néi pàhngyáuhge taaitáai yáuh móu bāt a?

12. Nīgo bīu haih m̀haih néi pàhngyáuh ga?

13. Gójèung boují haih bīngo ga?

14. Gógo yàhnge saimānjái leng ma?

15. Kéuih haih bīngoge pàhngyáuh a?

31. One of the basic principles of Chinese word order is that the
    qualifier precedes or is subordinated to the word it qualifies.
    Position alone is frequently sufficient to indicate this rela-
    tionship. 'Ge' is the qualifying or subordinating particle.
    What precedes 'ge' qualifies what comes after 'ge.' This holds
    true whether the qualifying construction is a word, phrase or
    clause.

32. 'Ga' is a fusion of 'ge' ≠ 'a'.

33. Nouns qualifying nouns.

    a. Certain nouns between which there is a particularly close
       personal relationship often omit 'ge':

       ngó bàhbā (voc.Les. 16)   my father
       kéuih màmā (voc.Les. 16)   his (or her) mother
       néi sìnsàang   your husband

b. Modifying nouns of place usually omit 'ge':

Jùnggwok yàhn   Chinese person
Méigwok syù   American book

c. Nouns qualifying inanimate objects usually take 'ge':

ngóge bīu   my watch
bīngoge bāt a?   whose pen?

d. Whenever the noun qualified is understood, 'ge' may not be
omitted:

Nīgo haih bīngo ga?   Whose is this?
Haih ngóge.   It's mine.

II. Nouns qualified by stative verbs.

    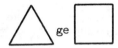

1. Yātjèung daaih tói
   a large table

2. léuhngjèung saige
   two small ones

3. hóu sànge
   a very new one

4. Daaih tói gwai, sai tói m̀gwai.
   Large tables are expensive, small ones are not expensive.

5. Ngó yiu léuhnggo saige, m̀yiu daaihge.
   I want two small ones, not large ones.

6. Kéuihdeih gogo dōu m̀haih yáuhchín yàhn.

7. Nījì haih yātjì hóu lengge bāt.

8. Gòuge saimānjái sing Chàhn, daihyihgo(saimānjái) sing Léih.

9. Gó léuhnggo saimānjái, daaihge gòu, saige m̀gòu.

10. Ngó yiu máai léuhnggo jūng, yātgo daaihge, yātgo saige.

34. Nouns qualified by stative verbs.

    a. When a noun is qualified by a stative verb, the relation-
ship may be shown by position alone, or by the use of the
subordinating particle 'ge':

        daaih tói or daaihge tói   a large table
        sàn syù or sànge syù   a new book

    b. When a stative verb is in itself qualified by an adverb the
particle 'ge' is used:

        hóu gòuge tói   very high table
        gam gwaige syù   so expensive a book

    c. Whenever the noun qualified is understood, 'ge' may not be
omitted:

        Kéuih móu saige.   He doesn't have small ones.
        Ngó yiu gógo sànge.   I want that new one.

    d. 'Dò' and 'síu' may not be used as modifiers of nouns unless
they in turn are modified by an adverb. When they are used
in such case, 'ge' is usually omitted.

        géi dò yàhn   quite a few people
        hóu síu pàhngyáuh   very few friends
        hóu dò chín   a lot of money

III. Numbers 100 and up.

yātbaak	100
yātbaak-lìhng-yāt	101
yātbaak-lìhng-yih	102
yātbaak-yātsahp	110
yātbaak-yāt	110
yātbaak-yihsahp-yāt	121
yātbaak-yah-yāt	121

yihbaak	200
sàambaak-luhksahp	360
sàambaak-luhk	360
chātbaak-sei'ah-yih	742
yātchìn	1,000
yātchìn-lìhng-yāt	1,001
yāt-lìhng-lìhng-yāt	1,001
yātchìn-lìhngyātsahp	1,010
yātchìn-yātbaak	1,100
bāatchìn-chātbaak-luhk'ah-ng̃	
	8,765
yātmaan	10,000
yātmaan-lìhng-yātsahp	10,010
yātmaan-lìhng-yātbaak	10,100
yātmaan-yātchìn	11,000
sahpmaan	100,000
sahpyihmaan	120,000
yātbaakmaan	1,000,000
yātchìnmaan	10,000,000
yātmaanmaan	100,000,000
seimaanmaan-ng̃chìnmaan	
	450,000,000

35. In fractional numbers above 100, the last measure of a series is often dropped:

yātbaak-yāt(sahp)   110
sàamchìn-ng(baak)   3,500
baatmaan-baat(chìn)   88,000

36. Where one or more digits in the middle of a number are zeros, the word 'lìhng' is inserted:

yātbaak-lìhng-yāt   101
yātchìn-lìhng-nǵ   1,005
yātmaan-lìhng-ngsahp   10,050

In giving numbers 'telephone-style', cardinal numbers without measures are used, and 'lìhng' is repeated for each zero:

yāt-lìhng-lìhng-yāt   1001
gáu-lìhng-gáu-lìhng   9090
yāt-gáu-lìhng-lìhng   1900

IV. Money expressions.

Dollars		Dimes	
Yāt	-go ngànchín	yāt	-hòuh jí
léuhng	-go ngànchín	léuhng	-hòuh jí
sàam	-go ngànchín	sàam	-hòuh jí
sei	-go ngànchín	sei	-hòuh jí
nǵ	-go ngànchín	nǵ	-hòuh jí
luhk	-go ngànchín	luhk	-hòuh jí
chāt	-go ngànchín	chāt	-hòuh jí
baat	-go ngànchín	baat	-hòuh jí
gáu	-go ngànchín	gáu	-hòuh jí
sahp	-go ngànchín	yāt	-go ngànchín
géi(dò)	-go ngànchín a?	géi(dò)	-hòuh jí a?

Cents	
yāt	-go sīn
léuhng	-go sīn
sàam	-go sīn
sei	-go sīn
nǵ	-go sīn
luhk	-go sīn

```
                    chāt    -go sīn
                    baat    -go sīn
                    gáu     -go sīn
                    yāt     -hòuh jí
                    géi(dò) -go sīn a?
```

yāt	-mān					$1.00
	go	bun¹				1.50
yāt	-go	-lìhng-		ng		1.05
	go	yāt				1.10
léuhng	-go	yih				2.20
sàam	-go	sàam				3.30
sei	-go	bun				4.50
ng	-go	ng	-hòuh	luhk(jí)		5.56
luhk	-go	luhk	-hòuh	chāt		6.67
chāt	-go	chāt	-hòuh	yāt		7.71
baat	-go	baat	-hòuh	yih		8.82
gáu	-go	gáu	(-hòuh)			9.90
sahp	-mān					10.00
sahpyāt	-go	yih				11.20
sahpyih	-go	-lìhng		sàam		12.03
yihsahp-yāt	-go	yih	-hòuh	yih		21.22
sàamsahp-yih	-go	sàam	-hòuh	sei		32.34
seisahp-ng	-go	luhk	-hòuh	sàam		45.63
chātsahp-gáu	-go	-lìhng		chāt		79.07
baatsahp-baat	-go	gáu	-hòuh	baat		88.98
gáusahp-gáu	-go	bun				99.50
yātbaak	-ngàn (or mān)					100.00

1. Néi yáuh chín ma? Móu.
   Do you have money?   No.

2. Néi yáuh géi(dò) chín a?   Ngó yáuh ng'ahmān.
   How many dollars do you have?   I have $50.00.

3. Nīgo jūng géidò chín a?   Ngmān.
   How much is this clock? $5.00.

1. The amounts from $1.10, 1.20 ... to 1.90 are always said as
   goyāt, goyih ... gogáu, the 'yāt' before 'go' is never in-
   cluded.

4. Nīdī bāt géi chín a?   Yáuhdī léuhngmān, yáuhdī sàammān.
   How much are these pens?   Some are $2.00, some are $3.00.

5. Bīndī léuhngmān, bīndī sàammān a?   Nīdī léuhngmān yātjì,
   gódī sàammān yātjì.
   Which are $2.00 and which are $3.00?   These are $2.00
   each, and those are $3.00 each.

6. Nībún syù maai géi chín a?   Nībún maai seigo ngànchín.

7. Nīgo bīu maai géi chín a?   Yihsahpmān.

8. Gógo nē?   Gógo hóu gwai, yiu chātsahpmān.   Chātsahpmān gam
   gwai àh?

9. Néi yáuh móu Jùnggwok bāt maai a?   Ngó yáuh.   Géi chín (yā
   jì a?   Léuhnghòuhbun (jì) yātjì.

10. Nījèung boují haih m̀haih seigo sīn a?   M̀haih, haih chātgo
    sīn.

11. Nīdī syù búnbún dōu maai léuhngmān.   Néi yiu géidòbún a?

12. Daaih bīu, sai bīu, gogo dōu maai yihsahpmān.   Néi jùngyi
    bīngo a?

13. Ngó yáuh gáugo sīn, séung máai yātjèung boují, m̀jì gau m̀gau
    chín nē?   M̀gau.

14. Néi séung yiu géidò chín a?   Ngó séung yiu gáusahpmān.

15. Ngó móu gáusahpmān, ńgsahpmān gau m̀gau a?   M̀gau.

16. Néidī pàhngyáuh yáuh móu seisahpmān a?   Kéuihdeih yáuh sàam
    sahpmān.

17. Néi daaihyihdī pàhngyáuh nē?   Kéuihdeih yáuh móu a?

18. Gógo sing Wòhngge yáuh (yāt)dī, gógo sing Léihge yáuh (yāt)
    dī, gógo sing...

19. Ngódeih yáuh yātbaakng'ahmān, ngódeih béi yātbaakyihsahpmān
    néi.

20. Ngó m̀yiu gamdò.   Ngódeih béi yātbaakmāan néi, hóu ma?   Hóu
    dòjeh, dòjeh.

37. '-dī' may be suffixed to the modifying element indicating the
    plural of the noun being modified.

    néidī saimānjái   your children

    Jùnggwokdī yàhn   the Chinese people

    daaihyihdī pàhngyáuh   other friends

Translate the following sentences:

1. Néi haih bīngwok yàhn a?
2. Nī léuhngbún syù géidò chín a?
3. Nībún chātmān, góbún nggo ngànchín.
4. Néi máai gamdò syù, néi gau mgau chín a?
5. Nīdī lengge haih bīngo ga?
6. Nī jèung daaih tói taai gauh, ngó mséung yiu, ngó séung máai
   jèung sànge.
7. Nī jì bāt haih sànge, gójì haih gauhge.
8. Daihyātjèung daaih tói haih Jèung sìnsàangge.
9. Chéng néi béi nīgo ngànchín daihsàamgo saimānjái.
10. Néi yáuh géidòbún Jùnggwok syù a?
11. Kéuih nīdī syù, yáuhdī haih sànge, yáuhdī haih gauhge.
12. Léih taaitáai yáuh léuhnggo saimānjái, daaihge hóu gòu,
    saige hóu leng.
13. Nīgo bīu haih néi pàhngyáuhge, gógo nē?
14. Yātgo ngànchín yáuh géidò hoují a?   Géidò hòuhjí haih yātgo
    ngànchín a?
15. Yāthòuhjí yáuh sahpgo sīn.   Sahpgo sīn haih yāthòuhjí.
16. Gódī lengge bāt taai gwai, jìjì dōu yiu (yāt)gogéi ngànchín.
17. Daihyāt gójì mhaih hóu bāt.   Néi yiu yihsahpyih mān taai
    gwai.
18. Ngó béi yāthòuhjí néi, néi béi sahpgo sīn ngó hóu ma?
19. Nīgo bīu gam leng, haih bīngo ga, haih mhaih néi ga?
20. Nī jèung yí sàammān, gójèung tói luhkmān, ngó gau chín máai
    jèung yí mgau chín máai jèung tói.

Translation of Dialogue

Use this as an exercise in translating back to Chinese and see how close you can come to the Chinese version printed at the beginning of the lesson.

Chàhn: Mr. Huang, do you have any money?
Wòhng: Yes. How much do you want? Will $2.00 be enough?
Chàhn: Do you have $5.00? I am thinking of buying a Chinese book.
Wòhng: I'll give you $10.00. Please buy two books. I want one too

****

Chàhn: Mr. Lee, do you sell books?
Léih: Yes. What books are you thinking of buying?
Chàhn: What books do you have?
Léih: I have both Chinese and American books.
Chàhn: Are Chinese books expensive?
Léih: Some are expensive and some are not too expensive.
Chàhn: Which ones are expensive, and which ones aren't?
Léih: The new ones are expensive, the old ones aren't.
Chàhn: How much is this one?
Léih: $6.00 per volume.
Chàhn: $6.00 a volume, so expensive?! How about $9.00 for two vol
Léih: $10.00 for two volumes; do you want them?
Chàhn: O.K. I'll buy two. (Chen pays him)
Léih: Thanks very much. Goodbye.
Chàhn: Goodbye.

REVIEW LESSON 1 — 6

I. Reading

Chàhn sìnsàang yáuh chātjèung tói. Kéuih séung jèungjèung dōu maai
yātbaakmān, daahnhaih kéuih gó chātjèung tói: Yáuhdī daaih, yáuhdī
sai, yáuhdī sàn, yáuhdī gauh. Wòhng sìnsàang jùngyi gójèung sànge,
kéuih séung máai gójèung sànge. Léih síujé jùngyi gójèung saige,
kéuih séung máai gójèung saige. Jèung taaitáai jèungjèung dōu
m̀jùngyi. Chàhn sìnsàang gójèung daaihge tói hóu hóu, daahnhaih taai
daaih, móu yàhn séung máai gam daaihge tói. Chàhn sìnsàang gójèung
gauhge tói géi leng, daahnhaih taai gauh, móu yàhn séung máai gam
gauhge tói.

II. Conversation

A. Gógo yàhn haih bīngo a?
Gógo haih nīgo yàhnge hóu pàhngyáuh.
Nīgo yàhn haih bīngo a?
Nīgo haih yātgo Méigwok yàhn.
Kéuih sing māt(yéh) a?
Kéuih sing Léih.
Kéuih pàhngyáuh nē?
Kéuihge pàhngyáuh sing Wòhng.
Kéuihge pàhngyáuh dōu haih Méigwok yàhn àh?
M̀haih, kéuihge pàhngyáuh haih Jùnggwok yàhn.
Kéuihdeih yiu mātyéh a?
Kéuihdeih séung máai (yāt)dī yéh.
Kéuihdeih séung máai mātyéh a?
Gógo Jùnggwok yàhn séung máai yātbún Méigwok syù.
Gógo Méigwok yàhn nē? Kéuih dōu séung máai Méigwok syù àh?
M̀haih, kéuih séung máai léuhngjí lengge Jùnggwok bāt.

B. Chàhn sìnsàang, néi hóu ma?
Hóu, néi nē?
Ngó dōu géi hóu. Néi taaitáai hóu ma?
Kéuih dōu hóu hóu, yáuhsàm.
Nīdī saimānjái haih m̀haih néi ga?

51

Yáuhdī haih, yáuhdī m̀haih.
Néi yáuh géidògo saimānjái a?
Ngó yáuh sàamgo saimānjái.
Bīnsàamgo haih néige saimānjái a?
Nī sàamgo. Néi haih m̀haih yáuh yātgo síujé a?
Haih, ngó yáuh yātgo.
Ngó yáuh yātjèung Méigwok boují, néi tái ma?
Dòjeh néi, ngó dōu yáuh Méigwok boují. Ngó séung tái Jùnggwok
   boují, néi yáuh Jùnggwok boují ma?
Ngó móu Jùnggwok boují, daahnhaih ngó yáuh Jùnggwok syù, néi
   yiu ma?

C. Néi nībún syù haih m̀haih sàn ga?
    M̀haih, nībún haih gauhge. Néi hóu jùngyi tái Jùnggwok syù àh?
    Haih, ngó hóu jùngyi tái Jùnggwok syù, daahnhaih ngó móu
       Jùnggwok syù.
    Ngó jìdou Wòhng sìnsàang yáuh géibaakbún gauhge Jùnggwok syù.
       Kéuih séung maai gódī gauh syù. Néi séung m̀séung máai géibún
       a?
    Ngó séung, daahnhaih m̀jìdou gódī syù gwai m̀gwai nē?
    M̀haih géi gwai, yātgo ngànchín yātbún. Néi jìdou bīngo haih
       Wòhng sìnsàang ma?
    Ngó jìdou. Ngo séung máai sahpbún, daahnhaih ngó m̀gau chín.
    Néi yáuh géidò chín a?
    Ngó yáuh ngmān.
    Ngó béi sahpngmān néi, chéng néi máai yihsahpbún.
    Néi dōu séung máai àh? Haih, ngó dōu séung máai sahpbún.
    Nīgo Wòhng sìnsàang haih m̀haih néige pàhngyáuh a?
    Haih, kéuih haih ngó yātgo hóu pàhngyáuh. Kéuih dōu maai jūng,
       bīu, tòih, yí. Néi yiu máai gódī yéh ma?
    Ngó yáuh gódī yéh, ngó m̀séung máai.

D. Néi haih m̀haih Wòhng sìnsàang a?
    Haih, ngó sing Wòhng. Néi gwaising a?
    Ngó sing Jèung. Wòhng sìnsàang, néi haih m̀haih maai gauhge
       Jùnggwok syù a?
    Haih, néi haih m̀haih séung máai a?
    Haih, ngó séung máai léuhngbún.
    Néi máai m̀máai tòih, yí a? Ngó daaih tói, daaih yí, sai tói,
       sai yí dōu yáuh.
    Dòjeh néi, ngó m̀máai. Nījèung tói gam leng, yiu géidò chín a?
    Saphyihgo ngànchín.
    Ngó hóu jùngyi nījèung tói, daahnhaih ngó séung máai syù, ngó
       m̀séung máai tói.

III. Sentence Drill

1. Bīngo yáuh bāt a? Ngó yáuh léuhngjì, kéuih yáuh sàamjì.
2. Ngó jìdou néi yáuh houdò chín, kéuih yáuh ngsahpgo ngànchín.
   Ngó nē, ngó yáuh yāthòuhjí.
3. Ngó yiu yātjì bāt, léuhngbún syù, sàamjèung boují.
4. Yātjì bāt léuhnghòuhbun; léuhngbún syù, seimān; sàamjèung boují
   gáugosīn.
5. Nībún gauh syù chātsahpmān taai gwai, ngó béi yihsahpmān néi
   maai m̀maai a?
6. M̀gòi néi béi góbún syù ngó hóu ma?
7. Ngó m̀yiu nījèung boují, m̀gòi néi béi daihyihjèung ngó, hóu ma?
8. Néi tái m̀tái nībún syù a? Néi m̀tái béi ngó tái, hóu ma?
9. Nījì bāt taai gwai, ngó móu gamdò chín, m̀gòi (néi) béi daihyihjì
   ngó hóu ma?
10. Néi jì m̀jì kéuih jùngyi bīnjì bāt a? Nījì hóu leng, daahnhaih
    m̀haih géi hóu, gójì hóu hóu, daahnhaih m̀haih géi leng, (ngó) m̀jì
    kéuih jùngi bīnjì nē?

IV. Translation

(Practice on Grammar Structure)

A. 1. That chair is big.
   2. They are not tired.
   3. He is very tall, his friend is also very tall.
   4. That table is very pretty, but it is too expensive.
   5. Are you tired? You are not tired!?
   6. I am very tired, are you also very tired?
   7. This table is rather pretty, but this chair is not (very
      pretty).
   8. Is this Mr. Huang's book?
   9. Is this a new book?
   10. Do you like this book?
   11. None of us knows about it.
   12. None of them wants to buy.
   13. All of these chairs are expensive.
   14. Would you please give me that newspaper?
   15. I give you five dollars, aren't you going to sell it?

B. A: Which one is Miss Chang?
    B: That one is Miss Chang.
    A: Do you like her?
    B: No, I don't like her very well.
    A: She is not pretty?
    B: No, she is pretty, but she is too tall!

C. A: Which two books do you like?
    B: I like those new ones.
    A: But those new ones are American books, not Chinese books.
    B: I want those old ones. I don't want those new noes.

V. Exercise

(Practice on Number, Measure, and Money Expressions)

A. Yātjèung boují seigosīn, léuhngjèung boují baatgosīn, sàamjèun
    géi(dò) chín a? Sàamjèung hòuhyihjí.
    Seijèung nē? Seijèung hòuhluhkjí.
    Ngjèung nē? Luhkjèung nē? Chātjèung nē? Baatjèung nē?
    Gáujèung nē? Sahpjèung nē?

B. Yātbún syù ngmān, sàambún syù géi(dò) chín a?
    Yātjèung yí luhkmān, léuhngjèung géi chín a?
    Yātgo bīu yātbaak sàamsahpmān, sahpgo bīu géidò chín a?
    Yātbaakgo bīu géidò chín a?
    Yātjèung tói ngsahp seimān, léuhngjèung tói géi chín a?

LESSON 7

AUXILIARY VERBS

Conversation

Wòhng: Néi jùngyi sihk tòhngchāan ma?
Léih: Ngó hóu jùngyi sihk tòhngchāan.
Wòhng: Néidī saimānjái nē? Kéuihdeih dōu jùngyi ma?
Léih: Kéuihdeih dōu hóu jùngyi.
Wòhng: Néi wúih góng Gwóngdùngwá ma?
Léih: Ngó wúih góng géigeui jē, daahnhaih ngódī saimānjái wúih. Kéuihdeih duhk Jùnggwok syù, wúih góng Gwóngdùngwá.
Wòhng: Gwóngdùngwá nàan m̀naan a?
Léih: Gwóngdùngwá m̀haih géi nàan góng, daahnhaih Jùnggwok jih hóu nàan sé.
Wòhng: Néidī saimānjái wúih sé Jùnggwok jih ma?
Léih: Kéuihdeih wúih sé yātdī jē.
Wòhng: Néi yìhgā jouh mātyéh sih a?
Léih: Ngó yìhgā jouhsàangyi.
Wòhng: Sàangyi hóu ma?
Léih: Yìhgā sàangyi hóu nàanjouh.

Vocabulary

sé   V: write
  séjih   VO: write

                     1. Néi sé mātyéh a?
                     2. Ngó sé Jùnggwok jih.

jih (M: go)   N: word, character (written word)

                     3. Bīn géigo jih leng a?
                     4. Nī géigo jih leng.

béichín   VO: pay

                     5. Bīngo béichín a?

55

sihk   V: eat
  sihkfaahn   VO: eat (intransitive)

                              6. Néi yiu sihk mātyéh a?
                              7. Kéuih m̀sihkfaahn àh?

faahn (M: nāp, 'grain')N: cooked rice
  faahn (M: chàan)   N: meal

                              8. Nīdī haih m̀haih faahn a?
                              9. Gódī faahn hóu hóusihk.
                             10. Néi sihk géidòchàan faahn a?

tòhngchāan (M: chàan) N: Chinese food

                             11. Néi sihk tòhngchāan ma?
                             12. Tòhngchāan haih m̀haih hóu gwai a?

sāichāan (M: chàan)   N: Western food

                             13. Ngó yiu sāichāan; néi nē?
                             14. Ngó dōu yiu sāichāan.

chāan (M: tíng,'type of') N: food, meal
  chāan (M: go)   N: meal (Western)

                             15. Néideih sihk bīntíng chāan a?
                             16. Nīgo chāan gwai m̀gwai a?

cheung   V: sing
  cheunggō   VO: sing (intransitive)

                             17. Bīn go cheunggō a?
                             18. Haih m̀haih Léih síujé cheunggō a?
                             19. Kéuih cheung mātyéh gō a?

gō (M: sáu)   N: song

                             20. Kéuih cheung léuhngsáu Jùnggwok gō.
                             21. Néi cheung géidò sáu gō a?

jouh   V: do
  jouhsih   VO: do (deeds, work), work (intransitive)
  jouhsàangyi   VO: do business, be in business

22. Kéuih jouh mātyéh sih a?
23. Gódī yàhn jouh mātyéh a?
24. Néi jùngyi jouhsàangyi ma?

sih, sihgon, sihchìhng(M:gihn) N: task, undertaking, project, job

25. Ngó jouh nīgihn sih, néi jouh gógihn
    sih .
26. Kéuih jouh bīn: géigihn sih a?

sàangyi (M: dàan,'item;' tíng,'kind') N: business of buying and selling
(the measure 'dī' can also be used instead of
'tíng '

27. Nīdàan sàangyi hóujouh ma?
28. Kéuih jouh dī mātyéh sàangyi a?

duhk   V: study; read (aloud)
  duhksyù   VO: study (intransitive); go to school

29. M̀gòi néi duhk nī yātgo jih.
30. Ngó m̀jùngyi duhksyù.
31. Kéuih m̀duhksyù àh?

wah   V: say (usually used in indirect speech),
                        think (expressing opinion)

32. Ngó wah néi hóu leng.
33. Ngó wah nī jèung tói m̀hóu.
34. Kéuih wah góbún syù m̀hóu àh?

góng   V: say; talk, speak; tell
  góngsyutwah   VO: talk, speak (intransitive)

35. Kéuih góng mātyeh a?
36. Kéuih góng kéuih hóu hóu.
37. Kéuihdeih góng mātyeh a?

góng...jì or   Ph: tell (someone something)
  góng...tēng
                        38. Kéuih góng ngó tìng kéuih m̀jùngyi nīgo bīu.

syutwah (M: geui, 'sentence') N: spoken words

39. Bīn go góngsyutwah a?
40. Nīgeui m̀haih hóu syutwah.

wá (M: júng, 'kind of') N: spoken language or dialect

                     41. Kéuih góng mātyéh wá a?
                     42. Nīgeui syutwah haih m̀haih Jùnggwok wá
                          a?

Gwóngjàu   TW: Canton

                     43. Néi haih m̀haih Gwóngjàu ga?(i.e. yàhn

Gwóngdùng   PW: province of Kwangtung

Gwóngdùngwá, Gwóngjàuwá N: Cantonese (dialect)

                     44. Kéuih góng Gwóngdùngwá ma?

yìhgā   TW: now, at present, at this time

                     45. Néi yìhgā yáuh chín ma?
                     46. Yìhgā ngó móu chín.
                     47. Néi yìhgā sihk àh?

nàan   SV: be difficult

                     48. Gwóngdùngwá nàan m̀nàan a?
                     49. Gwóngdùngwá m̀nàan.
                     50. Jùnggwok jih nàan m̀nàan a?

wúih   AV: can (know how to), be able to

                     51. Kéuih wúih góng Gwóngdùngwá ma?
                     52. Kéuih m̀wúih, ngó wúih.
                     53. Néi wúih tái Jùnggwok boují ma?

hóyíh   AV: can (be permitted), may

                     54. Ngó hóyíh sihk nīdī yéh ma?
                     55. Néi hóyíh.
                     56. Ngó hóyíh tái nījèung boují ma?

yiu   AV: want to, have to, must, need to, would
                         like to, be going to

                     57. Néi yiu máai mātyéh a?
                     58. Ngó yiu máai léuhngbún syù.

59. Ngó yiu tái nībún syù àh?

dāk   P: can (be possible), may[1]

60. Nīdī yéh sihk m̀sihkdāk a?
61. Nīdī sihkdāk, gódī m̀sihkdāk.
62. Bīndī haih sihkdāk ga?

jē   P: that's all, only (usually used when answer-
                        ing a compliment); not at all (negative)

63. Géigo ngàanchín jē.
64. Ngó yiu léuhngjèung yí jē.
65. Ngó yáuh yātgo saimānjái jē.

38. In the Vocabulary sentences, note carefully the difference between góngsyutwah, 'speak, talk', and góng... wá, 'speak a
language or dialect'.

39. Timewords (TW) have a double function; they may function as nouns,
standing as subject or object of a sentence; they may also - and
more commonly - function as moveable adverbs, modifying a verb (see
examples above under 'yìhgā')

Pattern Sentences

I. Use of auxiliary verbs:

1. Néi yiu máai mātyéh a?   Ngó yiu máai géibún syù.
   What do you want to buy?   I want to buy some books.

2. Néi jùngyi sihk (yāt)dī yéh ma?   Ngó jùngyi.
   Do you like to eat something?   Yes, I do.

1. 'dāk' is also used as a SV meaning 'O.K.; alright':

Dāk m̀dāk a?   Will that be all right?
Dāk or dāk la.   O.K.; Yes.

3. Néi séung sihk mātyéh a?   Ngó séung sihk tòhngchāan.
   What are you going to eat?   I want to eat Chinese food.

4. Néi hóu jùngyi sihk tòhngchāan àh?   Ngó hóu jùngyi sihk.
   Are you very fond of eating Chinese food?   I love to eat it.

5. Bīngo wúih cheunggō a?   Léih taaitáai.
   Who can sing?   Mrs. Lee.

6. Kéuih wúih cheung mātyéh gō a?   Jùnggwok gō, Méigwok gō,
   kéuih dōu wúih.

7. Kéuih wúih cheung géidòsáu Jùnggwok gō a?   Kéuih wúih cheung
   ńgluhksáu.

8. Kéuih hóyih béi góbún syù ngó ma?   Hóyíh.

9. Ngó hó-ṁhóyih máai nībún syù a?   Ṁhóyíh, nībún syù taai gwai

10. Ngó hó-ṁhóyih chéng kéuih sihkfaahn a?   Hóyíh, daahnhaih ngó
    ṁjì kéuih jùngṁjùngyi sihk tòhngchāan.

40. Auxiliary verbs (AV) normally take other verbs or verb-objects
    as their objects. Very few verbs serve this auxiliary function
    exclusively; many may be either functive (i.e. take a noun as
    object) or auxiliary. Such are 'jùngyi,' 'yiu,' 'séung.'

    Kéuih jùngyi cheunggō.   He likes to sing.
    Kéuih jùngyi Jùnggwok gō   He likes Chinese songs.
    Kéuih wúih góng Gwóngdùngwá. He knows how to speak Cantonese.
    Kéuih hóyíh tái nībún syù.   He may read this book.

41. When two syllable auxiliary verbs are used in the choice type
    question pattern, the full verb usually is not used both times:
    the first time only the first syllable is necessary, i.e.:
    hóyíh: hó-ṁhóyíh; jùngyi: jùng-ṁjùngyi.

II. Suffix '-dāk' as an auxiliary verb means 'can' or 'may'.

    1. Kéuih wah nībún syù taai nàan, kéuih ṁduhkdāk.
       He said this book is too difficult and he couldn't read it.

    2. Ngó ṁgau chín, ṁmáaidāk góbún syù.
       I haven't got enough money, I can't buy that book.

3. Nī jèung boují ngó táidāk ma?
   May I read this paper?

4. Nījèung yí taai gauh, m̀béidāk néi.
   This chair is too old, I can't give it to you.

5. Gógo bīu m̀haih kéuihge, kéuih m̀maaidāk.
   That isn't his watch, he can't sell it.

6. Kéuih jouhdāk bīngihn sih a?   Kéuih gihngihn sih dōu jouhdāk.

7. Ngódeih yìhgā hóyíh cheunggō ma?   Kéuihdeih yìhgā duhksyù,
   néideih m̀cheungdāk gō.

8. Néi wúih jouh nīgihn sih ma?   Ngó wúih jouh, daahnhaih ngó
   yìhgā taai guih, ngó m̀jouhdāk.

9. Néi yáuh léuhngjì bāt, néi béi nījí ngó, dāk m̀dāk a?

10. Nī jèung boují m̀haih géi hóu, néi m̀tái (kéuih) dāk m̀dāk a?
    M̀dāk, ngó jèungjèung dōu yiu tái.

11. Ngó góng kéuih jì, dāk m̀dāk a?

12. M̀dāk, néi yìhgā m̀góngdāk kéuih jì!

42. 'Góng (béi) ngó tèng' or 'góng (béi) ngó jì' literally mean
    'speak to me to hear or understand,' that is 'tell.'

III. 'Hóu' and 'nàan' as adverbial prefixes:

1. Gósáu gō hóucheung ma?
   Is that song easy to sing?

2. Nīdī jih nàansé ma?
   Are these characters difficult to write?

3. Tòhngchāan hóusihk.
   Chinese food tastes good.

4. Bīngihn sih(gon) hóu jouh a?
   Which piece of work is easy to do?

5. Nībún syù hóu(tái) m̀hóutái a?
   Is this book interesting?

6. Nībún syù hóu tái.

7. Méigwok chāan hóu(sihk) m̀hóusihk a?

8. Gódī jih nàan m̀nàan sé a?

9. Gódàan sàangyi hóu(jouh) m̀hóujouh a?

10. Nīgihn sih nàanjouh, gógihn sih hóujouh.

IV. Use of 'jē' as a final particle.

1. Jèung sìnsàang, néi yáuh géidògo saimānjái a?   Ngó yáuh yātg
   jē.
   How many children do you have, Mr. Chang?   I have only one.

2. Néi góng Gwóngjàuwá ma?   Ngó m̀wúih góng hóudò.   Ngó wúih
   góng yāt-léuhnggeuí jē.
   Can you speak Cantonese?   I can't speak very much.   I
   can only say one or two sentences, that is all.

3. Néideih yiu géidò chín a?   Kéuih yiu sahpmān, ngó yiu ńgmān
   jē.
   How much money do you want?   He wants ten dollars, I only wa
   five dollars.

4. Néi yiu mātyéh a?   Ngó yiu yātjèung tói.   Yí nē?   Ngó yiu
   tói jē, m̀yiu yí.
   What do you want?   I want a table.   How about chairs?   I
   need only a table, I don't need chairs.

5. Néi wúih sé nīdī jih ma?   Ngó wúih sé géigo jē.
   Can you write these characters?   I can only write a few.

V. Uses of 'yiu'.

1. <u>Yiu</u> in expressions for cost or price:

   Nībún syù yiu géidò chín a?
   Gójèung tói yiu géidò chín a?
   Yiu gam dò chín, ngó m̀máai.
   Yiu yātbaakmān yātgo.

2. <u>Yiu</u> as verb meaning 'want':

   Néi yiu géidòbún a?
   Kéuih yiu hóu dò yí àh?
   Nībún sàammān; néi yiu myiu a?
   Ngó yiu nīgo bīu, gógo jūng.

3. <u>Yiu</u> as verb used together with <u>séung</u> to mean 'would like' or
   'would like to have':

   Néi séung yiu dī mātyéh a?
   Néi séung mséung yiu nībún syù a?
   Néi séung yiu yāt jèung yí àh?
   Ngó séung yiu yātjì Jùnggwok bāt, mséung yiu yātjì Méigwok bāt.

4. <u>Yiu</u> as auxiliary verb meaning 'must', 'need to', 'have to':

   Ngó yiu máai nībún syù.
   Néi yiu góng kéuih jì àh?
   Kéuih yiu jouh nīgihn sih.
   Kéuih yiu sihk dī mātyéh a?

5. <u>Yiu</u> as auxiliary verb meaning 'would like to,' 'want to,' is
   going to':

   Wòhng sìnsàang yiu cheung mātyéh gō a?
   Néi yiu sihk dī mātyéh a?
   Kéuih yiu máai dī mātyéh a?
   Néi yiu tái mātyéh syù a?

VI. Verbs with generalized objects:

   1. góngsyutwah:

      Kéuih jùngyi góngsyutwah.
      Kéuih mgóngsyutwah àh?
      Chéng néi góng nīgeui syutwah.
      Bīngo góngsyutwah a?

   2. táisyù:

      Néi jùngyi táisyù ma?
      Néi jùngyi táisyù àh?
      Kéuih jùngyi tái mātyéh syù a?
      Ngó yiu tái léuhngbún syù.

3. duhksyù:

   Néi jùngyi duhksyù ma?
   Gógo saimānjái hóu jùngyi duhksyù.
   Néi duhk nībún syù àh?

4. séjih:

   Néi wúih m̀wúih séjih a?
   Ngó wúih sé léuhng-sàamgo (jih) jē.

5. sihkfaahn:

   Néi m̀sihkfaahn àh?
   Sihkfaahn m̀nàan, jouhsih nàan.
   Ngó jùngyi sihkfaahn, m̀jùngyi jouhsih.

6. béichín:

   Bīngo béichín a?
   Léih sìnsàang m̀béichín àh?
   Chàhn sìnsàang m̀beichín.
   Chàhn sìnsàang béichín.

7. cheunggō:

   Bīngo cheunggō a?
   Bīngo yiu cheunggō a?
   Léih síujé yiu cheunggō.
   Léih síujé cheung mātyéh gō a?
   Léih síujé cheung yātsáu Jùnggwok gō.

8. jouhsih:

   Ngó m̀jouhsih, hóu m̀hou a?
   Mhóu.
   Kéuih m̀jì kéuih jùngyi jouh mātyéh sih.
   Néi jouhsàangyi hóu m̀hóu a?

9. máaiyéh:

   Kéuih yiu máaiyéh.
   Kéuih yiu máai dī mātyéh a?
   Kéuih yiu máai hóudò yéh.

43. Verb-Object combinations (VO) usually possess one or more of the
    following qualities:

1. The verb and object form one single concept in English and
   are thus translated by a single English verb. For example,
   cheunggō is'to sing' in English, while the literal translation of the Chinese is 'sing song.'

2. The verb and the object can be separated by verbs suffixes
   or by other words further modifying the verb. For example,
   cheunggán gō indicates the progressive tense 'singing' (see
   Lesson 11). Cheung Jùnggwok gō, 'sing a Chinese song' illus-
   trates a modifier between the verb and the object.

3. The verb separated from its object does not necessarily
   carry the meaning that the combined form does. For example,
   chēut alone means'go out' and, combined with sai, meaning
   'world', chēutsai means 'to be born', literally: 'out to the
   world.'(see Lesson 13 Voc.)

Answer the following questions in Cantonese:

1. Hóyíh jouh nīgihn sih ma?
2. Néi séung sihk dī yéh ma?
3. Kéuih jùngyi tái syù ma?
4. Néi nē?   Néi jùngyi tái mātyéh syù a?
5. Néideih jùngyi m̀jùngyi sihk tòhngchāan a?
6. Néi gógo pàhngyáuh wúih m̀wúih góng Gwóngdùngwá a?
7. Néi wúih cheung nīsáu gō ma?
8. Néi yiu máai mātyéh a?
9. Gógihn sāangyi hóujouh m̀hóujouh a?
10. Néi wúih sé géidògo Jùnggwok jih a?
11. Jùnggwok jih nàan m̀nàan sé a?
12. Néi yìhgā yiu duhk syù ma?
13. Nībún Jùnggwok syù, néi duhkdāk ma?
14. Néi béi nīgo bīu ngó dāk m̀dāk a?
15. Néi yáuh géidò chín a?   Néi yìhgā máaidāk gójèung tói ma?

Translate the following sentences:

1. I want a small table and four chairs.
2. Does he have another one?
3. Please give this pen to Mr. Huang.
4. He has over 1,500 books.
5. The large clock costs $75.00, the small one costs $5.95.

Below are English translation of sentences used in the vocabulary
of this lesson as examples of usage. Translate these back into
Chinese (numbers correspond to those in Vocabulary section.)

1. What are you writing?
2. I am writing Chinese characters.
3. Which characters look good?
4. These look good.
5. Who's paying?
6. What do you want to eat?
7. He's not eating?
8. Is this rice?
9. That rice tastes very good.
10. How many meals do you eat (a day)?
11. Do you eat Chinese food?
12. Is Chinese food very expensive?
13. I want Western food, how about you?
14. I want Western food too.
15. What kind of food do you want to eat? (i.e. Chinese or Western)
16. Is this meal expensive?
17. Who is singing?
18. Is it Miss Lee who is singing?
19. What song is she singing?
20. She is singing two Chinese songs.
21. How many songs are you going to sing?
22. What kind of work does he do?
23. What are those people doing?
24. Do you like being in business?
25. I'll do this, you do that.
26. Which jobs is he going to do?
27. Will the transaction be a good (profitable) one?
28. What business is he in?
29. Please read this character aloud.
30. I don't like to study.
31. Doesn't she study?
32. I think you are very pretty.
33. I would say this table is no good.
34. Did he really say that book is not good?
35. What did he say?
36. He said he is fine.
37. What were they talking about?
38. He told me he doesn't like this watch.
39. Who is speaking?
40. This isn't proper talk.
41. What language does he speak?

42. Is this sentence Chinese? (Is this a Chinese sentence?)
43. Are you from Canton? (Are you Cantonese?)
44. Does she speak Cantonese?
45. Do you have any money now?
46. I haven't any money now.
47. You're eating now?
48. Is Cantonese difficult?
49. Cantonese is not difficult.
50. Are Chinese characters difficult?
51. Does he know how to speak Cantonese?
52. He doesn't, but I do.
53. Can you read Chinese newspapers?
54. May I eat these things?
55. You may.
56. May I read this newspaper?
57. What do you have to (need to, want to) buy?
58. I want to (need to) buy two books.
59. Do I have to read this book?
60. Are this things edible?
61. These are edible, but those are not.
62. Which things are edible?
63. A few dollars, that's all.
64. I want only two chairs.
65. I have one child, that's all.

LESSON 8

NOUNS MODIFIED BY CLAUSE -- CHANGED STATUS WITH 'LA' OR 'LO'

Reading

Ngó yáuh yātgo pàhngyáuh, sing Jàu. Jàu sìnsàang haih gaausyù ge. Kéuih yáuh hóudò hohksāang. Kéuih gódī hohksāang yáuhdī haih Jùnggwok yàhn, yáuhdī haih Méigwok yàhn. Yànwaih Jàu sìnsàang hóu wúih gaausyù, sóyíh kéuih gódī hohksāang hóu jùngyi kéuih.

Jàu sìnsàang haih Méigwok yàhn, daahnhaih kéuih taaitáai haih Jùnggwok yàhn. Jàu taaitáai hóu wúih jyú Jùnggwok faahn. Kéuih jyúge faahn dōu hóu hóusihk. Ngó hóu jùngyi sihk kéuih jyúge Jùnggwok faahn.

Jàu sìnsàang Jàu taaitáai yáuh léuhnggo saimānjái. Daaihge haih jái, saige haih néui. Kéuih nī léuhnggo saimānjái dōu hóu daaih lo. Kéuihdeih léuhnggo dōu hóu chùngmìng. Daaihge yìhgā mduhk syù la, saige juhng duhk. Gógo saige hóu wúih cheunggō. Kéuih cheung gódī gō dōu hóu hóutèng. Ngó hóu jùngyi tèng kéuih cheung gódī gō. Gógo daaihge hóu wúih góng Jùnggwok wá, kéuih yihk wúih tái Jùnggwok syù. Gógo saige yìhgā duhk Jùnggwok syù, daahnhaih kéuih yìhgā juhng mwúih góng Jùnggwok wá.

Vocabulary

Jàu	N:	surname: Chou, Chow

1. Jàu sìnsàang néi hóu ma?
2. Jàu taaitáai yáuh sàamgo saimānjái.

jái	N:	son

3. Kéuih yáuh géidògo jái a?
4. Nīgo haih mhaih Chàhn taaitáaige jái

néui	N:	daughter

5. Kéuih haih bīngoge néui a?

68

néui   BF: woman-, girl-

                              6. Gógo néuisìnsàang sing mātyéh a?

hohksāang   N: student

                              7. Kéuih haih bīngoge hohksāang a?
                              8. Wòhng sìnsàang yáuh géidògo hohksāang
                                 a?

Yìngmàn, Yìngmán   N: English (language)

                              9. Kéuih wúih m̀wúih góng Yìngmàn a?

Jùngmàn, Jùngmán   N: Chinese (language)

                              10. Bīngo wúih duhk Jùngmàn a?

daaihyàhn   N: adult

                              11. Léuhnggo daaihyàhn, yātgo saimānjái.
                              12. Gógo daaihyàhn haih bīngo a?

wái   M: for person (polite form)

                              13. Néi wái síujé jùngyi cheunggō ma?
                              14. Néi gó léuhngwái pàhngyáuh gwai sing a?

tèng   V: listen to

                              15. Néi jùngyi tèng cheunggō ma?
                              16. Ngó hóu jùngyi tèng cheunggō.
                              17. Néi jùngyi tèng mātyéh gō a?

jyú   V: cook
   jyúfaahn   VO: cook (intransitive)

                              18. Néi wúih jyúfaahn ma?
                              19. Ngó wúih jyú sāichāan.
                              20. Néi m̀wúih jyú tòhngchāan àh?

gaau   V: teach
   gaausyù   VO: teach (intransitive)

                              21. Néi jùng(yi) m̀jungyi gaausyù a?

22. Ngó wúih góng Yìngmàn, m̀wúih gaau
    Yìngmàn.
23. Bīngo gaau néideih góng Gwóngdùngwá aʼ

chùngmìng   SV: be clever, mentally bright, smart

24. Kéuihdī saimānjái chùngmìng ma?
25. Go néui hóu chùngmìng, go jái m̀haih
    géi chùngmìng.
26. Kéuihdī saimānjái gogo dōu hóu chùng-
    mìng àh?

yihk, yihkdōu   SV: also; too, as well

27. Kéuih wúih góng Jùnggwok wá yihk
    wúih sé Jùnggwok jih àh?
28. Haih, kéuih wúih góng yihk wúih sé.
29. Tòhngchāan ngó yihkdōu jùngyi sihk.

juhng   A: still, yet

30. Néi juhng m̀jì àh?
31. Ngó juhng m̀jì.
32. Néi juhng yáuh ma?

yànwaih   MA: because

33. Yànwaih néi móu chín àh?
34. Haih, yànwaih ngó móu chín.
35. Yànwaih Jùnggwok wá taai nàan, sóyíh
    ngó m̀wúih góng.
36. Ngó m̀wúih sé Jùnggwok jih, yànwaih...

sóyíh   MA: therefore, so
    yànwaih A, sóyíh B   Patt: A, so B; because A, therefore B
                                 (see lesson 15 Patt. IV)

37. Yànwaih góbún syù taai gwai, sóyíh
    ngó m̀máai.
38. Yànwaih kéuih m̀wúih sóyíh ngó gaau
    kéuih.
39. Yànwaih nīgihn sih hóu nàanjouh,
    sóyíh kéuih m̀wúih jouh.

la or laak, lo or lok P: indicating changed status

40. Gogo dōu hóu daaih la, wúih sé jih
    la.
41. Gogo dōu hóu daaih lo, wúih jouh
    sàangyi lo.
42. Ngó yìhgā wúih góng Gwóngdùngwá la.

làh   P: fusion of 'la' and 'àh'

43. Kéuihdī saimānjái hóu daaih làh?
44. Kéuih m̀cheung làh?
45. Néideih m̀sihk làh?

Useful Expressions

Chéng yuhng Yìngmàn sé nī géigeui syutwah (or 'wá' might be used).
Please write these sentences in English.

Chéng yuhng Yìngmàn góng nī géigeui syutwah.
Please say these sentences in English.

Chéng yuhng Gwongdùngwá góng nī géigeui syutwah.
Please say these sentences in Cantonese.

Chéng yuhng Gwóngdùngwá daap.
Please answer in Cantonese.

Pattern Sentences

I. Qualifying clauses in sentences of a general nature.

   A. Nouns qualified by a verb-object clause:

      1. yiu máai yéh ge yàhn...
         people who are going to (want to, need to) buy things...

      2. wúih sé jih ge saimānjái...
         children who know to write characters...

      3. jùngyi duhk syù ge hohksāang...
         students who like to study...

4. wúih góng Jùnggwok wá ge yàhn...
   people who know how to speak Chinese...

5. wúih gaausyù ge sìnsàang...
   teachers who know how to teach...

6. Wúih máaiyéh ge yàhn gogo dōu jùngyi nījèung tói.

7. Kéuihdeih haih wúih cheung Jùnggwok gō ge saimānjái.

8. Jùngyi duhksyù ge hohksāang dōu haih hóu hohksāang.

9. Wúih séjih ge Jùnggwok yàhn dōu wúih táisyù.

10. Wúih góng Jùnggwok wá ge Méigwok yàhn hóu síu.

11. Hohksāang dōu jùngyi wúih gaausyù ge sìnsàang.

12. Ngó yáuh hóudògo jùngyi sihk tòhngchāan ge Méigwok
    pàhngyáuh.

13. Kéuihdeih dōu haih wúih tái Jùnggwok boují ge Méigwok
    hohksāang.

14. Ngó m̀jùngyi gaau m̀jùngyi cheunggō ge saimānjái.

15. Kéuihdeih dōu haih wúih jyúfaahn ge taaitáai.

44. Qualifying clauses, like nouns and stative verbs, precede the
    nouns which they qualify. There are no Chinese equivalents for
    the relative pronouns 'who,' 'which,' and 'that.' For example,
    in English one says: 'The house that Jack built,' whereas in
    Chinese it is: 'The Jack-built house.' (compare English ex-
    pressions such as a 'self-made man,' 'home-cooked meals,' etc.)

45. Qualifying clauses in sentences of a general nature always
    take the particle 'ge.'

    tái boují ge hohksāang   students who read newspapers

    sihk faahn ge yàhn   people who eat (eat-food-ge-people)

46. A verb-object clause may be preceded by a specifier, in which
    case the 'ge' will come between the qualifier and the noun
    qualified.

Gógo góng syutwah ge yàhn haih ngóge pàhngyáuh.
That person who is talking is my friend.

Gógo wúih sé jih ge saimānjái hóu chùngmìng.
That boy who knows how to write is very clever.

Gógo séung máaiyéh ge yàhn yáuh hóu dò chín.
That person who wants to buy something has a lot of money.

B. Nouns qualified by a subject-verb clause:

1. kéuihdeih tái ge boují...
   the newspaper which they read...

2. gógo yàhn jouh ge sihgon...
   what that man does...

3. gówái taaitáai jyú ge faahn...
   the food which that lady cooks...

4. gówái síujé cheung ge gō...
   the song(s) which the young lady sings...

5. nīgo saimānjái sihk ge faahn...
   the food that this child eat...

6. Gógo saimānjái wúih sé ge jih hóudò.

7. Hohksāang jùngyi duhk ge syù dōu taai gwai.

8. Ngó mwúih sé Jùnggwok yàhn sé ge jih.

9. Nīgo yàhn yiu máai ge yéh haih mātyéh a?

10. Kéuih yiu duhk gógo sìnsàang gaau ge syù.

11. Kéuih máai ge yéh dōu hóu gwai.

12. Léih síujé wúih cheung ge dōu haih Jùnggwok gō.

13. Ngó hóu jùngyi sihk kéuih jyú ge tòhngchāan.

14. Kéuih jouh ge sih ngó mjouhdāk.

15. Nīgo yàhn góng ge wá haih Yìngmàn.

Speak cantonese

II. Qualifying clauese in sentences of a specific nature.

   A. Specified nouns qualified by a verb-object clause:

      1. góngsyutwah gógo yàhn...
         that man who is speaking...

      2. wúih séjih nīgo saimānjái...
         this child who knows how to write...

      3. jùngyi duhksyù gódī hohksāang...
         those students who like to study...

      4. yiu máaiyéh gógo sìnsàang...
         that adult who wants to buy something...

      5. wúih gaausyù gógo sìnsàang...
         that teacher who knows how to teach...

      6. Góngsyutwah gógo yàhn haih ngó ge hóu pàhngyáuh.

      7. Wúih séjih nīgo saimānjái hóu chùngmìng.

      8. Jùngyi duhksyù gódī hohksāang dōu haih hóu hohksāang.

      9. Yiu máaiyéh gógo daaihyàhn haih bīngo a?

     10. Wúih gaausyù gógo sìnsàang yiu sihkfaahn ma?

     11. Wúih góng Jùnggwok wá gógo Méigwok yàhn haih Jàu sìnsàang

     12. Ngó m̀jùngyi gaau m̀jùngyi cheunggō gódī saimānjái.

     13. Wúih jyú Jùnggwok faahn gógo pàhngyáuh haih Jàu taaitáai.

     14. Maai bīu gógo Jùnggwok yàhn hóu chùngmìng.

     15. Ngó yiu tái néi máai ge nībún sàn syù.

   B. Specified nouns qualified by a subject-verb clause:

      1. kéuihdeih tái gódī[1]boují...
         the newspapers they read...

1. Whenever 'gó' or 'gódī' is preceded by a modifying clause — for
  example: kéuih cheung gódī gō — the English will translate more
  smoothly as 'the' rather than 'that' or 'those.'

- 2. gógo yàhn jouh gógihn sih(gon)...
     the job that man does...

  3. ngó taaitáai máai nīgihn yéh...
     this thing my wife bought...

  4. Chàhn síujé cheung (ge) nīsáu gō...
     this song Miss Chen sings...

  5. Wòhng sìnsàang sé gódī syù...
     the books Mr. Huang writes...

  6. Nīgo yàhn góng nīdī wá haih mātyéh wá a?

  7. Nīgo saimānjái sé gó géigo jih leng ma?

  8. Ngó dōu hóyíh sé gógo Jùnggwok yàhn sé gódī jih.

  9. Kéuih máai nīgihn yéh hóu gwai.

  10. Kéuih gaau gódī syù hóu nàanduhk.

  11. Léih taaitáai cheung nīsáu gō haih Méigwok gō.

  12. Ngó tái gójèung boují haih Méigwok boují.

  13. Ngó hóu jùngyi sihk kéuih jyú gódī tòhngchāan.

  14. Ngó m̀wúih cheung gógo Jùnggwok yàhn cheung gódī gō.

  15. Ngó m̀jouhdāk kéuih jouh nīgihn sàangyi.

47. Usually when 'ge' and a measure (or specifier 'gó' or 'nī' plus
    measure) come together in a noun qualifying clause one or the
    other is dropped.

    maai boují ge saimānjái   góng syutwah ge yàhn
    maai boují gógo saimānjái   góng syutwah nīgo yàhn

III. Changed status with 'la' or 'lo.'

  1. Néige saimānjái hóu ma?   Hóu, kéuihdeih dōu daaih lo.
     How are your children?   Fine, they are all grown-up now.

  2. Néi juhng yiu sihk (yāt) dī yéh ma?   M̀sihk la, gau la.
     Do you want to eat some more?   I don't want to eat any-
     more, I have had enough.

3. Yìhgā ngó wúih góng Jùnggwok wá la.
   Now I am able to speak Chinese.

4. Yìhgā nīdī yéh juhng gwai m̀gwai a?   Yìhgā nīdī yéh m̀gwai 1
   Are these things still expensive?   No, they are not expens
   any longer.

5. Kéuih yìhgā hóyíh sé géidògo Jùnggwok jih a?   Kéuih yìhgā
   hóyíh sé yātbaak-lìhng-ńggo la.
   How many Chinese characters can he write now?   He can
   write 105 now.

6. Chàhn sìnsàang yáuh seigo saimānjái lo.

7. Néi juhng yiu chín m̀yiu a?   Ngó yáuh chín lo, m̀yiu lo.

8. Néi juhng m̀jìdou kéuih haih bīngo àh?   Ngó jì la, kéuih
   haih Wòhng sìnsàangge daaih jái.

9. Jèung taaitáaige sìnsàang yìhgā jouhsàangyi làh!?

10. Kéuih yìhgā yáuh chín lo, hóyíh máai nījèung tói lo.

48. The particle 'la' or 'lo' indicates that a new situation has
    arisen or that there is a changed condition or state of affairs
    'lo' lays a slightly stronger emphasis upon the change in the
    state of affairs. The negative with the particles 'la' or 'lo'
    has the force of 'no longer, no more.' With some speakers you
    will hear 'laak' or 'lok' instead of 'la' or 'lc.'

IV. The use of 'yihk 'dōu,' and yihkdōu.'

    'Yihk':

    1. Kéuih wúih cheung Jùnggwok gō, yihk wúih cheung Méigwok gō.
       She can sing Chinese songs and American songs too.

    2. Kéuih m̀jùngyi jouhsih, yihk m̀jùngyi duhksyù.
       He neither likes to work nor to study.

    3. Ngó yáuh Jùnggwok syù yihk yáuh Jùnggwok boují, néi jùngyi
       tái ma?
       I have a Chinese book and a Chinese paper. Do you want to
       see them?

'Dōu':

1. Néi m̀sihk ngó dōu m̀sihk.
   You don't eat it, neither do I.

2. Néi wúih góng Gwóngdùngwá àh?　Ngó dōu wúih góng.
   You can speak Cantonese!?　I can also speak it!

3. Yànwaih Jàu síujé hóu jùngyi cheunggō sóyíh kéuih yìhgā dōu
   hóu jùngyi cheunggō lo.
   Because Miss Chou is very fond of singing, he is also very fond
   of singing now!

'Yihkdōu':

1. Yànwaih Léih sìnsàang Léih taaitáai hóu wúih cheunggo, sóyíh
   kéuihdeih léuhnggo saimánjái yihkdōu hóu wúih cheunggō.
   Because Mr. and Mrs. Lee sing beautifully, their two children
   also can sing beautifully.

2. Nī léuhnggo hohksāang haih Méigwok yàhn, gó léuhnggo hohksāang
   dōu haih Méigwok yàhn, juhng yáuh léuhnggo yihkdōu haih Méigwok
   yàhn.
   These two students are Americans, those two are also, and there
   are two more also Americans.

3. Néi m̀duhksyù, kéuih m̀duhksyù, ngó yihkdōu m̀duhksyù lo!
   You don't study, he doesn't study, I won't study either!

49. Uses of 'yihk,' 'dōu,' and 'yihkdōu':

   'Yihk' is used when both halves of the sentence have the same
   subject: 'he <u>a</u>, and he also <u>b</u>.'

   'Dōu' is used when both halves of the sentence have the same
   verb or predicate: 'he <u>a</u> and I <u>a</u> too.'

   'Yihkdōu' can be used like both 'yihk' and 'dōu,' i.e. with
   same subject or with same predicate.

Translate the following sentences into English:

1. Wúih séjih ge yàhn dōu wúih táisyù.
2. Wúih duhksyù ge Jùnggwok yàhn dōu wúih sé Jùnggwok jih.

3. Ngó tái ge boují dōu haih Méigwok boují.
4. Kéuih jouh ge sàangyi dōu haih nàanjouh ge sàangyi.
5. Kéuih yiu máai ge syù dōu haih sànge Méigwok syù.
6. Néi wúih m̀wúih góng kéuih góng gójung wá a?
7. Kéuihdeih gogo dōu haih jùngyi duhksyù ge hóu hohksāang.
8. Jùngyi sihk tòhngchāan ge Méigwok yàhn hóudò, daahnhaih
   jùngyi sihk Méigwok chāan ge Jùnggwok yàhn hóusíu.
9. Gógo góngsyutwah ge síujé sing Léih.
10. Néi se nīdī jih hóu hóutái.
11. Kéuih máai gó léuhngjì bāt haih m̀haih Jùnggwok bāt a?
12. Wúih cheunggō gówái síujé haih Jèung sìnsàangge néui.
13. Kéuih jouh gógihn sihgon nàan m̀nàan a?
14. Maai syù gógo yàhn haih Jùnggwok yàhn, máai syù gógo yàhn
    haih Méigwok yàhn.
15. Ngó béi néi gójèung daaih tói haih yātjèung gauhge daaih tó

Translate the following sentences into Cantonese:

1. What is he doing? He is reading.
2. Do you know how to sing? I can a little.
3. Can you speak any Cantonese? Just a few sentences.
4. How many Chinese characters can you write? Only ten.
5. Do you like to eat Chinese food? I love it.

Below are English translations of sentences used in the vocabulary
of this lesson as examples of usage. Translate these back into
Chinese (numbers correspond to those in Vocabulary section).

1. How are you, Mr. Chou?
2. Mrs. Chou has three children.
3. How many sons has he?
4. Is this Mrs. Chen's son?
5. Whose daughter is she?
6. What is the name of that lady teacher?
7. Whose student is he?
8. How many students has Mr. Huang?
9. Does he know how to speak English?
10. Who can read Chinese?
11. Two adults, one child.
12. Who is that adult?
13. Does your daughter like to sing?
14. What are the (family) names of these two friends of yours?
15. Do you like listening to singing?
16. I'm very fond of listening to singing.

17. What kind of songs do you like to listen to?
18. Do you know how to cook?
19. I know how to cook Western food.
20. You don't know how to cook Chinese food!?
21. Do you like teaching?
22. I can speak English, but I can't teach it.
23. Who is teaching you to speak Cantonèse?
24. Are his children smart?
25. The daughter is very smart, the son isn't very smart.
26. His children are all very clever?
27. He can speak Chinese, and also can write Chinese characters?
28. Yes, he can speak and also can write.
29. I like to eat Chinese food too. (i.e. in addition to Western food)
30. You still don't know?
31. I still don't know.
32. Do you still have some?
33. Because you don't have any money?
34. Yes, because I don't have any money.
35. Chinese is too difficult, so I can't speak it.
36. I don't know how to write Chinese characters because...
37. That book is too expensive, so I won't buy (it).
38. He didn't know how, so I taught him.
39. This work is very difficult to do; therefore he doesn't know how to do it.
40. They're all grown up, they know how to write characters now.
41. They're all grown up, they know how to do business now.
42. I know how to speak Cantonese now.
43. His children are all grown up now?
44. She won't sing anymore?
45. You won't eat anymore?

LESSON 9

EXISTENCE AND LOCATION

Conversation

A: Bīngo a?
B: Ngó. Chéngman nīsyu haih m̀haih Jàu sìnsàangge ngūkkéi a?
A: Haih. Néi wán Jàu sìnsàang àh? Néi gwaising a?
B: Haih. Ngó sing Wòhng. Jàu sìnsàang hái (ngūk)kéi ma?
A: Deuim̀jyuh. Jàu sìnsàang m̀hái (ngūk)kéi. Néi wán kéuih yáuh
   mātyéh sihgon a?
B: Ngó yáuh (yāt)dī sih séung man kéuih. Kéuih yìhgā hái bīnsyu a?
A: Kéuih yìhgā hái hohkhaauhsyu.
B: Kéuih hái hohkhaauhsyu jouh mātyéh a?
A: Kéuih hái hohkhaauhsyu gaausyu.
B: Kéuih gógàan hohkhaauh hái bīnsyu a?
A: Hái sèhng ngoibihn.
B: Hái sèhng ngoibihn bīnsyu a?
A: Néi jì m̀jì(dou) sèhng ngoibihn gógàan maai syù ge poutáu a?
B: Ngó jì(dou).
A: Gógàan hohkhaauh hái gógàan poutáu hauhbihn.

Reading

Fóng léuihbihn yáuh yātgo yàhn, fóng ngoibihn yáuh yātgo yàhn.
Wòhng sìnsàang hái fóng léuihbihn, Wòhng taaitáai hái fóng ngoibihn.
Fóng léuihbihn gógo yàhn haih Wòhng sìnsàang, fóng ngoibihn gógo
yàhn haih Wòhng taaitáai.

Tói seuhngbihn yáuh yātbún syù. Syùge hahbihn haih tói, tóige
seuhngbihn haih syù. Syùge seuhngbihn móu yéh. Tóige hahbihn dōu
móu yéh.

Néi hái ngóge chìhnbihn, ngó hái néige hauhbihn. Ngóge chìhnbihn haih néi, néige hauhbihn haih ngó.

80

Vocabulary

ngūk (M: gàan)	N: house

    1. Gógàan ngūk haih m̀haih néi ga?
    2. Kéuih yáuh géidò gàan ngūk a?

ngūkkéi	PW: house of family

    3. Néi ngūkkéi yáuh géidògo yàhn a?

kéi	PW: house of family (cannot use as a **true** noún)

    4. Wòhng sìnsàang hái m̀hái kéi a?

fóng (M: gàan)	N: room

    5. Néi gàan ngūk géidògàan fóng a?
    6. Nīgàan fóng taai sai.

hohkhaauh (M: gàan)	N/PW: school

    7. Bīngàan haih Yìngmàn hohkhaauh a?
    8. Néi jùngyi gógàan hohkhaauh ma?

poutáu (M: gàan)	N/PW: store, shop

    9. Gógàan poutáu haih bīngo ga?
    10. Néi gàan poutáu (haih) maai mātyéh
        (ge) a?

sèhng (M: joh; go)	N: walled city; city, town

    11. Jùnggwok juhng yáuh sèhng ma?
    12. Néi jì m̀jì nīgo haih mātyéh sèhng a?

láu (M: joh)	N: building with two or more floors; storey, floor

    13. Gó joh láu haih bīngo ga?
    14. Yihláu sàamláu dōu móu yàhn.

làuhseuhng	PW: upstairs, second floor

    15. Làuhseuhng yáuh tói ma?
    16. Làuhseuhng yáuh sàamjèung tói.

làuhhah   PW: downstairs; the main floor

                                 17. Làuhhah haih mātyéh poutáu a?
                                 18. Làuhhah m̀haih maai bīu ge poutáu àh?

seuhngbihn   PW: top, above, on

                                 19. Tói seuhngbihn gódī (yéh) haih
                                     mātyéh a?
                                 20. Tói seuhngbihn gódī syù haih m̀haih
                                     Jùnggwok syù a?

hahbihn   PW: bottom, below, underneath, under

                                 21. Syù hahbihn haih mātyéh a?
                                 22. Gójì bāt hahbihn haih mātyéh a?

chìhnbihn   PW: front, in front of, before

                                 23. Syù chìhnbihn haih mātyéh a?
                                 24. Syù chìhnbihn haih bīu.

hauhbihn   PW: rear, in back of, behind

                                 25. Bīu hauhbihn haih mātyéh a.
                                 26. Bīu hauhbihn haih syù.

léuihbihn (or yahpbihn, PW: inside, in, within
          noibihn)
                                 27. Syù léuihbihn yáuh mātyéh a?
                                     Yáuh móu Jùnggwok jih a?
                                 28. Syù léuihbihn yáuh Jùnggwok jih.

ngoibihn (or chēutbihn) PW: outside

                                 29. Ngoibihn gógo yàhn haih bīngo a?
                                 30. Ngoibihn gógo saimānjái nē?

man   V: ask

                                 31. Néi man mātyéh a?
                                 32. Ngó man gógo yàhn sing mātyéh.
                                 33. Néi haih m̀haih man ngo a?

wán   V: look for; find

                                 34. Néi wán bīngo a?
                                 35. Ngó wán Léih sìnsàang.
                                 36. Néi wán bīnbún syù a?

hái   V: be located at, in, on
  hái   CV: from (see Les. 10, Patt. I)
   -hái   P: (see Les. 11, Note 59)

                                 37. Wòhng sìnsàang hái (ngūk)kéi ma?
                                 38. Kéuih mhái (ngūk)kéi.
                                 39. Kéuih haih mhaih hái poutáu a?

-syu (or -douh)   P: a place

                                 40. Ngó bún syù hái bīnsyu a?
                                 41. Néi bún syù hái gósyu.
                                 42. Kéuih bún syù hái bīnsyu a?

Useful Expressions

Jouh mātyéh a?	Móu yéh.	Móu mātyéh.
What's the matter?	Nothing.	Nothing.
Jouh māt(yéh) sihgon a?	Móu māt sihgon.	Mou yéh.
What's happened?	Nothing.	Nothing.
deuimjyuh	I'm sorry.	
chéngman, ...	May I ask...? Would you please tell me?..?	

Pattern Sentences

I. Place-words before 'yáuh' indicate existence.

   1. Seuhngbihn yáuh syù.
      There are books on top.

2. Tói seuhngbihn yáuh syù.
   There are books on the table.

3. Yí hahbihn yáuh yātjèung boují.
   There is a newspaper under the chair.

4. Tói hahbihn móu yéh.
   There is nothing under the table.

5. Hohkhaauh chìhnbihn yáuh yātgàan poutáu.
   There is a store in front of the school.

6. Sèhng ngoibihn yáuh géigàan daaih ngūk.

7. Kéuih chìhnbihn yáuh yātgo saimānjái.

8. Gójèung tói hahbihn móu yéh.

9. Nīgàan ngūk léuihbihn yáuh hóudò hohksāang.

10. Gwóngjàu yáuh hóudò daaihge poutáu.

11. Ngoibihn yáuh yàhn góng syutwah.

12. Gógàan hohkhaauh hauhbihn yáuh yātgàan maai syù ge poutáu.

13. Bīnsyu yáuh maai syù ge poutáu a?   Sèhng léuihbihn syusyu
    dōu yáuh.

14. Fóng léuihbihn yáuh yàhn ma?   Yáuh.

15. Néi ngūkkéi yáuh géidògo yàhn a?   Ńggo.

16. Yí hahbihn yáuh mātyéh a?   Yí hahbihn yáuh yātjèung boují.

17. Ngūk ngoibihn yáuh géidògo yàhn a?   Ngūk ngoibihn yáuh sàamgo
    yàhn.

18. Bīnsyu yáuh Jùnggwok hohkhaauh a?   Gósyu yáuh yātgàan Jùnggwok
    hohkhaauh.

19. Gójèung yí hauhbihn yáuh móu jūng a?   Móu jūng, yáuh (yāt)go
    bīu jē.

20. Gójèung tói seuhngbihn yáuh (yāt)dī mātyéh a?   Yáuhdī sihkge
    yéh.

50. Words indicating position or location are called placewords (PW). Some of these placewords are as follows:

léuihbihn	inside
ngoibihn	outside
seuhngbihn	'topside'
hahbihn	'bottomside'
chìhnbihn	'frontside'
hauhbihn	'backside'

These words may be modified by other nouns without the use of the particle 'ge': 'tói seuhngbihn,' 'on top of the table,' 'fóng chìhnbihn,' 'in the front of the room.' And these words can also used as modifiers to nouns, i.e. 'seuhngbihn góbún syù,' 'the book on the top'; 'chìhnbihn gógàan fóng,' 'the room at the front,' etc.

51. When a placeword preceds the verb 'yáuh,' it signifies that 'at x there is y':

léuihbihn yáuh yàhn	there are people inside
seuhngbihn móu yéh	there is nothing on top of it
tói hauhbihn yáuh jèung yí	there is a chair behind the table

II. Place-words after 'hái' indicate location.

1. Kéuih hái fóng léuihbihn.
   She is in the room.

2. Ngóge pàhngyáuh hái fóng ngoibihn.
   My friend is outside the room.

3. Wòhng taaitáai hái làuhseuhng.
   Mrs. Huang is upstairs.

4. Wòhng sìnsàang hái làuhhah.
   Mr. Huang is downstairs.

5. Yáuh yātbún syù hái tói seuhngbihn.
   There is a book on the table.

6. Ngó hái néi chìhnbihn.

7. Poutáu hái gógàan gòu láu(ge) hauhbihn.

8. Léih taaitáai hái gógàan ngūk léuihbihn.

9. Ngó gàan ngūk hái sèhng ngoibihn.

10. Kéuih gàan poutáu hái sèhng léuihbihn.

11. Boují hái góbún syù hahbihn.

12. Néige pàhngyáuh hái gógàan poutáu hauhbihn.

13. Ngó máai góbún syù hái fóng léuihbihn.

14. Jèung sìnsàang hái chìhnbihn, Jàu sìnsàang hái hauhbihn.

15. Néi máai gójèung boují hái gójèung sai tói seuhngbihn.

16. Kéuih hái bīnsyu a? Kéuih hái seuhngbihn.

17. Bīngo hái seuhngbihn a? Dī saimānjái hái seuhngbihn.

18. Chàhn síujé hái m̀hái nīsyu a? Kéuih m̀hái nīsyu, kéuih hái
    Gwóngjàu.

19. Néi gàan hohkhaauh hái bīnsyu a? Ngó gàan hohkhaauh hái
    sèhng léuihbihn.

20. Ngó góbún syù hái néisyu ma? M̀hái, néibún syù hái kéuihsyu.

52. The verb 'hái' followed by a placeword means 'is at/in/on...'

Kéuih hái fóng léuihbihn.   He is inside the room.
Syù hái tói seuhngbihn.   The book is on the table.
Hohkhaauh hái sèhng ngoibihn. The school is located outside
                                  the city.

53. 'Syu' and 'douh' are general positional suffixes that can be
    added to nouns and pronouns, making them into placewords.
    The meaning may be 'on, in, or at x.'

Gójèung tóisyu yáuh sàamjì bāt.
There are three pens on (or in) the table.

Kéuih gàan poutáu hái bīndouh a?
Where is his store?

Gójoh láusyu yáuh hóudò hohksàang.
There are quite a few students around(or in) that building.

Góbún syù m̀hái hohkhaauhsyu hái ngósyu.
That book is not in school, it's in my place.

M̀hái ngó nīdouh, yihk m̀hái kéuih gódouh, haih m̀haih hái néidouh
a?
It isn't in my place, it isn't in his place, could it be in your
place?

These positional suffixes, when they are added to the specifiers
'nī,' 'gó,' and 'bīn,' are translated in English as 'here,'
'there,' and 'where,' and when they are used in the duplicated
form, 'syusyu dōu' or 'douhdouh dōu,' they are translated as
'everywhere,' or 'anywhere.'

Nīsyu móu Jùnggwok sīnsàang.
There is no Chinese teacher here.

Gósyu móu Méigwok hohkhaauh.
There is no American school.

Bīnsyu yáuh maaisyù ge poutáu a?
Where is a bookstore?

Syusyu dōu yáuh.
It is everywhere.

III. 'Hái' as the co-verb of location:

1. hái ngūkkéi sihkfaahn
   eat at home

2. hái fóng léuihbihn tái boují
   read a newpaper inside the room

3. hái bīnsyu máaiyéh
   buy things where

4. hái nīsyu góngsyutwah
   talk here

5. hái sèhng ngoibihn jouhsih
   work outside the city

6. Kéuihdeih hái seuhngbihn sihkfaahn.

7. Ngó hái nīsyu tái boují.

8. Kéuihdī saimānjái hái gógàan hohkhaauh duhksyù.

9. Kéuih hái sèhng léuihbihn jouhsih.

10. Kéuih m̀hái nīsyu duhksyù.

11. Jàu sìnsàang hái gósyu jouh mātyéh a? Kéuih hái gósyu gaau-
    syù.

12. Bīngo hái léuihbihn cheunggō a? Chàhn síujé hái léuihbihn
    cheunggō.

13. Kéuihdeih hái bīnsyu jyúfaahn a? Hái gàan ngūk léuihbihn.

14. Kéuih hái bīngàan poutáusyu máaiyéh a? Hái gógàan Jùnggwok
    hohkhaauh hauhbihn gógàan.

15. Néi hái bīngàan hohkhaauh duhksyù a? Ngó hái gógàan Jùng-
    gwok hohkhaauhsyu duhksyù.

54. A co-verb (CV) with its object forms an adverbial phrase modi-
    fying the main verb of a sentence. Such a co-verbal phrase
    takes the place of a prepositional phrase in English. Many
    otherwise functive verbs are used co-verbally, but a few are
    consistently co-verbs.

                         Drill on 'Yáuh'

A. Used as 'have' in English.

    Ngódeih hohkhaauh yáuh sàamgo néui-sìnsàang.
    Nī sàamgo néui-sìnsàang gogo dōu yáuh géigo saimānjái.
    Kéuihdeihdī saimānjái yáuhdī yáuh Jùnggwok bāt yáuhdī yáuh Méi-
    gwok bāt.
    Gódī yáuh Jùnggwok bāt ge, jùngyi yiu Méigwok bāt; gódī yáuh
    Méigwok bāt ge, jùngyi yiu Jùnggwok bāt.
    Gó sàamwái néui-sìnsàang wah: "Ngódeih yáuh Jùnggwok bāt yihk
    yáuh Méigwok bāt. Néideih jùngyi yiu Méigwok bāt ge, ngódeih
    hóyíh béi Méigwok bāt néideih; néideih jùngyi yiu Jùnggwok bāt
    ge, ngódeih hóyíh béi Jùnggwok bāt néideih.

B. Used to indicate existence.

Sèhng ngoibihn yáuh yātgàan hóu daaihge hohkhaauh.
Hohkhaauh léuihbihn yáuh yātgàan maai syù ge poutáu.
Poutáu léuihbihn yáuh hóudò Jùnggwok syù.
Syù seuhngbihn yáuh Yìngmàn, yihk yáuh Jùnggwok jih.
Jùnggwok jih chìhnbihn, hauhbihn, dōu yáuh hóudò Yìngmàn, ngó
wúih duhk gódī Yìngmàn, ngó m̀wúih duhk gódī Jùnggwok jih.

<u>Comparison of the uses of</u> 'yáuh' <u>and</u> 'hái

Yáuh		Hái
bīnsyu	yáuh boují a?	boují hái bīnsyu a?
gósyu	yáuh boují.	boují hái gósyu.
nīsyu	yáuh boují.	boují hái nīsyu.
kéuihsyu	yáuh boují.	boují hái kéuihsyu.
hohkhaauhsyu	yáuh boují.	boují hái hohkhaauhsyu.
ngūkkéisyu	yáuh boují.	boují hái ngūkkéisyu.
fóngsyu	yáuh boují.	boují hái fóngsyu
poutáusyu	yáuh boují	boují hái poutáusyu.
tóisyu	yáuh boují.	boují hái tóisyu.
yísyu	yáuh boují.	boují hái yísyu.

Translate the following sentences into Cantonese:

1. Who is the gentleman who wants to buy books?
2. I am very fond of listening to the songs she sings.
3. Mr. Huang now is in business and is not studing anymore.
4. I don't know whether or not this is the book which he likes
   to read.
5. This book is very difficult (to read), therefore he doesn't
   want to read it anymore.

Below are English translations of sentences used in the vocabulary
of this lesson as examples of usage. Translate these back into
Chinese (numbers correspond to those in Vocabulary section.)

1. Is that house yours?
2. How many houses has he?

3. How many persons in your family?
4. Is Mr. Huang home?
5. How many rooms do you have in your house?
6. This room is too small.
7. Which one is an English school?
8. Do you like that school?
9. Whose store is that?
10. What kind of a store is yours?
11. Does China still have walled cities?
12. Do you know what this city is?
13. Who owns that tall building?
14. There was no one in the second and third floor.
15. Is there a table upstairs?
16. There are three tables upstairs.
17. What kind of store is downstairs?
18. It isn't a store that sells watches downstairs?
19. What are those things on the table?
20. Are those books on the table Chinese books?
21. What's underneath the books?
22. What's underneath that pen?
23. What's in front of the book?
24. It's a watch.
25. What's in back of the watch?
26. It's a book.
27. What's inside the book? Is there any Chinese character the
28. There are Chinese characters in the book.
29. Who is that person outside?
30. Who is that child outside?
31. What are you asking about?
32. I am asking what that gentleman's surname is.
33. Are you asking me?
34. Who are you looking for?
35. I'm looking for Mr. Lee.
36. Which book are you looking for?
37. Is Mr. Huang in?
38. He isn't in.
39. Is he in the store?
40. Where is my book?
41. Your book is over there.
42. Where is his book?

LESSON 10

MOTION AND DIRECTION -- CONVEYANCE AND PURPOSE

Conversation

A: Néideih heui bīnsyu a?
B: Ngódeih heui Hèunggóng.
A: Néideih chóh fóchè heui àh?
B: Mhaih, ngódeih chóh heichè heui.
A: Dímgáai mchóh fèigēi nē?
B: Hái nīsyu heui Hèunggóng móu fèigēi chóh.
A: Néi heui gósyu jouh mātyéh a?
B: Ngódeih heui taam léuhnggo pàhngyáuh. Ngódeih yihkdōu séung
   máai dī yéh.
A: Néideihge pàhngyáuh hái Hèunggóng bīnsyu a?
B: Hái daihbaatgāai.
A: Néideihdī saimānjái dōu heui ma?
B: Daaihge heui, saige mheui.
A: Dímgáai néideih mchéng néideihge pàhngyáuh lèih nīsyu nē?
B: Kéuihdeih hóu jùngyi lèih, daahnhaih kéuihdeih yáuh hóudò sih
   yiu jouh; saimānjái gogo dōu taai sai, sóyíh mlèihdāk.

Vocabulary

gàmyaht	TW:	today

1. Néi gàmyaht yáuh chín ma?
2. Néi yáuh gàmyahtge boují ma?

tìngyaht	TW:	tomorrow

3. Tìngyaht néi duhksyù ma?
4. Tìngyaht bīngo jyúfaahn a?

tìnhei	N:	weather

5. Nīsyu tìnhei hóu ma?

6. Nīsyuge tìnhei m̀haih géi hóu⁻.

(fó)chèjaahm   N/PW: railroad station

7. Fóchèjaahm hái bīnsyu a?

gāai (M: tìuh)   N/PW: street

8. Gógàan hohkhaauh hái bīntìuh gāai a?
9. Néi wán bīntìuh gāai a?

heuigāai   VO: go out (onto the street)

10. Néi heui m̀heuigāai a?

Seuhnghói   PW: Shanghai

11. Seuhnghói yáuh móu sèhng a?
12. Seuhnghói yìhgā móu sèhng.

Hèunggóng   PW: Hongkong

13. Hèunggóng yáuh móu maai Jùnggwok syù
    ge poutáu a?
14. Hèunggóng yáuh géidò Jùnggwok yàhn a?

lèih (or làih)   V: come

15. Kéuih lèih ma?
16. Kéuih m̀lèih.
17. Néi lèih m̀lèih ngó ngūkkéi a?

heui   V: go, go away, go to

18. Néi heui ma?
19. Ngó m̀heui la.
20. Kéuih nē? Kéuih dōu m̀heui àh?

jip   V: meet; receive (a letter)

21. Néi jip bīngo a?
22. Ngó jip ngóge pàhngyáuh.
23. Kéuih jip kéuihge pàhngyáuh àh?

| taam | V: visit |

24. Néi taam bīngo a?
25. Ngó taam Chàhn taaitáai.
26. Néi jì m̀jì kéuih taam bīngo a?

| chóh | CV: ride on, take, by (bus, train, ship, plane)
V: sit, drop in (for a visit); take a seat |

27. Ngódeih chóh fóche heui.
28. Néi chóh nīsyu, néi taaitáai chóh gósyu.
29. Chéng chóh! Chéng chóh!

| hohk | V: learn; study
AV: learn to, study how to |

30. Néi yìhgā hohk mātyéh a?
31. Ngó yìhgā hohk góng Gwóngdùngwá.
32. Hohk Gwóngdùngwá nàan m̀nàan a?

| fóchè (M: ga) | N: train |

33. Néi jùng(yi) m̀jùngyi chóh fóchè a?
34. Kéuih dōu jùngyi chóh fóchè àh?

| heichè, chè (M: ga) | N: automobile, car |

35. Néi ga heichè hái bīnsyu a?
36. Ngó ga heichè hái gógàan poutáu chìhnbihn.

| fèigèi (M: ga) | N: airplane |

37. Góga haih bīngwokge fèigèi àh?
38. Néi jùngyi chóh fèigèi ma?

| syùhn (M: jek) | N: ship, boat, steamship |

39. Bīnjek haih Méigwok syùhn a?
40. Nīsyu yáuh géidòjek Méigwok syùhn a?

| Hòh | N: Ho (surname) |

41. Bīnwái haih Hòh sìnsàang a?
42. Hòh taaitáai hái bīnsyu a?

Ng̀   N: Wu (surname)

                                     43. Néi wán Ng̀ sìnsàang àh?
                                     44. Néi jì m̀jì Ng̀ sìnsàang hái bīnsyu a?

jànhaih   A: certainly, really

                                     45. Néi jànhaih m̀wúih àh?
                                     46. Ngó jànhaih m̀wúih.
                                     47. Néi jànhaih m̀jùngyi sihk tòhngchāan à

dím, dímyéung   MA: how?

                                     48. Nígo jih dím sé a?
                                     49. Ngó m̀jì dím sé.
                                     50. Nīgihn sih dím jouh a?

dímgáai   MA: why? how is it that...?

                                     51. Dímgáai kéuih m̀jouh a?
                                     52. Ngó m̀jì dímgáai kéuih m̀jouh.
                                     53. Dímgáai néi juhng m̀wúih a?

mē   P: question ending expressing surprise,
                                         doubt, etc.

                                     54. Néi m̀jì mē?
                                     55. Kéuih m̀maai mē?
                                     56. Néi m̀jì kéuih jùng(yi) m̀jùngyi mē?

Useful Expressions

Dím(yéung) a?   How's everything? How's it coming?
Dím syun a?   What can be done about it?
Hóu noi m̀gin.   Haven't seen you for a long time.

Pattern Sentences

I. Co-verb of direction 'hái'

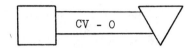

1. Néi hái bīnsyu lèih a? Ngó hái poutáu lèih.
   Where are you coming from? I am coming from the store.

2. Kéuih hái bīnsyu lèih a? Kéuih hái hohkhaauh lèih.
   Where is he coming from? He's coming from school.

3. Kéuihdeih haih mhaih hái hohkhaauh lèih a? Mhaih, kéuihdeih
   hái sèhng ngoibihn lèih.
   Will they come from school? No, they'll come from outside the
   city.

4. Kéuih haih mhaih hái poutáuoyu hcui a? Mhaih.
   Is he going there from the store? No.

5. Kéuih haih mhaih hái ngūkkéi heui a? Mhaih, kéuih haih hái
   hohkhaauh heui.
   Is he going from home? No, from school.

6. Kéuih yìhgā hái hohkhaauhsyu heui àh? Haih, kéuih yìhgā hái
   hohkhaauhsyu heui.
   Is he going from school now? Yes, he is going from school now.

55. 'Hái' which literally means 'be at, in, or on' is used as a
    coverb to indicate direction from, rather than the more formal
    co-verb 'chùhng':

    hái ngūkkéisyu lèih...   come from home...
    hái Meigwok lèih Jùnggwok...   come from America to China...
    hái Seuhnghói heui Hèunggóng...   go from Shanghai to Hong Kong...

II. Co-verb of conveyance 'chóh':

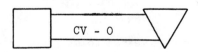

1. Néi dímyéung lèih a? Chóh fóchè lèih àh? Mhaih, ngó chóh
   heichè lèih.
   How are you going to get here, by train? No, I'll come by
   car.

2. Dímgáai néi mchóh fèigèi nē? Yànwaih tìnhei mhóu sóyíh ngó
   mchóh fèigèi.
   Why don't you take a plane? The weather isn't good, therefore I am not going to.

3. Chóh syùhn heui Seuhnghói gwai mgwai a? Mgwai, yihsahpgo
   ngànchín jē!
   Is it expensive to go to Shanghai by boat? No, it isn't
   expensive, only twenty dollars.

4. Ngó hó mhóyíh chóh syùhn heui Gwóngjàu a? Hóyíh.
   Can I go to Canton by boat? Yes, you can.

5. Néi chóh syùhn lèih àh, mhaih chóh fóchè lèih àh? Mhaih,
   ngó mchóh fóchè lèih, yihk mchóh syùhn lèih. Ngó chóh
   fèigèi lèih.
   You are coming here by boat, not by train, eh? No, I'm not
   coming by train or by boat. I'm coming by plane.

6. Gàmyaht tìnhei hóu, sóyíh hóudò yàhn chóh fèigèi.

7. Ngó mjùngyi chóh fèigèi, jùngyi chóh syùhn.

8. Néi gàmyaht dímyéung heui Hèunggóng a? Ngó chóh syùhn heui.

9. Gàmyaht tìnhei gam hóu, dímgáai mchóh fèigèi heui nē? Fèigèi
   taai gwai, ngó móu gamdòchín, dímyéung chóhdāk fèigèi a?

10. Tìngyaht heui Hèunggóng góga fèigèi haih mhaih hóu daaih ga?
    Haih, haih hóu daaihge hóu sànge.

56. 'Chóh' and its object form a co-verbal phrase indicating the
    means of conveyance adopted to get from one point to another.

    chóh syùhn heui...   go by ship...
    chóh fèigèi lèih...   come by plane...
    chóh heichè heui...   go by car...

    Note that since 'chóh' literally means 'to sit,' it is only
    used with respect to conveyances which provide places to sit
    down.

III. Purpose of coming and going

A: Néi tìngyaht heui fóchèjaahm jouh mātyéh a?
B: Ngó heui jip ngóge pàhngyáuh Hòh sìnsàang, Ng̀ sìnsàang.
A: Hòh sìnsàang lèih Jùnggwok jouh mātyéh a?
B: Kéuih lèih Jùnggwok gaausyù.
A: Kéuih lèih nīsyu juhng heui m̀heui daihyihsyu a?
B: Kéuih m̀heui daihyihsyu lo!
A: Ng̀ sìnsàang nē?
B: Ng̀ sìnsàang yiu heui Seuhnghói, yànwaih kéuih hái gósyu yáuh hóu daaihge sàangyi.
A: Dímgáai kéuih lèih Hèunggóng nē?
B: Kéuih lèih Hèunggóng máai dī yéh.
A: Ngó tìngyaht dōu heui fóchèjaahm jip pàhngyáuh.
B: Jip bīngo a?
A: Jip Léih sìnsàang.
B: Haih mē! Lèih sìnsàang jànhaih lèih mē! Kéuih lèih jouh mātyéh a?
A: Kéuih lèih ngódeih gàan hohkhaauh gaau cheunggō.
B: Ngó hóu séung hohk cheunggō, m̀jì kéuih jùng(yi) m̀jùngyi gaau ngó nē?

English translation of the above dialogue.

A: Why are you going to the railroad station tomorrow?
B: I am going there to meet my friends Mr. Ho and Mr. Wu.
A:. What is Mr. Ho coming to do in China?
B: He is coming to China to teach.
A: After he has come here, will he be going anywhere else?
B: He won't go anywhere else!
A: How about Mr. Wu?
B: Mr. Wu has to go to Shanghai, because he has a very big business there.
A: Why does he come to Hongkong?
B: He comes to Hongkong to buy a few things.
A: Tomorrow I am also going to the **railroad** station to meet a friend.
B: Who are you going to meet?
A: Mr. Lee.
B: Is that so! Is he really coming!? What is he coming for?
A: He is coming to our school to teach singing.
B: I would like very much to learn how to sing. I don't know whether or not he would like to teach me.

57. The purpose of coming from or going to a place is indicated by
    placing the purpose expression immediately after the main verb
    'lèih' or 'heui' plus its placeword object:

    lèih gaau syù...   come to teach...
    heui poutáu máai yéh...   go to the store to buy things..
    heui Seuhnghói jouh sàangyi...   go to Shanghai to do business..

Additional Sentences

1. Kéuih haih m̀haih hái Méigwok chóh fèigèi lèih a?
2. Ngó tìngyaht heui sèhng ngoi(bihn) gógàan poutáu máai yéh,
   néi dōu heui ma?
3. Ngó jùngyi chóh syùhn m̀jùngyi chóh fèigèi. Néi nē?
4. Chóh syùhn heui Méigwok gwai m̀gwai a?
5. Nīsyu yáuh móu heui Méigwok ge fèigèi a?
6. Néi yáuh géidògo pàhngyáuh yiu chóh fèigèi heui Hèunggóng a?
7. Néi wah (hái) nīsyu mou fèigèi heui Méigwok, hái Hèunggóng
   yihk móu fèigèi heui Méigwok àh?
8. Gaau cheung gō gówái sìnsàang haih m̀haih tìngyaht lèih a?
9. Néideih haih m̀haih séung chóh syùhn heui Hèunggóng, hái
   Hèunggóng chóh fèigèi heui Méigwok a?
10. Hóudò yàhn jùngyi chóh fèigèi dímgáai néideih m̀jùngyi chóh
    (fèigèi) nē?
11. Néige pàhngyáuh Wòhng sìnsàang kéuih lèih Jùnggwok jouh māt-
    yéh a?
12. Néidī pàhngyáuh haih m̀haih gogo dōu haih hái Méigwok lèih a?
13. Néidī pàhngyáuh haih hái Seuhnghói chóh syùhn lèih Hèunggóng
    m̀haih hái Méigwok chóh syùhn lèih Hèunggóng àh?
14. Gàmyaht tìnhei gam hóu, dímgáai néi m̀chóh fèigèi heui Hèung-
    góng nē?
15. Gógo hái Méigwok chóh syùhn lèih ge Méigwok yàhn, haih m̀haih
    néige hóu pàhngyáuh a?
16. Bīngo góng néi jì a? Néi dím jì gósyu móu fèigèi heui Hèung
    góng a?
17. Bīnjek syùhn haih heui Méigwok ga? Haih m̀haih gójek a?
18. Néi séung chóh bīnjek syùhn heui Seuhnghói a? Gójek Méigwok
    syùhn àh?
19. Heui Méigwok gódī fèigèi, haih m̀haih gaga dōu haih Méigwok
    fèigèi a?
20. Néideih gogo dōu jùngyi chóh fèigèi heui, m̀jùngyi chóh syùhn
    heui àh?

Translate the following sentences into Cantonese:

1. My car is behind that big house.
2. Why is my book underneath your table?
3. Do you know where the bookstore is?
4. There are many American students inside that school.
5. They are eating upstairs.

Below are English translations of sentences used in the vocabulary of this lesson as examples of usage. Tranalate these back into Chinese (numbers correspond to those in Vocabulary section).

1. Do you have money today?
2. Do you have today's paper?
3. Will you study tomorrow?
4. Who's going to cook tomorrow?
5. Is the weather here nice?
6. It isn't very good.
7. Where is the railroad station?
8. On what street is that school?
9. Which street are you looking for?
10. Are you going out?
11. Is there a walled city in Shanghai?
12. There isn't a walled city in Shanghai anymore.
13. Is there any Chinese bookstore in Hongkong?
14. How many Chinese are in Hongkong?
15. Does he come?
16. He doesn't.
17. Are you coming to my home?
18. Will you go?
19. I won't go.
20. How about him? Won't he go either?
21. Whom are you going to meet?
22. I'm going to meet my friends.
23. He is going to meet his friend, I suppose.
24. Whom are you going to visit?
25. I'm going to visit Mrs. Chan.
26. Do you know whom he is going to visit?
27. We will go by train.
28. You sit here, and your wife sit there.
29. Please sit down!
30. What are you learning?
31. I'm learning to speak Cantonese.
32. Is it difficult to learn Cantonese?
33. Do you like to ride on trains?

34. Does he also like to ride on trains?
35. Where is your car?
36. My car is in front of that store.
37. Which country's plane is that?
38. Do you like to ride in planes?
39. Which one is an American ship?
40. How many American ships are here?
41. Who is Mr. Ho?
42. Where is Mrs. Ho?
43. You are looking for Mr. Wu, eh?
44. Do you know where Mr. Wu is?
45. You really don't know how to do it?
46. I really don't know how to do it.
47. You really don't like to eat Chinese food?
48. How is this character written?
49. I don't know how to write it.
50. How is this to be done?
51. Why doesn't he do it?
52. I don't know why he doesn't do it.
53. Why don't you still know how to do it?
54. Don't you know?
55. Doesn't he want to sell it?
56. Don't you know whether she likes it or not?

LESSON 11

DIRECTIONAL VERBS -- CONTINUANCE WITH 'GAN'

Reading

Chàhn sìnsàang jyuhhái sèhng ngoibihn daihsàamgāai, kéuih yáuh gàan maai syù ge poutáu hái sèhng léuihbihn. Gàmjìujóu, Chàhn sìn-sàang m̀yahpdākheui kéuih gàan poutáu, yànwaih kéuih móu sósìh. Kéuih fàanheui ngūkkéi, kéuih taaitáai m̀hái (ngūk) kéi, kéuih yauh m̀yahpdākheui kéuihge ngūkkéi, yànwaih kéuih móu ngūkkéige sósìh. Kéuih kéihhái gāaisyu dáng kéuih taaitáai. Móugéinói, kéuih taai-táai fàanlèih la, man kéuih: "Néi kéihhái (nī)syu jouh mātyéh a"? Kéuih wah: "Ngó dáng néi béi poutáu tìuh sósìh ngó." Kéuih taai-táai wah: "Poutáu tìuh sósìh m̀hái ngósyu, m̀haih hái néi gàan fóng léuihbihn mē"? Chàhn sìnsàang yahpheui gàan fóng wán, yātjahngāan, kéuih chēutlèih wah: "Dímgáai móu nē? M̀hái néisyu, yihk m̀hái ngó gàan fóngsyu, hái bīnsyu a"? Chàhn taaitáai wah: "Haih m̀haih hái ga (hei)chèsyu"? Chàhn sìnsàang chēutheui ga chèsyu, séuhngheui ga chè, yauh lohklèih, yauh séuhngheui, yauh lohklèih, wah: "Yáuh la! Yáuh la! Ngó yìhgā fàanheui poutáu la. Joigin! Joigin"!

Vocabulary

gàmmáan   TW: tonight

                               1. Gàmmáan néi heui ma?
                               2. Gàmmáan ngó m̀heui.
                               3. Kéuih gàmmáan dōu m̀heui àh?

gàmjìujóu, gàmjìu   TW: this morning

                               4. Gàmjìujóu tìnhei hóu ma?
                               5. Gàmjìujóu tìnhei hóu hóu.
                               6. Gàmjìujóu néi sihk mātyéh a?

tìngjìujóu, tìngjìu   TW: tomorrow morning

                               7. Tìngjìujóu néi lèih ma?

8. Kéuih tìngjìujóu heui bīnsyu a?

tìngmáan   TW: tomorrow night

9. Tìngmáan bīngo lèih a?
10. Tìngmáan néi heui Hèunggóng ma?

yātjahnggāan   TW: (in) a moment, (after) a short while

11. Mgòi néi dáng ngó yātjahnggāan.

dākhàahn   SV: having free time

12. Néi tìngyaht dākhàahn ma?
13. Ngó tìngyaht dākhàahn.

mdākhàahn   SV: busy

14. Néi yìhgā mdākhàahn àh?
15. Kéuih mdākhàahn mē?

hàahng   V: walk, go or run (of watch, cars, etc.)
  hàahnglèih hàahngheuiPh: walk back and forth

16. Néi hàahngdāk ma?
17. Ngó mhàahngdāk, yànwaih ngó taai gui
18. Néige bīu hàahng mhàahng a?

jáu   V: run; leave (to depart)
  jáulèih jáuheui   Ph: run back and forth

19. Kéuih jáu mātyéh a?
20. Ngó mjì kéuih jáu mātyéh.
21. Ngó jáu la, néi jáu mjáu a?
22. Ngó dōu jáu la.

jyuh   V: stay, live (at a place)

23. Néi jyuhhái bīnsyu a? (See Note 59)
24. Ngó jyuhhái gógàan ngūksyu.
25. Kéuih jyuhhái bīnsyu a?

kéih   V: stand

26. Néi kéihhái nīsyu jouh mātyéh a?
(See Note 59)

27. Ngó kéihhái nīsyu dáng yātgo pàhng-
    yáuh.
28. Kéuih kéihhái gósyu jouh mātyéh a?

dáng   V: wait

29. Néi dáng bīngo a?
30. Ngó dáng Chàhn sìnsàang.

sósìh (M: tìuh; 'bunch', chàu) N: key

31. Néi yáuh gógàan fóngge sósìh ma?
32. (Ngó) m̀jì nītìuh haih m̀haih nē?

hóu   AV: may, should (used only in questions)

33. Ngó hóu heui ma?
34. Néi m̀hóu heui.
35. Ngó hóu m̀hóu man kéuih a?
36. Ngó hóu m̀hóu máai nībún syù a?

m̀hóu   AV: better not, don't (imperative), should not

37. Haih m̀haih m̀hóu heui a?
38. Haih, m̀hóu heui.
39. Kéuih dōu m̀hóu heui àh?
40. M̀hóu góng syutwah la!
41. M̀hóu cheung gō la!

gám   A: in this(or that) way; in that case;
                             then...; well, ...

42. Gám sé ngāam m̀ngāam a?
43. Gám sé ngāam la.
44. Gám ngó m̀heui lo!
45. Gám kéuih nē? Kéuih heui m̀heui a?
46. Nīsáu gō gám cheung hóu m̀hóu a?
47. Nīsáu gō m̀hóu gám cheung, yiu gám
    cheung.

yauh   A: again

48. Néi tìngyaht yauh heui àh?
49. Haih, ngó tìngyaht yauh heui.
50. Néi yauh sihkfaahn làh?

yātdihng   A: definitely, certainly, sure

                                51. Néi haih m̀haih yātdihng heui a?
                                52. Haih, ngó yātdihng heui.
                                53. Haih m̀haih yātdihng yáuh a?

gán   P: indicating continuance of action

                                54. Kéuih jouhgán mātyéh a?
                                55. Kéuih duhkgán syù.
                                56. Néi táigán mātyéh a?

lā   P: sentence final used with mild commands,
                                suggestions, request; or to express fin
                                decision

                                57. Néi lèih lā!
                                58. Néi sé lā!
                                59. Gám, ngó dōu heui lā!

waih, wái   P: Hello! (on the telephone) Hey! (only 'w
                                can be used in this sense)

                                60. Waih! (or wái) Néi haih bīnwái a?
                                61. Waih! Néi heui m̀heui a?

                            Useful Expressions

Yáuh māt jígaau a?   Is there anything I can do for you
                                        (Lit. Any instructions?)
M̀gáamdòng!   You are flattering me!
                                        (Lit. I am not entitled to...)
Móugéinói, ...   After a while, ...
                                        (Lit. Not very long.)
M̀gòi néi dángháh   Please wait a minute.

Pattern Sentences

I. Verbs of motion compounded with 'lèih' and 'heui':

séuhnglèih	come up	séuhngheui	go up
lòhklèih	come down	lohkheui	go down
yahplèih	come in	yahpheui	go in
chēutlèih	come out	chēutheui	go out
fàanlèih	come back	fàanheui	go back

1. Chéng yahplèih chóh yātjahngāan lā!
   Please come in and sit down awhile!

2. Chéng séuhnglèih làuhseuhng chóh hóu ma?
   Please come upstairs and have a seat!

3. Ñgòi néi chēutlèih ngoibihn, ngó yáuhdī yéh béi néi.
   Please come out, I have something to give you.

4. Kéuih fàan(lèih) mfàanlèih ngūkkéi sihkfaahn a?
   Does he or doesn't he come home to eat?

5. Kéuih yahpheui gógàan poutáu máai boují.
   He goes in that store to buy a newspaper.

6. Néi yìhgā fàanheui poutáu jouh mātyéh a?

7. Néi hái seuhngbihn jouh mātyéh, dímgáai juhng mlohklèih a?

8. Néi chēutheui jouh mātyéh a? Ngó chēutheui máai dī yéh.

9. Ngó séung lohkheui làuhhah gógàan poutáu máai dī yéh.

10. Kéuih jáulèih jáuheui, mjì kéuih jouh mātyéh nē!

58. 'Lèih' and 'heui' may be affixed to certain verbs of motion to
    form directional compounds, 'lèih' indicating direction toward
    the speaker, and 'heui' direction away from the speaker and
    toward some definite place.

yahplèih		come in	chēutheui	go out
séuhnglèih		come up	lohkheui	go down
hàahnglèih		walk over	jáuheui	run to
hàahnglèih ngósyu			jáuheui kéuihsyu	
walk over to where I am			run (or go) to his place	

II. 'Hái' as a suffix to verbs of location.

   1. Néi chòhhái gósyu jouh mātyéh a?
      What are you sitting there for?

   2. Dímgáai néi chòhhái jèung tói seuhngbihn a?
      Why are you sitting on the table?

   3. Kéuih kéihhái gógàan gòu láu chìhnbihn maai boují.
      He stands in front of that high building and sells papers.

   4. Ngó jyuhhái sahpngláu.
      I live in the fifteenth floor (British: fourteenth floor)

   5. Néi yìhgā mjyuhhái hohkhaauhsyu mē! Gám, néi jyuhhái bīnsyu
      You are not living at school now!? Then, where do you live?

59. 'Hái' has already been presented as a main verb and as a co-ver
    (See Lesson 9 & 10). 'Hái' may also be used as a suffix to
    certain verbs of location, such as 'chóh' (sit), 'kéih' (stand)
    'jyuh' (live), etc. Used in this way, 'hái' becomes part of th
    action itself. (Compare English prepositions which are related
    to verbs, such as stand <u>on</u>, sit <u>on</u>, live <u>at</u>, etc.) In all cases
    'hái' requires a placeword as an object.

chòhhái yísyu	sit on the chair
kéihhái poutáu chìhnbihn	stand in front of the store
jyuhhái làuhseuhng	live upstairs

III. Continuance with '-gán.'

     1. Wòhng sìnsàang hái (gó) syu jouhgán mātyéh a? Wòhng sìnsàa
       hái (gó)syu gaaugán syù.
       What is Mr. Huang doing there? He is teaching.

     2. Wòhng taaitáai hái syu jouhgán mātyéh a? Wòhng taaitáai hái
       syu jyúgán faahn.
       What is Mrs. Huang doing? Mrs. Huang is cooking dinner.

     3. Léih sìnsàang hái syu jouhgán mātyéh a? Léih sìnsàang hái
       syu cheunggán gō.
       What is Mr. Lee doing there? Mr. Lee is singing.

     4. Léih síujé hái syu jouhgán mātyéh a? Léih síujé hái syu
       duhkgán syù.
       What is Miss Lee doing there? Miss Lee is studying.

5. Néi hái syu jouhgán mātyéh a? Ngó hái syu táigán boují.
   What are you doing there? I am reading a newspaper.

6. Hàahnggán gāai m̀hóu sihk yéh; sihkgán yéh m̀hóu góng syutwah.

7. Néi hái bīnsyu jouhsih a? Ngó móu jouhsih, ngó yìhgā juhng
   duhkgán syù.

8. Nī jèung boují ngó táigán, néi tái daihyihjèung hóu ma?

9. Kéuih hái fóngsyu jouhgán mātyéh a? Kéuih hái fóngsyu ségán
   jih.

10. Kéuihdeih yìhgā jouhgán sàangyi, gogo dōu m̀dākhàahn.

60. 'Gán' may be suffixed to most functive verbs to indicate that
    the action of the verb is going on at the moment of speaking
    or time referred to.

Ngó táigán syù.	I am reading a book.
Kéuih sihkgán faahn.	He is eating.
Kéuih gàmjìujóu jyúgán faahn gójahnsí	While she is cooking this morning... (See '...gójahnsí' in Less. 12)

Often the phrase 'hái syu,' or 'hái douh' (is there, is in the
act of) is used together with '-gán'; see sentences 1-5 above.

IV. Compound verbs with 'gán' and 'dāk.'

1. Sìnsàang yahpgánlèih la, m̀hóu góng syutwah la!
   The teacher is coming in now, silence!

2. Hái Hèunggóng lèih ge fèigèi yìhgā lohkgánlèih la!
   The plane which came from Hongkong is landing now.

3. Ngó yahpdāklèih ma?
   May I come in?

4. Kéuihdeih gogo dōu yahpdākheui, dímgáai néi m̀yahpdākheui a?
   They all got in, how come you couldn't?

5. Kéuih yìhgā hái Jùnggwok chóh fèigèi fàangánlèih la. Ngó
   tìngyaht heui jip kéuih.

6. Hái hohkhaauh chēutgánlèih gógo yàhn, haih Wòhng sìnsàangge
   pàhngyáuh Léih sìnsàang.

7. Nīgàan fóng taai sai, ngó m̀yahpdākheui.

8. Kéuih hái poutáu hóu m̀dākhàahn, yìhgā m̀fàandāklèih.

9. Gógàan láu taai gòu, ngó m̀séuhngdākheui.

10. Kéuih hái làuhhah séuhnggánlèih la!

11. Hái làuhseuhng lohkgánlèih gógo haih bīngo a?

12. Néidī saimānjái (kéuihdeih hái hohkhaauh) dākhàahn ma?
    Kéuihdeih chēut (dāklèih) m̀chēutdāklèih sihk faahn a?
    Kéuihdeih dākhàahn daahnhaih m̀chēutdāklèih.

61. In compound verbs of motion, 'gán' or 'dāk' (See Less. 7) is
    placed in between the first verb and 'lèih' or 'heui.'

séuhnggánlèih	coming up
lohkgánheui	going down
yahpgánlèih	coming in
chēutdākheui	can go out
m̀fàandāklèih	can't come back

Conversation

A CHAT ON THE TELEPHONE

A: Waih! Néi haih bīnwái a? Néi haih Hòh sìnsàang àh?
B: M̀gáamdòng, ngó haih Hòh Gwok-sàn, néi haih bīnwái a?
A: Ngó haih Léih Yaht-jān.
B: Oh! Léih síujé, yáuh māt jígaau a?
A: Néi taaitáai hái (ngūk)kéi ma? Ngó yáuh geui wá séung man kéuih.
B: Kéuih hái làuseuhng jyugánfaahn... Oh! Kéuih yìhgā lohkgánlèih la
A: Hòh taaitáai àh? Néi gàmmáan heui sèhng ngoibihn gógàan poutáu
   máai yéh ma?
C: Gàmyaht tìnhei m̀hóu, ngo m̀séung heui lo!
A: Tìngjìujóu néi heui ma?
C: Tìngjìujóu ngó m̀dākhàahn, Ǹg taaitáai lèih taam ngó, ngó m̀heuidāk
A: Tìngmáan nē?
C: Tìngmáan ngó yātdihng heui.
A: Gám ..., ngó dōu tìngmáan heui, tìngmáan hái gósyu gin (see)néi
   lā, tìngmáan gin!

62. a. 'Lā' added to a command, changes its aspect to a mild com-
       mand, request, or suggestion. This is particularly true if
       the tone is prolonged.

    Heui lā! Dímgáai néi m̀heui a?
    Let's go! Why aren't you going?

    Lèih lā! Ngódeih heui sihkfaahn lā!
    Come along! Let's go to eat!

    Gám lā! Hóu ma? M̀hóu, ngó m̀jùngyi gám.
    How about this way? No, I don't like this way.

  b. Statements beginning with 'gám' and ending with 'lā' indicate
     final decision after some prior discussion.

    Gám, ngó dōu tìngyaht heui lā!
    Well then I'll go tomorrow.

    Gám, ngó tìngyaht góng néi tèng lā!
    Well then I'll tell you tomorrow.

    Gám, ngó jyúfaahn, néi duhksyù lā!
    Then I'll cook and you study.

                      Additional Sentences

1. Néi kéihhái (nī)syu jouh mātyéh a? Dímgáai juhng m̀séuhngheui
   làuhseuhng sihkfaahn a?
2. Kéuih haih m̀haih m̀dākhàahn a? Kéuih yìhgā jouhgán mātyéh a?
3. Wòhng sìnsàang, néi yáuh go pàhngyáuh hái ngoibihn dánggán néi.
4. Ngó yìhgā dākhàahn la, chéng kéuih yahplèih chóh lā!
5. Kéuih haih jyuhhái làuhseuhng gógo hohksāang.
6. Kéihhái ngoibihn gógo (yàhn) haih bīngo a?
7. Néi yìhgā fàan(dākheui) m̀fàandākheui Gwóngjàu a? M̀fàandāk lo!
   Yānwaih yìhgā móu syùhn heui Gwóngjàu la!
8. Cheunggán gō gógo haih bīngo a? Haih Chàhn sìnsàangge néui.
9. Ngó yìhgā m̀dākhàahn néideih m̀yahpdāklèih.
10. Bīngo sēuhnggánlèih a? Haih m̀haih Ǹg sìnsàang a?
11. Haih m̀haih gogo dōu m̀yahpdākheui a? M̀haih, godī taai saige
    m̀yahpdākheui jē.
12. Hái fóchè lohkgánlèih gógo haih m̀haih néige sìnsàang a?

13. Tìngmáan néi fàan(dāklèih) m̀fàandāklèih a? Fàandāklèih.
14. Néidī saimānjái yahpdāk(heui) gógàan hohkhaauh duhk syù ma?
    M̀dāk, yànwaih kéuihdeih m̀wúih góng Gwòngjàuwá.
15. Séuhnggán fèigèi gógo Méigwok yàhn, m̀haih néige pàhngyáuh mē?

Translate the following sentences into Cantonese:

1. I came from America by plane.
2. Why don't you like to go by ship?
3. I come here to learn Cantonese.
4. Who is the friend of yours who came from America?
5. What is your friend Mr. Jone's coming to do in China?

Below are English translations of sentences used in the vocabulary
of this lesson as examples of usage. Translate these back into
Chinese (numbers correspond to those in Vocabulary section.)

1. Are you going tonight?
2. I am not going tonight.
3. He isn't going tonight either?.
4. How was the weather this morning? (Or, How is the weather
   this morning?)
5. This morning's weather was beautiful.
6. What did you eat this morning? (What are you going to eat
   this morning?)
7. Are you coming tomorrow morning?
8. Where will he go tomorrow morning?
9. Who'll come tomorrow night?
10. Are you going to Hongkong tomorrow night?
11. Please wait for me a short while.
12. Are you free tomorrow? (Lit. Do you have leisure tomorrow?)
13. I'm free tomorrow.
14. Are you (really) busy now?
15. Is he busy??? (I doubt it).
16. Can you walk?
17. I can't, because I'm too tired.
18. Does your watch run?
19. What's he running for?
20. I don't know why he's running.
21. I'm going to leave, how about you?
22. I'm going to leave also.
23. Where do you live?
24. I live in that house.
25. Where does he live?
26. What are you standing here for?
27. I'm standing here waiting for a friend.

28. What's he standing there for?
29. Who are you waiting for?
30. I'm waiting for Mr. Chen.
31. Do you have the key to that room?
32. I don't know whether this is the one; (Do you?)
33. May I go?
34. You may not. (You better not.)
35. May I ask him? (Is it all right that I ask him?)
36. Is it all right that I buy this book?
37. Do you mean that it's better not to go?
38. Yes, it's better not to go.
39. (Does that mean) he'd better not go either?
40. Don't speak anymore.(or, Silence!)
41. Stop singing!
42. Isn't this the way to write it?
43. Yes, that's the way to write it.
44. In that case, I won't go anymore.
45. Well, how about him, is he going?
46. Is this the way to sing this song?
47. Don't sing it that way, you should sing it this way.
48. You'll go again tomorrow?
49. Yes, I'll go again tomorrow.
50. You are eating again???
51. Are you definitely going?
52. Yes, definitely.
53. Are you certain you have it?
54. What is he doing?
55. He's studying.
56. What are you reading?
57. Why don't you come? (a suggestion)
58. Come on, write it! (gentle urging)
59. Well then I'll go.
60. Hello! Who is this? (answering the telephone)
61. Hey! Are you going?

LESSON 12

COMPLETED ACTION WITH 'JÓ' AND 'YÙHN'

Reading

Ngóge pàhngyáuh Má sìnsàang hái Hèunggóng chóh fóchè lèih taar
ngó, ngó kàhmyahtjīu heui fóchèjaahm jip kéuih. Yànwaih tìnhei
m̀hóu, tìuhtìuh gāai dōu hóu nàanhàahng, ngó dou fóchèjaahm gójahnsi
fóchè yìhgìng dōujó lo! Ngó jáuheui léuihgún wán kéuih, hái léuihgún jouhsih gódī yàhn, gogo dōu wah Má sìnsàang juhng mei lèih.

Doujó johkmáan ngó yauh heui fóchèjaahm jip kéuih. Yātjahngāar
fóchè lèih la, gogo yàhn dōu hái fóchè lohksaailèih la, juhng mei
(tái)gin Má sìnsàang. Ngó yauh jáuheui léuihgún wán kéuih, léuihgúndī yàhn wah: "Má sìnsàang móulèihgwo!"

Ngó hái léuihgún fàanheui ngūkkéi, táigin Má sìnsàang chóhhái
ngó jèung yísyu táigán boují, ngó wah: "Dímgáai...?" Kéuih wah:
"Jànhaih deuim̀jyuh néi lo! Ngó móu chóh fóchè lèih, ngó chóhjó
fèigēi lèih!"

Vocabulary

kàhmyaht, johkyaht,   TW: yesterday
   chàhmyaht

       1. Kàhmyaht tìnhei hóu ma?
       2. Kàhmyaht néi hái bīnsyu a?

kàhmmáan, johkmáan,   TW: last night
   chàhmmáan

       3. Kàhmmáan néi hái bīnsyu a?
       4. Kàhmmáan ngó hái hohkhaauhsyu duhksyì

kàhmyahtjīu, johkyahtjīu   TW: yesterday morning

       5. Kàhmyahtjīu néi hái m̀hái (ngūk)kéi a'
       6. Kàhmyahtjīu néi hái bīnsyu a?

112

géisí, géisìh   TW: when? at what time?

                                7. Néi géisí heui a?
                                8. Ngó gàmmáan heui.
                                9. Kéuih géisí lèih a?

gójahnsí...   TW: at that time...; meanwhile

                         10. Gójahnsí ngó jyuhhái pàhngyáuhsyu.
                         11. Gójahnsí yáuh géidò hohksāang a?
                         12. Gójahnsí ngó ṁjì dím syun!

...gójahnsí   TW: when (while)...; at the time of...

                         13. Néi sihkfaahn gójahnsí (néi) tái
                                boují ma?
                         14. Ngó sihkfaahn gójahnsí ṁtái boují.
                         15. Néi duhksyù gójahnsí (néi) jyuhhái
                                bīnsyu a?

dou   V: arrive (at), reach

                         16. Kéuih géisí dou Hèunggóng a?
                         17. Kéuih tìngjìujou dou.
                         18. Ngódeih tìngyaht doudāk Hèunggóng ma?

táigin   RV: see

                         19. Néi táigin kéuih (gó)ga heichè ma?
                         20. Ngó táigin la.
                         21. Néi táigin mātyéh a?

gin   V: meet (somebody by prior arrangement);
                            pay a visit to (rather formally)

                         22. Néi séung gin kéuih ma?
                         23. Ngó séung gin kéuih.
                         24. Néi heui gin bīngo a?
                         25. Ngó heui gin ngóge sìnsàang.

ṁginjó   V: lost; be lost, become lost

                         26. Ṁhóu ṁginjó góbún syù!
                         27. Góbún syù ṁginjó làh?
                         28. Ṁginjó lo!

sĩk   V: know (a person,subject, etc.); recogniz
                                     become acquainted with
                                 AV: know how to

                                     29. Néi sĩk m̃sĩk kéuih a?
                                     30. Ngó sĩk kéuih, kéuih haih Wòhng sìn-
                                         sàangge pàhngyáuh.
                                     31. Néi sĩk m̃sĩk gógo yàhn a?
                                     32. Néi sĩk m̃sĩk góng Gwóngjàu wá a?
                                     33. Ngó sĩk góng géigeui jē.

léuihgún, jáudim   PW: hotel
   (M: gàan)
                                     34. Nĩsyu yáuh móu léuihgún a?
                                     35. Nĩsyu yáuh yatgàan hóu saige léuih-
                                         gún.

Má   N: Ma (surname)

                                     36. Má sìnsàang hái m̃hái (nĩ)syu a?
                                     37. Má sìnsàang hái bĩnsyu a?

-fo   M: lesson

                                     38. Nĩfo haih daihgéifo a?
                                     39. Nĩfo haih daihsahpyihfo.

-jó   P: verb suffix, indicating completed actio

                                     40. Néi sihkjó faahn làh?
                                     41. Sihkjó la!
                                     42. Kéuih dōu sihkjó làh?

-gwo   P: verb suffix, indicating experience (See
                                     note 66)

                                     43. Néi yáuh móu sihkgwo tòhngchāan a?
                                     44. Néi yáuh móu heuigwo Jùnggwok a?

-yùhn   P: verb suffix,indicates the finishing of
                                     an action

                                     45. Néi jouhyùhn gógihn sih làh?
                                     46. Ngó jouhyùhn la.
                                     47. Néi séyùhn gódĩ jih làh?

-saai   P: verb suffix, used as 'all' or 'whole'

                               48. Kéuih sésaai gódī jih mei a?
                               49. Kéuih sésaai la.
                               50. Néi maaisaai gódī syù làh?

yíhgìng   MA: already

                               51. Néi yíhgìng maaisaai gódī syù làh?
                               52. Ngó yíhgìng maaisaai lo.
                               53. Kéuih yíhgìng maaijó gójì bāt làh?

mei   P: negative indicating that the action has
                                   not yet been performed

                               54. Néi mei sihkfaahn àh?
                               55. Ngó mei sihk(faahn).
                               56. Kéuih juhng mei heui àh?
                               57. Néi sihkjó faahn mei a?
                               58. Mei.

                          Useful Expressions

Chéng chóh lā!   Please sit down!
Dāk mei a?   Is it ready? Is it done yet?
                                    Is that all right now?
Mei dāk! Dāk la!   Not yet! O.K. !
Gau mei a?   Is that enough?
Mei gau. Gau la!   Not yet. It's enough!

                          Pattern Sentences

I. Completed action with suffix '-jó,' and negation of completed
   action with 'mei.'

   1. Wòhng sìnsàang lèihjó mei a? Lèihjó la.
      Has Mr. Huang come yet? Yes, he has come.

2. Jèung sìnsàang jáujó mei a?   Juhng mei jáu.
   Has Mr. Chang left yet?   No, not yet.

3. Juhng yáuh bīngo[1] leihjó a?   Chàhn sìnsàang lèihjó.
   Has anyone else come?   Mr. Chen has come.

4. Kéuihdeih sihkjó faahn mei a?   Kéuihdeih mei sihk.
   Have they had their meal?   They have not eaten yet.

5. Ngódeih sihkjó faahn séung tèng Léih sìnsàang cheunggō m̀jì
   Léih sìnsàang lèihjó mei nē?
   When we have finished eating, we want to hear Mr. Lee sing,
   I don't know whether he has come or not.

6. Léih sìnsàang heuijó hohkhaauh gaausyù, kéuih yìhgā fàangán
   lèih la!

7. Léih sìnsàang néi lèihjó làh!?   Néi gàmyaht hái hohkhaauh
   gaaujó géidòfo (syù) a?

8. Ngó gaaujó léuhngfo jē!

9. (Gó)dī hohksāang wúih duhk mei a?

10. Gogo dōu mei wúih, gogo dōu wah: "Jànhaih nàan lo!"

63.
   a. The verb suffix 'jó' indicates completed action, and is
      usually translated by the perfect tense in English. After
      stative verbs, it imparts the meaning 'has become...'

      sihkjó   has eaten
      jouhjó   has done
      gauhjó   has become old

      This suffix is different from the final particle 'la (lo),'
      which indicate change of state or new situation:

      sihkjó faahn   has eaten
      sihk faahn la   is eating now (and wasn't before)
      sihk faahn la   is eating <u>rice</u> now (and was eating
                                 gruel before)

1. See note 76, Lesson 16.

The two used together indicate that an action has just been completed (producing a new situation.) The effect is more lively and immediate than when 'jó' is used alone:

sihkjó faahn la   has eaten
lèihjó la   has come

In answer to a question containing 'jó,' the particle 'la' is usually used:

Kéuih lèihjó mei a?   Has he come?
Kéuih lèihjó la.   He has come.

In questions using a question word, where the interrogative particle would follow 'la,' the two reduce to 'la':
'la' + 'a' — 'la.'

Néi táijó géidòbún la? How many (book) have you read?

The combination 'la' + 'àh' becomes 'làh.' To make a question from a statement containing 'jó' or 'la,' the particle 'làh' is used (never 'ma').

Kéuih heuijó la.   He has gone.
Kéuih heuijó làh?   Has he gone?

b. The negative 'mei' expresses the opposite of 'jó' and 'la' — that the action has not yet been completed or a new situation reached. To negate a single action in the past, 'móu' is used:

Kéuih mei heui.   He hasn't gone.
Kéuih móu heui.   He didn't go.

The usual question form when 'móu' is used is 'yáuh móu V...?' (a choice-type question: 'did he V...?'). When 'móu' is used, 'jó' and 'la' may not be used after it.

64. Question forms with 'jó' may be expressed

a. as a choice-type question with 'mei' as the second half:

Néi sihkjó faahn mei a? Have you eaten yet?

Sihkjó la.   Yes, I have already eaten.
Mei sihk.   Not yet.
Ngó mei sihk.   I haven't eaten yet.

b. in statements of the form '... jó... la,' by changing 'la' to 'làh':

Néi sihkjó faahn làh?   Have you eaten (your meal) already?

Sihkjó la.   Yes, I have already eaten.
Mei.   Not yet.

c. by using a question-word with 'a' in the usual manner:

Néi máaijó dī mātyéh béi   What have you bought for her?
keuih a?

Ngó máaijó yātjì bāt béi   I have bought her a pen.
keuih.

II. Completed action with verb suffix '-yùhn.'

1. Néideih sihkyùhn faahn mei a? Sihkyùhn la! Chéng yahplèih chóh lā!
   Have you finished your meal? We have already finished.
   Please come in and have a seat!

2. Néi séyùhn jih mei a? Ngó mei séyùhn.
   Have you finished writing those characters? No, I haven't finished yet.

3. Néi táiyùhn nī léuhngbún syù mei a? Ngó táiyùhn nībún jē, góbún juhng mei táiyùhn.
   Have you finished reading these two books? This book I have finished, that one, not yet.

4. Kéuih jouhyùhn gógihn sih mei a? Kéuih yìhgā juhng jouhgán, kéuih wah tìngyaht hóyíh jouhyùhn la!
   Has he finished that work? He is still working on it, he says tomorrow it may be finished.

5. Néi géisí hóyíh duhkyùhn nībún syù a? Ngó tìngmáan hóyíh duhkyùhn la!
   When can you finish reading this book? I might finish it tomorrow night.

6. Ngó yiu néi duhkge góbún syù, néi duhkyùhn mei a? Deuimjyuh sìnsàang, ngó juhng mei duhkyùhn.

7. Keuih yìhngìng sihkyùhn faahn la, yìhgā hái làuhseuhng lohkgán-
leih la!

8. Sìnsàang! Ngódeih duhkyùhn nībún syù, ngódeih wúih góng Gwóngdùngwá mei a?

9. Dímgáai ngó yíhgìng duhkyùhn yātbún syù, néi juhng mei táiyùhn
yātjèung boují a?

10. Kéuih yíhgìng duhkyùhn syù lo, dímgáai juhng m̀jouhsih a?

65. 'V-yùhn' means 'finish V-ing.' 'mei' may be used with 'yùhn':
mei V-yùhn, 'has not finished V-ing.'

Kéuih sihkyùhn faahn mei a?	Has he finished his meal?
Mei sihkyùhn.	Not yet.
Néi duhkyùhn géidòbún syù la?	How many books have you read?
Ngó duhkyùhn seibún (syù) la.	I have finished four already.
Néi tìngyaht hóyíh jouhyùhn	Can you have this work finished
nīgihn sih ma?	by tomorrow?
Hóyíh.	Yes.

III. Experiential suffix '-gwo.'

A. Néi duhkgwo nībún syù ma?
B: Ngó duhkgwo (yāt)dī jē.
A: Góbún nē?
B: Góbún haih mātyéh syù a?
A: Góbún haih gaau yàhn góng Gwòngdùngwáge syù.
B: Néi yáuh móu duhkgwo a?
A: Ngó yìhgā duhkgán, Chàhn sìnsàang gaugán ngó.
B: Néi wúih góng Gwòngdùngwá mei a?
A: Ngó wúih góng dī, ngó hái Jùnggwok gójahnsí hohkgwo géigeui.
B: Bīngo gaaugwo néi a?
A: Yáuh yātwái sing Wòhngge síujé gaaugwo ngó. Kéuih gaau ngó
góngwá, yihk gaau ngó cheunggō.
B: Néi yáuh móu tènggwo kéuih cheunggō a? Kéuih haih m̀haih
hóu wúih cheung a?
A: Kéuih jùngyi cheungge gō, sáusáu ngó dōu tènggwo, kéuih jàn-
haih hóu wúih cheung!
B: Néi yìhgā juhng sīk cheung Jùnggwok gō ma?
A: Yìhgā móu yàhn gaau ngó, ngó m̀sīk lo! Néi sīk bīngo wúih
gaau cheunggō ge ma?
B: Ngó m̀sīk.

English translation of the above.

> A: Have you read this book?
> B: I have read some of it.
> A: How about that one
> B: What book is that?
> A: That is a book for teaching people to speak Cantonese.
> B: Have you studied it?
> A: I am studying it, Mr. Chen is teaching me.
> B: Can you speak Cantonese now?
> A: I can speak a little, I learned a few sentences (when I was in China.
> B: Who taught you there?
> A: There was a Miss Wang who taught me. She taught me to spea and also taught me to sing.
> B: Have you heard her sing? Did she really know how to sing?
> A: I heard all of the songs she liked to sing, she really know how to sing.
> B: Do you still know how to sing the Chinese songs?
> A: There is no one teaching me, I don't know how to sing now. Do you know someone who is able to teach?
> B: I don't know.

66. The verb suffix 'gwo' indicates that the subject has had the experience of performing the action at some time in the past. The negative forms are 'mei V-gwo' and 'mou V-gwo.' 'Mei V-gwo' means 'have not yet V-ed (but might in the future)'; 'mou V-gwo' means 'never V-ed' with no indications about the future.

   Question forms involving 'gwo' may be made in all the ways described in Note 64. In addition, the sentence particle 'ma' may be used. The most frequent question form is 'yáuh móu V-gwo a?'

   1. Néi táigwo bīnbún syù a?   Which book have you read?
      Ngó táigwo nībún syù.   I have read this one.

   2. Néi yáuh móu heuigwo Méigwok   Have you ever been to the U.S. a?
      Heuigwo.   Yes.
      Ngó heuigwo.   I have been there.
      Heuigwo, ngó heuigwo.   Yes, I have been there.
      Heuigwo, ngó heuigwo Méigwok.   Yes, I have been to the U.S.

Móu.   No.
Móu heuigwo.   (I) have never been there.
Ngó móu heuigwo.   I have never been there.
Móu, ngó móu heuigwo.   No, I have never been there.
Móu, ngó móu heuigwo Méigwok.   No, I have never been in the U.S.

3. Kéuih heuigwo Méigwok mei a?   Has he been in the U.S.?
   Mei.   Not yet.
   Mei heuigwo.   (He) hasn't yet.
   Kéuih mei heuigwo.   He hasn't yet.
   Mei, kéuih mei heuigwo.   No, he hasn't yet.

4. Néi sihkgwo tòhngchāan ma?   Have you ever eaten Chinese food?
   Ngó sihkgwo.   Yes, I have eaten (it).
   Ngó móu sihkgwo.   No, I haven't eaten (it).
   Ngó mei sihkgwo.   No, I haven't eaten (it) yet.

'Gwo' may sometimes be used like 'jó' to express completed action:

5. Néi sihkgwo faahn mei a?   Have you eaten yet?

6. Néi sihkgwo faahn làh?   You have eaten (your meal) already?

IV. 'Saai,' 'yùhnsaai,' 'gwosaai.'

1. Néi sésaai gódī jih mei a?   Ngó mei sésaai, juhng yáuh léuhnggo (jih) mei sé.
   Have you written all of those characters? No, not yet. I
   still have two more I haven't written.

2. Ngó juhng mei jouhyùhnsaai nīdī sih, ngó yìhgā mei fàandāk
   ngūkkéi.
   I haven't finished all of those affairs yet, I can't go home
   right now.

3. Néi sihkyùhnsaai nīdī yéh, néi juhng séung sihk (yāt)dī mātyéh a?
   When you finish eating up all these things, what else do you
   want (to eat)?

4. Néi táiyùhnsaai gó géibún syù mei a?   Mei, ngó juhng yáuh
   léuhngbún mei dākhàahn tái.
   Have you finished reading all of those books? Not yet, there
   are two of them I still haven't had time to read.

5. Kéuihdeih yìhgìng jáusaai lo, néi juhng lèih jouh mātyéh a? They have all gone, what is the use of your coming (or what are you coming for)?

6. Ngódī saimānjái gogo dōu heuisaai duhksyù lo, néi lèih chóh lā!

7. Kéuih séung máaisaai gamdòbún syù, daahnhaih kéuih móu gamdò chín.

8. Néi wah m̀ginjó néi góbún Jùnggwok syù, néi wángwosaai gamdò-gàan fóng mei a?

9. Néi gingwosaai ngó nì géiwái pàhngyáuh mei a?

10. Kéuih mangwosaai gamdògo sìnsàang, gogo dōu wah nīgo jih m̀ha Jùnggwok jih.

67. The verb suffix '-saai' means 'all.' It may refer backward to t subject or forward to an object, and may designate all members a group or all parts of a whole.

Dī yàhn jáusaai la.   The people have all left.
Ngó jouhsaai gódī sih la.   I have done all those things.
Nei hó m̀hóyíh táisaai gódī   Can you finish reading all those
  syù a?   books?

In some cases '-saai' has the sense of 'thoroughly': jìngfàan-saai 'completely fixed up.' (Les. 19, Patt.II, -fàan)

Note the idiomatic usage Dòjehsaai 'Thank you very much.'

The forms '-yùhnsaai' and '-gwosaai' also occur:

jouhyùhnsaai   have finished them all
táigwosaai   have read them all

Forms involving '-saai,' '-yùhnsaai' and '-gwosaai' can be made into questions in the three ways mentioned in Note 64; 'ma' is not used after these forms.

68. In sentences including a number-measure combination in the object, the forms with 'jó' translate to the simple past in English:

Néi sihkjó géidò faann a?   How much rice <u>did</u> you eat?
Ngó sihkjó hóudò.   I <u>ate</u> a lot.
Kéuih táijó sàambún syù.   He <u>read</u> three books.

With the particle 'la' added, the meaning can be rendered by
the perfect in English :

Néi sihkjó géidò faahn la?   How much rice <u>have</u> you eaten?
Ngó sihkjó hóudò la.   I <u>have</u> eaten a lot.
Kéuih táijó sàambún syù la.   He <u>has</u> read three books.

Translate the following sentences into Cantonese:

1. My good friend Mr. Jones is coming back from America by plane.
2. Are you free? Can you come out and have dinner (with us)?
3. That car is too small, he can't get in.
4. Do you know why he is standing in front of that tall building?
5. Is he teaching now? Well, I'll come to visit him tomorrow.

Below are English translations of sentences used in the vocabulary
of this lesson as examples of usage. Translate these back into
Chinese (numbers correspond to those in Vocabulary section).

 1. How was yesterday's weather?
 2. Where were you yesterday?
 3. Where were you last night?
 4. I studied at school last night.
 5. Were you home yesterday morning?
 6. Where were you yesterday morning?
 7. When will you go?
 8. I'll go tonight.
 9. When will he come?
10. At that time I lived with my friend.
11. How many students had they at that time?
12. Meanwhile, I don't know what can be done about it!
13. Do you read the paper while you're eating?
14. I don't read the paper while I'm eating.
15. Where did you live at the time of your schooling?
16. When will he arrive Hong Kong.
17. He'll arrive tomorrow.
18. Can we arrive at Hong Kong tomorrow?
19. Do you see his car?
20. Yes, I see it.
21. What have you seen?

22. You want to see (or meet) him?
23. Yes, I wish to see (or meet) him?
24. Whom are you going to visit?
25. I'm going to visit my teacher.
26. Don't lose that book!
27. That book is lost?
28. Yes, it's lost.
29. Do you know him?
30. I know him, he's Mr. Huang's friend.
31. Do you know English?
32. Do you know how to speak Cantonese?
33. I only know how to speak a few sentences.
34. Is there a hotel here?
35. There's a very small hotel here.
36. Is Mr. Ma here?
37. Where is Mr. Ma?
38. Which lesson is this?
39. This is Lesson 12.
40. You've already eaten?
41. Yes, I have.
42. Has he also eaten?
43. Have you ever eaten Chinese food?
44. Have you ever been in China?
45. You've finished that work, I suppose.
46. Yes, I have.
47. You've finished writing those characters?
48. Has he finished writing all those characters?
49. He has already finished.
50. You've sold all those books, I suppose?
51. You've already sold those books, I suppose?
52. Yes, I have.
53. He has already sold that pen, I suppose?
54. You haven't eaten yet?
55. I haven't eaten yet.
56. He still hasn't gone?
57. Have you eaten?
58. No, not yet.

I. Reading

Wòhng sìnsàang hái Gwóngjàu yáuh yátgàan poutáu, kéuih gàan poutáu
m̀haih géi daaih, daahnhaih hóu hóusàangyi. Poutáu léuihbihn yáuh
Jùnggwok syù, yihk yáuh Yìngmàn syù. Séung hohk Yìngmàn ge yàhn,
gogo dōu heui kéuihsyu máai Yìngmàn syù.

Yáuh yātyaht, yáuh (yāt)go hohksāang yahpleih Wòhng sìnsàang gàan
poutáu, yiu máai léuhngbún Yìngmàn syù, Wòhng sìnsàang séuhngheui
làuhseuhng wán, yātjahngāan, kéuih lohkleih béi léuhngbún syù gógo
hohksāang. Gógo hohksāang wah: "M̀haih nī léuhngbún!" Wòhng sìnsàang yauh séuhngheui làuhseuhng, yauh wángwosaai gamdòbún syù,
lohkleih wah: "Gódī Yìngmàn syù yìhgìng maaisaai la!" Gógo hohksāang wah: "Jànhaih maaisaai làh! Gaau ngódeih Yìngmàn gowái
Wòhng sìnsàang wah néi juhng yáuh hóudò, néi lohkheui làuhhah wángwo mei a?" Wòhng sìnsàang lohkheui làuhhah yauh wángwosaai gamdòbún syù, séuhngleih wah: "Janhaih maaisaai lo!"

Gógo hohksāang hàahngjó chēutheui, yahpheui daihyihgàan poutáu,
Wòhng sìnsàang wah: "M̀sīk Yìngmàn jànhaih m̀dāk! Jànhaih m̀dāk!
NGÓ YĀTDIHNG YIU HOHK YÌNGMÀN!"

II. Conversation

A.

A: Jèung sìnsàang néi géi hóu ma?
B: Hóu, Wòhng sìnsàang néi heuijó bīnsyu a? Gam noi m̀gin néi a?
A: Ngó heuijó Jùnggwok duhksyù.
B: Néi hái Jùnggwok bīnsyu duhksyù a?
A: Ngó hái Gwóngjàu duhk(syù).
B: Gám, néidī Gwóngjàuwá yātdihng hóu hóu la, néi gaau géigeui
   ngó dāk m̀dāk a?
A: Néidī Gwóngjàuwá dōu géi hóu lā! Bīngo gaaugwo néi a?
B: Yáuh yātwái sing Chàhnge sìnsàang gaaugwo ngó, daahnhaih ngó
   yìhgā juhng m̀haih géi sīk góng. Ngódeih yáuh luhkgo yàhn
   hohk Gwóngjàuwá, Chàhn sìnsàang wah ngódeih gogo dōu hóu
   chùngmìng, daahnhaih...

B: ... Daahnhaih gogo góngsaai Yìngmàn, m̀góng Gwóngjàuwá, sóyíh
juhng m̀haih géi sīk góng.

B.

A: Chàhn sìnsàang néi jyuhjái bīnsyu a?
B: Ngó jyuhhái sèhng ngoibihn gógàan léuihgún.
A: Jyuhhái gógàan léuihgún làuhseuhng àh?
B: M̀haih, làuhhah jē!
A: Làuhhah daihgéigàan fóng a?
B: Làuhhah hauhbihn daihsàamgàan. Ngó jùngyi hauhbihn dī fóng,
yànwaih chìhnbihn gótluh gāai taai dò chè...
A: Géi(dò) chín yātmáan a?
B: M̀haih géi gwai jē! Léuhnggobun ngànchín.
A: Néi haih m̀haih tìngyaht heui Seuhnghói a?
B: M̀haih, ngó tìngjìujóu chóh syùhn heui Hèunggóng.
A: Chóh fèigèi heui m̀hóu mē?
B: Hóu, daahnhaih nī léuhngyaht tìnhei m̀hou, sóyíh ngó m̀séung
chóh fèigèi.
A: Néi jì fóchèjaahm hái bīnsyu ma?
B: Léuihgúndī yàhn yíhgìng góng ngó jì la, kéuihdeih wah hái
sèhng léuihbihn, daahnhaih ngó hóyíh hái léuihgúnsyu chóh
kéuihdeihge heichè heui.
A: Néi hái Hèunggóng fàanlèih, chéng lèih ngó ngūkkéisyu sihk
máanfaahn lā, hóu ma?
B: M̀sáihaakhei lo! Ngó fàanlèih yātdihng heui taam néi, joigin,
joigin!

C.

A: Léih sìnsàang, néi lèih nīsyu jouh mātyéh a?
B: Ngó lèih nīsyu duhksyù.
A: Néi lèih nīsyu duhk mātyéh syù a?
B: Ngó lèih nīsyu duhk Jùnggwok syù.
A: Néi lèih duhk mātyéh Jùnggwok syù a?
B: Ngó lèih duhk hohk góng Gwóngjàuwá ge Jùnggwok syù.

A: Néi heui Jùnggwok jouh mātyéh a?
B: Ngó heui Jùnggwok jouhsàangyi.
A: Néi heui Jùnggwok jouh mātyéh sàangyi a?
B: Ngó heui Jùnggwok jouh maai syù ge sàangyi.
A: Néi dímyéung heui a?
B: Ngó chóh fèigèi heui.
A: Néi géisí heui a?
B: Ngó tìngjìujóu heui.

III. Drill

A. Drill on sentence particles jē, la, lo, làh, mē, lā and a.

Translate the following conversation into English:

A: Hohk Gwóngjàuwá m̀haih hóu nàan jē! Dímgáai néi m̀hohk la?
B: Ngóge pàhngyáuh Jèung sìnsàang wah hóu nàan sóyíh ngó m̀séung hohk lo!
A: Néi jànhaih m̀séung hohk làh!
B: Ngó jànhaih m̀séung hohk lo!
A: Hohk lā! Ngó hohkgán Gwóngjàuwá, ngó jìdou m̀haih géi nàan jē!
B: Haih mē! Néi hohkgán mē!
A: Haih, ngó hái nīgàan hohkhaauh hohkgán, ngó yìhgā yíhgìng sīk góng hóudò la!
B: Gám, ngó tìngyaht dōu lèih hohk, Joigin! Joigin!

Fill in the following blanks with appropriate final particles:

1. Ngó taai guih, ngó m̀heui _____ !
2. Ngó wúih góng géigeui _____ !
3. Kéuih sihkjó hóudò _____ !?
4. Ngó yìhgā móu chín _____ Ngó m̀heuidāk Jùnggwok _____ !
5. Haih _____ ! Kéuih haih néige pàhngyáuh _____ !
6. Néi hai léuihgún sihkjó faahn _____ !? Dímgáai m̀lèih ngósyu sihk a?
7. Johkmáan sihkyùhnfaahn, m̀haih kéuih béi chín, haih néi béi chín _____ !?
8. Sihk _____ ! Juhng yáuh hóudò!
9. Ngó yìhgā hóu dākhàahn, néi lèih chóh _____ !
10. Ngó m̀haih géi sīk sé Jùnggwok jih, ngó hohkjó housíu _____ !

(Make sentences by following the pattern of each sentence shown above).

Sentence Particle 'a' vs. 'la':

Néi máaijó géidò yéh a?   Ngó máaijó hóudò yéh.
Néi máaijó géidò yéh la?   Ngó máaijó hóudò yéh la.
Néi kàhmyaht máaijó géidò yéh a? Ngó kàhmyaht máaijó hóudò yéh.
Néi yìhgā máaijó géidò yéh la?   Ngó yìhgā máaijó hóudò yéh la.

Néi séjó géidògo jih a?   Ngó séjó sàambaakgo jih.
Néi séjó géidògo jih la?   Ngó séjó sàambaakgo jih la.

Néi kàhmyaht séjó géidògo jih a?   Ngó kàhmyaht séjó sàambaakgo j
Néi yìhgā séjó géidògo jih la?   Ngó séjó sàambaakgo la.

Néi duhkjó géidòfo syù a?   Ngó duhkjó baatfo syù.
Néi duhkjó géidòfo syù la?   Ngó duhkjó baatfo la.
Néi kàhmyaht duhkjó géidòfo   Ngó kàhmyaht duhkjó baatfo syù
  syù a?
Néi yìhgā duhkjó géidòfo syù la?   Ngó yìhgā duhkjó baatfo la.

Néi hohkjó géidògeui Gwóngjàuwá   Ngó hohkjó ńg-luhkgeui.
  a?
Néi hohkjó géidògeui Gwóngjàuwá   Ngó hohkjó ńg-luhkgeui la.
  la?
Néi kàhmyaht hohkjó géidògeui   Ngó kàhmyaht hohkjó ńg-luhkgeu
  Gwóngjàuwá a?
Néi yìhgā hohkjó géidògeui   Ngó yìhgā hohkjó ńg-luhkgeui l
  Gwóngjàuwá la?

Answer the following questions:

1. Néi táijó géidòbún syù la?   2. Néi jouhjó géidògihn sih la
   Néi kàhmyaht táijó géidòbún   Néi kàhmyaht jouhjó géidògi
   (syù) a?   (sih) a?

3. Néi maaijó géidòjì bāt la?   4. Néi máaijó géidòjèung yí la
   Néi kàhmyaht maaijó géidòjì   Néi kàhmyaht máaijó géidòjè
   (bāt) a?   (yí) a?

5. Néi gaaujó géidòfo syù la?   6. Néi cheungjó géidòsáu gō la
   Néi kàhmyaht gaaujó géidòfo   Néi kàhmyaht cheungjó géidò
   (syù) a?   (gō) a?

B. Drill on compound verbs and placewords.

    ngó jùngyi yahpheui   kéuih jùngyi chēutlèih
    ngó jùngyi séuhngheui   kéuih jùngyi lohklèih
    ngó yahpheui léuihbihn   kéuih chēutlèih ngoibihn
    ngó séuhngheui làuhseuhng   kéuih lohklèih làuhhah
    ngó jáuheui chìhnbihn   kéuih jáulèih hauhbihn
    ngó séuhngheui seuhngbihn   kéuih lohklèih hahbihn
    ngó hái nīsyu   kéuih heui gósyu
    ngó heui gósyu   kéuih lèih nīsyu

(For drilling purposes, use 'séung,' 'yiu' to replace 'jùngyi,'
and substitute other placewords for the ones used.)

Fill in the following blanks with appropriate words:

1. Yáuh pàhngyáuh lèih taam ngó, ngó chéng kéuihdeih _____ chóh.
2. Gógàan poutáu hái bīnbihn yahpheui a? Hái _____ _____ , m̀haih hái _____ _____ .
3. Hóudò hohksāang hái gógàan hohkhaauh _____ , _____ gógàan poutáu máai yeh sihk.
4. Néi séung m̀séung _____ Jùnggwok a?
5. Kéuih hái làuhhah _____ , yātjahngāan yauh _____ .
6. Tói _____ yáuh jèung yí, yí _____ yáuh jèung boují.
7. Dímgáai néi juhng m̀_____ ngūkkéi a?
8. Ngó hái ngūkkéi _____ gójahnsí, kéuih juhng mei fàanheui ngūkkéi.
9. Kéuihge saimānjái hái làuhseuhng _____ man kéuih, "Ngó yìhgā_____ ngoibihn wán ngóge pàhngyáuh dāk ma?
10. Néi bún syù hái _____ , m̀haih hái _____ .

C. 'M̀' vs. 'móu.'

Dímgáai néi m̀heui a?	Ngó m̀jùngyi heui.
Dímgáai néi kàhmyaht m̀heui a?	Ngó m̀dākhàahn heui, or:
	Ngó m̀jùngyi heui.
Dímgáai néi gàmyaht m̀heui a?	Ngó m̀dākhàahn heui, or:
	Ngó m̀jùngyi heui.
Dímgáai néi tìngyaht m̀heui a?	Ngó m̀dākhàahn heui, or:
	Ngó m̀jùngyi heui.

Dímgáai néi móu heui a?	Ngó m̀dākhàahn heui.
Dímgáai néi kàhmyaht móu heui a?	Ngó m̀dākhàahn heui, or:
	Ngó m̀jùngyi heui.
Dímgáai néi gàmyaht móu heui a?	Ngó m̀dākhàan heui, or:
	Ngó m̀jùngyi heui.
Dímgáai néi tìngyaht m̀heui a?	Ngó m̀dākhàan heui, or:
	Ngó m̀jùngyi heui.

Dímgáai kéuih m̀lèih a?	Kéuih m̀dākhàahn, m̀lèihdāk.
Dímgáai kéuih kàhmyaht m̀lèih a?	Kéuih m̀dākhàahn, m̀lèihdāk.
Dímgáai kéuih gàmyaht m̀lèih a?	Kéuih m̀dākhàahn, m̀lèihdāk.
Dímgáai kéuih tìngyaht m̀lèih a?	Kéuih m̀dākhàahn, m̀lèihdāk.

Dímgáai kéuih móu lèih a?	Kéuih yáuh sih, m̀dākhàahn lèih.
Dímgáai kéuih kàhmyaht móu lèih a?	Kéuih yáuh sih, m̀dākhàahn lèih.
Dímgáai kéuih gàmyaht móu lèih a?	Kéuih yáuh sih, m̀dākhàahn lèih.
Dímgáai kéuih tìngyaht m̀lèih a?	Kéuih yáuh sih, m̀dākhàahn lèih.

Dímgáai néi m̀jyúfaahn a?   Ngó m̀sīk jyúfaahn.
  Dímgáai néi kàhmyaht m̀jyú-   Ngó m̀dākhàahn jyú.
  faahn a?
  Dímgáai néi gàmyaht m̀jyú-   Ngó m̀dākhàahn jyú.
  faahn a?
  Dímgáai néi tìngyaht m̀jyú-   Ngó m̀dākhàahn jyú.
  faahn a?

Dímgáai néi móu jyúfaahn a?   Ngó yáuh sih, m̀dākhàahn jyú.
  Dímgáai néi kàhmyaht móu   Ngó yáuh sih, m̀dākhàahn jyú.
  jyúfaahn a?
  Dímgáai néi gamyaht móu   Ngó yáuh sih, m̀dākhàahn jyú.
  jyúfaahn a?
  Dímgáai néi tìngyaht m̀jyú-   Ngó yáuh sih, m̀dākhàahn jyú.
  faahn a?

Dímgáai néi m̀wán kéuih a?   Ngó m̀jì dím(yéung) wán kéuih.
  Dímgáai néi kàhmyaht m̀wán   Ngó m̀jì dím(yéung) wán kéuih.
  kéuih a?
  Dímgáai néi gàmyaht m̀wán   Ngó m̀jì dím(yéung) wán kéuih.
  kéuih a?
  Dímgáai néi tìngyaht m̀wán   Ngó m̀jì dím(yéung) wán kéuih.
  kéuih a?

Dímgáai néi móu wán kéuih a?   Ngó m̀dākhàahn wán kéuih.
  Dímgáai néi kàhmyaht mou wán   Ngó m̀dākhàahn wán kéuih.
  kéuih a?
  Dímgáai néi gàmyaht móu wán   Ngó m̀dākhàahn wán kéuih.
  kéuih a?
  Dímgáai néi tìngyaht m̀wán   Ngó m̀dākhàahn wán kéuih.
  kéuih a?

(The use of 'móu' before the functive verbs is limited to the
past tense but 'm̀' is free from any limit of tense.)

IV. Exercise

A. Exercise on verb suffixes and question forms (Verb suffixes: 'jó'
  'yùhn,' 'saai,''yùhnsaai,' 'gwosaai,' 'hái,' 'dāk,' 'gán'.)

  1. Kàhmyaht ngó tái _____ syù kéuih yahplèih man ngó tái _____
     góbún syù_____ ?
  2. Ngó mei tái _____ nībún syù, ngó m̀jì nībún haih mātyéh syù.
  3. Kéuih wán _____ gamdògàan poutáu, gàangàan dōu maai ____

4. Néi jouh _____ gamdōgihn sih ____ a?
5. Nījèung yī taai gauh, mchóh ____ lo!
6. Kéuih kàhmyaht heui ___ Jùnggwok lo, yìhgā chóh ____ fèigèi
   la!
7. Dīmgáai kéuih msihk _____ faahn a?
8. Néi gàmmáan tái _____ góbún syù, _____ m_____ a?
9. Gógàan poutáuge Yīngmàn syù, kàhmyaht yìhgìng maai _____lo!
10. Néi man ____ Jàu taaitáai _____ a? Jàu sìnsàang heui ____
    Meigwok mei a?
11. Ngó yìhgā jyuh ____ léuihgún, tìngmáan chóh fóchè heui
    Hèunggóng.
12. Kéuih _____ poutáu chìhnbihn tái ____ boují gógo yàhn,
    haih mhaih Hòh sìnsàang a?
13. Kéuih hóu jùngyi chóh ____ fóchè léuihbihn tái boují.
14. Ngó hái Jùnggwok gójahnsī, ngó jyuh ____ pàhngyáuh ŋgūkkéi,
    ngóge pàhngyáuh gaau ____ ngó geigeui Gwóngdùngwá.
15. Gógo maai boují ge saimānjái, kéuih maai _____ boují,
    yìhgìng fàan _____ ngūkkéi lo!

B. Question form 'yáuh móu ...' and answer.

Néi yáuh móu máai gódī yéh a?
(Have you bought those things?)
  Ngó yáuh. (I have.)   Ngó móu (máai). (I haven't.)
Néi yáuh móu máaigwo gódī yéh a?
(Have you ever bought those things?)
  Ngó máaigwo. (I have.)   Ngó móu máaigwo. (I never have.)
Néi yáuh móu tai góbún syù a?
  Ngó yáuh.   Ngó móu.
Néi yáuh móu táigwo góbún syù a?
  Ngó táigwo.   Ngó móu táigwo.
Néi yáuh móu chéng kéuih sihkfaahn a?
  Ngó yáuh.   Ngó móu.
Néi yáuh móu chénggwo kéuih sihkfaahn a?
  Ngó chénggwo.   Ngó móu chénggwo.
Néi yáuh móu tèng kéuih cheunggō a?
  Ngó yáuh.   Ngó móu.
Néi yáuh móu tènggwo kéuih cheunggō a?
  Ngó tènggwo.   Ngó móu tènggwo.

Néi yáuh móu sé gódī jih a?
(Hve you written those characters?)
  Ngó yáuh. (I have.)   Ngó móu. (I haven't.)
Néi yáuh móu sésaai gódī jih a?
(Have you finished writing those characters?)
  Ngó sésaai la. (I have.)   Ngó móu sésaai. (I haven't finished)

Néi yáuh móu máai gódī syù a?
  Ngó yáuh.   Ngó móu.
Néi yáuh móu máaisaai gódī syù a?
  Ngó máaisaai la.   Ngó móu máaisaai.
Néi yáuh móu sihk gódī yéh a?
  Ngó yáuh.   Ngó móu.
Néi yáuh móu sïhksaai gódī yéh a?
  Ngó sihksaai la.   Ngó móu sihksaai.
Néi yáuh móu jouh gó géigihn sih a?
  Ngó yáuh.   Ngó móu.
Néi yáuh móu jouhsaai gógéigihn sih a?
  Ngó jouhsaai la.   Ngó móu jouhsaai.

Néi yáuh móu gaau gófo syù a?
(Have you taught that lesson?)
  Ngó yáuh. (I have.)   Ngó móu. (I haven't.)
Néi yáuh móu gaauyùhn gófo syù a?
(Have you finished teaching that lesson?)
  Ngó gaauyùhn la. (I have.) Ngó móu gaauyùhn. (I haven't.)
Néi yáuh móu cheung gósáu gō a?
  Ngó yáuh.   Ngó móu.
Néi yáuh móu cheungyùhn gósáu gō a?
  Ngó cheungyùhn la.   Ngó móu cheungyùhn.
Néi yáuh móu jouh gó géigihn sih a?
  Ngó yauh.   Ngó móu.
Néi yáuh móu jouhyùhnsaai gó géigihn sih a?
  Ngó jouhyùhnsaai la.   Ngó móu jouhyùhnsaai.

C. Answer the following questions:

1. Gójahnsí néi yáuh móu heui Jùnggwok a?
   Néi yáuh móu heuigwo Jùnggwok a?
2. Néi yáuh móu tái gójèung boují a?
   Néi yáuh móu táigwo gójèung boují a?
3. Kàhmyaht néi yáuh móu sihk tòhngchāan a?
   Néi yáuh móu sihkgwo tòhngchāan a?
4. Gójahnsí néi yáuh móu jouhsàangyi a?
   Néi yáuh móu jouhgwo sàangyi a?
5. Gójahnsí néi yáuh móu hohk Gwóngdùngwá a?
   Néi yáuh móu hohkgwo Gwóngdùngwá a?
6. Néi yáuh móu tái gó géibún syù a?
   Néi yáuh móu táisaai gó géibún syù a?
7. Néi yáuh móu jouh gógihn sih a?
   Néi yáuh móu jouhyùhn gógihn sih a?

8. Néi yáuh móu mangwo néidī pàhngyáuh a?
   Néi yáuh móu mangwosaai néidī pàhngyáuh a?
9. Néi yáuh móu tái góbún syù a?
   Néi yáuh móu táisaai góbún syù a?
10. Néi yáuh móu jyuhgwo gógàan léuihgún a?
    Néi yáuh móu jyuhgwosaai gó géigàan léuihgún a?

V. Translation

Translate the following questions and answer each of them, giving a reason why:

1. Do you want to go to China?
2. Which job do you like to take?
3. What did you come here for?
4. Are you looking for him?
5. What do you want to ask him?
6. Why doesn't he want to go by plane?
7. Have you finished that book?
8. Where does he live?
9. You don't want to learn Chinese, I suppose!?
10. You said you liked that book, why don't you buy it?
11. Are you going to that store to buy something?
12. Why don't you speak Cantonese?
13. Have you been to his home?
14. Have you ever eaten Chinese food?
15. Can you sing a Chinese song?

TIME WHEN AND TIME SPENT -- DIRECTIONAL COMPLEMENTS

Vocabulary

Gauhnín	TW: last year
gàmnín	TW: this year
chēutnín	TW: next year
chìhnnín	TW: year before last
hauhnín	TW: year after next
yāt-gáu-yāt-yihnín	TW: 1912
yāt-gáu-ńg-sàamnín	TW: 1953
yāt-sei-gáu-yihnín	TW: 1492
yātchìn-chātbaak-chātah-chātnín	TW: 1777

1. Gauhnín néi hái bīnsyu a?
2. Néi gàmnín heui mheui Seuhnghói a?
3. Chēutnín kéuih lèih ma?
4. Ngó chìhnín hái gógàan hohkhaauh
   gaaugwo (syù).
5. Hauhnín haih yāt-gáu-chāt-sàamnín.
6. Néi gauhnín yáuh móu heuigwo Hēung-
   góng a?
7. 1941nín néi hái bīnsyu a?
8. 1754nín yáuhjó nīgàan hohkhaauh mei a
   1754nín yíhgìng yáuhjó nīgàan hohkhaa
   la.

-nìn	M: year
géidònìn	TW: how many years

9. Néi duhkjó géidònìn Yìngmàn a?

yātnìn   TW: one year

10. Ngó duhkgwo yātnìn Yìngmàn.

nìnnìn   TW: every year

11. Néi nìnnìn dōu heui Jùnggwok a?

géinìn   TW: several (few) years
  hóugéinìn   a good many years

12. Ngó (hóu) géinìn móu heui lo.

bīnnìn (or bīnnín)   TW: which year

13. Néi bīnnìn heuigwo a?

chìhngéinìn   TW: several years ago

14. Ngó chìhngéinìn heuigwo.

daihyātnìn   TW: the first year

15. Kéuih daihyātnìn hohk góng Jùnggwok
    wá, daihyihnìn hohk sé Jùnggwok jih.

gónìn (or gónín)   TW: that year

16. Gónìn néi hái bīnsyu a?

gó-sàamnìn   TW: those three years

17. Gó-sàamnìn ngó hái Hèunggóng gaausyù.

yuht   N: month

Jìngyuht   TW: the first month of the Lunar year

Yātyuht   Yātyuht haih January
Yihyuht   Yihyuht haih February
Sàamyuht   Sàamyuht haih March
Seiyuht   Seiyuht haih April
Ngyuht   Ngyuht haih May

Luhkyuht	Luhkyuht haih June
Chātyuht	Chātyuht haih July
Baatyuht	Baatyuht haih August
Gáuyuht	Gáuyuht haih September
Sahpyuht	Sahpyuht haih October
Sahpyātyuht	Sahpyātyuht haih November
Sahpyihyuht	Sahpyihyuht haih December

bīngo yuht   Ph: which month

    18. Bīngo yuht néi dākhàahn a?

seuhnggo yuht   Ph: last month

    19. Seuhnggo yuht néi heuijó Hèunggóng àh?

hahgo yuht   Ph: next month

    20. M̀gòi néi hahgo yuht lèih lā.

chìhngo yuht   Ph: month before last month

    21. Chìhngo yuht ngó móu heuigwo.

géidògo yuht   Ph: how many, months

    22. Néi heuijó géidògo yuht a?

chātgo yuht   Ph: seven months

    23. Ngó heuijó chātgo yuht.

baatgo yuht   Ph: eight months

    24. Ngó lèihjó baatgo yuht la.

bīngéigo yuht   Ph: which few months

    25. Bīngéigo yuht sàangyi hóu a?

nīgéigo yuht   Ph: these few months

    26. Nīgéigo yuht m̀hóu, gógéigo yuht hóu.

chìhngéigo yuht   Ph: several months ago

27. Ngó chìhngéigo yuht wángwo kéuih.

láihbaai   N: week

Bīngo láihbaai a?	Which week?
Nīgo láihbaai	This week.
Gógo láihbaai	That week.
Seuhnggo láihbaai	Last week.
Hahgo láihbaai	Next week.
Daihyihgo láihbaai	Next week.
Chìhngo láihbaai	Week before last (or last week).
Chìhnléuhnggo láihbaai	Two weeks ago.
Láihbaaigéi a?	Which day in the week?
Láihbaaiyāt	Monday.
Láihbaaiyih	Tuesday.
Láihbaaisàam	Wednesday.
Láihbaaisei	Thursday.
Láihbaaing	Friday.
Láihbaailuhk	Saturday.
Láihbaaiyaht	Sunday.

28. Seuhnggo láihbaaigéi a? Seuhnggo
    láihbaaiyāt.
29. Hahgo láihbaaigéi a? Hahgo láih-
    baaisàam.
30. Bīngo láihbaaiyāt a? Nīgo láih-
    baaiyāt.[1] Seuhnggo láihbaaiyāt.
    Hahgo láihbaaiyāt.
31. Néi láihbaaigéi dākhàahn a? Láih-
    baaisei dākhàahn. Bīngo láihbaaisei
    a? Nīgo láihbaaisei, m̀haih hahgo-
    láihbaaisei.

1. In the Chinese reckoning Monday is the first day of the week, i.e.,
the range of week is Monday .... Sunday. Whenever any week-day is mentioned within the range of a week, nīgo láihbaaiyāt, nīgo láihbaaisàam
is used, no matter whether that day is past or not:

nīgo láihbaaiyāt   last Monday (spoken on, say, Friday)
nīgo láihbaaisàam   last Wednesday (spoken on, say, Friday)
                          or this coming Wednesday (spoken, say, Monday)

yaht	M:	day
bīnyaht	Ph:	which day
		32. Néi bīnyaht lèihgwo a?
kàhmyaht, chàhmyaht, johkyaht	TW:	yesterday
		33. Ngó kàhmyaht lèihgwo.
gàmyaht	TW:	today
		34. Néi gàmyaht heui m̀heui a?
tìngyaht	TW:	tomorrow
		35. Néi tìngyaht dākhàahn ma?
chìhnyaht	TW:	day before yesterday
		36. Ngó chìhnyaht heuijó Hèunggóng.
hauhyaht	TW:	day after next
		37. Hauhyaht ngó m̀dākhàahn.
daaihchìhnyaht	TW:	the day before the day before yesterday (three days ago)
		38. Daaihchìhnyaht haih láihbaaigéi a?
daaihauhyaht	TW:	the day after the day after tomorrow.
		39. Ngó daaihhauhyaht heui Hèunggóng.
géidòyaht?	Ph:	how many days
		40. Néi heuijó géidòyaht a? Ngó heuijó léuhngyaht jē.
yahtyaht	Ph:	every day
		41. Kéuih yahtyaht dōu gam m̀dākhàahn àh? Haih, kéuih yahtyaht dōu gam m̀dākhà:
-houh	M:	day (of the month); number (of house, ro etc.)

42. Gàmyaht géi(dò)houh a? Gàmyaht
(haih) yāthouh.

yihhouh, sàamhouh,....
sahpyāthouh, sahpyihhouh, ...
yahyāthouh, yahyihhouh, ...
sà-ahhouh, sà-ahyāthouh
43. Gàmyaht haih géiyuht géihouh a?
Gàmyaht haih yihyuht sàamhouh.
44. Gàmyaht haih yātgáugéinìn géiyuht
géihouh a? Gàmyaht haih yātgáungng-
nìn yātyuht sahphouh.
45. Kéuih jyuhái daihgéihouh fóng a?
Kéuih jyuhái daihsàamhouh fóng.
46. Dàihsàamgāai daihgéihouh a? Daihsàamgāai daihgáuhouh.

sàangyaht   N: birthday

47. Gàmyaht haih bīngoge sàangyaht a?
48. Gàmyaht haih néige sàangyaht àh?
49. Gàmyaht ṁhaih ngóge sàangyaht haih
kéuihge sàangyaht.

Bākgìng   PW: Peking

50. Néi heuigwo Bākgìng ma?
51. Bākgìng hái bīnsyu a?
52. Bākgìng juhng yáuh sèhng ma?

seun (M: fùng)   N: letter

53. Ngó yiu sé léuhngfùng seun.
54. Ngó yáuh mou seun a?
55. Gófùng seun haih bīngo ga?

chēutsai   VO: be born (for"give birth to," sàng is used)

56. Néi géisí chēutsai ga?
57. Saimānjái chēutjósai mei a? Kéuih
chēutjósai la.

gaausyù   VO: teach

58. Néi yáuh móu gaaugwo syù a? Ngó
gaaugwo (syù).

59. Néi jùngyi gaausyù ma?

táu   V: rest

60. Ngó táu yātjahnggāan dāk ma?
61. Ngó hóu guih, séung táuháh.
    (see Les. 15, Pat. V)
62. Néi táuháh lā.

bùn   V: move
   bùn(ngūk)   VO: to move from one dwelling to another

63. Kéuih bùnjó heui bīnsyu a?   Kéuih
    bùnjó heui Seuhnghói.
64. Néi bùnjó gójèung tói mei a?

daai   V: take or bring along

65. Néi yáuh móu daai chín a?
66. Néi daai ngó heui dāk ma?
67. Ngó m̀daaidāk néi heui.

nīk, nìng   V: hold (in one hand); hold (in general);
                            bring or take (something somewhere; in
                            this sense always used with -heui or
                            -lèih)

68. Néi nīkdāk ma?   Ngó nīkdāk.
69. Néi yiu ngó nīkheui bīnsyu a?

ló   V: get, fetch

70. Néi heui ló mātyéh a?   Kéuih heui ló
    chín.
71. Néi nē? Néi yihkdōu heui ló chín àh?
    Haih, ngó yihkdōu heui ló chín.
72. M̀gòi néi (heui) lóleìh lā.

sung   V: deliver (a thing); escort, send off; take
                            (a person somewhere); present (a gift)

73. Néi géisí hóyíh sungheui a? (see
    Patt. III)
74. Bīngo sung kéuih fàan ngūkkéi a?

75. Ngó heui sung kéuih fàan Jùnggwok.
76. Ngó séung sung dī yéh (béi)¹ kéuih.

gei   V: send (something by mail), mail

77. Gófùng seun néi geijó mei a? Ngó
    géijó la.
78. Ngó séung gei nībún syù fàan Méigwok.

yéung   N: style, appearance (look)

79. Néi jùngyi nīgo yéung ge ma? Ngó
    m̀jungyi nīgo yéung ge.
80. Néi jùngyi dím(ge)yéung ga?
81. Kéuihge yéung leng ma?

hóuyéung   SV: good-looking

82. Nījèung tói hóu hóuyéung, ngó hóu
    jùngyi.

cháuyéung   SV: ugly

83. M̀haih géi cháuyéung lā.

noi, nói   SV: a long time

84. Haih m̀haih yiu dáng hóu noi a?
    M̀sái dáng géi noi jē.
85. Néi lèihjó géi nói a?

When noi is preceded by géi (used as 'how') in a question form, it is
always pronounced as nói.

mui   SP: each, every

86. Múi (yātgo) yàhn yáuh jì bāt.
87. Múibún syù dōu yiu yáuh nīgo jih.
88. Múigàan fóng yáuh léuhngjèung tói.

1. The word 'béi' may also be placed after certain verbs e.g. sungbéi
(to present a gift to), geibéi (to mail to) etc.

-màai   P: up to, over to, against; near (only with
                                  verbs of motion)

                             89. Hàahngmàai kéuih gósyu.
                             90. Chéng néi chóhmàai jèung tóisyu.
                             91. Kéuih ga chè pungmàai[1]ngó ga chèsyu.

The V-màai combination is followed by place-words; ordinary nouns
must have '-syu' or '-douh' added.

-gwolèih   P: over, over to, across, across to
  -gwoheui
                             92. Kéuih jáugwoheui gàan poutáusyu.
                             93. Hái gósyu hàahnggwolèih.

-hòi   P: away from, away

                             94. Hàahnghòi gósyu.
                             95. Hàahnghoi!

géi   A: how
  géi   NU: few, several; odd, more than; which (of
                                  series)

                             96. Kéuih géi gòu a?   or
                                 Kéuih yáuh géi gòu a?
                             97. Góga chè géi daaih a?
                             98. Géidò chín a? Géimān jē.
                             99. Yáuh géidò hohksāang a? Géigo jē.
                            100. Ngó hái gósyu jyuhjó gogéiyuht.
                            101. Nībún syù gogéi ngànchín.
                            102. Kéuih heuijó gogéilàihbaai la.
                            103. Daihgéihouh fóng a? Daihluhkhouh.

as an adverb:

géi hóu, géi leng.   fairly good, fairly pretty.
mhaih géi hóu, mhaih géi leng.   not very good, not very pretty.
géi chèuhng a?   how long (in length)
géi nói la?   how long (in time)
dángjó géi noi a.   waited very (to any extent) long.
dángjó (dōu) géi noi la.   waited quite (to some extent) long.

1. Pung 'collide with' is introduced in Book II, Lesson 12.

as a number:

géi(dò) go a?	how many?
géigo (see Les. 16, Patt. I)	few, several
sahpgéigo (" " ")	'en-several,' 'ten-odd.'
yahgéigo, sà'ahgéigo	'twenty-several,' 'thirth-odd,' etc.
gogéi (ngànchín)	more than one dollar
géi(dò) houh a?	which number?

Useful Expressions

Mhóuyisi	I'm sorry!
Jauh gám lā!	Good, let's do it that way.
Dáng ngó táiháh	Let me see.
Móu mantàih!	No problem at all.

Conversation

A: Yātnìn yáuh géidòyaht a?
B: Yātnìn yáuh sàambaak-luhk-ah-ng-yaht.
A: Yātnìn yáuh géidògoyuht a?
B: Yātnìn yáuh sahpyihgoyuht.
A: Yātgoyuht yáuh géidòyaht a?
B: Yáuhdī yáuh sàamsahpyaht, yáuhdī yáuh sà-ah-yātyaht.
A: Yihyuht dōu yáuh sàamsahpyaht gam dò mē?
B: Móu, yihyuht móu sàamshapyaht gam dò, yihyuht yáuh yahbaatyaht jē.
A: Yātgoyuht yáuh géidògo láihbaai a?
B: Yātgoyuht yáuh seigo láihbaai, yātnìn yáuh ng-ah-yihgo láihbaai.
A: Múigo láihbaai yáuh géidò yaht a?
B: Múigo láihbaai yáuh chātyaht.
A: Gàmyaht haih láihbaaigéi a?
B: Gàmyaht haih láihbaaiyāt.
A: Kàhmyaht nē?
B: Kàhmyaht haih láihbaaiyaht.
A: Chìhnyaht nē?
B: Chìhnyaht haih láihbaailuhk.
A: Gàmnín haih yātchìn-gáubaak-chāt-ah-géinìn a?
B: Gàmnín haih yātchìn-gáubaak-chāt-ah-yātnìn.

A: Nīgoyuht haih géiyuht a?
B: Nīgoyuht haih luhkyuht.
A: Gàmyaht haih géiyuht géihouh a?
B: Gàmyaht haih luhkyuht sà'ahhouh.
A: Gàmyaht haih m̀haih néige sàangyaht a?
B: M̀haih, gàmyaht haih kéuihge sàangyaht.
A: Géisí haih néige sàangyaht a?
B: Chātyuhtseihouh haih ngóge sàangyaht.

Pattern Sentences

I. Time When Expressions.

   1. Kéuih géisí lèih a? Kéuih gàmyaht lèih.
      When will he come? He'll come today.

   2. Néi géisí heui Hèunggóng a? Ngó tìngyaht heui.
      When will you go to Hongkong? I'll go tomrrow.

   3. Néideih géisí heui Jùnggwok a? Ngódeih chēutnín heui.
      When will you go to China? We'll go next year.

   4. Léih sìnsàang géisí hái Bākgìng lèih a? Kéuih hahgo yuht lè:
      When will Mr. Lee come from Peking? He'll come next month.

   5. Wòhng sìnsàang géisí heui Gwóngjàu a? Kéuih hauhyaht heui.
      When will Mr. Huang go to Canton? He'll go day after tomorr◀

   6. Néi haih m̀haih gàmmáan lèih a? M̀haih, ngó tìngmáan lèih.

   7. Néi géisí hóyíh táiyùhn níbún syù a? Ngó tìngyaht hóyíh tái◀
      yùhn la.

   8. Néi géisí béi nībún syù kéuih a? Ngó daihyihgo láihbaai béi
      kéuih.

   9. Kéuih haih m̀haih tìngyaht chóh syùhn heui a? M̀haih, kéuih
      tìngyaht chóh fóchè heui.

   10. Hahgo láihbaai gaau bīngéifo syù a? Hahláihbaaiyāt gaau daih◀
       sàamfo, hahláihbaaiyih gaau daihseifo.

11. Kéuih géisí lèih ga?   Kéuih kàhmyaht lèih ge.

12. Néi géisí heui Hèunggóng ga?   Ngó chìhnyaht heui ge.

13. Néideih géisí heui Jùnggwok ga?   Ngódeih yāt-gáu-sàam-yih
    nín heui ge.

14. Léih sìnsàang géisí hái Bākgìng lèih ga?   Léih sìnsàang
    seuhnggoyuht lèih ge.

15. Wòhng sìnsàang géisí heui Gwóngjàu ga?   Wòhng sìnsàang
    chìhnyaht heui Gwóngjàu ge.

16. Néi géisí lèih ga?   Ngó kàhmmáan lèih ge.

17. Néi géisí táiyùhn góbún syù ga?   Ngó chìhnmáan táiyùhn ge.

18. Néi géisí béi nībún syù kéuih ga?   Ngó seuhnggoláihbaai
    béi kéuih ge.

19. Kéuih géisí chóh syùhn lèih ga?   Kéuih kàhmmáan chóh syùhn
    lèih ge.

20. Seuhnggoláihbaai gaaujó bīngéifo a?   Seuhngláihbaaisàam
    gaaujó daihyātfo, (seuhng) láihbaaisei gaaujó daihyihfo.

69. Time When: In indicating the time when or within which an
    action occurred, or failed to occur, whether it is a point of
    time or stated period, the time element always comes somewhere
    before the main verb of the sentence or clause. The entire
    expression thus functions as a movable adverb, and serves as a
    setting for the action.

    Gàmyaht ngódeih sihk tòhngchāan.
    Ngódeih gàmyaht sihk tòhngchāan.

II. Time Spent (Measured Time).

    1. Néi lèihjó géi nói la?   Ngó lèihjó léuhngyaht la.
       How long have you been here?   I have been here two days.

    2. Kéuih jáujó géi nói la?   Kéuih jáujó yātgoyuht la.
       How long has he left?   He left a month ago.

    3. Fóchè doujó géi nói la?   Fóchè doujó hóu noi lo.
       How long ago did the train arrive?   It has been here quite
       a while.

4. Gójek syùhn doujó mei a? Gójèk syùhn doujó léuhng-sàam-
   yaht la.
   Has that ship arrived yet? That ship has been two or three
   days.

5. Kéuih heuijó Jùngwok géi nói la? Kéuih heuijó Jùnggwok
   sàammìn la.
   How long since he went to China? He went to China three
   years ago.

6. Néi hái Seuhnghói jyuhgwo géidògoyuht a? Ngó hái Seuhnghói
   jyuhgwo léuhnggo làihbaai jē.

7. Chàhn sìnsàang séung hái Seuhnghói jyuh géi nói a? Kéuih
   séung hái Seuhnghói jyuh bunnìn.

8. Néi hohkjó géi nói ge Gwóngjàuwá la? Ngó hohkjó léuhnggogéi-
   yuht ge Gwóngjàuwá la.

9. Léih sìnsàang fàanjó Jùnggwok géi nói la?

10. Néi gaunín hái Hèunggóng jyuhjó géi nói a? Ngó gauhnín hái
    Hèunggóng jyuhjó gogéiyuht.

11. Chàhn sìnsàang yáuh móu gaaugwo néi a? Yáuh, Chàhn sìnsàang
    gaaugwo ngó sàamgo yuht.

12. Néi yáuh móu hái gógàan léuihgún jyuhgwo a? Seuhnggo làih-
    baai ngó hái gógàan léuihgún jyuhgwo léuhngmáan, ngó mjùng-
    yi gógàan léuihgún.

13. Néi haih mhaih hái (nī)syu dángjó hóu noi la? Haih, ngó
    dángjó hóu noi la.

14. Nīfo syù gaaujó géidòyaht la? Néideih sīk mei a? Nīfo syù
    gaaujó seiyaht la, daahnhaih ngódeih juhng mei sīk.

15. Néi sīkjó Wòhng sìnsàang hóu noi làh? Ngó sīkjó Wòhng sìn-
    sàang hóu noi lo, Wòhng sìnsàang hái Méigwok gójahnsí hái
    ngó ngūkkéi jyuhgwo hóu géinìn.

70. Time Spent constructions:

  a. Time Spent is expressed by a Number-Measure-Noun phrase
     (sàamgo yuht) or a Number-Measure phrase (sàamnìn) after
     the verb.

     Ngódeih hàahngjó léuhngyaht. We walked for two days.

     In verb-object constructions, the time-spent expression
  comes between verb and object. The particle 'ge' may be
  inserted after the time-spent expression.

     Ngó hohkjó sàamgo yuht ge   I studied Chinese for three
        Jùnggwokwá.   months.

  b. Note the idiomatic use of 'lèih,' 'heui' and 'jáu,' where
     English has 'be here,' 'be there,' 'be gone.'

     Kéuih lèihjó géi nói la?   How long has he been here?
     Kéuih heui géi nói a?   How long will he be there?
     Ngó heuijó luhkjo yuht.   I was there six months.
     Ngó lèihjó luhkgo yuht la. I have been here for six months.
     (For 'jó' and 'la' with number-measure combinations, see
     Lesson 12, Note 68.)

     When 'lèih,' 'heui' and 'hái' take a placeword
  object, the object follows the verb directly and the time-
  spent expression follows the object.

     Kéuih yìhgìng hái nīsyu   He has already been here for
        léuhngnìn la.   two years.
     Kéuih yìhgìng lèihjó nīsyu   He has already been here for
        léuhngnìn la.   two years.

  c. To express that for a certain period of time something has
     not been done, the time-spent expression comes before the
     verb and is followed by the negative 'móu.'

     Kéuih sàamgo yuht móu   He didn't work for three
        jouhsih.   months.
     Kéuih léuhnggo yuht móu   He has't eaten Chinese
        sihk tòhngchāan la.   food for two months.

     Note that in this construction, 'la' may occur even though
  'móu' is used.

III. Directional Complements 'lèih' and 'heui.'

    A.

        1. Kéuih hái làuhhah jáuséuhnglèih.
           He runs up from downstairs.

        2. Ngó hái làuhseuhng jáulohkheui.
           I run down from upstairs.

        3. Kéuih jáuséuhnglèih wán ngó.
           He runs up to look for me.

        4. Ngó jáulohkheui wán kéuih.
           I run down to look for him.

        5. Kéuih hái gógàan hohkhaauhsyu hàahngchēutlèih.
           He walks out from that school.

        6. Kéuih hàahngyahpheui gógàan poutáu máai yéh.

        7. Saimānjái néi hàahngmàailèih, ngó yáuh dī yéh béi néi.

        8. Ñgòi néi hàahnggwoheui gósyu dáng ngó.

        9. Saimānjái m̀hóu hàahnghòiheui, gósyu hóudò chè.

      10. Dímgáai néi m̀nīkséuhnglèih a?

      11. Nībún syù nīkheui gósyu, góbún syù nīklèih nīsyu.

      12. Ñgòi néi nīkmàailèih nīsyu.

      13. M̀hóu nīkgwoheui kéuihsyu la, nīkgwolèih ngósyu lā.

      14. Bīndī haih nīkséuhngheui fóchè ga?

      15. Gódī haih nīkfàanheui ngūkkéi ge, nīdī haih nīkfàanheui
           hohkhaauh ge.

    B.

        1. Ñgòi néi ló gódī yéh lèih (béi) ngó.
           Please go and get those things for me.

        2. Kéuih nīk (gó)dī yéh heui bīnsyu a?
           Where is he taking those things to?

3. Ṁgòi néi nīk nībún syù heui (béi) kéuih.
   Please take this book to her.

4. Néi géisí nīk nībún syù heui (béi) kéuih a?
   When are you going to take this book to him?

5. Ṁgòi néi bùn nījèung yí séuhngheui làuhseuhng, bùn gójèung tói lohklèih nīsyu.
   Please move this chair upstairs and move that table
   down here.

6. Dímgáai néi ṁdaai néidī saimānjái lèih a?

7. Hahgo láihbaai ngó yātdihng daai kéuihdeih lèih taam
   néideih.

8. Néi tìngyaht nīk góbún syù lèih hóu ma?

9. Ngó séung gei fùng seun heui Hèunggóng.

10. Néi sung Jèung taaitáai ge saimānjái fàan ngūkkéi dāk ma?

C.

1. Néi nīkjó gó-léuhnggihn yéh fàanheui ngó ngūkkéi mei a?
   Ngó nīkjó fàanheui lo.
   Have you taken those two things to my home? Yes, I have.

2. Kéuih sungjó gódī yéh heui Wòhng sìnsàang ngūkkéi mei a?
   Has he sent those things to Mr. Huang's home?

3. Néi bùndāk nījèung tói séuhngheui ma? (or Nījèung tói
   bùndākséuhngheui ma?) Ngó ṁbùndākséuhngheui.
   Can you move this table up? No, I can't.

4. Kéuih bùnjó jèung tói lohklèih mei a? Kéuih yìhgā bùn-
   gán lohklèih.
   Has he moved the table down? He's moving it down now.

5. Néi bùnsaai ngódī syù heui bīnsyu a? Ngó bùnsaaiheui
   hohkhaauh la.
   Where did you move all my books? I moved all of them
   to school.

6. Ngó kàhmyaht nīkjó nīléuhngbún syù séuhngheui làuhseuhng,
   bīngo yauh nīkfàan lohklèih a?

7. Néi yíhgìng sungjó gódī yéh heui la, dímgáai néi yauh
nīkfàanlèih a? Yanwaih móu yàhn hái (ngūk)kéi sóyíh
ngó nīkfàanlèih.

8. Néi yáuh móu geigwo chín fàan(heui) Jùnggwok a? Ngó
chìhnléuhngnìn geigwo fàanheui yìhgā móu lo.

9. Bīngo sung néidī saimānjái fàan hohk(haauh) a? Ngó
taaitáai yíhgìng sungjó kéuihdeih heui lo.

10. Néi bùnsaai gódī tói chēutheui mei a? Ngó bùnsaai gódī
tói chēutheui la, juhng yáuh léuhngjèung yí mei bùn jē.

71. Directional verbs of motion like <u>lèih</u>, <u>heui</u> and directional
compounds formed with <u>leih</u> and <u>heui</u> may be placed after certain
verbs to indicate the direction of the action:

nīklèih	'take hold of come'	...bring
nīkheui	'take hold of go'	...take away
nīkséuhnglèih	'take hold of ascend'	...bring up
nīklohkheui	'take hold of down'	...take down
nīkyahplèih	'take hold of enter'	...bring in
nīkchēutheui	'take hold of go out	...take out
nīkfàanlèih (or -heui)	'take hold of return'	...bring back (take
nīkmàailèih (or -heui)	'take hold of come close'	...bring close to (take)
nīkgwolèih (or -heui)	'take hold of come	...bring (it) over (take)

Verb with directional complements are split by the direct objec
and followed by placewords:

Kéuih nīk jì bāt <u>heui</u> gósyu.
Kéuih <u>nīk</u> bún syù <u>lohklèih</u> nīsyu.

Verbal suffixes <u>gán</u>, <u>dāk</u>, <u>jó</u>, <u>gwo</u>, <u>saai</u>, are attached to the
main verb:

Kéuih nīkgán jì bāt heui bīnsyu a?
Kéuih nīkjó bún syù lohklèih làuhhah mei a?
Néi bùnsaai dī yéh chēutheui mei a?
Néi bùndāk dī tói séuhngheui làuhseuhng ma?

Additional Sentences

1. Néi chēutnín juhng lèih m̄lèih nīsyu a?
2. Néi chìhnnín yáuh móu heuigwo Seuhnghói a?
3. Néi chēutsai gónìn haih bīnnìn a?
4. Néi gógàan hohkhaauh gauhnín yáuh géidò hohksāang a?
5. Néi duhkgwo géidònìn Yìngmàn a?
6. Néi chēutnín juhng duhk m̄duhk syù a?
7. Néi haih m̄haih lèihjó nīsyu léuhngnìn la?
8. Má sìnsàang hahgoyuht géidòhouh lèih nīsyu a?
9. Néi seuhnggoyuht yàthouh hái bīnsyu a?
10. Néi daihyihgoyuht gáuhouh juhng hái (nī)syu ma?
11. Néi géisí sàangyaht a?
12. Yātgoyuht yáuh géidògo láihbaai a?
13. Léih taaitáai haih m̄haih nīgo láihbaai lèih taam néi a?
14. Nīgo láihbaai haih nīgoyuhtge daihgéigo láihbaai a?
15. Kéuih heui Seuhnghói gógo láihbaai néi hái bīnsyu a?
16. Néi seuhnggoyuht géihouh heuigwo Gwóngjàu a?
17. Néi daihyihgo láihbaai heui m̄heui Gwóngjàu a?
18. Kàhmyaht haih m̄haih láihbaaisàam a?
19. Tìngyaht nē, tìngyaht haih m̄haih láihbaaing a?
20. Néi séung nīgo láihbaaigéi heui Hèunggóng a?
21. Wòhng sìnsàang nīgo láihbaaigéi lèih a?
22. Néi nīgo láihbaailuhk heui Jèung sìnsàangsyu ma?
23. Nīgo láihbaaigéi haih kéuihge sàangyaht a?
24. Hahgo láihbaaigéi yáuh yàhn heui Hèunggóng a?
25. Kéuih haih m̄haih nīgo láihbaaisei lèih a?

Translate the following questions into Cantonese and answer each
in Cantonese:

1. Are you going to Mr. Ho's home for supper tomorrow evening?
2. What is he doing upstairs now?
3. How many lessons have you studied already?
4. Have you ever been to Canton?
5. Have you finished all I told you to do?
6. Have you had your meal, I haven't eaten yet, how about
   (going out) getting something to eat?
7. Has she finished singing those songs? When she is finished,
   I want to invite her to have some Chinese food.
8. Have you finished studying that lesson (taught by the teacher)?
9. Have you asked all of them? Were they all busy?
10. Have you sold that book which I gave you last night?

Below are English translations of sentences used in the vocabulary
of this lesson as examples of usage. Translate these back into
Chinese (numbers correspond to those in Vocabulary section).

1. Where were you last year?
2. Are you going to Shanghai this year?
3. Is he coming next year?
4. I taught at that school year before last.
5. The year after next is 1973.
6. Were you in Hongkong last year?
7. Where were you in 1941?
8. Did this school already exist in 1754? In 1754, this school
   already existed.
9. How many years of English have you studied?
10. I studied one year of English.
11. Do you go to China every year?
12. I haven't been there for quite a few years.
13. Which year were you there?
14. I was there several years ago.
15. He learns to speak Chinese the first year, and learns to
    write the next year.
16. Where were you that year?
17. I taught at Hong Kong those three years.
18. Which month will you be free?
19. Did you go to Hong Kong last month?
20. Please come next month.
21. I didn't go there last month.
22. How many months were you there?
23. I was there seven months.
24. I have been here eight months already.
25. Which months is business good?
26. These months are not good, those months are good.
27. I looked him up (or called on him) a few months ago.
28. Which day of last week? Last Monday (the Monday of last wee
29. Which day of next week? Next Wednesday.
30. Which Monday? Last Monday. The Monday of last week. This
    coming Monday.
31. Which weekday are you free? Thursday. Which Thursday?
    (I mean) This (coming) Thursday, not next week Thursday.
32. Which day did you come here?
33. I came here yesterday.
34. Are you going today?
35. Are you free tomorrow?
36. I went to Hong Kong day before yesterday.
37. Sorry, I'll be busy day after tomorrow.

38. Which day of the week was the day before the day before yesterday?
39. I'll go to Hong Kong three days from now (the day after the day after tomorrow).
40. How many days have you been there? I have only been there two days.
41. Is he that busy everyday? Yes, he is that busy everyday.
42. Which day of the month is it today? Today is the first day of the month.
        the Second, the Third, ...
        the 11th, 12th, ...
        the 21th, 22nd, ...
        the 30th, 31st.
43. Which day of which month is it today? Today is February 3rd.
44. Today is which day of which month of what year (19??)? Today is January 10, 1955.
45. In which room does he live? (What number?) He lives in room 3.
46. What number Third Street? Nine Third Street.
47. Whose birthday is it today?
48. Today is your birthday, isn't it?
49. It isn't my birthday, it is his.
50. Have you been to Peking?
51. Where is Peking?
52. Is Peking still a wall city?
53. I have to write two letters.
54. Do I have any mail?
55. Whose letter is that?
56. When were you born? (When is your birthday?)
57. Has the baby been born? Yes, he has.
58. Did you ever teach? I did.
59. Do you like to teach?
60. May I rest a while?
61. I'm very tired, I want to rest.
62. Rest yourself a while.
63. Where did he move? He moved to Shanghai.
64. Have you moved that table?
65. Have you brought some money along?
66. Can you take me there? (Can you bring me along?)
67. I can't take you there.
68. Can you carry it? I can.
69. Where do you want to take it to?
70. What is he going to get? He's going to get some money.
71. How about you? Are you also? Yes, I'm going to also.
72. Please go and get it for me.

73. When can you send it over?
74. Who is going to take (escort) her home?
75. I'm going to see him off to China.
76. I want to give him some gifts. (don't use béi)
77. Have you mailed that letter? I have already mailed it.
78. I want to send this book back to the U.S.A.
79. Do you like one of this style? I like one of that style.
80. Which style do you like?
81. Is she pretty?
82. This table is very pretty, I like it very much.
83. Not very ugly, I think.
84. Do I have to wait very long? You don't have to wait very lor
85. How long have you been here?
86. Each one has a pen.
87. Each book must have this character.
88. Each room has two tables.
89. Walk over toward him.
90. Please have a seat by the table.
91. His car ran into my car.
92. He ran across to the shop.
93. Walk over (here) from there.
94. Go away from there.
95. Go away!
96. How tall is he?
97. How big is that car?
98. How much? Only a few dollars.
99. How many students are there? Only a few of them.
100. I lived there more than a month.
101. This book costs more than a dollar.
102. He has been gone more than a week.
103. Which room? Room No. 6.

USES OF TÙHNG
STRESSING ATTENDANT CIRCUMSTANCE

Vocabulary

jihgéi (or jihgēi)   N: self, oneself

1. Kéuih jihgéi lèih àh? Haih, kéuih
   jihgéi lèih.
2. Néi jihgéi hái nīsyu jyuh àh?

Faatgwok   PW: France

3. Néi haih Faatwok yàhn àh? Mhaih,
   kéuih haih Faatgwok yàhn.
4. Néi yáuh móu heuigwo Faatgwok a?

Dākgwok   PW: Germany

5. Néi go pàhngyáuh haih mhaih Dākgwok
   yàhn a? Kéuih mhaih Dākgwok yàhn,
   kéuih haih Faatgwok yàhn.
6. Dímgáai kéuih góng Dākgwok wá a?
   Kéuih hái Dākgwok jyuhgwo luhknìn.

Bàlàih   PW: Paris

7. Kéuih wah kéuih séung heui Bàlàih
   jyuh géinìn.
8. Ngó wah ngó yihkdōu séung heui Bàlàih
   jyuh géinìn.

faatjí   N: method, way, device

9. Néi yáuh móu faatjí bùn nījèung tói
   séuhngheui làuhseuhng a?
10. Ngó jihgéi móu faatjí bùn dāk seuhng-
    heui.

11. Kéuih mchóh fèigèi lèih, yáuh mātyéh
    faatjí lèih a?

wáan   V: play, enjoy or amuse oneself, play
                           musical instruments

12. Néi jùngyi heui bīnsyu wáan a?
    Ngó jùngyi heui Bàlàih wáan géiyaht.
13. Nīgo láihbaaiyaht néi heui bīnsyu
    wáan a?

giu   V: call, order(dishes)
                       CV: call, tell, order

14. Bīngo giu néi a? Ngó pàhngyáuh giu
    ngó.
15. Kéuih giu néi jouh mātyéh a?
16. Kéuih giu ngó chéng kéuih sihk tòhng
    chāan.
17. Mgòi néi giu kéuih lèih nīsyu.
18. Ngó giujó kéuih hóu noi la, kéuih
    juhng mei lèih mē?

hóuwáan   SV: amusing, interesting

19. Bàlàih hóuwáan ma? Bàlàih hóu hóu-
    wáan néi móu heuigwo mē?
20. Jànhaih gam hóuwáan chēutnín ngó
    yātdihng heui wáan géiyaht.

jài   V: put
  jàihái   V: put at
  jài...hái   Ph: put something at

21. Gógihn yéh néi jàihái bīnsyu a?
    Gógihn yéh ngó jàihái jèung tói
    hahbihn.
22. Kàhmyaht ngó jàihái nīsyu gógihn yéh
    dímgáai mginjó a?

tùhng(màai)   CV: with, and, for

23. Ngó yiu nīgo tùhng gógo.
24. Néi tùhng(màai) ngó heui hóu ma?
25. Nījèung boují haih ngó tùhng kéuih
    màai ge.

sìn   A: first (in Cantonese <u>sìn</u> as an adverb
                                      can be used after the verb)

                                      26. Bīngo sìn lèih ga? Kéuih sìn lèih
                                          ge.
                                      27. Néi heui sìn lā.

yātchái (or yātchàih) A: together

                                      28. Néideih yātchái lèih gàh? Haih, ngó-
                                          deih yātchái chóh fèigèi lèih ge.
                                      29. Dímgáai néideih ṁyātchái heui nē?

yùhgwo (or yeuhkhaih) MA: if, in case

                                      30. Yùhgwó néi dāknàahn néi heui ma?
                                      31. Yùhgwó néi ṁheui, ngó dōu ṁheui.
                                      32. Yùhgwó tìnhei ṁhóu néi juhng heui ma?

tíng (or yeuhng)   M: kind, sort

                                      33. Néi jùngyi bīntíng a?
                                      34. Néi sīk góng bīntíng Jùnggwok wá a?

-màai   P: indicating 'with,' 'along with,' 'also
                                      with'

                                      35. Dímgáai néi ṁtùhngmàai kéuih heui a?
                                      36. Dímgáai néi ṁdaaimàai kéuih heui a?
                                      37. Mgói néi nīkmàai góbún Jùnggwok syù
                                          lèih.

jīkhāak   A: immediately, at once

                                      38. Chéng néi jīkhāak lèih.
                                      39. Ṁgòi néi jīkhāak lólèih béi ngó.
                                      40. Nīgihn sih yiu jīkhāak jouh.

sāam (M: gihn, tyut)   N: clothes, dress, gown, coat; suit

                                      41. Néi gihnsāam jànhaih leng la.
                                      42. Ngó yìhgā séung heui máai géigihn
                                          sāam.
                                      43. Néi daai bīntyut sāam heui a?

jeuk   V: wear

                            44. Néi jeuk bīngihn sāam heui a?
                            45. Nīgihn sāam néi jeukgwo mei a?
                            46. Nītyut sāam néi jeukjó géinói la?

gàyàhn (M: dī)   N: the family (members)

                            47. Néidī gàyàhn hái bīnsyu a?
                            48. Néidī gàyàhn géisí lèih a?
                            49. Kéuihge gàyàhn hái (nī)syu ma?

kìnggái   VO: chat, converse

                            50. Ngó séung wán néi kìnggái, néi dāk-
                                hàahn ma?
                            51. Ngódeih kàhmmáan kìngjó hóu noi.
                            52. Bīngéiwái hái (gó)syu kìnggángái a?

lohkyúh   VO: rain
   yúh   N: rain

                            53. Tìngyaht wuih lohkyúh ma?
                            54. Gam daaih yúh m̀hóu heui lo!

                            Conversation

A: Chàhn sìnsàang chìhngo yuht ngó heui taam néi, néi m̀hái kéi,
   seuhnggo yuht ngó heui taam néi yauh m̀hái kéi, néi heuijó bīn-
   syu a?
B: Oh, ngó heuijó Faatgwok sóyíh m̀hái kéi jàn(haih) deuim̀jyuh la.
A: Néi chìhngo yuht géidòhouh heui ga?
B: Ngó sahpluhkhouh heui ge.
A: Néi yáuh móu tùhngmaai dī gàyàhn heui a?
B: Móu, yànwaih dī saimānjái yiu duhksyù m̀dākhàahn, sóyíh móu tùhng
   kéuihdeih heui.
A: Néi haih m̀haih chóh fèigèi heui ga?
B: M̀haih, ngó sìn chóh syùhn heui Yìnggwok, hái Yìnggwok chóh fóchè
   heui Bàlàih ge.
A: Néi hái Bàlàih jyuhjó géi nói a?
B: Jyuhjó léuhnggo láihbaai jē, yànwaih ngó yiu heui Dākgwok taam
   géigo pàhngyáuh.

A: Bàlàih hóuwáan ma?
B: Bàlàih hóu hóuwáan.
A: Néi yáuh móu hái Faatgwok daai dī yéh fàanlèih béi néi taaitáai
   a?
B: Ngó tùhng kéuih hái Bàlàih máaijó léuhngtyut sāam kéuih hóu
   jùngyi. Néi chìhnnín heui Faatgwok gójahnsí, móu heuigwo Bàlàih
   mē?
A: Mou, ngó heuiyùhn Dākgwok jauh (see Les. 15) jīkhāak fàanlèih
   la. Chēutnín luhkyuht ngó juhng yiu heui Dākgwok, gójahnsí,
   ngó yātdihng heui Bàlàih wáan géiyaht.

                     Pattern Sentences

I. Uses of tùhng or tùhngmàai:

A. As co-verb meaning 'with' or 'together with.'

   1. Ngó tùhng kéuih hcui Hèunggóng.
      I am going to Hong Kong with him.

   2. Néi tùhng mtuhng ngódeih yātchái heui a?
      Are you going with us?

   3. Dímgáai néi mtùhng néidī saimānjái yātchái lèih a?
      Why don't you come with your children?

   4. Néi tùhngmàai ngó yātchái heui Hèunggóng máai dī yéh hóu ma?
      How about going to Hong Kong with me to buy something?

   5. Yùhgwó néi mtùhng ngó heui, gám ngó jihgéi heui la.
      If you won't go with me, I'll go by myself.

   6. Néidī Gwóngjàuwá tùhng bīngo hohk ga?

   7. Ngó tùhng Wòhng sìnsaang hohkjó sàamgo láihbaai, tùhng Léih
      sìnsàang hohkjó léuhngnìn.

   8. Ngó tìngyaht tùhng néi heui Hèunggóng taam kéuih hóu ma?

   9. Ngó sìn tùhng kéuih yātchái cheung, yātjahngāan ngó tùhng
      néi yātchái cheung.

10. Kéuih tùhng Wòhng sìnsàang chēutjóheui, ngó móu man kéuih-
    deih heui bīnsyu.

11. Chìhnnín ngó tùhng kéuih yātchái heui Jùnggwok ge, kéuih
    yìhgā juhng hái Jùnggwok mei fàanlèih.

12. Ngó tùhng kéuih yātchái duhkgwo léuhngnìn syù, gauhnín kéuih
    fàanjó Jùnggwok lo.

13. Chìhnnín ngódeih hái Jùnggwok gójahnsí ngó tùhng kéuih yāt-
    chái hái yātgàan hohkhaauh gaausyù.

14. Gogo láihbaai(yaht) Jèung sìnsàang Jèung taaitáai dōu tùhng
    kéuihdeihdī saimānjéi chēutheui sihk tòhngchāan.

15. Nī géiyaht tìnhei gam mhóu néi tìngyaht tùhngmàai ngódeih
    chóh syùhn heui mhóu chóh fēigèi heui lo.

B. As co-verb meaning 'for' or 'for the benefit of'

   1. Bīngo tùhng néideih jyúfàahn a?
      Who cooks for you?

   2. Néi tùhng ngó jouh nīgihn sih dāk ma?
      Can you do this for me?

   3. Mgòi néi tùhng ngó giu kéuih lèih nīsyu dāk ma?
      Can you tell him to come over here (for me)?

   4. Néi tùhng ngó heui Hèunggóng máai dī yéh hóu ma?
      (compare with Patt. I A. 4 above)
      How about going to Hong Kong and buying something for me?

   5. Gám ngó tùhng néi sé jih néi tùhng ngó jyúfàahn la.
      (Then)I'll write those characters for you and you cook for
      me.

   6. Ngó tùhng néi jouhjó gam dò sih néi juhng mdòjeh ngó àh?

   7. Nībún Yìngmàn syù haih kéuih hái Méigwok tùhng néi máai gàh?

   8. Néi jùng(yi) myùngyi ngó tùhng néi hái Méigwok máai ge gógo
      bīu a?

   9. Ngó gàmyaht mdākhàahn mgòi néi tùhng ngó gaau nīfo syù dāk
      ma?

10. Kéuih tùhng ngó sé gógéigo jih jànhaih leng la.

11. Bīngo tùhng ngó bùnjó jèung tói séuhngheui làuhseuhng a?
    Jànhaih m̀gòi kéuih lo.

12. M̀gòi néi tùhng ngó heui Wòhng sìnsàangsyu ló gó léuhngbún
    Yìngmàn syù fàanlèih dāk ma?

13. Yātjahngāan néi heui gāai máai yéh gójahnsí, néi tùhng ngó
    geijó nīfùng seun dāk ma?

14. Néi tīngyaht dāk m̀dākhàahn tùhng ngó sung dī saimānjái fàanhohk
    a?

15. Néideih géiwái tùhng ngó jouhjó gam dò sih   ngó jànhaih dòjeh
    néideih lo.

C. As a commecting word 'and'

1. Ngó tùhng kéuih haih hóu pàhngyáuh.
   He and I are good friends.

2. Ngó tùhng kéuih dōu haih Chàhn sìnsàang ge hohksāang.
   He and I both are Mr. Chen's students.

3. Ngó chēutnìn yiu heui Faatgwok tùhng Dākgwok.
   I'll go to France and Germany next year.

4. Ngó gàmmáan yiu chēutgāai máai yéh tùhngmàai taam yātgo pàhngyáuh. (chēutgāai, or heuigāai, 'going out')
   I am going downtown shopping and to see a friend tonight.

5. Néi chēutnìn séung heui Seuhnghói tùhng Bākgìng àh?
   Do you want to go to Shanghai and Peking next year?

6. Néi gauhnìn heuigwo Faatgwok tùhng bīngwok a?

7. Néi kàhmmáan tùhng chìhnmáan hái bīnsyu jyuh a?

8. Ngó gauhnìn tùhng Jèung sìnsàang hái Bàlàih wáanjó sàamgo
   làihbaai.

9. Wòhng síujé tùhng kéuih dī pàhngyáuh dímyéung heui Méigwok ga?

10. Ngó tùhng ngó taaitáai dōu mei heuigwo Jùnggwok.

11. Néi tùhng néi taaitáai gàmmáan lèih ngódeih syu sihkfaahn hóu ma?

12. Chàhn sìnsàang tùhng Chàhn taaitáai dōu heuijó gāai àh?

13. Kéuih tùhng Wòhng sìnsàang léuhngwái dōu haih hái Méigwok duhkyùhn syù fàanlèih ge.

14. Néi tùhng Léih sìnsàang haih hóu pàhngyáuh, ngó tùhng Léih sìnsàang yihk haih hóu pàhngyáuh, sóyíh néi tùhng ngó yihk haih hóu pàhngyáuh.

15. Kéuih ge saimānjái tùhng ngó ge saimānjái tùhngmàai hái yātgàan hohkhaauh duhk syù, sóyíh ngó sīk kéuih.

72. In mentioning a number of coordinate nouns in succession tùhng may be used to link them together:

Kéuih tùhng ngó haih hóu pàhngyáuh.
Kéuih tùhng ngó yiu heui Hèunggóng tùhng Seuhnghói.

II. Stressing attendent circumstance:

A. Stressing Time:

1. Chàhn sìnsàang lèihjó mei a? Kéuih lèihjó la.
   Has Mr. Chen come? Yes, he has.

   Kéuih géisí lèih ga? Kéuih kàhmyaht lèih ge.
   When did he come? He came yesterday.

2. Léih sìnsàang jáujó mei a? Léih sìnsàang jáujó la.
   Has Mr. Lee left? Yes, he has.

   Kéuih géisí jáu ga? Kéuih seuhnggoláihbaai jáu ge.
   When did he leave? He left last week.

3. Nījèung tói néi géisí máai ga? Ngó chìhnyaht máai ge.
   When did you buy this table? I bought it the day before yesterday.

   Néi géisí béi chín kéuih ga? Ngó kàhmyaht béi chín kéuih ge.
   When did you pay him? I paid him for it yesterday.

4. Jèung sìnsàang doujó Hèunggóng mei a? Jèung sìnsàang doujó la.

Has Mr. Chang arrived in Hong Kong? He has already arrived.

Kéuih haih mhaih chóh fèigèi heui Hèunggóng ga? Haih, kéuih
haih chóh fèigèi heui ge.
Was he going there by plane? Yes, he was going by plane.

Kéuih géisí heui ga? Kéuih kàhmyaht heui ge.
When did he go? He went yesterday.

5. Kéuih wúih góng Gwóngjàuwá mei a? Kéuih wúih góng hóu géigeui la.
   Does he know how to speak Cantonese now? He can speak quite
   a few sentences now.

   Kéuih géisí hohk ga? Kéuih gauhnìn hái nīsyu hohk ge.
   When did he learn it? He learned it here last year.

B. Stressing Place:

1. Néi sihkjó fàahn mei a? Ngó sihkjó la.
   Have you eaten? I have already eaten.

   Néi hái bīnsyu sihk ga? Ngó hái Chàhn sìnsàangsyu sihk ge.
   Where did you eat? I ate at Mr. Chen's place.

2. Néi sīk Wòhng síujé ma? Ngó sīk kéuih.
   Do you know Miss Huang? Yes, I know her.

   Néi hái bīnsyu sīk kéuih ga? Ngó hái Chàhn taaitáai ngūkkéi
   sīk kéuih ge.
   Where did you meet (get to know) her? I met (got to know)
   her at Mrs. Chen's home.

3. Néi máaijó boují mei a? Ngó máaijó la.
   Have you bought the newspaper? I bought it already.

   Néi hái bīnsyu máai ga? Ngó hái gógàan poutáu máai ge.
   Where did you buy it? I bought it from that store.

4. Néi yáuh chín mei a? Ngó yáuh chín la.
   Have you got the money? I've got it.

   Hái bīnsyu ló ga? Hái pàhngyáuhsyu ló ge.
   Where did you get it from? I got it from a friend.

5. Gójek syùhn géisí dou ga? Gàmjìujóu dou ge.
   When did that ship arrive? It arrived this morning.

   Hái bīnsyu lèih ga? Hái Méigwok lèih ge.
   Where did it come from? It came from the U.S.A.

C. Stressing Conveyance:

   1. Léih síujé lèihjó mei a? Léih síujé lèihjó la.
      Has Miss Lee arrived yet? Yes, she has arrived.

      Kéuih dímyéung lèih ga? Kéuih chóh heichè lèih ge.
      How did she come here? She came here by car.

   2. Jèung sìnsàang fàanjóheui Méigwok mei a? Kéuih faanjóheui
      hóu noi la.
      Has Mr. Chang gone back to America? He returned a long time
      ago.

      Kéuih chóh syùhn fàanheui gàh? Mhaih, kéuih chóh fèigèi
      fàanheui ge.
      Did he go by ship? No, he went back by plane.

   3. Néi géisí hái Gwóngjàu lèih ga? Ngó gàmjìujóu lèih ge.
      When did you come from Canton? I came this morning.

      Néi chóh syùhn lèih gàh? Ngó chóh fóchè lèih ge.
      Did you come by boat? I came here by train.

   4. Néi tùhng kéuih yātchái lèih gàh? Mhaih, kéuih chóh chè
      lèih ge, ngó hàahnglèih ge.
      Did you come here with him? No, he came here by car, I
      walked.

   5. Léih sìnsàang néi fàanjólèih làh? Haih, ngó kàhmmáan fàan-
      lèih ge.
      Oh! Mr. Lee you returned? Yes, I returned last night.

      Néi dímyéung fàanlèih ga? Ngó chóh syùhn fàanlèih ge.
      How did you return? I returned by boat.

D. Stressing Purpose:

   1. Chàhn sìnsàang lèihjó mei a? Chàhn sìnsàang lèihjó la.
      Has Mr. Chen arrived? Yes, Mr. Chen has arrived.

Kéuih (haih) lèih jouh mātyéh ga? Kéuih (haih) lèih gaausyù
ge.
What did he come here for? He came here to teach.

2. Néidī saimānjái géisí lèih ga? Kéuihdeih gàmnín yihyuht lèih
ge.
When did your children come? They came here last February.

Kéuihdeih lèih Hèunggóng jouh mātyéh ga? Kéuihdeih lèih duhksyù ge.
What did they come here for? They came here to study.

3. Néi sīk gógéiwái Dākgwok yàhn ma? Ngó sīk.
Do you know those gentlemen from Germany? Yes, I do.

Kéuihdeih lèih nīsyu jouh mātyéh ga? Kéuihdeih lèih nīsyu
jouhsàangyi ge.
What did they come here for? They came here to do business.

4. Néideih séung géisí bùnheui gógàan ngūksyu a? Ngódeih séung
yìhgā bùn.
When are you going to move into that house? We want to move
right now.

Gógéigo yàhn lèih jouh mātyéh ga? Kéuihdeih lèih bùn yéh ge.
What did those men come for? They came to move things.

5. Néi wán mātyéh a? Ngó wán yātjek syùhn.
What are you looking for? I'm looking for a boat.

Gójek syùhn lèih nīsyu jouh mātyéh ga? Gójek syùhn (haih)
lèih nīsyu jip ngódeih ge.
What (purpose) did the boat come for? The boat came here to
meet us.

E. Stressing Person:

1. Chàhn sìnsàang lèihjó mei a? Léihjó la.
Has Mr. Chen arrived yet? Yes, he has.

Kéuih tùhng bīngo lèih ga? Kéuih tùhng dī saimānjái yātchái
lèih ge.
With whom did he come? He came with the children.

2. Néi taaitáai géisí fàan Méigwok ga? Kéuih seuhnggoyuht fàanheui ge.

When did your wife go back to America?   She went back last
month.

Kéuih tùhng bīngo yātchái fàanheui ga?   Kéuih tùhng dī saimānjái yātchái fàanheui ge.
With whom did she go?   She went with the children.

3. Léih síujé heuijó cheunggō mei a?   Heuijó la.
   Has Miss Lee gone to sing?   She has already gone.

   Kéuih tùhng bīngo heui ga?   Kéuih tùhng Léih sìnsàang yātchái heui ge.
   With whom did she go?   She went with Mr. Lee.

4. Néi gójì bāt jànhaih leng la, géisí máai ga?   Ngó gauhnín
   hái Méigwok máai ge.
   Your pen (fountain pen) is really beautiful, when did you
   buy it?   I bought it last year in the States.

   Néi tùhng bīngo heui máai ga?   Ngó tùhng ngó taaitáai yātch₁
   heui máai ge.
   With whom did you go to buy it?   I went to buy it with my
   wife.

5. Má sìnsàang néi géisí lèih ga?   Ngó kàhmmáan lèih ge.
   When did you come Mr. Ma?   I came here last night.

   Néi tùhng bīngo lèih ga?   Ngó tùhng ngó taaitáai yātchái
   chóh syùhn lèih ge.
   With whom did you come?   I came with my wife by boat.

73. Sometimes it is not the action expressed by the main verb, but
    an attendant circumstance expressed by an adverb or coverb
    phrase which is the real point of the sentence. To stress an
    attendant circumstance such as time an action occurred, the
    place where the action occurred or started from, what conveyan
    was needed, the pupose of coming or going, or the person with
    whom the action occurred, sentence final ge is used instead of
    the completed action form of the verb. The addition of haih
    before the elements to be stressed is common but not required.

Kéuih géisí lèih ga?
Kéuih kàhmyaht lèih ge.

Kéuih hái bīnsyu lèih ga?
Kéuih hái Hèunggóng lèih ge.

Kéuih dímyéung lèih ga?
Kéuih chóh syùhn lèih ge.

Kéuih lèih jouh mātyéh ga?
Kéuih lèih gaausyù ge.

Kéuih tùhng bīngo lèih ga?
Kéuih tùhng kéuihge saimānjái yātchái lèih ge.

Note:the question forms may be ga (ge ≠ a) or gàh (ge ≠ àh).
Ga is used after choice-type question forms or when a question
word appears in the sentence. Gàh occurs when the speaker is
in agreement or indicates surprise, i.e.

Néi kàhmyaht lèih gàh?   You came yesterday?
Néi chóh fèigèi lèih gàh?   You came here by plane?

III. Verbal modifier following the object.

  A.

    1. Gàmyaht yáuh móu yúh lohk a?   Gàmyaht móu yúh lohk.
       Is it going to rain today? No.

    2. Gógàan poutáu yáuh móu tòhngchāan sihk a?
       Do they sell Chinese food in that store?

    3. Gàmyaht yáuh móu fèigèi chóh a?   Gàmyaht móu fèigèi chóh,
       yànwaih fèisaaiheui Hèunggóng la.
       Is there any plane available (for a ride)? No, because
       they all flew to Hong Kong.

    4. Néi chēutnìn juhng yáuh syù duhk ma?   Móu la, yànwaih ngó
       móu chín duhk la.
       Can you carry on your study next year? I can't because
       I'm out of money.

    5. Gógàan poutáu yáuh móu Yìngmàn boují maai a? Yáuh, daahn-
       haih gàmjìujóu yíhgìng maaisaai la.
       Does that store sell English papers? Yes, they do, but
       the papers were sold out this morning.

B.

  1. Kéuih yìhgā wángán sìh jouh àh? Kéuih yìhgā wángán sìh
     jouh.
     Is he looking for a job? He is looking for a job.

  2. Kéuih heui jouh mātyéh a? Kéuih heui jyú fàahn sihk.
     What is she going to do? She is going to cook.

  3. Néi heui máai mātyéh a? Ngó heui máai yéh sihk.
     What are you going to buy? I'm going to buy something to
     eat.

  4. Ngódī sāam taai gauh la, sóyíh ngó séung heui máai géigihn
     sāam jeuk.
     My clothes are too old, therefore I want to buy some new
     clothes to wear.

  5. Kéuih heui Hèunggóng jouh mātyéh a? Wán sìh jouh àh?
     M̀haih, kéuih séung wán sàangyi jouh.
     What is he going to Hong Kong for? Looking for a job?
     No, he wants to look for some business to do.

74. Verbal modifier following the object: In some sentences a verb
    form may follow the object and modify what precedes. Such a
    form is usually translated into English as 'to ≠ V': i.e. 'to
    eat, to wear.' Use of this construction after the verb 'yáuh'
    — 'there is' — is common.

    Yáuh yéh sihk ma?   Is there anything to eat?
    Móu yéh maai la.   There is nothing more to sell.
    máai sāam jeuk.   buy clothes to wear.
    wán sih jouh   look for work (to do)

75. Uses of the verb 'yáuh':

  a. Impersonal use, indicating existence or presence.

     yáuh yātgo yàhn   there is a man
     yáuh yéh maai   there are things for sale

  b. Indicating existence or presence after a placeword.

     Tóisyu yáuh jèung boují. There is a newspaper on the table.
     (Note that to use the form 'boují hái tóisyu' would mean
     'the (previously mentioned) paper is on the table.')

The choice-type question form for the above two uses is:

Yáuh móu yàhn hái syu a? Is there anybody around?
Yáuh móu yàhn hái kéi a? Is there anybody home?
Gósyu yáuh móu hohkhaauh a? Is there a school there?

c. Coverbal use with 'gam' to indicate equality in a comparision (introduced in Les. 20)

d. Use in measurement (introduced in Les. 21)

e. 'Yáuh móu' as a question form when the verb is followed by a particle (see Les. 12, note 66)

Kéuih kàhmyaht yáuh móu lèihgwo a?
Did he come yesterday?
Néi yáuh móu heuigwo seuhnghói a?
Have you ever been to Shanghai?
Kéuih yáuh móu sésaai gódī jih a?
Has he written all those characters yet?

76. When certain verbs are followed by the particle 'jó,' 'gwo,' 'gán,' the place phrase with 'hái' _precedes_ rather than follows the verb.

Kéuih hái Hèunggóng jyuhgwo géi nói a?
How long did he live in Hong Kong?
Ngó hái nīsyu dángjó bundímjūng la.
I have been waiting here for half an hour.
Kéuihdeih hái gótiuh kiuhsyu hàahnggán.
They are walking on that bridge.
(see also Voc. sentence 6 in this lesson)

Additional Sentences

1. Néi géisí tùhng kéuih chóh syùhn lèih ga?
2. Néi tùhng kéuih hái Méigwok chóh fèigèi lèih gàh?
3. Néi giu kéuih lèih tùhng néi jouh mātyéh a?
4. Tùhngmàai néi lèih gógo haih bīngo a?
5. Kàhmyaht bīngo tùhng néi heui ga?
6. Nībún Yìngmàn syù bīngo tùhng néi máai ga?
7. Mgòi néi tùhng ngó giu kéuih lèih nīsyu dāk ma? Ngó yáuh dī sih yiu man kéuih.

8. Ńgòi néi giu kéuih tùhng ngó máai jèung boují dāk ma?
9. Kéuih tùhng bīngo hái làuhseuhng kìnggángái a?
10. Néi yáuh mātyéh yiu ngó tùhng néi daaifàanheui ngūkkéi ge ma?
11. Ngó séung tùhng néi kìng géigeui néi dākhàahn ma?
12. Ńgòi néi tùhng ngó jīkhāah heui máai jèung boují ngó séung jìd(
    tìngyaht yauh móu fèigèi heui Méigwok.
13. Néi séung tìngyaht tùhng néidī gàyàhn heui bīnsyu wáan a?
14. Yùhgwó néi heui Faatgwok tùhng Dākgwok wáan, néi séung heui bīr
    gwok sìn a?
15. Tìngmáan Wòhng sìnsàang chéng sihkfaahn néi séung jeuk bīntyut
    sāam heui a?
16. Ńgòi néi dáng yātjahngāan, dáng ngó lómàai bún syù lèih tùhng
    néi yātchái duhk hóu ma?
17. Néi tìngyaht heui fóchèjaahm jip Jèung sìnsàang néi dáaimàai néi
    gàyàhn heui ma?
18. Néi yáuh móu faatjí nīkmàai gógéigihn yéh a?
19. Nījèung tói tùhng gójèung yí néi séung jàihái bīnsyu a?
20. Kéuih tùhng néi góng mātyéu wá a? Yìngmàn àh?

Translate the following sentences:

1. Where were you last Monday?
2. I wasn't here last Monday, but I was here the Monday of last we
3. Which day of next month are you going to Hong Kong?
4. Isn't his birthday December the twelfth.
5. How long have you waited for me?
6. I lived in China for two months in 1947.
7. When are you going to mail this letter?
8. We have already studied Cantonese for six weeks.
9. Please go and get a pen for me.
10. Who brought my book here?

Below are English translations of sentences used in the vocabulary
of this lesson as examples of usage. Translate these back into
Chinese (numbers correspond to those in Vocabulary section.)

1. Is he coming by himself? Yes, he is coming by himself.
2. Do you live here alone?
3. Are you a Frenchman? No, I'm not, but he is.
4. Have you ever been to France?
5. Is your friend a German? He isn't a German, he is a Frenchman.
6. How come he speaks German? Because he has lived there for six
   years.
7. He said that he would like to live in Paris for a few years.
8. I said I also would like to live in Paris for a few years.

9. Do you have any way of moving this table upstairs?
10. I can't move it up by myself.
11. If he is not going to come here by plane, how can he get here?
12. Where would you like to go to enjoy yourself? I would like to enjoy myself in Paris for a few days.
13. Where are you going to spend this Sunday?
14. Who called you? My friend called me.
15. What did he call you for?
16. He told me to invite him to have some Chinese food.
17. Please tell him to come here.
18. I have been calling him for quite a while already, hasn't he come yet?
19. Is Paris very interesting? Yes, it is, haven't you been there?
20. If it really is, next year I certainly will spend a few days there.
21. Where did you put that thing? I put that thing underneath the table.
22. Why has that thing I put there yesterday disappeared?
23. I want this one and that one.
24. How about going with me?
25. This paper is the one I bought for him.
26. Who came first? He is the one who came first.
27. You go first.
28. Did you all come together? Yes, we came here together by plane.
29. Why don't you go (all) together?
30. If you are free, are you going?
31. If you won't go, I won't go either.
32. If the weather is bad, do you still want to go?
33. Which kind do you like?
34. Which kind of Chinese do you speak (i.e. which dialect)
35. Why don't you go with him?
36. Why don't you take him along along (with you)?
37. Please bring that Chinese book along.
38. Please come here at once.
39. Please fetch it for me at once.
40. This thing should be done at once.
41. Your dress is really beautiful.
42. I want to go to buy some clothes.
43. Which suit are you bringing along with you?
44. Which dress are you going to wear (to the party)?
45. Has this dress ever been worn?
46. How long have you worn this suit.
47. Where is your family?
48. When will your family come?
49. Is his family here?
50. I want to chat with you, are you free?
51. We chatted quite a while last night.
52. Who are the ones chatting there?
53. Will it rain tomorrow?
54. Since it's raining so hard, I think we'd better not go.

PAIRED CLAUSES

Vocabulary

faaijí (M: sèung)   N: chopsticks

                        1. Ńgòi nīk sèung faaijí (béi) ngó.
                        2. Nīsèung faaijí hái bīnsyu máai ga?
                        3. Nīsèung faaijí haih ngó hái Jùnggwok
                            daailèih ge.

jáugún, jáugā (M: gàan)N: restaurant

                        4. Nīsyu yáuh géidògàan jáugún a?
                        5. Nīsyu yáuh sàamgàan jáugún.
                        6. Ngó hóu noi móu heuigwo jáugún la.

dōu (M: bá)   N: knife
  doujái   N: pocket knife

                        7. Ńgòi néi béi bá dōu ngó.
                        8. Nībá dōu géi chín a?
                        9. Néi yáuh dōujái ma?

chā (M: jek)   N: fork

                     10. Néi dī dōu chā gau ńgau a?
                     11. Ngó ńginjó léuhngjek chā.
                     12. Néi tùhng ngó heui máai léuhngjek
                           chā dāk ma?

chàh   N: tea

                     13. Néi yámgwo chàh ma?
                     14. Ngó yámgwo chàh.
                     15. Néi yámge haih bīngwokge chàh a?

-fu   M: set

                             16. Néi nīfu dōu chā jànhaih leng la.
                             17. Nīfu dōu chā haih ngó hái Méigwok
                                 daailèih ge.
                             18. Nīfu tòih yí haih m̀haih Jùnggwok
                                 tòih yí a?

yú   N: fish

                             19. Nītiuh yú géi chín a?
                             20. Néi jùngyi sihk yú ma?
                             21. Bīnsyu yáuh yú maai a?

sung (M: dihp)   N: dish of food

                             22. Néi jùngyi sihk mātyéh sung a?
                             23. Nīdihp sung haih bīngo jyú ga?
                             24. Néi wúih m̀wúih jyú sung a?

choi (M: dihp or mei)   N: (formal dish of food as those served in
                              the restaurants)
   choi (M: tíng - kind)N: vegetable

                             25. Néi jùngyi sihk choi ma?
                             26. Néi jùngyi sihk bīntíng choi a?
                             27. Bīngàan jáugúnge choi hóu a?
                             28. Gógàan jáugúnge choi hóu hóu.
                             29. Ngódeih giu sàamgo choi gau mei a?

tòng (M: wún)   N: soup

                             30. Néi jùngyi choi tòng ma?
                             31. M̀gòi néi béi wún tòng ngó.
                             32. Néideih yiu géidòwún tòng a?

wún (M: jek)   N: bowl
                             M: bowl

                             33. Nījek haih m̀haih Jùnggwok wún a?
                             34. Nījek Jùnggwok wún nei géisí máai ga?
                             35. Nījek wún géidò chín a?

jáu (M: -bùi)   N: wine

                             36. Nīdī jáu hái bīnsyu lèih ga?

37. Nīdī haih m̀haih Faatgwok jáu a?
38. Gógàan poutáu yáuh mòu jáu maai a?

būi (M: -jek)   N: glass, cup

deihfòng (M: daat)   N: place

39. Néi heuigwo gódaat deihfòng ma?
40. Gódaat deihfòng jànhaih hóu la.
41. Néi wah(ge) gódaat deihfòng hái bīn-
    syu a?

yám   V: drink

42. Yám bùi jáu hóu ma?
43. Ngó m̀sīk yám jáu.
44. Néi jùngyi yám jáu ma?

ngo (or tóuhngo)   SV/V: hungry

45. Néi ngo ma?
46. Ngó hóu ngo.
47. Kéuih ngojó géi nói la?
48. Kéuih ngojó léuhngyaht la.

sái   V: use, spend
                        CV: send, tell (someone to do something)
                        AV: need to, have to (see Les. 16, Patt. II A

49. Ngó sái nīji bāt dāk ma?
50. Kéuih sáijó hóu dò chín.
51. Néi seuhnggo lòihbaai sáijó géi dò
    chín a?
52. Néi tìngyaht sái m̀sái duhk syù a?

jauh   A: then (introducing subsequent action), at
                             once; only, just (see Les. 18)

53. Béi ngmān kéuih jauh maai la.
54. Kéuih jauh lèih la.
55. Ngó jauh yáuh yātgo jē.

-háh   P: (do something) once, a little (see note 7

56. Ngó séung tùhng néi kìngháh.

57. Béi ngó táiháh dāk ma?
58. Ngódeih chēutheui hàahngháh hóu ma?

Useful Expressions

mgányiu (or móugányiu) IE: never mind, it doesn't matter

        59. Néi heui mheui mgányiu.
        60. Haih mhaih móugányiu a?
        61. Bīngo wah mgányiu a?

tèngginwah   IE: hear(d) it said that

        62. Tèngginwah yìhgā dī yéh hóu gwai
            haih mhaih a?
        63. Tèngginwah néi yiu heui Hèunggóng
            haih mhaih a?
        64. Tèngginwah néi yìhgā hóu mdākhàahn
            haih mhaih a?

chèuihbín   MA: as one pleases (lit. follow convenience),
                      at random

        65. Chèuihbín néi géisí lèih dōu dāk.
        66. Ngó chèuihbín máaijó léuhngjèung.
        67. Chèuihbín chóh!

Conversation

A: Ngó séung gàmmáan heui sihk tòhngchāan, néi heui mheui a?
B: Dáng ngó táiháh ngó dāk(hàahn) mdākhàahn tùhngmàai néi heui,
   Oh! ngó gàmmáan mdākhàahn mheuidāk.
C: Ngó mei sihkgwo tòhngchāa... Ngó tùhng néi heui hóu ma?
A: Hóu. Néi sīk sái faaijí ma?
C: Ngó msīk. Haih mhaih msīk sái faaijí jauh msihkdāk tòhngchāan a?
A: Mhaih. Néi jànhaih msīk sái faaijí àh?
C: Ngó jànhaih msīk.
A: Móugányiu, néi hóyíh sái dōu chā, jáugúnsyu yáuh dōu chā. Yùh-
   gwó néi séung hohk sái faaijí ngó hóyíh gaau néi.

C: Hohk sái faaijí haih m̀haih hóu nàan a?
A: M̀haih hóu nàan jē.
C: Néi géisí hohk ga?
A: Ngó chìhnnín hái Hèunggóng hohk ge.
C: Néi tùhng bīngo hohk ga?
A: Ngó tùhng ngó dī Jùnggwok pàhngyáuh hohk ge.
C: Haih m̀haih yiu hohk hóu noi a?
A: Oh, néi gam chùngmìng, yāt hohk jauh sīk la.
C: Hóuwah, hóuwah, ngódeih heui bīngàan jáugún sihk a?
A: Sèhng léuihbihn daihbaatgāai yáuh yātgàan jáugún, tèngginwah gó-
   gàan jáugúnge choi hóu hóu.
C: Gám ngódeih jauh heui gógàan lā.
A: Néi jùngyi sihk mātyéh sung a?
C: Chèuihbín lā.
A: Néi jùngyi sihk yú ma?
C: Ngó hóu jùngyi sihk yú.
A: Gám ngódeih jauh sihk yú lā. Ngódeih yiu go mātyéh tòng a?
C: Choi tòng hóu ma?
A: Hóu, hóu, ngódeih giu yātgo tòng léuhnggo choi ngó tái m̀gau,
   ngódeih giu yātgo tòng sàamgo choi hóu ma?
C: M̀hou lo, gau lo, gau lo.

(after a short while)

A: Sái m̀sái giu kéuihdeih ló dī dōu chā lèih a?
C: M̀sái la m̀sái la.

Paired Clauses

When two clauses are placed side by side in a single sentence,
their relationship may be described as either free or bound. A
'free clause' is one which may stand alone as a complete sentence,
while a 'bound clause' is one which is incomplete in meaning without the presence of a free clause before or after it.

I. Free -- Free

   1. Néi heui, ngó dōu heui.
      If you go, I'll go too.

   2. Kéuih m̀hái kéi, ngódeih jáu lo.
      He is not home, let's go.

3. Ngó tái syù, m̀tái boují.
   I read books, not newspapers.

4. Ngó máai tói, m̀máai yí.
   I'll buy table, not a chair.

5. Ngó máaijó syù, móu máai boují.
   I bought the book, not the paper.

6. Ngó sihk tòhngchāan m̀sihk sāichāan.

7. Ngó jùngyi nīgo m̀jùngyi gógo.

8. Ngó sīk góng Yìngmàn, m̀sīk góng Gwóngdùngwá.

9. Ngó lójó ngó bún syù, móu ló néi bún syù.

10. Ngó heui wángwo Chàhn sìnsàang, móu heui wángwo Léih sìnsàang.

II. Free -- Bound

A. ..., daahnhaih...; ..., sóyíh...

1. Ngó séung heui Faatgwok wáanháh, daahnhaih móu chín.
   I'd like to go to France to have some fun, but I have no
   money.

2. Ngó móu chín sóyíh m̀heuidāk.
   I have no money so I can't go.

3. Ngó séung jīkhāak heui, daahnhaih yìhgā m̀dākhàahn.
   I'd like to go right away, but now I'm very busy.

4. Kéuih gàmjìujóu heui jip kéuihge gàyàhn, sóyíh kéuih m̀dākhàahn.
   He went to meet his family, therefore he hasn't any (leisure)
   time.

5. Nīgo faatjí hóu hóu, daahnhaih ngódeih mei hohkgwo.
   This is a very good method, but we haven't learned it yet.

6. Ngódeih móu hohkgwo gám jouh, sóyíh m̀sīk.

7. Kéuih hóu jùngyi kìnggái, daahnhaih kéuih jouhgán sih gójahnsí
   kéuih m̀kìnggái.

8. Kéuihdī gàyàhn hái Méigwok lèihjó sóyíh kéuih hóu m̀dākhàahn

9. Ngó giu kéuih jīkhāak lèih, daahnhaih kéuih wah kéuih m̀dākh

10. Kéuih m̀dākhàahn tùhng ngó yātchái lèih sóyíh ngó sìn lèih.

11. Kàhmmáan ngó hóu guih, sóyíh ngó móu duhk syù.

12. Ngó hóu noi móu jipgwo kéuihdeih ge seun la, daahnhaih ngó jìdou kéuihdeih gogo dōu hóu hóu.

13. Bàlàih jànhaih hóuwáan la, sóyíh ngódeih hái gósyu jyuhjó géigoyuht.

14. Kéuih giu ngó tùhngmàai kéuih yātchái heui, sóyíh ngó yìhgā hái nīsyu dáng kéuih.

15. Ngó hái gósyu dángjó nei hóu noi la, juhng mei gin néi, sóy ngó lèih nīsyu wán néi.

B. ... , yànwaih ....

1. Kéuih kàhmyaht bùn ge, yànwaih kéuih ge gàyàhn lèihjó.
   He moved yesterday, because his family is here.

2. Ngódeih m̀heuidāk, yànwaih gàmyaht móu fèigèi fèi(heui) Bākgìng.
   We can't go because there's no plane flying to Peking today

3. Ngó kàhmyaht móu lèih taam néi yànwaih ngó hóu m̀dākhàahn.
   I didn't come to vist you yesterday, because I was very bus

4. Ngó móu hohkgwo sé Jùnggwok jih, yànwaih gójahnsí móu yàhn gaau ngó.
   I didn't learn to write Chinese because there was no one to teach me at that time.

5. Ngó móu faatjí man kéuih hái syu jouhgán mātyéh, yànwaih kéuih m̀sīk góng Yìngmàn ngó m̀sīk góng Gwóngdùngwá.
   I had no way to ask him what he was doing there, because he didn't speak English and I didn't speak Cantonese.

C. ... , jauh ....

1. Kéuih heuijó léuhngyaht jauh fàanlèih la.
   He was gone for two days and then came back.

2. Ngó duhkjó yātgo yuht jauh móu duhk la.
   I studied it for a month and then quit.

3. Ngó heui gaai máai dī yéh jauh fàanlèih.
   I am going out to buy something; I'll be back soon.

4. Kéuihdeih hái Bàlàih jyuh yātgo làihbaai jauh chóh fóchè
   heui Dākgwok.
   They will stay at Paris for a week and then they will leave
   for Germany by train.

5. Kéuihdeih hái Bàlàih jyuhjó yātgo làihbaai jauh chóh fóchè
   heuijó Dākgwok.
   They stayed at Paris for a week and then they left for Germany by train.

6. Chàhn sìnsàang hái syu jyuhjó léuhngmáan jauh jáujó la.
   Mr. Chàhn left here after staying for two nights.

7. Ngó yámjó léuhngbùi jauh móu yám la.
   I quit after I had two drinks.

8. Góbún syù ngó táijó yātyaht jauh táiyùhn la.
   1 finished reading that book in one day. (see Les. 18 Patt.
   III, B.2)

9. Ngó séyùhn nīfùng seun jauh heui la.
   I'll go after I finish writing this letter.

10. Jàihá. gósyu jauh dāk la.
    Just leave it there.

III. Bound -- Free

Yùhgwó ..., ...
Yànwaih ..., ...

1. Yùhgwó néi m̀máai ngó dōu m̀máai.
   If you don't buy it, I won't either.

2. Yùhgwó móu yàhn man néi néi m̀hóu góng.
   If no one asks you, don't say anything. (Don't say anything
   unless someone ask you.)

3. Yànwaih kéuihge gàyàhn lèihjó, kéuih nīgéiyaht hóu m̀dākhàahr
   kéuih léuhngyaht móu lèihgwo nīsyu la.
   He is very busy these past few days because his family is
   here; he hasn't been here the last two days.

4. Yànwaih gàmjìujóu ngó m̀dākhàahn (ngó) móu heui fóchèjahm
   jip néi jànhaih m̀hóuyisi lo.[1]
   Because I was very busy this morning I didn't go to meet you
   at the station. I'm very sorry!

5. Yànwaih gàmyaht tìnhei m̀hóu, fèigèi m̀fèidāk, kéuih wah kéuih
   chóh fóchè lèih.
   Because today's weather is not good, the plane can't take
   off; she said she'll come by train.

6. Yùhgwó ngó m̀sīk ngó wúih man néi.

7. Yùhgwó néi gàmyaht m̀dākhàahn, (néi) tìngyaht dākhàahn ma?

8. (Yùhgwo) ńgó dākhàahn jauh lèih.[2]

9. Yùhgwó móu gàyàhn tùhngmàai néi yātchái heui dímgáai néi
   m̀chóh fèigèi nē?

10. Yùhgwó néi gàmmáan m̀dākhàahn néi tìngmáan lèih lā, ngó yáuh
    dī sih séung tùhng néi kìnghàh.

11. Yànwaih Gwóngjàu tùhng Seuhnghói dōu móu syùhn lèih, sàangyi
    m̀hóu, ngódeih gauhnín maaijó gógo sàangyi lo.

12. Yànwaih kéuih m̀yám (jáu) léuhngjek būi gau la.

13. Yànwaih gódaat deihfòng taai sai móu sàangyi jouh, kéuih
    maaijó gógo sàangyi bùnjó lèih nīsyu hóu noi lo.

1. The expression 'jànhaih SV' is usually accompanied by either
   'la' or 'lo' at the end of the sentence, i.e. Jànhaih leng la!
   (Gee, it's really beautiful!)

2. The sentence "I'll come if I am free." Can also be said in
   these ways: (Yùhgwó) dākhàahn jauh lèih." or "Ngó (yùhgwó)
   dākhàahn jauh lèih." Be sure to distinguish this sentence
   from "Ngó (yāt) dākhàahn jauh lèih." (I'll come as soon as
   I'm free.) (see this lesson Patt. IV, B.)

14. Yànwaih gàan fóng taai sai m̀jàidāk gam dò yéh, ngó bùnjó
    hóu dò séuhngheui làuhseuhng.

15. Yànwaih ngó m̀wúih góng Seuhnghóiwá móufaatjí man kéuih, m̀gòi
    néi tùhng ngó manhàh kéuih dāk ma?

IV. Bound -- Bound

A. Yànwaih ..., sóyíh ....

1. Yànwaih ngó kàhmyaht m̀dākhàahn sóyíh móu lèih.
   Because yesterday I was busy, (therefore) I didn't come.

2. Yànwaih ngó jìdou néi hóu jùngyi sihk yú, sóyíh ngó máaijó
   léuhngtìuh yú.
   Because I know that you like fish (therefore) I bought two
   of them.

3. Yànwaih gógàan jáugún móu sāichāan sihk sóyíh ngódeih lèih
   nīsyu.
   Because they don't serve Western meals in that restaurant
   (therefore) we came over here.

4. Yànwaih móu dōu chā m̀sihkdāk sāichāan sóyíh ngó heui máaijó
   léuhngfu fàanlèih.
   Because we didn't have knives and forks we were not able to
   eat a Western meal, (therefore) I went out and bought two
   sets of them.

5. Yànwaih ngó m̀jìdou kéuih jyuhhái bīnsyu sóyíh ngó móu heui
   wán kéuih.
   Because I don't know where he lives (therefore) I didn't
   look him up.

6. Yànwaih néi móu mangwo ngó sóyíh ngó móu góng néi tèng.

7. Yànwaih ngó seuhnggoláihbaai móu lèih sóyíh ngó móu duhkgwo
   nīfo syù.

8. Yànwaih ngó móu chín sóyíh ngó móu máai gógihn sāam.

9. Yànwaih nīgéiyaht móu syùhn lèih sóyíh dī yéh gam gwai.

10. Yànwaih ngó tèngginwah Bàlàih gam hóuwáan sóyíh ngó gauhnín
    heui wáanjó géigo láihbaai.

B. Yāt ... jauh .... (as soon as; whenever...)

1. Ngó yāt doujó Méigwok jauh sé seun béi néi.
   As soon as I arrive in the United States I'll write to you.

2. Ngó yāt gin néi jauh jìdou néi haih Jùnggwok yàhn.
   As soon as I saw you, I knew you were a Chinese.

3. Kéuih yāt sihkyùhn fàahn jauh chēutjóheui la.
   As soon as he finished his meal he went out. (or left.)

4. Léih sìnsàang yāt gaauyùhn syù jauh fàanjó ngūkkéi la.
   Mr. Lee returned home as soon as he finished teaching.

5. Ngó yāt doujó Méigwok jauh máaijó nīga chè la.
   As soon as I arrived in the United States I bought this car

6. Néi jànhaih chùngmìng la, gógo jih néi yāt tái jauh sīk la.

7. Gwóngjáuwá gam nàanhohk yáuh móu faaijí yāthohk jauh sīk a?

8. Kéuih yāt yáuh chín jauh máai sāam ngó yāt yáuh chín jauh maai jáu.

9. Ngó yāt sihk tòhngchāan jauh séung yám jáu.

10. Ngó yāt dākhàahn jauh lèih. (c.f. Ngó géisí dākhàahn jauh lèih. 'I'll come whenever I'm free.')

C. Yùhgwó (or yeuhkhaih) ..., jauh .... (in common practice yùhgwó or yeuhkhaih is usually omitted)

1. Yùhgwó tìnhei hóu, ngódeih jauh heui.
   If the weather is good, we will go.

2. Yùhgwó móu dōu chā jauh yiu sihk tòhngchāan la.
   If we haven't forks and knives then we will have to eat a Chinese meal.

3. Yùhgwó ngó heui Seuhnghói jauh mheui Bākgìng.
   If I go to Shanghai then I'll not go to Peking.

4. Yùhgwó kéuih tìngyaht mlèih kéuih jauh hauhyaht lèih.
   If he won't come tomorrow then he'll come day after tomorrow

5. Néi yùhgwó m̀sihk fàahn jauh sihk mātyéh a?
   If you don't eat the regular meal (or cooked rice), then
   what do you to eat.

6. Néi yùhgwó m̀jouhyùhn nīgihn sih ngó jauh m̀béi chín néi.

7. Yùhgwó ngó yáuh chín ngó jauh m̀jouhsih la.

8. Yùhgwó néi m̀sé seun béi ngó, ngó jauh m̀sé seun béi néi.

9. Yùhgwó néi m̀tùhng ngó heui ngó jauh m̀heui la.

10. Yùhgwó ngó dākhàahn (ngó) jauh lèih. or (Yùhgwó) Ngó dākhàahn
    jauh lèih.

V. 'Jauh' or 'jauhlèih' with 'la' means'about to, right away, pretty
   soon, immediately.'

1. Néi géisí lèih a? Ngó jauh lèih (la).
   When will you come? I'll come right away.

2. Jèung sìnsàang lèihjó mei a? Mei, kéuih wah kéuih jauh
   lèih la.
   Has Mr. Chang come already? Not yet, he said he'll come
   right away.

3. Kéuihdeih sihkyùhn faahn mei a? Kéuihdeih jauh sihkyùhn la.
   Have they finished eating? They'll be finished in a minute.

4. Wòhng sìnsàang géisí fàanlèih a? Kéuih jàuh fàanlèih la.
   When will Mr. Huang be back? He'll be back pretty soon.

5. Néi géisí fàan ngūkkéi a? Ngó jauh(lèih) fàan ngūkkéi la.
   When will you go home? I'll go home right away.

6. Kéuih géisí heui Seuhnghói a? Kéuih jauhlèih heui la.

7. Néidī saimānjái fàanlèih mei a? Mei, kéuihdeih jauh fàanlèih la.

8. Dímgáai kéih juhng mei lèih a? Kéuih góng ngó tèng jauhlèih
   lèih la.

9. M̀gòi néi dánghah kéuih lā kéuih jauhlèih sihkyùhn faahn la.

10. Kéuih wah kéuih jīkhāah lèih dímgáai kéuih juhng mei lèih
    a? Yùhgwó kéuih juhng m̀lèih ngó jauh heui wán kéuih la.
    Yùhgwó kéuih juhng m̀lèih ngó jauhlèih heui wán kéuih la.

VI. Verbal Suffix <u>háh</u>

1. Ngódeih chēutheui hàahngháh hóu ma?
   How about going out and taking a walk?

2. Néi táiháh ngāam m̀ngāam?
   See whether it is right or not?

3. Ngó tèngháh dāk ma?
   May I listen to it?

4. Dáng ngó séungháh.
   Let me think about it.

5. Chéng yahplèih chóh(háh) la.
   Please come in and stay for a while.

6. Ngó séung heui taam(háh) kéuih.

7. Dímgáai néi m̀manháh kéuih nē?

8. Yáuh go pàhngyáuh séung heui Hèunggóng ginháh kéuih.

9. Kéuih séung heui Seuhnghói jyuhháh.

10. Ngó hóu guih ngó séung táuháh.

11. Néi yáuh móu hái Seuhnghói jyuhgwo a? Ngó hái Seuhnghói
    jyuhgwoháh.

12. Kéuih haih m̀haih hóu m̀dākhàahn a? Haih, m̀gòi néi dángháh lā

13. Néi yáuh móu hohkgwo Gwóngdùngwá a? Ngó chìhngéinìn hohk-
    gwoháh.

14. Wòhng sìnsàang kàhmmáan yáuh móu lèihgwo a? Wòhng sìnsàang
    kàhmmáan lèihgwoháh.

15. Léih sìnsàang yáuh móu lèihgwo a? Léih sìnsàang gàmjìujóu
    lèihgwo yauh jáujó lo.

16. Léih taatáai jùng(yi) m̀jùngyi gójèung tói a? Kéuih táijóhah gójèung tói kéuih wah gójèung tói taai daaih kéuih m̀jùngyi.

17. Gógihn sih jànhaih nàanjouh lo, néi jìdou dím jouh ma? Gógihn sih ngó séungjóhah yihkdōu m̀jì dím jouh.

18. Néi kàhmmáan lófàanlèih góbún syù néi táigwo mei a? Ngó gàmjìujóu táigwohah la.

19. Néi wah néi sihkgwo tòhngchāan néi wúih jyú ma? Ngó sihkgwohah tòhngchāan daahnhaih ngó m̀wúih jyú.

20. Wòhng sìnsàang néi haih m̀haih hái gósyu gaaugwo syù a? Haih, ngó hái gósyu gaaugwohah, yànwaih gósyu tìnhei m̀hóu sóyíh ngó lèih nìsyu.

77. Háh as a verbal suffix has the force of 'a little.' It may be translated by such phrases as:

táiháh	take a look at
táiháh syù	read a little
chóhháh	sit a while
séungjóháh	thought for a while

(A verb with suffix háh is equivalent to the reduplicated verb in Mandarin.)

Translate the following conversation into English:

A: Ngó gàmmáan séung chéng léuhnggo pàhngyáuh fàanlèih sihkfaahn, néi wah jyú dī mātyéh sung hóu a?
B: M̀jì néi séung chéng kéuihdeih sihk tòhngchāan sihk sāichāan nē?
A: Yùhgwó ngódeih chéng kéuihdeih sihk tòhngchāan, ngódeih yáuh faaijí ma?
B: Dáng ngó táiháh gau m̀gau, yùhgwó ngódeih yáuh seisèung jauh gau la.
A: Yùhgwó sihk tòhngchāan néi wah jyú mātyéh sung hóu a?
B: Ngūkkéi yáuh yú yáuh choi, nītìuh yú gam daaih, hóyíh jouh sàamdihp sung gódī choi hóyíh jouh tòng, gám hóyíh gau la.
A: Kéuihdeih mei yámgwo Jùnggwok jáu, ngūkkéi juhng yáuh Jùnggwok jáu ma?
B: Juhng yáuh, daahnhaih móu géi dò la, m̀gányiu, ngó yātjahngāan chēutheui máai.

A: Néi chēutheui máai jáu gójahnsí, máai géijek būi fàanlèih.
B: Néi yiu géijek mātyéh būi a?
A: Ngó yiu seijek chàh-būi, seijek jáu-būi. Chàh-būi m̀hóu máai
   gódī taai sai ge, jáu-būi m̀hóu máai gódī taai daaih ge.
B: Néi chéng nī léuhnggo pàhngyáuh kéuihdeih sing mātyéh a?
A: Yātgo sing Chàhn, yātgo sing Léih, kéuihdeih léuhnggo dōu
   lèih ngódeihsyu sihkgwo faahn ge la.
B: Kéuihdeih dī gàyàhn lèihjó mei a?
A: Juhng mei lèih, gàmmáan haih làihbaailuhkmáan, sóyíh ngó
   séung chéng kéuihdeih sihk chàan faahn.
B: Ngāam la, néi jìdou gàmyaht haih géisí ma? Gàmyaht haih
   baatyuht sahpng.

Translate the following sentences into Cantonese:

1. With whom did you study your English?
2. Do you have time to go to Hong Kong tonight?
3. I bought that chair for you yesterday, it's twelve and a
   half dollars.
4. Did you mail that letter for me this morning?
5. Both he and I are Americans, we came here by ship last week.
6. Mr. Johnson already arrived! With whom did he come?
7. I came by plane last night with my family.
8. Do they sell clothes in that store?
9. Has he got a job yet?
10. I heard that it's going to rain tonight, is that true?

Below are English translations of sentences used in the vocabulary
of this lesson as examples of usage. Translate these back into
Chinese (numbers correspond to those in Vocabulary section.)

1. Please get a pair of chopsticks for me.
2. Where did you buy this pair of chopsticks?
3. I brought this pair of chopsticks with me from China.
4. How many restaurants do you have here?
5. There are three of them.
6. I haven't been to a restaurant for a long time.
7. Please hand me a knife.
8. How much for this knife?
9. Do you have a pocket knife?
10. Do you have enough knives and forks?

11. I lost two forks.
12. Can you go and buy a couple of forks for me?
13. Have you ever drunk tea before?
14. Yes, I have.
15. Which kind of tea (lit. the tea from which country) did you drink?
16. This set of silver (knife and fork) of yours is very pretty.
17. I brought this set of silver along with me from the United States.
18. Is this set of table and chairs from China?
19. How much is this fish?
20. Do you like to eat fish?
21. Where can I buy some fish?
22. What kind of dish do you like?
23. Who prepared this dish?
24. Do you know how to prepare any dishes?
25. Do you like vegetables?
26. Which kind of vegetable do you like to eat?
27. Which restaurant has famous dishes (of food)?
28. That restaurant has some very good dishes (of food).
29. Do you think if we order three dishes it will be enough?
30. Do you like vegetable soup?
31. Please give me a bowl of soup.
32. How many bowls of soup do you want?
33. Is this a Chinese bowl?
34. When did you buy this Chinese bowl?
35. How much for this bowl?
36. Where is this wine from?
37. Is this French wine?
38. Do they sell wine in that store?
39. Have you ever been to that place?
40. That place is really wonderful.
41. Where is the place you are talking about?
42. How about having a drink?
43. I don't (know how to) drink.
44. Do you like to drink?
45. Are you hungry?
46. I am very hungry.
47. How long has he been hungry?
48. He has been hungry for two days.
49. May I use this pen?
50. He spent a lot of money.
51. How much money did you spend last week?
52. Do you have to study tomorrow?
53. Give him five dollars, he'll sell it.

54. He'll come at once.
55. I only have one.
56. I'd like to have a talk with you.
57. Could you let me have a look?
58. How about taking a walk?
59. It doesn't matter whether you go or not.
60. Doesn't it really matter?
61. Who said that it doesn't matter?
62. I hear it said that nowadays the things are very expensive, is that true?
63. I heard that you wanted to go to Hong Kong, is that true?
64. I heard that you are very busy now, is that true?
65. You may come anytime you please.
66. I picked up two pieces at random.
67. Make yourself at home; sit down please. (lit. Sit anywhere you please.)

LESSON 16

INDEFINITES - CV SÁI, YUHNG, ETC.

Vocabulary

múi

N: younger sister

1. Néi yáuh géidògo múi a?
2. Néige múi hái bīnsyu duhk syù a?

méng

N: name

3. Nei jì m̀jì kéuih ge méng a?
4. Néi jì m̀jì gójek sy'ihnge méng a?

seui

N: years (old)

5. Kéuih yìhgā géi(dò) seui la? Kéuih
   yìhgā sàamseui la.
6. Kéuih yìhgā m̀haih seiseui (la) mē?

yisi

N: meaning, idea, intention

7. Nīgo jih mātyéh yisi a?
   Nīgo jih haih m̀haih yáuh géigo yisi a?
8. Néige yisi haih m̀haih gàmyaht m̀heui a?
   Ngó móu gám ge yisi.
9. Kéuihge yisi (haih) séung hohk góng
   Jùnggwok wá m̀haih séung hohk sé Jùnggwok jih.

makséuibāt (M: jì)

N: fountain pen

10. Néi jì makséuibāt hái bīnsyu máai ga?
    M̀haih máai ge, haih yātgo pàhngyáuh
    sung ge.
11. Néi jì makséuibāt (haih) hái Méigwok
    máai gàh?

189

chìhgāng (M: jek)   N: spoon
  -gāng (or -gàng)   M: spoonful

                           12. Chìhgāng yáuh hóugéitíng, yáuh chàh-
                               gāng, tònggāng...
                           13. Léuhng(chìh)gāng gau mei a? Yātgàng
                               jauh gau la.

bàhbā, lóuhdauh,   N: daddy, father
  fuhchàn (formal)

                           14. Kéuih bàhbā yáuh móu lèih a? Kéuih
                               bàhbā móu lèih.
                           15. Néi bàhbā hái bīnsyu a?

màmā, lóuhmóu,   N: mother
  móuchàn (formal)

                           16. Néi màmā hái (ngūk)kéi ma?
                           17. Néi màmā fàanjólèih mei a?

nàu   SV: angry, getting angry

                           18. Néi nàu mātyéh a? Ngó móu nàu mātyéh
                           19. Mhóu nàu lo.

faai(cheui)   SV: fast

                           20. Bīnga chè faai a? Góga chè faai.
                           21. Chóh syùhn faai, chóh fóchè faai a?

maan   SV: slow

                           22. Chóh syùhn heui haih mhaih hóu maan
                               Mhaih géi maan jē.
                           23. Dímgáai nījek syùhn gam maan ga?

geidāk   V: remember

                           24. Néi geidāk kéuih haih bīngo ma? Ngó
                               geidāk kéuih haih néige hohksāang.
                           25. Dímgáai néi wúih mgeidāk a?
                           26. Néi geidāk gógo jih dím sé ma?

mgeidāk   V: unable to remember — forget (but can't
                                use in the meaning of 'let go out of the
                                mind' as in 'Forget it!'

27. Néi yauh m̄geidākjó la? Ngó yauh
    m̄geidākjó la.
28. Néi wúih m̀wúih m̄geidāk a?

giu(jouh)   EV: named, is called, considered as

29. Kéuih giu(jouh) mātyéh méng a? Kéuih
    giu(jouh) Jèung Baak-san.
30. Néige saimānjái giu(jouh) mātyéh méng
    a?

bòng   V: help
                           CV: help (see Patt. II. A.)

31. Kéuih yáuh móu bòng néi a? Kéuih
    móu bòng ngó.
32. Néi sái m̀sái ngó bòng néi a?
33. Néi bòngháh ngó dāk ma?

hòi   V: open; start away (train, bus, ship)

34. Néi wúih hòi ma? Ngó m̀wúih hòi.
35. Fóchè hòijó mei a?

mìngbaahk   V: understand

36. Ngó m̀mìngbaahk kéuihge yisi.
37. Néi yìhgā mìngbaahk mei a? Ngó yìhgā
    juhng mei mìngbaahk.

chi, tong   M: a time or occasion
  lèuhng-sàamchi[1]   Ph: a couple of times

38. Néi heuigwo géidòchi a? Ngó heuigwo
    hóudòchi la.
39. Néi sihkgwo géidòchi tòhngchāan a?

yuhng   V/N: use

40. Ngó yuhngháh néi jì bāt dāk ma?
    Ngó yìhgā m̀yuhng néi yuhng lā.

1. But: sahpchi-baatchi, nine or ten times (literally ten times,
   eight times.)
   Also sahpng̀-luhkchi, fifteen or sixteen times, etc.

41. Bāt yáuh mātyéh yuhng a? Bāt hóyíh
yuhngléih sé jih.

yáuhyuhng   SV: useful, helpful

42. Nījì bāt haih m̀haih hóu yáuhyuhng a?
Haih, nījì bāt hóu yáuhyuhng.
43. Kéuih haih m̀haih hóu yáuhyuhng a?

móuyuhng   SV: useless

44. Gójì bāt taai gauh, móuyuhng la.
45. Nījèung tói yíhgìng móuyuhng la.
46. Néi dím jì nījì bāt móuyuhng a?

joi   A: once more, ...more, (joi V NU M), again

47. Néi joi séungháh!
48. Ngó séung joi heui léuhngchi.
49. Ngó hóu guih ngó móufaatjí joi duhk
la.
50. Néi tìngyaht joi lèih lā!
51. Hóu, ngó tìngyaht joi lèih.

juhnghaih   A: still, as before, as usual (the addition
haih to certain adverbs such as juhng,
jauh, jàn, etc., serves to make them
more emphatic.)

52. Ngó juhnghaih m̀sīk.
53. Nījek syùhn jauhhaih la.
54. Néi jànhaih m̀sīk àh?

jīkhaih   A: is precisely, is (emphatic), is none
other than

55. Nījek syùhn jīkhaih gójek syùhn.

tàuh   BF: first (ordinalizing prefix denotes the
first one or more persons or things)

56. Nīchi haih néi tàuhyātchi chóh fèigèi
àh? M̀haih tàuhyātchi haih daihyihchi
la.
57. Nīchi haih m̀haih néi tàuhyātchi sihk
tòhngchāan a?

mouleuhn   MA: no matter..., whether... or not

                                58. Mouleuhn gei hou ngo dou mmaai.
                                59. Nīfo syù ngo mouleuhn dim duhk dōu
                                     msīk.
                                60. Mouleuhn (haih) sànge gauhge, ngo
                                   dōu yiu.

peiyuh(wah)   MA: for instance, if, in case

                                61. Peiyuh(wah) nei yìhgā yauh hou dò chín...
                                62. Peiyuh keuih mlèihdāk jauh dim a?
                                63. Peiyuh gàmyaht mou fèigèi heui Hèung-
                                 góng nei choh mātyeh heui a?

tìm   P: a sentence final meaning 'more' when it
                            is used in a form such as '(juhng) or
                            (joi) V NU M tìm.'; meaning 'also' in
                            'V N tìm.'

                                64. Keuih seung maai leuhnggo tìm.
                                65. Ngo seung (juhng) sihk dī tìm.
                                66. Keuih seung heui Faatgwok tìm.
                                67. Ngo seung maai bīu tìm.

seuhngtòhng   VO: go to class
   lohktòhng   VO: finish class

                                68. Nei gàmyaht seuhngjo geidò tòhng
                                   la? Ngo seuhngjo seitòhng la.
                                69. Geisi seuhngtòhng a?
                                70. Geisi lohktòhng a?
                                71. Nei heui bīnsyu seuhngtòhng a?

Useful Expressions

Nei wah....	Do you think....?
Nei wah....	Don't you think....?
Nei wah ngāam mgāam a?	Do you think it's alright?
Nei wah goga chè leng mleng a?	Don't you think that car is good-looking?

Reading

Saimúi gàmnín luhkseui la. Séuhnggoláihbaai haih kéuih daihyātyaht heui hohkhaauhsyu duhksyù. Kéuih bàhbā wah: "Gàmyaht
néi heui hohkhaauhsyu duhksyù, ngó tùhng néi màmā béi yātgo sànge
méng néi, giujouh Méi-hóu, néi sing Chàhn, sóyíh giujouh Chàhn Méi-
hóu, néi jùngyi nīgo méng ma?" Saimúi wah: "Haih m̀haih ngó yìhgā
yáuh léuhnggo méng, yātgo giujouh Saimúi, yātgo giujouh Chàhn Méi-
hóu a?" Kéuih bàhbā wah: "Haih la."

    Tàuhyātyaht séuhngtòhng gójahnsí, sìnsàang wah: "Chàhn Méi-
hóu, néi hàahngmàailèih nīsyu." Bīngo dōu m̀jì sìnsàang giugán
bīngo.

    Daihyihyaht kéuih bàhbā man kéuih: "Saimúi néi geidāk néige
sànge méng giujouh mātyéh ma?" Saimúi wah: "Haih m̀haih giujouh
'Néi-hóu' a, bàhbā?" Kéuih bàhbā wah: " M̀haih 'Néi-hóu,' haih 'Méi-
hóu.' Daahnhaih góyaht hái hohkhaauhsyu kéuih yauh m̀geidākjó
kéuihge méng la. Kéuih bàhbā jauh wah: "Saimúi néi jìdou néige
méng haih mātyéh yisi ma? 'Méi' jauhhaih Méigwok gógo 'Méi' jih,
'hóu' jauhhaih 'hóu m̀hóu gógo 'hóu' jih, peiyùh ngó gám góng néi
jauh mìngbaahk la, néi sìng Chàhn, néi haih hái Méigwok chēutsai
ge, néi chēutsai nīdaat deihfòng jànhaih hóu la, sóyíh néi giujouh
Chàhn Méi-hóu. Chàhn Méi-hou jauhhaih Saimui jauhnaih néi, néi
geidāk mei a?" Saimúi wah: "Nīchi ngó dím dōu geidāk la."

    Gómáan, kéuih bàhbā yáuh go pàhngyáuh lèih taam kéuihdeih,
kéuin man Saimúi: "Néi giujouh mātyéh méng a?" Saimúi wah: "Ngó
hái ngūkkéisyu bàhbā màmā gogo dōu giu ngó jouh Saimúi, hái hohkhaauhsyu sìnsàang giu ngó jouh Chàhn Méi-hóu, Chàhn Méi-hóu jauhhaih Saimúi, Saimúi jauhnaih ngó."

Pattern Sentences

I. Question Words as Indefinites; Inclusiveness and Exclusiveness

   A. Question Words as Indefinites:

      1. Néi séung yiu mātyéh a? Ngó m̀yiu mātyéh.
         What do you want? I don't want anything.

2. Néi gauhnín yáuh móu heuigwo bīnsyu wáan a? Móu heuigwo
   bīnsyu.
   Did you go somewhere to 'enjoy' yourself last year? I
   didn't go anywhere.

3. Néideih gàan hohkhaauh yáuh géidò hohksāang a? Móu géidò
   jē.
   How many students do you have in your school? Not very
   many.

4. Néi yáuh géidòbún Jùnggwok syù a? Móu géidòbún jē.
   How many Chinese books do you have? Not very many.

5. Néi táigwo bīnbún Yìngmàn syù a? Ngó móu táigwo bīnbún
   Yìngmàn syù.
   Which English book did you read? I didn't read any English
   books.

6. Fóchè doujó géi nói la? Móu géi nói jē.

7. Tói seuhngbihn yáuh mātyéh a? Móu mātyéh.

8. Bīngo hái fóng léuihbihn a? Móu bīngo.

9. Kéuih wúih cheung géidòsáu gō a? Móu géidòsáu jē.

10. Néi béijó kéuih géidò chín a? Móu géidò chín jē.

78. Note: Question words like mātyéh, bīngo, etc. are commonly used
    as indefinites like English 'anything,' and 'anyone.'

    (Question Word géi used as 'indefinite.' See examples at the
    end of Voc. Les. 13.)

B. Inclusiveness and Exclusiveness:

   1. Néi yiu mātyéh a? Ngó mātyéh dōu yiu. Ngó mātyéh dōu ṁyiu.
      What do you want? I want everything. I don't want anything.

   2. Néi jùngyi bīnyeuhng a? Ngó yeuhngyeuhng dōu jùngyi. Ngó
      yeuhngyeuhng dōu ṁjùngyi.
      Which kind do you like? I like any (or all) of them. I
      don't like any of them.

3. Bīngo jì(dou) nīgihn sih a? Bīngo dōu jì. (Gogo dōu jì.)
   Bīngo dōu m̀jì. (Gogo dōu m̀jì.)
   Who knew about this? Everybody knows about it. Nobody
   knows about it.

4. Bīnsyu yáuh jáu maai a? Syusyu dōu yáuh. Syusyu dōu móu.
   Where can we buy some wine? You can get it anywhere.
   You can't get it anywhere.

5. Bīnjì bāt haih néi ga? Jìjì bāt dōu haih ngó ge. Jìjì
   bāt dōu m̀haih ngóge.
   Which pen is yours? All of them are mine. None of them
   are mine.

6. Néi géisí lèihdāk ngósyu a? Géisí dōu dāk.

7. Néi wah bīnsáu gō hóutèng a? Sáusáu dōu hóu hóutèng.

8. Néideih bīngo hohkgwo cheunggō a? Ngódeih gogo dōu hohkgwo. Ngódeih gogo dōu mei hohkgwo.

9. Néideih bīngo wúih góng Yìngmàn a? Ngódeih dōu wúih.
   Ngódeih gogo dōu m̀wúih.

10. Néi wah bīngihn sāam leng a? Gihngihn sāam dōu hóu leng.
    gihngihn dōu m̀haih géi leng.

79. Note: To express inclusive ideas such as 'everything' and 'eve
    one,' and exclusive ideas such as 'nothing,' and 'no one,' inde
    nites plus dōu are used.

C. Exclusiveness Intensified with yāt + M followed by dōu:

1. Néi yiu géidò a? Ngó yātdī dōu m̀yiu.
   How much do you want? I don't want <u>any</u>.

2. Néi yiu géidògo a? Ngó yātgo dōu m̀yiu.
   How many do you want? Not one.

3. Néi sīk sé géidògo Jùnggwok jih a? Ngó yātgo dōu m̀sīk.
   How many Chinese characters can you write? I can't even
   write one.

4. Néi heuigwo Seuhnghói ma? Ngó yātchi dōu mei heuigwo.
   Have you ever been to Shanghai? Not even a single trip.

5. Néi yáuh géidò chín a? Ngó yātgosīn dōu móu.
   How much money do you have? I haven't even got a penny.

6. Néi sáisaai néidī chín mei a? Ngó yātgo sīn dōu mei sái.

7. Néi jì kéuihdeih góng mātyéh ma? Ngó yātdī dōu m̀jì.

8. Bīnga chè leng a? Yātga dōu m̀leng.

9. Néi nīgoláihbaai yáuh móu ségwo seun a? Ngó yātfùng seun
   dōu móu ségwo.

10. Néi haih m̀haih lèihgwo nīsyu hóudòchi la? Ngó yātchi dōu
    mei lèihgwo.

D. Inclusiveness and Exclusiveness intensified with:

   (Mòuleuhn) dím...dōu...   meaning 'no matter how...'
   (Mòuleuhn) géi...dōu...   meaning 'no matter how...'
             (Sentence 1-5)
   (Mòuleuhn) mātyéh N   S dōu... meaning 'no matter what...'
   (Mòuleuhn) bīn M (N)   S dōu... meaning 'no matter who, which...'
   (Mòuleuhn) bīn M (N) ge S dōu... meaning 'no matter whose...'
   (Mòuleuhn) géisí   S dōu... meaning 'no matter when...'
             (Sentence 6-10)
   (Mòuleuhn) V m̀ V   S dōu... meaning 'whether... or not,...'
   (Mòuleuhn) SV m̀ SV   S dōu... meaning 'whether... or not,...'
             (Sentence 12-13)[1]
   (Mòuleuhn)...clause...   dōu... meaning 'no matter...'
      (with question word)
             (Sentence 14-15)

1. Kéuih dím dōu m̀lèih.
   No matter what he won't come.

2. Dím dōu dāk.
   Anyway you like it. (lit. no matter what, it suits me fine.)

3. Ngó dím man kéuih dōu m̀góng.
   No matter how I ask him, he just won't say anything.

1. In common practice, in the first three patterns 'mòuleuhn' is
   often omitted.'

4. Góga chè géi leng ngó dōu m̀jùngyi.
   No matter how nice tnat car is, I just don't like it.

5. Kéuih hóu jùngyi gógihn sāam kéuih wah géi gwai kéuih dōu
   máai.
   She likes that dress very much, no matter how expensive it
   is she says she'll buy it.

6. Mātyéh syù kéuih dōu jùngyi tái.

7. Bīngo wah kéuih dōu m̀tèng.

8. Bīngo yiu kéuih dōu m̀béi.

9. Bīnjì bāt kéuih dōu yiu séháh.

10. Bīngoge chè kéuih dōu yiu chóhháh.

11. Gógàan poutáu géisí dōu yáuh yéh maai.

12. Tìngyaht tìnhei hóu m̀hóu ngó dōu yiu heui.

13. Gwai m̀gwai ngó dōu yiu.

14. (Mòuleuhn) kéuih haih bīngo dōu yiu béichín.

15. (Mòuleuhn) ngó heui bīnsyu dōu geidāk néi.

II. Co-verb 'sái,' 'yuhng' and 'bòng'

A. 'Sái' as co-verb, meaning 'to send,' 'to tell'; when it is
   used meaning 'need to,' or 'have to,' it can only be used
   in questions or in negative answer.

   1. Néi sái kéuih heui jouh mātyéh a? Ngó sái kéuih heui
      máai dī yéh.
      What did you send him to do? I sent him to buy something.

   2. Néi sái kéuih heui bīnsyu a? Ngó sái kéuih heui Hèung-
      góng tùhng ngó máai dī yéh.
      Where did you send him to? I sent him to Hong Kong to
      buy something for me.

   3. Dímgáai kéuih m̀sái néi heui, sái ngó heui a? Kéuih wah
      ngó taai guih, m̀heuidāk.

Why didn't he send you instead of me? He said, I'm too
tired, I can't go.

4. Kéuih sái néi gám jouh dímgáai néi ṅgám jouh a? Yànwaih
ngó móu hohkgwo gám jouh.
He told you to do it that way; why don't you do it that
way? Because I haven't learned how to do it that way.

5. Dímgáai néi kàhmyaht ṅgóng ngó tèng nē? Kéuih sái ngó
ṁhóu góng néi tèng, sóyíh ngó móu góng néi tèng.
Wny didn't you tell me yesterday? She told me not to tell
you, therefore I didn't.

6. Kéuih sái ngó heui Jùnggwok hohk Gwóngjàu wá, ngó wah ṁsái
heui Jùnggwok hohk, ngó hóyíh hái nīsyu hohk.

7. Gàmmáan ngó sái lèih ma?[1] Néi gàmmáan ṁsái lèih, tìngmáan
lèih lā.

8. Sái ṁsái ngó tùhng néi heui a? Ṁsái, ngó jihgéi heui dāk
la.

9. Néi tìngyaht sái ṁsái gaausyù a? Tìngyaht haih láihbaailuhk ngó ṁsái gaausyù.

10. Chàhn sìnsàang ngódeih sái ṁsái duhksaai nīfo syù a?
Néideih ṁsái duhksaai nīfo, daahnhaih yiu duhksaai gófo.

B. (1) Yuhng... (lèih) meaning 'use...to or for...'; by using;
with

1. Néi yuhng bīnbún syù (lèih) hohk Gwóngdùngwá ga?
Which book did you use to learn Cantonese?

2. Néi yuhng mātyéh lèih yám tòng a?
What do you eat (drink) soup with?

3. Néi hóyíh yuhng makséuibāt (lèih) sé Jùnggwok jih ma?
Can you write Chinese characters with a pen?

1. The affirmative answer for 'sái...? is yiu.' e.g. Gàmmáan ngó
sái lèih ma? Gàmmáan néi yiu lèih.

4. Néi haih m̀haih yuhng nīga chè (lèih) gaau kéuihdeih a?
   Are you using this car to teach them (how to drive)?

5. Ngó hóyíh yuhng nījèung jí sé seun ma?
   Can I use this paper to write a letter?

(2) Haih yuhnglèih (or ngoilèih, yiulèih)... ge, meaning
'is used for ...'; Haih yuhng ... jouhge, meaning
'is made of ...'

1. Bīnbún syù haih yuhnglèih hohk Gwóngdùngwá ga? Nībún
   syù haih yuhnglèih hohk Gwóngdùngwá ge.
   Which book is used for learning Cantonese? This book
   is used for learning Cantonese.

2. Wún tùhng faaijí haih yuhnglèih jouh mātyéh ga? Wún tùhn
   faaijí haih yuhnglèih sihk tòhngchāan ge.
   What are bowls and chopsticks used for? Bowls and chopsticks are used for eating Chinese food.

3. Mātyéh haih yuhnglèih yám tòng ga? Chìhgāng haih yuhnglè
   yám tòng ge.
   What does one use to eat soup with? The spoon is used fo
   eating soup.

4. Nīdī yéh haih ngoilèih jouh mātyéh ga? Nīdī yéh haih ngo
   lèih wáan ge, gódī yéh haih ngoilèih sihk ge.
   What are these things used for? These things are for play
   ing, those things are for eating.

5. Góga fèigèi haih yuhng mātyéh jouh ga? Góga fèigèi haih
   yuhng jí jouh ge.
   What is that plane made of? That plane is made of paper.

C. Bòng as a CV meaning 'for' or 'help'

1. M̀gòi néi bòng ngó sé fùng seun hóu ma?   •
   Would you please write a letter for me?

2. Néi bòng ngó jouh nīgihn sih dāk ma?
   Can you do this thing for me?

3. Kéuih bòng néi jouhgwo géinói a?
   How long did he work for you?

4. Néi yiu ngó bòng néi jouh mātyéh a?
   What do you want me to do for you?

5. Nīga chè bīngo bòng néi máai ga?
   Who bought this car for you?

6. Ngó séung giu léuhnggo yàhn bòng ngó nīk dī yéh heui
   chèjaahm.

7. Néi bòng ngó séuhngheui làuhseuhng giu kéuih lohklèih dāk
   ma?

8. Ṁgòi néi bòng ngó séungháh, kéuihge méng haih ṁhaih giujouh Dāk-faat a?

9. Yùhgwó kéuih hóyíh bòng néi jyú faahn, ngó bòng néi jyú
   sung, yātjahngāan ngódeih jauh yáuh fàahn sihk la.

10. Néi sái ṁsái ngó bòng néi (bùn nīdī tói) a? Nījèung (tói)
    ṁsái la, ngó jihgéi dāk la. Néi bòng ngó bùnháh gójèung
    dāk ma?

III. Time Element 'chi' or 'tong'

A. Time When:

1. Seuhngchi dímgáai néi ṁlèih a?
   Why didn't you come last time?

2. Nīchi haih ngó daihyihchi sihk tòhngchāan.
   This is the second time that I have eaten Chinese food.

3. Néi nīchi heui Hèunggóng haih ṁhaih chóh fèigèi heui a?
   Are you going by plane to Hong Kong this time?

4. Néi seuhng(yāt)chi dímyéung lèih nīsyu ga?
   How did you come here last time?

5. Néi seuhngchi tùhng bīngo heui Hèunggóng ga?
   Who went to Hong Kong with you last time?

6. Néi góchi heui Seuhnghói yáuh móu wángwo kéuih a?

7. Néi chìhngéichi heui wán kéuih kéuih hái ṁhái (ngūk)kéi a?

8. Ngó múichi heui kéuih ngūkkéi kéuih dōu chéng ngó hái
   kéuihsyu sihkfaahn, jànhaih m̀hóuyisi.

9. Tàuléuhngtong kéuihdeih dōu hóu haakhei, nīléuhngtong
   móu gam haakhei la.

10. Seuhng(yāt)chi ngó m̀dākhàahn móu tùhng néi heui jànhail.
    m̀hóuyisi la, daihyihchi ngó yātdihng tùhng néi heui,

B. Time Spent:

1. Néi lèihgwo nīsyu géidòchi la?
   How many times have you been here?

2. Ngó heuigwo Jùnggwok hóudòchi.
   I have been to China many times.

3. Ngó gàmnín heui taamgwo kéuih yātchi jē.
   I have only called on him once this year.

4. Kéuih góngjó sàam-seichi ngó juhng mei mìngbaahk kéuih
   góng mātyéh.
   He said it three or four times but I still couldn't
   understand what he was talking about.

5. M̀gòi néi joi góng yātchi dāk ma?
   Can you say it once again?

6. Ngó chóhgwo nījek syùhn hóudòchi la, chichi dōu haih gam
   maan ge.

7. Dímgáai ngó giujó kéuih léuhngchi kéuih juhng mei lèih a

8. Ngó gauhnín sihkgwo léuhngchi tòhngchāan, gàmnín mei sih
   gwo.

9. Nīfo syù ngódeih gàmyaht joi gaau yātchi.

10. Ngó wánjó kéuih hóudòchi kéuih dōu m̀hái (ngūk)kéi, ngó
    séung tingyaht joi heui wán kéuih yātchi tīm.

IV. Giu(jouh); giu N jouh....

1. Néi duhksyù gógàan hohkhaauh giujouh mātyéh méng a? Giujou
   Jùng-Méi hohkhaauh.

What is the name of the school you are in? The name is the
Sino-American School.

2. Néi geidāk gógàan jáugun giujouh mātyéh méng ma? Ngó yātdī
dōu m̀geidāk la.
Do you remember what that restaurant is called? I can't
remember at all.

3. Bīngo giujouh Chàhn Yaht-sàn a? (compare with Bīngo giu
Chàhn Yaht-sàn a?) Kéuih giujouh Chàhn Yaht-sàn.
Whose name is Chàhn Yaht-sàn? His name is Chàhn Yaht-sàn.

4. Kéuih léuhnggo néui giujouh mātyéh méng a? Kéuihge daaih
néui giujouh Daaihmúi, sainéui giujouh Saimúi.
What are the names of his two daughters? The elder one is
named Daaihmui, the younger one is named Saimui.

5. Néi jauhhaih Wòhng Dāk-faat la, haih m̀haih? Ngó sing Wòhng
daahnhaih ngóge méng m̀giujouh Dāk-faat.
You are Wohng Dak-faat, aren't you? My last name is Wohng,
but my given name is not Dak-faat.

6. Nījèung tói haih ngoilèih sihkfaahn ge sóyíh ngódeih giu
kéuih jouh sihkfaahntói, gójèung haih yuhnglèih séjih ge
sóyíh giu kéuih jouh séjihtói.
This table is used for eating, therefore we call it a dining
table; that one is used for writing, therefore we call it a
desk.

7. Dímyéung giujouh hóu hohksāang a? Haih m̀haih gódī hóu jùngyi
duhk syùge hohksāang ngódeih giu kéuihdeih jouh hóu hohksāang
a?
Whom can we consider as good students? Aren't those who are
very fond of studying good students?

●

Additional Sentences

1. Gógihn sāam yātdī dōu m̀leng dímgáai néi gam jùngyi a?
2. Gódī jih haih kéuih jihgéi sé ge, ngó yātdī dōu móu bònggwo kéuih.
3. Gihngihn yéh dōu hóu yáuhyuhng, daahnhaih ngó móu gam dò chín
   máai.
4. Yahtyaht dōu yáuh syùhn heui Hèunggóng, daahnhaih bīnjek faai,
   bīnjek maan ngó jauh m̀jì la.

5. Jek syùhn yìhgìng hòijó léuhngyaht la, kéuih juhng yātdī dōu m̀j
6. Bàlàih jànhaih houwáan la, ngó juhng séung heui léuhngchi tìm.
7. Néi m̀geidāk kéuihge mēng móuganyiu, néi geidāk kéuih sing mātyé
   ma?
8. Makséuibāt ngoilèih sé Yìngman hóu hóu, yùhgwó yiu sé Jùnggwok
   jih juhnghaih yuhng Jùnggwok bāt hóu.
9. Yeuhkhaih néi m̀góng ngó jì, ngó yìhgā juhng mei jì nīgihn yéh
   haih ngoilèih jouh mātyéh ge.
10. Néi nīgo yisi hóu hóu, nīgihn yéh yùhgwó gám yuhng jauh hóu yáu
    yuhng la.
11. Peiyùh kéuih yātgeui Gwóngdùngwá dōu m̀sīk, ngó tùhng kéuih góng
    Yìngmàn kéuih wúih mìngbaahk ngóge yisi ma?
12. Peiyùh yātjèung boují (gám), yùhgwó móu yàhn tái, gám yáuh māt-
    yéh yuhng a?
13. (Mòuleuhn) néi dím nàu dōu móuyuhng la, giu kéuih daihyihchi
    m̀hóu m̀geidāk jauh dāk la.
14. Mòuleuhn géisí yáuh syùhn dōu chéng néi góng ngó jì.
15. Mòuleuhn nīgihn yéh géidò chín, yùhgwó nīgihn yéh yáuhyuhng,
    jauh géi gwai dōu m̀gwai.

Translate the following sentences into Cantonese:

1. I'd like to go to Hong Kong right away, but there is no plan
   going there this week.
2. He told me that I didn't have to wait for him, therefore I
   came back.
3. We'll stay here for two days then we will return to the Unit
   States by plane.
4. We can't stay here overnight, because there is no hotel.
5. If today's weather isn't good, then we'll go tomorrow.
6. Because she didn't tell me where you were living I couldn't
   visit you last time.
7. I'll be back as soon as I finish shopping.
8. If I don't have enough money, I'll pay you tomorrow, is tha
   alright?
9. Let me see, didn't he come here by plane last week?
10. Last night I glanced over that book you gave me; it is very
    interesting.

Below are English translations of sentences used in the vocabulary of this lesson as examples of usage. Translate these back into Chinese (numbers correspond to those in Vocabulary section.)

1. How many younger sisters do you have?
2. Where does your younger sister go to school?
3. Do you know his name?
4. Do you know the name of that ship?
5. How old is she now? She is three years old.
6. Isn't she four years old now?
7. What is the meaning of this character? Are there several meanings for this character?
8. Do you mean you're not going today? I don't mean that. (I haven't any such idea.)
9. He intends (lit. His intention is) to learn to speak Chinese, not to write Chinese characters.
10. Where did you buy this fountain pen? I didn't buy it, it was given to me by a friend.
11. Did you buy this pen in the Unite States?
12. There are quite a few kinds of spoons, such as teaspoons, tablespoons, etc.
13. Will two spoonfuls be enough? One will be enough.
14. Has his father come? His father hasn't come.
15. Where is your daddy?
16. Is your mother home?
17. Has your mother returned?
18. What are you angry about? I'm not angry about anything.
19. Please don't be angry anymore.
20. Which car is faster? That car is faster.
21. Which is faster, going by ship or by train?
22. Is it very slow to go by boat? Not very slow.
23. Why is this ship so slow?
24. Do you remember who he is? I remember that he was your student.
25. How come you forgot?
26. Do you remember how to write that character?
27. You forgot again? Yes, I did.
28. Do you think you might forget it?
29. What is his name? His name is Jeung Baak-san.
30. What is your child's name?
31. Did he help you? He didn't.
32. Do you need my help?
33. Could you help me?
34. Do you know how to open it? No, I don't.
35. Has the train started?

36. I don't understand what he means.
37. Do you understand now? I still don't understand.
38. How many times have you been there? I have been there many
    times.
39. How many times have you eaten a Chinese meal?
40. May I use your pen? I'm not using it now, go ahead.
41. What is the use of a pen? A pen can be used to write with.
42. Is this pen very useful? Yes, it is.
43. Is he very helpful?
44. That pen is too old, it's useless.
45. This table is useless.
46. How can you tell this pen is useless?
47. Think it over again.
48. I want to go two more times.
49. I'm very tired, I can't study any more.
50. Please come again tomorrow!
51. Alright, I'll come again tomorrow.
52. I still don't know how.
53. This is the boat.
54. You really don't know how?
55. This is exactly the same boat. (i.e., this is exactly the
    boat which you saw or was mentioned, etc.)
56. Is this the first time you are riding on a plane? No, it's
    the second time now.
57. Is this the first time you are eating Chinese food?
58. No matter how good it is, I won't buy it.
59. No matter how I studied that lesson, I couldn't learn it.
60. Whether it's old or new, I'll take it.
61. For instance, now you have a lot of money....
62. If he can't come, then what?
63. In case there are no planes to Hong Kong, then how will you
    go?
64. He would like to buy two more.
65. I'd like to eat some more.
66. He also wants to go to France.
67. I also want to buy a watch.
68. How many classes have you had today? I had four classes
    already.
69. When will the class start?
70. When will the class be dismissed?
71. Where do you go to class?

READING OF THE CLOCK

Vocabulary

jìu(tàuh)jóu   TW: morning
 jìu   M: morning

     1. Néi jìu(tàuh)jóu jouh mātyéh a?
      Ngó jìu(tàuh)jóu duhksyù.
     2. Néi gàmjìujóu jouh mātyéh a? Ngó
      gàmjìujóu māt(yéh) dōu móu jouh.
     3. Néi tìngjìujóu lèih ma? Ngó tìngjìujóu
      m̀lèih, hauhyaht jìujóu lèih.
     4. Kéuih chìhnyaht jìujóu hái bīnsyu a?
      Kéuih chìhnyaht jìujóu juhng hái Hèung-
      góng mei fàanlèih.

máantàuhhāak   TW: night, evening, nighttime
 (or máanhāak, máantáu)
 máan   M: night

     5. Néi máantàuhhāak duhksyù ma? Ngó
      máantàuhhāak m̀duhksyù.
     6. Máanhāak gótìuh gāai hóu nàanhàahng,
      m̀hóu heui lo.
     7. Ngó gàmmáan tìngmáan dōu m̀dākhàahn ngó
      hauhmáan lèih dāk ma?
     8. Yātmáan léuhngmáan móugányiu, yùhgwó
      máanmáan haih gám jauh m̀dāk la.

yahttáu   TW: daytime
 yahttáu   N: sunshine

     9. Kéuih tìngyaht yahttáu dākhàahn ma?
      Kéuih yahttáu m̀dākhàahn, máantáu
      dākhàahn.
     10. Gàmyaht yahttáu jànhaih hóu la.
     11. Kéuih yìhgā yahttáu jouhsih máantáu
      duhksyù àh?

ngaanjau   TW: noontime
                            N: lunch

                            12. Néi ngaanjau hái bīnsyu sihkfaahn a?
                                 Ngó ngaanjau fàan ngūkkéi sihkfaahn.
                            13. Néi hái bīnsyu sihk ngaanjau a? Ngó
                                 hái ngūkkéi sihk ngaanjau.

seuhngjau   TW: forenoon
hahjau   TW: afternoon

                            14. Néi tìngyaht seuhngjau dākhàahn ma?
                                 Ngó seuhngjau m̀dākhàahn, hahjau dāk-
                                 hàahn.
                            15. Néi hahjau géidímjūng lohktòhng a?

dím(jūng)   M: o'clock

                            16. Yìhgā géidím(jūng) la? Yìhgā sàam-
                                 dím(jūng) la.
                            17. Néi géidímjūng fàan ngūkkéi a?

jūngdím   N: hour
dímjūng   M: hour (people frequently use this form
                                 when it refers to a period of time)

                            18. Kéuih heuijó gósyu léuhnggo jūngdím
                                 la juhng mei fàanlèih.
                            19. Ngó múiyaht duhk sàamgo jūngdím syù
                                 jauh hóu guih la.

fān(jūng)   M: minute (Whenever time of day is referred
                                 to, jūng is usually omitted)

                            20. Yātdímjūng yáuh géidòfānjūng a?
                                 Yātdímjūng yáuh luhksahpfānjūng.
                            21. Hái nīsyu heui Hèunggóng ge syùhn
                                 géifānjūng yātchi a?

yātgogwāt   NM: one quarter (gwāt, is the transliterati⊙
                                 of "quarter" in English)
sàamgogwāt   NM: three quarters

                            22. Kéuih wah kéuih léuhngdím sàamgogwāt
                                 lèih nīsyu.

23. Yìhgā sàamdím yātgogwāt mei a?
    Yìhgā sàamdím yātgogwāt la.

jóuchāan   N: breakfast

24. Néi sihkjó jóuchāan mei a? Ngó mei
    dākhàahn sihk.
25. Néi múiyaht géidímjūng sihk jóuchāan
    ga?

máanchāan   N: supper

26. Géidímjūng sihk máanchāan a? Ngó-
    deih luhkdímbunjūng sihk máanchāan.
27. Néi sihkjó máanchāan mei a?

louh (M: tìuh)   N: road

28. Nītìuh louh heui bīnsyu ga? Nītìuh
    louh heui Hèunggóng ge.
29. Hàahng nītìuh louh heui Hèunggóng
    ngāam ma?

deihjí (or jyuhjí)   N: address

30. Néi béi néige deihjí ngó dāk ma?
31. Néi geidāk kéuihge deihjí ma?

mùnpàaih (M: houh)   N: number of house, (lit. doorplate)

32. Gógàan ngūk géidòhouh mùnpàaih a?
    Kéuih jyuhhái Seuhnghói louh,
    sahpchāthouh mùnpàaih.
33. Néi gósyu mùnpàaih géidòhouh a?

fangaau   VO: sleep
fan   V: sleep

34. Néidī saimānjái fanjó gaau mei a?
    Kéuihdeih fanjó hóu noi lo.
35. Néi múimáan fan géidòdímjūng a?

ngaangaau   N: a nap

36. Kéuih fangán ngaangaau àh? Mhaih,
    kéuih gàmyaht móu fan ngaangaau.

37. Néi haih m̀haih yahtyaht dōu fan
    ngaangaau a?

héisàn   VO: get up

38. Kéuih héijósàn làh? Kéuih mei héi-
    sàn juhng fangán.
39. Néi gàmjlujóu géidímjūng héisàn ga?

jóu   SV: early

40. Yìhgā hóu jóu jē.
41. Kéuih gam jóu lèih jouh mātyéh a?
42. M̀gòi néi góng kéuih tèng tìngjlujóu
    m̀sái gam jóu lèih.

chìh   SV: late (for a certain time, usually used
                              as a RVE; ref. Les. 19); later

43. Dímgáai gam chìh a?
44. Daihyihchi m̀hóu gam chìh la.
45. Kéuih wah kéuih chìh léuhngyaht lèih

ngaan   SV: late (in the day)

46. Dímgáai gam ngaan kéuih juhng mei lè
47. Yìhgā haih m̀haih hóu ngaan la? Yìh-
    gā hóu ngaan la, luhkdímgéijūng la.

ngāam   SV: be right; fit

48. Ngó gám góng ngāam ma? Néi gám góng
    ngāam la.
49. Nīgihn sāam ngāam m̀gāam a?
50. Kéuih wah nīgo ngāam, ngó wah gógo
    ngāam néi wah bīngo ngāam a?

ngāamngāam   MA: just (a moment ago), luckily
jingwah   MA: just (a moment ago)

51. Kéuih ngāamngāam jáujó.
52. Kéuih ngāamngāam hái Méigwok fàanlèi
53. Jingwah yahplèih gógo haih bīngo a?
54. Ngó jingwah heuijó máai yéh, néi dán
    jo ngó hóu noi làh?
55. Ngāamngāam tìngyaht yáuh ga fèigèi
    heui Méigwok.

séng (fanséng)   SV: awake
    giuséng   RV: to wake (somebody) up (ref. Les. 19)

> 56. Kéuih sengjó mei a? Kéuih yìhgā
>   sénggán.
> 57. Néi gàmjlujóu géidímjūng séng ga?
> 58. Kéuih yìhgā juhng mei seng àh, néi
>   heui giuséng kéuih hóu ma?

fàangùng   VO: go to work
    fàanhohk   VO: go to school

> 59. Néi tìngyaht sái fàangùng ma? Ngó
>   tìngyaht msái fàangùng.
> 60. Néi saimānjái fàansaaihohk mei a?
> 61. Néi jlutàuhjóu géidímjūng fàanhohk a?

fonggùng   VO: stop work (at the end of the day)
    fonghohk   VO: get out of school (at the end of the day)

> 62. Kéuih géidímjūng fonggùng a? Kéuih
>   ngdímjūng fonggùng.
> 63. Néi géidímjūng fonghohk a?

jàang   V: lack, be short, differ by, owe

> 64. Juhng jàang géidò chín a? Juhng jàang
>   léuhngmān.
> 65. Néi haih mhaih jàang kéuih chín a?
> 66. Néi jàang kéuih géidò chín a? Ngó
>   jàang kéuih sàambaakmān.

gwo   V: past, exceed

> 67. Gwojó sàamdím(jūng) mei a? Gwojó
>   hóu noi lo.
> 68. Gwojó géi nói la?
> 69. Gwojó nīgo yuht kéuih jauh fàanlèih la.

yīkwaahk, waahkhaih   MA: or (as in 'whether...or...')
    dihng(haih)   MA: or (as in 'whether...or...')

> 70. Néi jùngyi nīgo yīkwaahk gógo a?
> 71. Haih néi heui dinhghaih kéuih heui a?
> 72. Hái nīsyu yahp(heui) yīkwaahk hái
>   gósyu yahp(heui) a?

73. Gàmyaht haih láihbaaiyāt díhng(haih)
    láihbaaiyih a?

waahkjé   MA: may, maybe; perhaps; or (only used in
                               answer)

74. Tìngyaht ngó waahkjé m̀dākhàahn.
75. Ngó waahkjé heui waahkjé m̀heui.
76. Waahkjé kéuih jì.
77. Kéuih wah kéuih waahkjé lèih.
78. Néi jùngyi bīngo a? Nīgo waahkjé
    (or yīkwaahk or waahkhaih) gógo dōu
    dāk.

yáuhsìh   MA: sometimes

79. Ngó yáuhsìh jùngyi sihk sāichāan
    yáuhsìh jùngyi sihk tòhngchāan.
80. (Nīgoláihbaai) yáuhsìh yáuh yáuhsìh
    móu.
81. Néi haih m̀haih yáuhsìh hóu jùngyi
    yám jáu a?

yìngfahn   MA: ought to, should
(or yìnggòi)

82. Ngó yìngfahn gàmyaht heui, daahnhaih
    ngó yìhgā m̀dākhàahn.
83. Néi yìngfahn góng ngó jì gógihn sāam
    géidò chín.
84. Nīgihn sih yìngfahn bīngo jouh a?

Conversation

A: Yātyaht yáuh géidòdímjūng a?
B: Yātyaht yáuh yahseidímjūng.
A: Yātdímjūng yáuh géidòfānjūng a?
B: Yātdímjūng yáuh luhksahpfānjūng.
A: Dímyéung giujouh yātgojih a?
B: Múi ngfānjūng giujouh yātgo jih.
A: Gám, yātdímjūng haih m̀haih yáuh sahpyihgo jih a?
B: Haih, yātdímjūng yáuh sahpyihgo jih.
A: Géidòfānjūng haih yātgogwāt(jūng) a?

B: Sahpngfānjūng haih yātgogwāt.
A: Gám, yātgogwāt jīkhaih sàamgo jih haih m̀haih a?
B: Haih, yātgogwāt jīkhaih sàamgo jih. Yìhgā géidímjūng la?
A: Yìhgā....eh....
B: Yìhgā ngāamngāam sàamdím.
A: Dímgáai néi m̀wah sàamdímjūng nē?
B: Wah sàamdím yīkwaahk sàamdímjūng dōu dāk.
A: Peiyùh ngó man néi, néi kàhmmáan duhkjó géi_nói syù a? Gám néi
   dím góng a?
B: Yùhgwó néi gám man,ngó jauh wah ngó kàhmmáan duhkjó léuhnggo
   jūngdímge syù, waahkjé wah ngó kàhmmáan duhkjó léuhngdímjūngge
   syù.
A: Peiyùh ngó man néi lèihjó géinói la?
B: Ngó hóyíh wah ngó lèihjó léuhngdímbunjūng la. Waahkjé léuhnggo
   bun jūngdím la.
A: Dímgáai néi m̀wah léuhngdím luhkgo jih yīkwaahk léuhngdím léuhng-
   gogwāt nē?
B: Yànwaih bundímjūng jauhhaih bundímjūng. Yáuhsìh yáuhdī yàhn wah
   léuhnggogwāt ge.
A: Ngó hóyíh wah sàamsahpfānjūng ma?
B: Hóyíh, néi hóyíh wah, bundímjūng waahkjé sàamsahpfānjūng dōu dāk.
   Yìhgā géidímjung la?
A: Yìhgā sàamdím.... sàamgo jih ngāam m̀gāam a?
B: Ngāam la, yùhgwó néi m̀wah sàamdím sàamgo jih, néi dím wah a?
A: Ngó hóyíh wah sàamdímyātgogwāt waahkjé sàamdímsahpngfān, ngāam
   m̀gāam a?
B: Hóu ngāam. Yìhgā gau sàamdímsàamgogwāt mei a?
A: Mei.
B: Juhng jàang géi nói a?
A: Juhng jàang yātgo jih.
B: Gám, jīkhaih géi(dò)dím(jūng) a?
A: Sàamdímsei'ahfān.
B: Gám, juhng jàang géidògo jih seidím a?
A: Juhng jàang seigo jih seidím.
B: Yìhgā gwojó sàamdímsàamgogwāt mei a?
A: Mei, yìhgā ngāamngāam sàamdímsàamgogwāt.

Pattern Sentences

I. Reading of the Clock

Yātdím
    Yātdím lìhng léuhnggān.
    Yātdím yātgo jih, (or) yātdím lìhng ngfān.

Léuhngdím
    Léuhngdím lìhng chātfān.
    Léuhngdím sahpfān, (or) Léuhngdím léuhnggo jih.

Sàamdím

Seidím
    Seidím sahpyihfān.
    Seidím sahpngfān (or) seidím yātgogwāt (or) seidím sàamgo jih.

Ngdím
    Ngdím yahngfān (or) ngdím nggo jih.

Luhkdím
    Luhkdím sà'ahfān (or) luhkdímbun (but not) luhkdím luhkgo jih.

Chātdím
    Chātdím sei'ah-ngfān (or) chātdím sàamgogwāt (or) chātdím gáug
    jih.

Baatdím, gaudím, sahpdím, sahpyātdím, sahpyihdím.

II. Uses of gau, gwo, dou, jàang, chìh, jóu, ngaan to indecate time

    A: Yìhgā haih mhaih hóu ngaan la?
    B: Mhaih géi ngaan jē.
    A: Ngó gàmyaht (lèih)chìhjó, mjì gau jūng mei nē?
    B: Mei, yìhgā juhng jóu.
    A: Juhng jàang géi noi gau gáudím a?
    B: Juhng jàang yihsahpfānjūng.
        (a little while later)
    A: Doujó gáudím mei a?
    B: Yìhgìng gwojó lo.
    A: Gwojó géi noi la?
    B: Gwojó yātgojih la.
    A: Yìhgā gau gáudím léuhnggojih mei a?
    B: Mei, juhng jàang seifānjūng.

III. Further use of <u>jauh</u> and <u>jē</u>:

A. <u>Jauh</u> <u>V NU M</u> ...jē,[1] means 'only,' and 'that's all there is to it.'

1. Ngó jauh heuigwo léuhngchi jē.
   I've been there only twice.

2. Ngó jauh yáuh sàammān jē.
   I have only three dollars.

3. Ngó jauh sīk góng géigeui jē.
   I only can speak a few phrases.

4. Ngó jauh máaijó géigo jē.
   I bought only a few.

5. Ngó jauh táigwo yātchi jē.
   I read it once and that is all there is to it.

6. Gauh<u>nín</u> ngó jauh gingwo kéuih yātchi jē.

7. Nīsyu jauh haih kéuih yātgo wúih góng Yìngmàn jē.

8. Ngó gàmyaht jauh séuhngjó yāttòhng jē.

9. Ngó kàhmmáan (jauh) fanjó léuhngdímjūng(ge gaau) jē.

10. Ngó jauh chìhjó bunfānjūng jē, fóchè yìhging hòijó lo.

B. Ṁhaih géi ...jē, 'isn't really very...(at all)'

1. Ṁhaih géi <u>ng</u>aan jē, dī saimānjái juhng mei fonghohk.
   It isn't that late, the children haven't come back (from school) yet.

2. Nīgo bīu ṁhaih géi gwai jē, dímgáai néi ṁmáaibéi kéuih nē?
   This watch isn't really very expensive, why don't you buy it for her?

3. Nīgeui wá ṁhaih géi nàan hohk jē, néi hohk géichì tìm jauh sīk la.

---

1. In common practice, jauh is optional whenever it is used with the jē. (See Les. 7, Patt. V)

This sentence isn't that hard, you'll learn it after a
couple of times more.

4. Mhaih géi chìh jē, juhng mei séuhngtòhng.
It isn't very late at all, the class hasn't begun yet.

5. Nībún syù mhaih géi hóutái jē.
This book isn't really very expensive, why don't you buy
it for her?

IV. Address:

A: Chàhn sìnsàang hóu noi móu gin, néi géi hóu ma? Dī gàyàhn
dōu géi hóu ma?
B: Gogo dōu hóu,yáuhsàm. Néi yìhgā ngāamngāam fonggùng àh?
A: Haih la, ngāamngāam fonggùng. Néi yìhgā dākhàahn ma? Chéng
gwolèih ngósyu chóhhàh lā?
B: Néi yìhgā haih mhaih juhnghaih hái Seuhnghóigāaisyu jyuh a?
A: Mhaih, ngó seuhnggoyuht ngāamngāam bùnjónggūk, ngó jauh jyuh-
hái nītluh gāai jē, hàahnggwoheui géigàan jauhaih la.
B: Yìhgā géidímjūng la?
A: Yìhgā ngdímsàamgogwāt.
B: Ngó ngāamngāam luhkdímjūng yáuh dī sih, yiu heui gin yātgo
pàhngyáuh, daihyihyaht ngó yātdihng lèih taam néi. Néi gósyu
mùnpàaih géidòhouh a?
A: Ngó gósyu mùnpàaih luhk'achchāthouh, néi haih mhaih juhng
jyuhhái Bākgìng louh a?
B: Oh, ngó mgeidāk góng néi jì, ngó seuhnggoyuht yihkdōu bùnjó,
yànwaih ngódī gàyàhn hái Gwóngjàu lèihjó, ngó jyuhgán gódaat
deihfòng taai sai, sóyíh bùnjoheui Gáulùhng (Kowloon — the
peninsula opposite Hong Kong), ngó yìhgā ge deihjí haih:

Gáulùhng, Bàlàih louh, sàambaakseiahchāthouh yihláu.
Géisí dākhàahn chéng lèih ngódeihsyu wáanháh lā, yìhgā jauhlèih luhkdím la, ngó yiu heui la, daih(yih)yaht gin, daih(yih)
yaht gin.

Drills on Dates and Addresses

A. Give the following years in Cantonese:

1245, 1894, 1951, 1789, 1953, 1914, 1600, 1932, 1940

B. Translate the following dates:

July 3rd, 1756; December 24th, 1941; January 15, this year;
24th, next month; August 29th, last year; first month of last
year; May 5, 1955; first week of last month; February 2nd,
next year.

C. Questions to be answered:

1. Néi jì m̀jì Wòhng sìnsàang jyuhhái bīnsyu a?
2. Néi jyuhhái nītluh gāai géidòhouh mùnpàaih a?
3. Néige deihjí haih bīnsyu a?
4. Néi hái Méigwokge deihjí haih bīnsyu a?
5. Néi hohkhaauhge deihjí haih bīnsyu a?

Additional Sentences

1. Yìhgā géi(dò)dím jūng a?   Yìhgā seidímbun.
2. Néi lèihjó nīsyu géinói la?   Lèihjó dímgéijūng la.
3. Néi ngūkkéi hàahnglèih nīsyu yiu géinói a?   Yiu dímbunjūng.
4. Fóchè hòijó géinói la?   Ngāamngāam hòijó jē.
5. Néi hohkhaauh géidímjūng sèuhngtòhng a?   Jìutàuhjóu baatdím.
6. Néi màantáu duhksyù ma?   Ngó gwojó gáudím jauh m̀uhk la.
7. Lèuhngdímjūng mei a?   ('doujó' is understood here)   Juhng jàang
   géinói a?   Mei dou lèuhngdímjūng, juhng jàang lèuhngfānjūng.
8. Yìhgā gwojó (yāt)dímbunjūng mei a?   Yìhgā sàamdímgéi lo.
9. Gwojó géinói a?   Gwojó hóu noi lo.
10. Nīga fèigēi géidímjūng hòi a?   Chìh bundímjūng hòi.
11. Néideih múiyaht sèuhng géidòdímjūng tòhng (or fo) a?   Ngódeih
    múiyaht sèuhng luhkdímjūng tòhng.
12. Néideih yìhgìng duhkjó géidòdímjūng syù la?   Ngódeih duhkjó sàam-
    dímjūng syù la.
13. Kéuih fàanjóheui géinói la?   Kéuih fàanjóheui dímgéijūng la.
14. Néi dángjó ngó géinói a?   Móu géinói jē.
15. Néi múimàan (abbr. of múiyaht màantàuhhāk) fan géidògojūngdím
    gaau a?   Ngó múimàan yiu fan baatgojūngdímge gaau.
16. Néi múimàan géidímjūng fangaau a?   Ngó múimàan sahpdímjūng fangaau.
17. Néi múijìu (abbr. of múiyaht jìutàuhjóu) géidímjūng héisàn a?
    Ngó múijìu luhkdímjūng héisàn.
18. Néideih tìngyaht géidímjūng heui a?   Ngódeih tìngyaht sahpyātdím-
    jūng heui.
19. Néi hahgo làihbaaiyāt géidímjūng lèih a?   Ngó hahgo làihbaaiyāt
    sèuhngjau gáudímyātgogwāt lèih.
20. Chàhn sìnsàang tùhng Lèih sìnsàang heuijó géinói la?   Kéuihdeih
    heuijó sàamseidímjūng (or sàam-seigo jūngdím) la.

21. Gau mei a? Yùhgwó mei gau juhng jàang géidò a? Juhng jàang hóu
    dò.Néi jīkhāak heui ló lā.
22. Dímgáai néi gam chìh lèih a? Ngó jingwah mdākhàahn sóyíh lèih
    chìhjó.
23. Néi juhng geidāk néi jàang ngó géidò chín ma? Ngó juhng jàang
    néi chín mē? Dímgáai ngó yātdī dōu mgeidāk a?
24. Kéuih haih mhaih jlutàuhjóu hóu jóu héisàn ga? Yáuh (yāt)go
    yàhn jlutàuhjóu mséung heisàn, màantàuhhāk mséung fangaau, néi
    jldōu gógo yàhn haih bīngo ma? Gógo yàhn jauhhaih kéuih la.
25. Néi tìngyaht chóh syùhn yīkwaahk chóh fèigèi heui Hèunggóng a?
    Ngó waahkjé chóh syùhn heui, yànwaih ngó tùhng yātgo pàhngyáuh
    heui, kéuih jùngyi chóh syùhn.

Translate the following sentences into Cantonese:

1. There are not very many good restaurants here.
2. These clothes are so pretty, I'd like to buy them all.
3. None of us has ever been to France.
4. I haven't had one Chinese meal.
5. No matter how pretty it is, I won't buy it.
6. Do you have to go to class this morning?
7. I don't know how to use chopsticks.
8. Do you remember the name of that ship?
9. Please help me move this table away.
10. I called on him more than ten times, he wasn't home even once

Below are English translations of sentences used in the vocabulary
of this lesson as examples of usage. Translate these back into
Chinese (numbers correspond to those in Vocabulary section.)

1. What do you do in the morning? I study in the morning.
2. What did you do this morning? I didn't do anything this
   morning.
3. Are you coming tomorrow morning? Not tomorrow, but I'll come
   the day after.
4. Where was he the day before yesterday morning? He was still
   in Hong Kong and had not returned.
5. Do you study at night? No, I don't study at night.
6. That street is very dark at night, it is better not to go.
7. I'll be busy tonight and tomorrow night, I'll come the night
   after, all right?
8. That'll be all right for one or two nights, but it is not
   permitted every night.

9. Is he free tomorrow during the day? He isn't free during the day but will be in the evening.
10. What lovely sunshine we have today.
11. He works in the daytime and studies in the evening, isn't that right?
12. Where do you eat your lunch? I go home to eat my lunch.
13. Where do you eat your lunch? I eat my lunch at home.
14. Are you free tomorrow morning? Not in the morning, but I'll be free in the afternoon.
15. When will school be over in the afternoon?
16. What time is it now? Now it is three o'clock.
17. What time will you go home?
18. He has (already) been there for two hours and still hasn't returned.
19. Each day after studying three hours, I become very tired.
20. How many minutes are there in an hour? There are sixty minutes in one hour.
21. What is the time schedule for the ferry from here to Hong Kong?
22. He said he would be here at quarter to three.
23. Is it quarter past three yet? Yes, it is.
24. Have you had your breakfast? I haven't had time to eat yet.
25. What time do you usually have your breakfast?
26. When are we going to have supper? We eat at six thirty.
27. Have you had your supper?
28. Where does this road lead to? This road leads to Hong Kong.
29. Can I get to Hong Kong by taking this road?
30. Would you give me your address?
31. Do you remember his address?
32. What's the number of the house? He lives at No. 17, Shanghai Road.
33. What's the number of your place?
34. Have your children gone to bed? They have already been asleep a long time.
35. How many hours do you sleep each night?
36. Is he taking a nap? No, he didn't take a nap today.
37. Do you take a nap every day?
38. He got up already? He hasn't risen yet, he is still sleeping.
39. When did you get up this morning?
40. It is still early!
41. Why does he come so early?
42. Please tell him he doesn't have to come so early tomorrow morning.
43. How come it is so late?
44. Next time don't be so late.
45. He said he'd come two days later.
46. How come it's already so late and he still hasn't come?

47. Is it very late now? Yes, it is already past six.
48. Is it correct if I say it this way? Yes, if you say it that way, it is right.
49. Does this dress fit?
50. He said this one is correct, I said that one is correct, which one do you say is correct?
51. He just left.
52. He just came back from America.
53. Who just came in?
54. I went out to get something just a moment ago, have you been waiting long?
55. Luckily, there is a plane going to America tomorrow.
56. Has he awakened? He is waking up.
57. When did you wake up this morning?
58. He hasn't awakened yet, would you please go wake him up?
59. Do you have to go to work tomorrow? No, I don't.
60. Have all your children gone to school?
61. What time do you go to school each morning?
62. When will he be off from work? He'll be off at 5 o'clock.
63. When will you be through school?
64. How much is it short? There is still two dollars short.
65. Do you owe him any money?
66. How much do you owe him? I owe him three hundred dollars.
67. Is it already past three? It's a long time past.
68. How long past is it?
69. After this month he'll be back.
70. Do you like this one or that one?
71. Are you going or is he going?
72. Do you enter here or there?
73. Is today Monday or Tuesday?
74. Tomorrow I may not have time.
75. I may go or I may not.
76. Perhaps he knows.
77. He said he might come.
78. Which one do you like? This one or that one, it makes no difference.
79. Sometimes I like to eat Western food, sometimes I like Chinese food.
80. (This week) sometimes we will have it, sometimes we won't.
81. Are there times when you like to drink a lot?
82. I should go today, but I can't get away now.
83. You should tell me how much that cloth is.
84. Who should take care of this matter?

LESSON 18

RELATIVE TIME

Vocabulary

Yandouh   PW: India

     1. Néi heuigwo Yandouh ma? Ngó ngāam-
        ngāam hái Yandouh fàanlèih.
     2. Yandouh hóuwáan ma?

Nàamgìng   PW: Nanking

     3. Néi hái Nàamgìng jyuhgwo ma? Ngó hái
        Nàamgìng jyuhgwo hóu noi.
     4. Néi hái Nàamgìng jyuhgwo géi noi a?

Tìnjèun   PW: Tientsin

     5. Tìngyaht yáuh syùhn heui Tìnjèun ma?
     6. Nīdī jáu hái (or haih) Tìnjèun lèih ge.

faaichè   N: express

     7. Néi chóh faaichè heui àh? Haih, m̀jì
        gàmyaht yáuh móu faaichè nē?
     8. Yùhgwó móu faaichè ngó jauh chóh fèigèi
        heui lo.

gaaisiuh   V: introduce

     9. Ngó tùhng néideih léuhngwái gaaisiuhhàh.
     10. Néi gaaisiuh ngó heui ginhàh kéuih hóu
        ma?
     11. Chàhn sìnsàang jingwah yíhgìng gaaisiuh-
        gwo la.

dásyun   V/N: plan to, plan

     12. Ngó dásyun chēutnín heui Jùnggwok.

221

13. Kéuih dásyun géisí heui a? Kéuih mā
    yéh dásyun dōu móu.
14. Néi nīgo láihbaailuhk dásyun heui bī
    syu wáan a?

gokdāk   V: feel

15. Néi gokdāk dím a? Ngó gokdāk hóu hó
16. Néi gokdāk nīgihn sih gám jouh ngāam
    ma?

dájeung   VO: make war, fight

17. Seuhngchi dájeung gójahnsí néi hái
    bīnsyu a? Dájeung gójahnsí ngó hái
    Jùnggwok.
18. Bīnnìn dáyùhnjeung ga, néi geidāk ma

deui   CV/V: to, towards (lit. facing)

19. Kéuih deui ngó wah....
20. Néi deui kéuihdeih góng(jó) mātyéh a
21. Ngó deui nīgihn sih yātdī dōu m̀jì.
22. Néi deui ngódeih jànhaih hóu la.

hòisàm   SV: amused, happy, contented

23. Ngó gokdāk hóu hòisàm.
24. Néi tái dī saimānjái géi hòisàm!
25. Dímgáai gàmyaht kéuih gam hòisàm a?

jihjoih   SV: comfortable (suggests satisfied respons
                            ness of a sense organ)

26. Gójèung yí hóu jihjoih.
27. Kéuih ga chè hóu jihjoih, ngó chóh(
    yātyaht dōu m̀gokdāk guih.
28. Chóh fèigèi néi gokdāk jihjoih ma?

ngònlohk   SV: contented, comfortable

29. Kéuih yìhgā hóu ngònlohk la.
30. Nīgàan ngūk jànhaih ngònlohk la.
31. Chìh géinìn néi jauh hóu ngònlohk la

chēutméng	SV: famous

32. Nīsyu bīngàan chāangún chēutméng a?
    Nīsyu móu bīngàan chēutméng ge chāan-
    gún.
33. Nīgàan chāangún bīngo choi chēutméng a?

pèhng	SV: inexpensive, cheap

34. Gógàan poutáu yeuhngyeuhng yéh dōu hóu
    pèhng.
35. Gwaige hóu gwai pèhngge hóu pèhng.
36. Néi yiu gwai ga yiu pèhng ga?

fòngbihn (or bihn)	SV: convenient

37. Yùhgwó m̀fòngbihn jauh m̀hóu lo.
38. Yáuh ga chè jànhaih fòngbihn lo.
39. Haih m̀haih hóu m̀(fòng)bihn a?

wúih	AV: may, would, likely

40. Ngó tīngyaht wúih heui.
41. Kéuih wúih lèih ma? Kéuih m̀wúih lèih.
42. Néi chēutnín wúih heui Jùnggwok ma?

yíhchìhn	MA: formerly, before, previously

43. Néi yíhchìhn sihkgwo tòhngchāan mei a?
    Ngó yíhchìhn mei sihkgwo.
44. Néi yíhchìhn sīk kéuih ma?

yíhhauh	MA: (t)hereafter, afterwards, from now on

45. Yíhhauh ngó m̀chóh syùhn heui la.
46. Yíhhauh kéuih móu lèih(gwo) la.
47. Kéuih yíhhauh dím a?

| ....jìchìhn
(or yíhchìhn)	MA: ....before....; ago

48. Ngó jáu jìchìhn yātdihng lèih taam néi.
49. Ngó múiyaht chātdímjūng yíhchìhn héi-
    sàn.
50. Ngó tīngyaht gáudím yíhchìhn lèih wán
    néi.

....jìhauh   MA: after....
 (or yíhhauh)
                            51. Ngó fàangùng jìhauh yáuh móu yàhn lèi
                                wàngwo ngó a?
                            52. Ngódeih duhkyùhn nībún syù jìhauh
                                juhng yiu duhk géi noi a?
                            53. Néi jáujó jìhauh yātjahngāan kéuih
                                jauh fàanlèih la.

gauhsìh, gauhsí   MA: formerly, in the past
 (or chùhngchìhn, wòhngsí)
                            54. Gauhsìh kéuih móu chín, yìhgā kéuih
                                hóu yáuhchín la.
                            55. Gauhsìh dī ngūk m̀haih gám yéung ge.

chùhnglòih dōu...   Ph: all along; have always...
 yātheung dōu...
                            56. Ngó chùhnglòih dōu haih gám jouh ge.

chùhnglòih mei   Ph: never have (done something)
 (or m̀, móu)
 yātheung m̀ (or móu)   57. Ngó chùhnglòih mei sihkgwo gam hóusìk
                                ge tòhngchāan.
                            58. Ngó chùhnglòih m̀jì kéuih wúih góng
                                Jùnggwokwá.

jèunglòih   MA: in the future

                            59. Bīngo dōu m̀jì jèunglòih dímyéung.
                            60. Yìhgā duhk ge syù jèunglòih yātdihng
                                yáuhyuhng.
                            61. Nīgihn sih jèunglòih yātdihng hóu
                                nàanjouh.

búnlòih   MA: originally

                            62. Bùnlòih ngó m̀jùngyi sihk, yìhgā ngó
                                hóu jùngyi sihk.
                            63. Kéuih búnlòih haih gaausyù ge sìn-
                                sàang, yìhgā kéuih haih duhksyù ge
                                hohksaang.
                            64. Ngó búnlòih m̀séung heui, daahnhaih ng
                                yìhgā móu sih jouh, ngódeih heui tái-
                                háh hóu ma?
                            65. Néi búnlòih haih jouh mātyéh ga?

hauhlòih (or sāumēi)   MA: afterwards, later on

          66. Hauhlòih dím a?
          67. Sāumēi kéuih yáuh móu joi lèihgwo a?
          68. Hauhlòih kéuih m̀yám la.

sāumēi   A: last ....(i.e. last one, etc.)
  sāumēi NU M....   last NU M of a period of time (see sent 69)

          69. Sāumēi go géinìn keuih móu cheung gō la.
          70. Ngó jùngyi sāumēi gógo.
          71. Sāumēi góga chè haih bīngo ga? (Note
              the sāumēi here may take as an MA
              meaning afterwards)

gahnlói   MA: recently

          72. Gahnlói géi hóu ma?
          73. Ngó gahnlói móu heui.
          74. Kéuih gahnlói yáuh seun ma?

tàuhsīn (or jingwah)   MA: just a while ago

          75. Tàuhsīn ngó m̀dākhàahn.
          76. Néi tàuhsīn heuijó bīnsyu a?
          77. Tàuhsīn néi góng mātyéh a?

sìhsìh   A: often, always, frequently

          78. Chéng sìhsìh lèih chóh lā!
          79. Ngó sìhsìh dōu séung máai ga sàn chè.
          80. Néi haih m̀haih sìhsìh sihk tòhngchāan
              a?

pìhngsìh   MA: usually, ordinarily

          81. Kéuih pìhngsìh m̀yám jáu ge, daahnhaih
              yáuhsìh yám hóu dò.
          82. Pìhngsìh nībún syù maai sàammān.
          83. Néi pìhngsìh hái bīnsyu sihk ngaanjau
              a?

ji   A: not....until, must...., then and only
                      then, only

          84. Kéuih tìngyaht ji lèih.

85. Ngó duhkyùhn syù ji heui.
86. Ji léuhngmān jē.

jihmjím   MA: gradually

87. Ngó jihmjím m̀geidāksaai la.
88. Jihmjím jauh móu gam nàan la.
89. Kéuih jihmjím wúih hàahng la.

maanmáan   A: slowly, gradually

90. Maanmáan (jouh) dōu m̀chìh!
91. Ngó maanmáan wúih la.
92. Gójek syùhn maanmáan hòigán la.

jouhmātyéh   MA: why (used interchangeably with dímgáai)

93. Jouhmātyéh kéuih m̀lèih a?
94. Jouhmātyéh fóchè juhng mei lèih a?
95. Kàhmyaht jouhmātyéh nei móu lèih taam
    ngódeih a?

daap   V: to answer

96. Dímgáai nei m̀daap ngó a? Ngó m̀jì dím
    daap nei.
97. Nīgeui wáh hóu nàam daap.

Yahtbún   PW: Japan

98. Néi yáuh móu heuigwo Yahtbún a?

Useful Expressions

maanmāan hàahng	Depart slowly. (said to departing gues
doihmaansaai	I have treated you shabbily. (said to departing guests; a polite formula not to be taken literally!)
chéng wùih	Please return. Don't escort me furth (said to a host accompanying his de parting guest)
chéng néi tùhng ngó manhauh...	Please give my regards to...
yātlouh seuhnfùng	A pleasant journey (to you)

Reading

Ngó mei lèih Méigwok jìhchhn hái Hèunggóng jyuhgwo hóugéininn.
Gójahnsí ngó hái yātgàan hohkhaauh gaausyù, yàuh yātgo Yìnggwok
yàhn kéuih yihk hái gósyu gaausyù. Kéuih sìhsìh wah séung heui
Bākgìng wáanháh, daahnhaih sìhsìh dōu m̀dākhàahn, sāumēi doujó 1941
nìn sahpyihyuht, yáuh yātyaht kéuih deui ngó wah: "Chàhn sìnsàang
ngó sìhsìh dōu wah heui Bākgìng wáanháh, nī yātchi jànhaih heui la!
Néi gauhsìh hái Bākgìng jyuhgwo, néi gaaisiuh géigo pàhngyáuh béi
ngó dāk ma?" Ngó wah: "Dāk! néi géisí heui a?" Kéuih wah: "Hahgo
làihbaai ngāamngāam yáuh ga fèigèi heui Bākgìng, ngó dásyun hái Bākgìng jyuh léuhnggo làihbaai; fàanlèih gójahnsi, ngó heui Seuhnghói
Nàamgìng wáan géiyaht."

Gógéiyaht kéuih hóu m̀dākhàahn, kéuih máaijó hóu dò yiu yùhng ge
yéh. Kéuih yāt gindóu (See Les. 19 Voc.) kéuih dī pàhngyáuh jauh
góng kéuihdeih jì kéuih jauhlèih yiu heui Bākgìng la.

Yáuh yātyaht kéuih yauh lèih wán ngó. Kéuih wah: "Néi hahjau
dākhàahn ma? Tùhng ngó chēutheui yám chàh hóu ma?" Ngó wah:
"(yùhgwó) Néi chéng yám chàh ngó géisí dōu dākhàahn."

Góyaht hahjau ngódeih yám chàh gójahnsí, kéuih wah kéuih heui
Bākgìng jìchìhn séung hohk géigeui Jùnggwokwá. Yùhgwó yātgeui Jùnggwokwá dōu m̀sīk yātdihng hóu m̀(fòng)bihn ge. Kéuih chéng ngó gaau
kéuih géigeui.

Ngó gaaujó kéuih géiyaht, múiyaht hahjau gaau yātgo jūngdím,
kéuih múiyaht jìutàuhjóu héisàn jìhauh jihgéi duhk léuhnggo jūngdím.
Hohkjó géiyaht jē, kéuih jauh wúih góng géigeui la, kéuih gokdāk
hóu hòisàm.

Làihbaaiyaht gómáan, kéuih chéng ngó hái jáugún sihk máanfaahn,
kéuih góng ngó tèng kéuih mātyéh dōu yuhbeihsaai la (See Les. 19
Voc.), gàmmáan kéuih hái Hèunggóng fan, tìngmáan kéuih jauh hái Bākgìng fan la. Ngó wah: "Ngó jànhaih séung fàanheui Bākgìng wáanháh
yùhgwó ngó hóyíh tùhng néi yātchái heui néi wah géi hóu a!"

Daiyihyaht làihbaaiyāt, jīkhaih sahpyihyuht baathouh, Yahtbún
tùhng Yìnggwo Méigwok dájeung. Ngóge Yìnggwok pàhngyáuh móufaatjí
heui Bākgìng, kéuih gokdāk hóu m̀ngònlohk.

1945nìn dáyùhnjeung la, yáuh yātyaht kéuih lèih wán ngó, kéuih
wah kéuih tìngyaht heui Bākgìng, ngó wah: "Nīchi jànhaih heui la!"
Kéuih wah: "Ngó m̀jì, tìngyaht chóh fèigèi doujó Bākgìng sìnji jì."
Ngó man kéuih: "Néi yíhchìhn hohk gódī Jùnggwokwá juhng geidāk ma?"
Kéuih wah: "Ngó yìhgā yātgeui dōu m̀geidāk la."

Pattern Sentences

I. General Relative Time:

yìhchìhn (formerly, before, previously)
yìhhauh (afterwards, (t)hereafter, from now on)

chùhnglòih dōu (all along; have always...)
chùhnglòih mei(or m̀, móu) (never have...)

yātheung dōu (all along; have always...)
yātheung m̀(or móu) (never have...)

gauhsìh, wòhngsí, chùhngchìhn (formerly, in the past)
yìhgā (now, at the present time)
jèunglòih (in the future)

búnlòih (originally)
hauhlòih (afterwards, later on)

gahnlói, gahnlòih (recently)
sāumēi (afterwards, later on)

1. Néi yìhchìhn hái bīnsyu jyuh a (or ga)?
   Where did you live formerly?

2. Yìhchìhn ngó yātgeui Gwóngdùngwá dōu m̀sīk, yìhgā ngó sīk góng
   hóugéigeui la.
   Formerly I couldn't speak a word of Cantonese; now I can spea
   quite a little.

3. Néi yìhchhn yáuh móu heuigwo Jùnggwok a?
   Have you ever been to China before?

4. Néi yìhchìhn sīk kéuih ma? Ngó sīk(jó) kéuih hóu noi lo.
   Did you know him previously? I know him a long time ago.

5. Néi yìhhauh dásyun jouh mātyéh (sih) a?
   What are you going to do (for a living) after this?

6. Seuhnghói jànhaih hóuwáan la, ngó yìhhauh juhng séung heui.

7. Néi giu kéuih yìhhauh m̀hóu lèih la.

8. Yìhhauh ngó móu ségwo seun béi kéuih.

9. Gauhsìh yáuh go saimānjái.... Gauhsìh yáuh go chēutméngge
   yàhn wahgwo. "..............."

10. Gauhsìh kéuih jùngyi yám jáu daahnhaih yìhgā kéuih yātbùi
    dōu myám la.

11. Gauhsìh yeuhngyeuhng yéh dōu pèhng, yìhgā yeuhngyeuhng yéh
    dōu gwai.

12. Néi gauhsìh haih mhaih hóu jùngyi sihk tòhngchāan ga?

13. Ngó chùhnglòih dōu hóu jùngyi sihk tòhngchāan ge.

14. Ngó chùhnglòih mei chóhgwo fèigèi nīchi haih daihyātchi.

15. Néi jèunglòih duhkyùhn syù dásyun jouh mātyéh(sih) a?

16. Kéuih jànhaih yātdī dásyun dōu móu yìhgā jauhlèih duhkyùhn
    syù la, juhng mjì jèunglòih jouh mātyéh.

17. Néi búnlòih séung heui bīnsyu ga?

18. Jèung sìnsàang hauhlòih (or sāuméi) yáuh móu heui Seuhnghói a?

19. Ngó búnlòih kàhmyaht séung lèih taam néideih, sāuméi ngó mdāk-
    hàahn, sóyíh móu lèih.

20. Búnlòih ngó yātgeui Gwóngdùngwá dōu msīk góng, sāuméi ngó hái
    Yèhlóuh Daaihhohk hohkjó léuhnggo yuht, ngó yìhgā sīk gong
    géigeui la.

80. General relative time follows the time-when pattern. The time
    words must come before the main verb of the sentence; they may
    either precede the subject or come after it similarly to movable
    adverbs (MA).

    Yíhchàhn ngó mei sihkgwo tòhngchāan. Yíhhauh ngó yātdihng yiu
    sìhsìh sihk.
    I have never eaten Chinese food before. I certainly will eat
    it often after this.

II. Specific Relative Time:

    A. ...jìchìhn (or yíhchìhn, means 'before', 'ago')

        1. Néi fangaau jìchìhn yám myám chàh a?
           Would you like (to drink) some tea before going to bed?

        2. Léuhngnìn (jì)chìhn ngó lèihgwo nīsyu yātchi.
           Two years ago, I was here once.

        3. Gó (yāt)nìn jìchìhn ngó móu heuigwo Hèunggóng.
           I hadn't been to Hong Kong before that year.

        4. Néi máai yéh jìchìhn yātdihng yiu manháh sìn gógihn yéh gé
           (dò) chín.
           You should ask how much the article is before you buy it.

        5. Hóu, ngó gàmmáan baatdím(jūng) yíhchìhn yātdihng dou.
           All right, I'll be here before eight tonight.

    B. ...jìhauh (or yíhhauh, means 'after')

        1. Kéuih doujó Bākgìng jìhauh yáuh móu ségwo seun béi néi a?
           Did he write to you after he arrived in Peking?

        2. Kéuihdeih sihkyùhn faahn jìhauh jauh chēutjóheui wáan la.
           They went outside to play after they had their meal.

        3. Léuhngnìn jìhauh kéuih jauh fàanlèih la.
           He'll be back after two years.

        4. Gwojó tàuh léuhnggo yuht jìhauh jauh hóu (yùhng)yih la.
           After the first two months it'll be very easy.

        5. Kéuih sihkyùhn sàamwún faahn jìhauh juhng séung sihk sàam-
           wún tìm.
           After finishing three bowls of rice, he still wants to eat
           another three.

    C. ...gójahnsí (while; when)

        1. Néi chìhnyaht lèih taam ngó gójahnsí ngó ngāamngāam chēut-
           jóheui, mhóuyisi.
           When you came to see me two days ago I had just gone out,
           I'm sorry.

2. Ngó yám jáu gójahnsí jùngyi yáuh yàhn tùhng ngó kìnggái.
   I like to have someone to chat with while I drink.

3. Ngó góng Gwóngjàuwá gójahnsí chéng néi mhóu man ngó góng
   ge haih mātyéh wá.
   When I speak Cantonese please don't ask me what language
   I'm talking.

4. Gauhnín sàamyuht gójahnsí ngó heuigwo yātchi.
   I went there once during March last year.

5. Gauhnín gójahnsí ngó juhng hái Jùnggwok.
   About that time last year I was still in China.

81. Specific Relative Time: To express temporal relationship to a
    specific event or point in time, a phrase made up of a noun,
    noun phrase or clause plus one of the timewords jìchìhn (or
    yìhchìhn), jìhauh (or yìhhauh), gójahnsí is used. The phrase
    behaves like a movable adverb.

góyaht jìhauh...	after that day ...
duhksyù gójahnsí...	while studying ...
Néi jáu jìchìhn, mgòi néi góng ngó jì.	Before you go, please let me know.

With number-measure time expressions, jìchìhn may mean "before
or ago" and jìhauh may mean "later."

léuhngnìn jìchìhn...	two years ago ...
sàamgoyuht jìhauh...	three months later ...

For jìhauh, note the following idiomatic use:

Ngó tèng kéuih gám góng jìhauh, ... When I heard him say that,...
                                    (Lit., After I...)

III. Ji or sìnji means "only then." It is used to express such
     ideas as "not until, not before, only after."

A. .....ji.....indicates   not.....until.....
                            not.....before.....
                            ....only after then.....
                            ....before............

1. Ngó yiu duhkyùhn syù ji heui.
   I can't go until I have finished studying. (I want to
   finish studying and then I'll go.)

2. Kéuih heuiyùhn Faatgwok ji heui Dākgwok.
   He will go to Germany only after he has visited France.

3. Néi yiu géidímjūng ji dākhàahn a? Ngó (yiu) hahjau sàamdím ji dākhàahn.
   When can you be free? I won't be free until three o'clock
   this afternoon.

4. Kéuih yiu géidò chín ji maai a? Kéuih yiu yihsahpmān ji
   maai.
   What's the lowest price he will sell it for? He'll sell
   it for not less than $20.

5. Kéuih wah sahpgo ngànchín m̀gau, yiu yah-ńgmān ji gau.
   He said ten dollars wasn't enough, it will take $25.

6. Nībún syù yiu sīk Yìngmàn ji duhkdāk.

7. Kéuih wah kéuih yiu maaijó kéuih gàan ngūk ji yáuh chín.

8. Kéuih wah kéuih gàmmáan m̀fàanlèih, tìngmáan ji fàanlèih.

9. Ngó sìn sung kéuih fàan ngūkkéi ji lèih jip néi hóu ma?

10. Néi yiu sihkgwo Tòhngchāan ji jìdou Tòhngchāan hóusihk.

11. Ngó doujó kàhmyaht ji jì kéuih gàmyaht m̀lèih.

12. Kéuih jingwah ji góng ngó tèng.

13. 1951nìn ngó ji lèih Méigwok ge.

14. Kéuih géisí ji fàanlèih ga? Kéuih (jidou) gàmjÌujóu ji
    fàanlèih ge.

15. Ngódeih tìngyaht ji heui hóu ma? Hóu, ngódeih tìngyaht ji
    heui.

82. The clause before __ji__ often servers as the condition of limiting
    circumstance to the latter; the limiting circumstance is an
    'imperative condition' to the action. After ji or __sìnji__ in a
    contemplated action, expressions like __yātdihng yiu__ (must), and
    __sìn__ (first) can be added.

Ngó (yiu, or yātdihng,yātdihng yiu, sìn) sihkjó faahn ji yám jáu.
I won't drink until I have eaten.

The difference between a sentence with and without ji may be
illustrated by the following sentences:

Ngó tìngyaht lèih.   I'll come tomorrow.
Ngó tìngyaht ji lèih.   I won't come until tomorrow.

In sentences 11 - 15 above, when ji or sìnji is used in the
following pattern: (doujó or jidou...'until') Time expression
ji ...., it always can be translated into English as 'not until
...' or 'not.... until....'

B. Ji and jauh compared:

_____ ji____ indicates   not......until......
_____ jauh__ indicates   when ....(then).....
(see Sent. 1-4)   whenever ..., ...
                            as soon as..., ...

Time expression ji_____   implies later than expected.
Time expression jauh___   implies sooner than expected.
(see Sent. 5-7)

_____ ji V NU M ... jē   indicates only
__ jauh V NU M ... jē   indicates only
_____ ji   NU M ... jē   indicates only
(see Sent. 8-10)

1. Ngó sihkjó faahn ji heui. Ngó (yāt) sihkjó faahn jauh heui.
   I won't go until I have eaten. As soon as I have eaten
   I'll go.

2. Ngó maaijó ga chè ji yáuh chín. Ngó maaijó ga chè jauh
   yáuh chín la.
   I won't have any money until I sell my car. When I sell
   my car, then I'll have money.

3. Néi (yiu) jouh sih ji yáuh chín. Néi jouh sih jauh yáuh
   chín.
   You won't have any money until you work. When you work
   you'll have money.

4. Kéuih wah kéuih dākhàahn ji lèih. Kéuih wah kéuih dākhàahn
   jauh lèih.

He said he won't come until he is free. He said he will
come when he is free.

5. Kéuih géidímjūng lèih ga? Kéuih baatdímjūng ji lèih ge.
   Kéuih baatdímjūng jauh lèihjó la.
   When did he come? He didn't come until eight o'clock.
   He came when it was only eight o'clock.

6. Néi kàhmmáan géidímjūng fan ga? Ngó kàhmmáan sahpyihdím
   ji fan ge. Ngó kàhmmáan baatdím jauh fan(jó) la.
   When did you go to sleep last night? I didn't go to slee
   until twelve o'clock. I went to bed when it was only
   eight o'clock.

7. Néi ga chè géisí máai ga? Ngó gauhnín ji máai ge. Ngó
   chìhnnín jauh máaijó la.
   When did you buy your car? I just bought it last year.
   I bought it two years ago.

8. Ngó ji heuigwo yātchi jē. Ngó jauh heuigwo yātchi jē.
   I've been there only once. I've been there only once.

9. Ngó ji yáuh sàamgo ngànchín jē. Ngó jauh yáuh sàamgo
   ngànchín jē.
   I've only three dollars. I've only three dollars.

10. Yìhgā géidímjūng la? Yìhgā ji sàamdím jē. (not 'yìhgā
    jauh sàamdím jē.')
    What time is it now? It's only three o'clock.

83. Summary of the ways of expressing Time Relationship in Cantone

1. with timewords alone: gàmyaht, kàhmyaht, hauhyaht; yìhgā,
   gauhsí, jèungloìh; seuhnggoyuht, hahláihbaaiyāt, chēutnín,
   etc. (see Les. 13)

2. with timeword phrases: jìchìhn, jìhauh, gójahnsí, etc.
   (see Les. 18)

3. with adverbs or auxiliary verbs and the sentence final 'la'
   jauh(lèih) ... la; jauh yiu ... la. (see Les. 15)

4. with particles such as: -jó, -gán, -gwo, etc. after the ver
   (see Les. 12)

Additional Sentences

1. Yìhgā kéuih gam wúih duhksyù, jèunglòih kéuih yātdihng hóu wúih jouhsih.
2. Kéuih chùhngchìhn yātgo láihbaai lèih sàamchi, yìhgā yātgo láihbaai lèih seichi, yíhhauh kéuih yahtyaht dōu yiu lèih.
3. Kéuih búnlòih dásyun duhkyùhn syù (jauh) heui Seuhnghói jouhsih, sāumēi kéuih móu chín duhk la, sóyíh kéuih yihk móu heui Seuhnghói.
4. Ngó sihkfaahn jìchìhn heui wángwo kéuih yātchi, sihkjó faahn jì- hauh, ngó yauh heui wángwo kéuih yātchi, kéuih dōu m̀hái (ngūk)kéi.
5. Néi heuijó máaiyéh jìhauh yáuh léuhnggo yàhn lèih taamgwo néi.
6. Yáuh yàhn wah sihkfaahn jìchìhn m̀hóu yám jáu, yáuh yàhn wah sihk- faahn jìhauh m̀hóu yám jáu, néi wah bīnyeuhng ngāam a?
7. Tàuhsīn dímgáai néi m̀lèih a? Tàuhsīn ngó yiu lèih gójahnsí ngāam- ngāam yáuh yàhn lèih wán ngó, ngó tùhng kéuih góngjó léuhnggeui- (wá) sóyíh chìhjó.
8. Yíhchìhn ngódeih hái Gwóngjàu jyuh, sāumēi ngódeih bùnjó heui Seuhnghói.
9. Gógàan jáugún ge choi gam gwai, ngódeih yíhhauh m̀hóu heui la.
10. Néideih bùnlèih jìhauh sìhsìh chéng lèih chóh lā.
11. Cheunggán gō gójahnsí chéng néideih m̀hóu góng syutwah.
12. Ngó heui Seuhnghói jìhauh juhng séung heui Bākgìng wáan géiyaht.
13. Kéuih yātdímjūng gójahnsí juhng hái nīsyu kìnggángái, waahkjé yìhgā kéuih yìhgìng fàanjó ngūkkéi lo.
14. Ngó sihkgán faahn gójahnsí yáuh móu yàhn lèih wángwo ngó a?
15. M̀gòi néi dángháh ngó, ngó sahpfānjūng jìhauh jauh fàanlèih.
16. Pìhngsìh kéuih fàangùng jìchhn yātdihng (or gáng) lèih wán ngó ge, m̀jì kéuih gàmyaht jouhmātyéh m̀lèih nē?
17. Gahnlòi kéuih jihmjím wúih sái faaijí la, sóyíh ngódeih sìhsìh heui sihk tòhngchāan.
18. 1939nìn ngó búnlòih séung heui Bālàih wáan ge, sāumēi Dākgwok tùhng Faatgwok dájyung sóyíh ngó móu heui.
19. Yìhgā kéuihdī saimānjai jihmjím daaih lo, gogo dōu hóyíh bòng- dākháh kéuih lo, chìh géinìn tìm kéuih jauh hóu ngònlohk lo.
20. Yíhchìhn hái Méigwok heui Jùnggwok yiu chóh sahpgéiyaht syùhn, yìhgā chóh fèigèi sàamyaht jauh hóyíh dou la, jèunglòih waahkjé léuhng-sàamdímjūng jauh hóyíh dou la.

Translate the following sentences:

1. Ngó pìhngsìh sihkyùhn faahn ji duhksyù duhkyùhn syù ji séjih.
2. Ngó yiu hohkyùhn Gwóngdùngwá ji heui Hèunggóng.
3. Ngódeih yiu sìn hohk góngwá, hohkyùhn góngwá ji hohk séjih.
4. Wòhng taaitáai wah kéuih yiu máaiyùhnsaai yéh ji fàan ngūkkéi.

5. Néi jì m̀jì kéuih géisí dākhàahn a? Kéuih gàmmáan ji dākhàahn
6. Kéuih wah gam dò juhng mei gau, yiu hóu dò ji gau.
7. Ngó máanmáan (dōu) yiu sihk dī yéh ji fandāk.
8. M̀ganyiu ngó gáudím ji fàangùng.
9. M̀hóu giuseng kéuih, kéuih wah kéuih gàmjlujóu baatdímjūng ji fàangùng.
10. Syùhn géidímjūng hòi a? Sahpdím ji hòi, maanmáan dōu m̀chìh. (take your time)

Below are English translations of sentences used in the vocabulary of this lesson as examples of usage. Translate these back into Chinese (numbers correspons to those in Vocabulary section.)

1. Have you been in India? I just came back from India.
2. Is India a very interesting place?
3. Have you lived in Nanking? I lived there for a long time.
4. How long did you live in Nanking?
5. Is there any ship going to Tientsin tomorrow?
6. This wine came from Tientsin.
7. Are you going by express? Yes, is there any express on the schedule today?
8. If there isn't any express then I'll go by plane.
9. Let me introduce you two (to each other).
10. Could you introduce me to (see) him?
11. Mr. Chen already introduced us a while ago.
12. I plan to go to China next year.
13. When does he plan to go? He has no plans at all.
14. Where are you going to spend this Saturday?
15. How do you feel? (or what do you think?) I feel fine. (or I think it is very good.)
16. Do you think it is right to do it this way?
17. Where were you during the last war? I was in China during the war.
18. When did the war end, do you remember?
19. He said to me ....
20. What did you tell them?
21. I don't know anything about it.
22. You are very nice to us.
23. I feel very happy.
24. See how happy the children are!
25. Why is he so happy today?
26. That chair is very comfortable.
27. His car is very comfortable riding, I don't feel tired after riding in it all day.
28. Do you feel comfortable riding on a plane?

29. He is very contented now.
30. Say, this house is really cosy!
31. After a few more years you'll be acclimatized.
32. Which restaurant is famous here? There isn't any famous restaurant here.
33. What dish in this restaurant is famous?
34. Everything in that store is quite inexpensive.
35. The expensive ones are very expensive, the cheap ones are very cheap.
36. Do you want an expensive one or a cheap one?
37. If it is inconvenient, please don't bother!
38. It's really convenient having a car!
39. Is it very inconvenient (for you)?
40. I may go tomorrow.
41. Is she likely to come? She isn't likely to come.
42. Are you likely to go to China next year?
43. Have you ever eaten Chinese food? No, I haven't.
44. Did you know him previously?
45. Hereafter I won't go by boat.
46. He hasn't come since.
47. What happened to him afterwards?
48. I'll come to see you before I leave.
49. I get up before seven each morning.
50. I'll call you up tomorrow morning before nine.
51. Did anyone come to see me after I went to work?
52. After we finish studying this book, how much longer do we have to study?
53. He came back right after you left.
54. In the past he was poor, but now he is rich.
55. Those houses didn't use to look like this.
56. I've always done it this way.
57. I never tasted such delicious Chinese food before.
58. I have never before had the slightest idea that he could speak Chinese.
59. Nobody knows what the world will be like in the future.
60. What you learn today certainly will be useful in the future.
61. This task certainly will be hard to do in the future.
62. Originally I didn't like to eat it, but now I like it very much.
63. Originally he was a teacher, now he is a student.
64. Originally I didn't want to go, but I have nothing to do now, so let's go and have a look.
65. What was your own line of work?
66. What happened afterwards?
67. Did he come again afterwards?
68. Later on he quit drinking.

69. He hasn't sung any for the last few years.
70. I like the last one.
71. To whom did that car belong finally?
72. How are you these days?
73. I haven't been there recently.
74. Have you heard from him recently?
75. I was busy a while ago.
76. Where were you a while ago?
77. What did you say just now?
78. Please drop in to see us often.
79. I am always wanting to buy a new car.
80. Do you eat Chinese food very often?
81. He doesn't usually drink, but sometimes he drinks a lot.
82. Ordinarily this book sells for three dollars.
83. Where do you usually eat your lunch?
84. He won't come until tomorrow.
85. I must finish my studying before I go.
86. It's only two dollars.
87. Gradually I forgot all of them.
88. It'll gradually become easier.
89. She will gradually be able to walk.
90. No hurry!
91. I'm picking it up now.
92. That ship is moving slowly.
93. Why doesn't he come?
94. Why has the train not arrived yet?
95. Why didn't you come to see us yesterday?
96. Why don't you answer me? I don't know how to answer you.
97. This question (sentence) is very hard to answer.
98. Have you ever been in Japan?

I. Reading

Yāt-gáu-sei-gáu nìn sei yuht, ngó hái Méigwok chóh syùhn heui Jùng-gwok. Hái syùhn seuhngbihn ngó sīkjó yātgo pàhngyáuh, kéuih sing Jèung. Kéuih haih yāt-gáu-yih-sei nìn hái Méigwok chēutsai ge, chùhnglòih mei fàangwo Jùnggwok.

Jèung sìnsàang yāt séuhng syùhn jauh sīkjó yātwái hái Méigwok duhk-yùhn syù fàan Hèunggóng ge síujé, nīwái síujé sing Hòh.

Syùhn hòijó jìhauh, daihyātyaht, Jèung sìnsàang chéng Hòh síujé yám chàh. Kéuihdeih góng Méigwokge tìnhei, Jùnggwokge tìnhei, Hèunggóng ge tìnhei.......... .

Daihyihyatht, Jèung sìnsàang yauh chéng Hòh síujé yám chàh. Kéuih-deih góng Méigwokge hohkhaauh tùhng Jùnggwokge hohkhaauh, Méigwokge hohksāang Jùnggwokge hohksāang tùhng Jùnggwok hái Méigwokge hohk-sāang.

Daihsàamyaht, kéuihdeih yātchái sihk tòhngchāan, kéuihdeih góng Méi-gwok bīndaat bīndaat deihfòng hóu wáan, bīngàan bīngàan chāangúnge chāan hóusihk.

Daihseiyaht, Jèung sìnsàang chéng Hòh síujé yám jáu. Hòh síujé wah: "Ngó m̀wúih yám jáu." Góyaht Jèung sìnsàang jihgéi yātgo yàhn yámjó dī jáu jìhauh, góngjó hóudò wá. Hòh síujé chóhhái jèung yísyu yāt geuí wá dōu móu góng.

Daihngyaht, daihluhkyaht, daihchātyaht, kéuihdeih yātchái sihkfaahn, yātchái cheunggō, yātchái wáan, kéuihdeih léunggo hóu hòisàm.

Daihbaatyaht gómáan, kéuihdeih sihkyùhn faahn, hái syùhn seuhngbihn hàahnglàih hàahngheui[1]. Hòh síujé man Jèung sìnsàang yíhchìhn hái bīnsyu duhkgwo syù hái bīnsyu jouhgwo sih, kéuih yìhgā heui Hèung-góng jouh mātyéh, jèunglòih hái Jùnggwok dásyun jouh mātyéh. Jèung sìnsàang tènggin Hòh síujé gám man kéuih, jīkhāak yātdī dōu góngsaai béi Hòh síujé tèng.

1. V làih   V heui ....   back and forth

Doujó daihsahpyaht, (syùhn) juhng jàang seiyaht jauh dou Hèunggóng
la, Jèung sìnsàang chéng Hòh síujé sihkfaahn. Jèung sìnsàang wan:
"Ngódeih yámdī jáu hóu ma?" Hòh síujé wah: "Chèuihbín lā!" Hòh
síujé yámjó dī jáu jìhauh deui Jèung sìnsàang wah: "Ngó yáuh geui
wá séung man néi." Jèung sìnsàang wah: "Mātyéh nē!" Hòh síujé
wah: "Yàhnyàhn dōu wah Jùnggwokwá hóu nàanhohk, néi wah haih mhaih
a?" Jèung sìnsàang wah: "Haih!"

Hòh síujé wah: "Néi yìhchìhn yáuh móu hohkgwo a?" Jèung sìnsàang
wah: "Ngó chùhnglòih mei hohkgwo." Hòh síujé wah: "Néi dásyun
hohk ma?" Jèung sìnsàang wah: "Ngó mei yáuh nīgo dásyun." Hòh
síujé wah: "Néi haih mhaih gokdāk kéuih yātdihng hóu nàan sóyíh
mséung hohk a?" Jèung sìnsàang wah: "Haih!"

Hòh síujé wah: "Néi chùhnglòih mei hohkgwo dímjì kéuih yātdihng
hóu nàan nē?" Jèung sìnsàang séungjó hóu noi sìnji daap kéuih (wah
"Hòh síujé ngó mìngbaahk néige yisi, néige yisi haih ...."

Daihsahpsàamyaht, syùhn juhng jàang yātyaht jauh dōu Hèunggóng lo.
Kéuihdeih léuhnggo yātchái sihkfaahn. Ngàamngàam ngó yihk chohhái
gójèung tóisyu, Jèung sìnsàang gaaisiuh ngó sīk Hòh síujé. Hòh
síujé wah: "Jèung sìnsàang néi haih Méigwok yàhn dímgáai néi gam
wúih góng Jùnggwokwá a?" Ngó wah: "Mgaamdòng! Ngó bunlòih haih há
Bākgìng chēutsai ge, doujó sahpyih seui sìnji fàanlèih Méigwok.
Léuhngnìn (yih)chìhn ngó séung heui Jùnggwok jouhsih, daahnhaih yáu
hóudò Jùnggwokwá ngó yìhgìng mgeidākjó lo, sóyíh Ngó chéngjó yātwái
sìnsàang gaau ngó. Ngó gauhnín hohkjó yātnìn, sóyih ngó yìhgā ji
hóyíh yuhng Jùnggwokwá tùhng néideih góng wá." Hòh síujé tènggin
ngó gám góng, móu góng mātyéh jauh hàahngjó chēutheui.

Daihyihyaht, syùhn doujó Hèunggóng. Hòh síujé deui ngódeih góng,
kéuih mséung hái léuihgún jyuh, kéuih yiu jīkhāak heui Seuhnghói,
hái Seuhnghói heui Bākgìng gin kéuih màmā. Gójahnsí Seuhnghói yìhgìng dagánjeung, móu syùhn heui Seuhnghói, yiu chóh fóchè ji heui-
dāk. Jèung sìnsàang wah: "Hòh síujé, ngó tùhng néi yātchái heui
hóu ma?" Hòh síujé wah: "Dòjeh néi la, Jèung sìnsàang! Hái Jùnggwok mSīk góng Jùnggwokwá haih hóu mfòngbihn ge, néi chìh yāt-léuhn
nìn lèih Bākgìng taam ngó lā!"

Jèung sìnsàang tùhng ngó sung Hòh síujé heui fóchèjaahm. Ngódeih
dáng fóchè hòijó, ji hái fòchèjaahm hàahngchēutlèih. Jèung sìnsàan
jihgéi deui jihgéi wah:

"Yùhgwó léuhngnìn yíhhauh ngó ji sīk kéuih, gám kéuih jauh mwúih
wah ngó haih yātgo mwúih góng Jùnggwokwá ge Jùnggwok yàhn lo!"
(to be continued in Les. 24)

II. Conversation

A: Ngāamngāam ngó tènggin yáuh yàhn wah syùhn gàmmáan jauh hóyíh
   dou Hèunggóng la, m̀jì haih m̀haih nē?
B: Ngó tèngginwah gàmmáan baatdím jūng yíhchìhn jauh hóyíh dou la,
   gám ngódeih juhng yáuh (or jàang) seidímgéi jūng jauh hóyíh dou
   Hèunggóng lo.
A: Néige bīu yìhgā géidím a?
B: Jàang (yāt)go gwāt seidím, ngāam m̀ngāam a?
A: Ngóge bīu yihgā haih jìutàuhjóu sahpdím jūng, néige bīu haih
   m̀haih m̀hàahng a?
B: M̀haih lā! Ngóge bīu yìhgā juhng hàahnggán.
A: Gám, waahkjé haih ngóge bīu m̀hàahng la, daahnhaih kàhmmáan sihk-
   yùhn faahn jìhauh ngó mangwo hái syùhn seuhng(bihn) jouhsih ge
   yàhn, kéuih wah ngóge jūng ngāam.
B: Gàmyaht haih m̀haih sahpyihyuht chāthouh a?
A: M̀haih, gàmyaht haih sahpyihyuht baathouh.
B: Ngó geidāk ngó mei séuhng syùhn jìchìhn, yáuh yàhn góng ngó jì,
   chóh sahpseiyaht syùhn jauh hóyíh dou Hèunggóng la. Ngó haih
   seuhnggo yuht yahseihouh lohksyùhn ge, doujó gàmyaht ngāamngāam
   sahpseiyaht. Sahpyātyuht yahsei, yahng, yahluhk ......sahpyih-
   yunt yāthouh, yihhouh ......dímgáai gàmyaht m̀haih chāthouh nē?
A: Ngó jìdou dímgáai la! Hái yāthouh góyaht néi m̀geidākjó, gwojó
   yāthouh jauh haih sàamhouh.......
B: Haih la! Haih la! Ngó gómáan tùhng néi yātchái sihkfaahn yámjó
   hóudò jáu, yámyùhn jáu jìhauh ngó jīkhāak heui fangaau. daihyihyaht, ngó fanjó yātyaht, m̀geidāk hái gósyu síujó yātyaht.
A: Néi géisí chēutsai ga?
B: Ngó? Ngó 1914 nìn sahpyihyuht chēutsai ge.
A: Sahpyihyuht bīnyaht a?
B: Sahpyihyuht yihhouh, ... Oh! nīgo yuht yíhhouh jauh haih ngóge
   sàangyaht, Gám, ngó gàmnìn m̀haih móujó sàangyaht.

III. Drill

Drill on M̀hóu and M̀....dāk

M̀hóu	M̀hóu	M̀-dāk
(better not)	(not fit; not good)	(can't be...)
M̀hóu jouh nīgihn sih	Nīgihn sih m̀hóujouh	Nīgihn sih m̀jouhdāk
M̀hóu sihk gódī yéh	Gódī yéh m̀hóusihk	Gódī yéh m̀sihkdāk

Mhóu tái nībún syù	Nībún syù mhóutái	Nībún syù mtáidāk
Mhóu tèng nīsáu gō	Nīsáu gō mhóutèng	Nīsáu gō mtèngdāk
Mhóu sái nīga chè	Nīga chè mhóusái	Nīga chè msáidāk
Mhóu yám gódī jáu	Gódī jáu mhóuyám	Gódī jáu myámdāk
Mhóu chóh nījèung yí	Nījèung yí mhóuchóh	Nījèung yí mchóhdāk
Mhóu hàahng gótluh	Gótluh gāai mhóu-	Gótluh gāai
gāai	hàahng	mhàahngdāk

Drill on chìhn-, hauh-, seuhng-, hah-

Kàhmyahtge kàhmyaht haih chìhnyaht.
Kàhmyahtge chìhnyaht haih daaihchìhnyaht.

Tìngyahtge tìngyaht haih hauhyaht.
Tìngyahtge hauhyaht haih daihhauhyaht.

Gàmnín haih 1955 nìn, chìhnnín haih 1953 nìn daaihchìhnnín haih
   1952 nìn.
Gàmnín haih 1955 nìn, hauhnín haih 1957 nìn, daihhauhnín haih 1958
   nìn.

Nīgo láihbaai haih nīgo yuht daihyātgo láihbaai, seuhnggo láihbaai
   haih seuhnggo yuht daihseigo láihbaai.
Nīgo láihbaai haih nīgo yuht daihseigo láihbaai, hahgo láihbaai
   haih hahgo yuht daihyātgo láihbaai.

Nīgo yuht haih baatyuht, seuhnggo yuht haih chātyuht, hahgo yuht
   haih gáuyuht.
Nīgo yuht haih yihyuht, seuhnggo yuht haih yātyuht, hahgo yuht
   haih sàamyuht.

Nīgo yuht haih sahpyihyuht, seuhnggo yuht haih sahpyātyuht, hahgo
   yuht haih chēutnín yātyuht.
Nīgo yuht haih yātyuht, seuhnggo yuht haih gauhnín sahpyihyuht,
   hahgo yuht haih gàmnín yihyuht.

IV. Translation

Translate the following questions and answer each of them:

   1. Where do you plan to go in August?
   2. Do you need my help in writing these letters?
   3. Can you go with him, and move that table over here to me?

4. I liked this place as soon as I saw it; I don't know how you feel about it.
5. Where were you last week?
6. Are you going to China next.month or next year?
7. Is it five minutes before two or five minutes past two?
8. After you have learned how to speak Cantonese, are you still going to learn to read the characters?
9. Why didn't you tell me before you went to the station?
10. Where were you before and after 1949?
11. Where did you live before you moved down here?
12. Were you teaching in China before you came to America?
13. Haven't you ever been to Hong Kong before?
14. Do you know who called on me just a while ago?
15. Where do you usually have fun ?   (play)

LESSON 19

RESULTATIVE COMPOUND VERBS

Vocabulary

fā   N: flower

> 1. Néi yáuh móu fā maai a? Yáuh, néi
>   jùngyi nīdī fā ma?
> 2. Nīdī fā gwai m̀gwai a?

mùn (M: douh)   N: door, gate

> 3. Gódouh mùn hái bīnsyu a? Gódouh mùn
>   hái gàan fóng hauhbihn.
> 4. Néi hái bīndouh mùn yahplèih ga?

chēungmún or chēung   N: window
  (M: go or douh)

> 5. Nīgàan fóng yáuh géidògo chēungmún a?
>   Yáuh luhkgo chēungmún.
> 6. Nīgo chēung hòidāk ma?

dihnyàuh (M: jek)   N: gasoline

> 7. Néiga chè yáuh móu dihnyàuh a? Ngó
>   ga chège dihnyàun sáisaai la.
> 8. Nīsyu dihnyàuh gwai ma?

sàandéng   N: summit

> 9. Néi yáuh móu séuhnggwo nīgo sàandéng
>   Ngó móu séuhnggwo nīgo sàandéng, kéui
>   séuhnggwo.
> 10. Nīgo sàandéng seuhngbihn yáuh ngūk ma

dāng (M: jáan)   N: lamp, light

> 11. Dímgáai nīgàan fóng móu dāng a?
>   Nīgàan fóng búnlòih yáuh léuhngjáan
>   dāng, daahnhaih .....

244

12. Gógàan fóng nē? Gógàan fóng dōu móu
dāng àh?

chaahk   N: thief, bandit

13. Néideih nīsyu yáuh móu chaahk ga?
Yìhgā yātgo dōu móu la.
14. Gógo chaahk móu ló mātyéh, lójó léuhngbún syù heui jē.

ngànhòhng   N: bank

15. Néi heui ngànhòhng jouh mātyéh a?
Ngó heui ngànhòhng ló chín.
16. Néi heui bīngàan ngànhòhng a? Ngó
heui Méigwok ngànhòhng.

tāai or léhngdáai   N: necktie
(M: tìuh)

17. Néi tùhngmàai ngó heui máai tìuh tāai
dāk ma? Néi tìuh tāai jànhaih leng la.

je   V: to borrow
   je ... béi   V: to lend

18. Ngó je yihsahp mān dāk ma? (Néi)
Je yihsahp mān béi ngó dāk ma?
Ngó móu yihsahp mān je béi néi.

màn   V: to smell

19. Ngó mànháh nīdī fā dāk ma?
20. Néi m̀jùngyi màn àh?
21. Néi yáuh móu màngwo nīdī fā a?

jíng   V: to repair, to fix; to prepare (dishes)

22. Néi sīk jíng bīu ma? Ngó m̀sīk jíng.
23. Néige bīu yáuh móu jínggwo a?
24. Gàmmáan jíng mātyéh sung a?

sàan   V: to close (door, gate)
(refer to note 84, -màai)

hahp   V: to close (book, eye, box, etc.)
(refer to note 84, -màai)

gáai   V: to untie
  (refer to note 84, -hòi)

dá   V: to hit
  dá- (refer to note 84, -hóu and hòi)
  dáhòi   RV: open
  dájih   VO: to type

                         25. Kéuih yáuh móu dágwo néi a? Móu;
                             kéuih móu dágwo ngó.
                         26. Bīngo dá néi a?

só (M: bá)   N/V: lock/ to lock

                         27. Néi sójó ga chè mei a? Ngó sójó la.
                         28. Néi sái m̀sái yuhng sósih só a?
                             M̀sái, ngó ga chè m̀sái yuhng sósih só
                             ge.

yuhbeih   V: prepare

                         29. Wòhng sìnsàang, néi giu ngódeih yuh-
                             beih daihgéifo a? Yuhbeih daihseifo
                             daihngfo léuhngfo.
                         30. Daihluhkfo sái m̀sái yuhbeih a?

jūk   V: to catch; to net

                         31. Kéuihdeih hái gósyu jūk mātyéh a?
                             Kéuihdeih hái gósyu jūk chaahk.
                         32. Gógo yàhn hái gósyu jūk mātyéh a?
                             Gógo yàhn hái gósyu jūk yú.

laahn   AV: be broken; rotten; overripe

                         33. Gójèung tói laahnjó làh? Laahnjó
                             hóu noi lo.
                         34. Nījèung yí laahnjó, m̀gòi néi chóh
                             gójèung lā.

láahn   SV: lazy

                         35. Kéuih haih m̀haih hóu láahn ga?
                             Haih, kéuih haih hóu láahn ge, māt-
                             (yéh) dōu m̀jouh.
                         36. Néi m̀hóu gam láahn dāk ma?

hèung   SV: fragrant

                              37. Nīsyu yáuh móu hèung ge fā a?
                                   Nīsyu yáuh hóudò hèung ge fā.
                              38. Bīndī fā hèung a?

hāak (or hāk)   SV: black; dark

                              39. Ngoibihn haih m̀haih hóu hāak a?
                                   Haih, ngoibihn hóu hāak.
                            40. Néi jùng(yi) m̀jùngyi nījì hāak ga?

lohkyúh   VO: raining

                            41. Gàmyaht yáuh móu yúh lohk a? Gàm-
                                 yaht móu yúh lohk.
                            42. Kàhmyaht haih m̀haih lohk hóu daaih
                               yúh a?

bàan (or bāan)   M: (measure for a group of persons)

                            43. Nībàan yàhn lèih nīsyu jouh mātyéh a?
                          44. Néideih hohkhaauh yáuh géidòbāan
                               hohksāang a? Ngódeih hohkhaauh yáuh
                               sahpbāan.

Reading

    Gauhsìh yáuh yātgo saimānjái kéuih hóu láahn, kéuih m̀jùngyi duhk-
syù yihk m̀jùngyi jouhsih ......

    Kéuih hái hohkhaauh fàanlèih ngūkkéi jìhauh kéuih màmā yāt giu
kéuih duhksyù kéuih jauh wah: "Ngó táimgin, ngó m̀duhkdāk syù."
Kéuih màmā wah: "Dímgáai néi táimgin a?" Kéuih wah: "Nīgàan fóng
taai hāak." Kéuih màmā wah: "Dímgáai néi m̀hòijeuhk jáan dāng nē?"
Kéuih wah: "M̀ ....!"

    Kéuih màmā man kéuih: "Néi bàhbā giu néi sé gófùng seun néi
séhéi mei a?" Kéuih wah: "Mei séhéi, ngó jì bāt laahnjó." Kéuih
màmā wah: "Juhng mei jíngfàan(hóu) mē? Gám, néi gójì Méigwok bāt
nē?" Kéuih wah: "Saimúi jejó juhng mei béifàan ngó."

    Kéuih bàhbā gaauyùhn syù hái hohkhaauh fàanlèih, táigin kéuih
hái ngoibihn wáan, kéuih man kéuih: "Ngó giu néi sung gobún syù

béi Chàhn sìnsàang, néi sungjó heui mei a?"   Kéuih wah: "Chàhn
sìnsàang jyuh gósyu haih m̀haih gógo sàandéng a?"   Gógo sàandéng
gam gòu, ngó m̀hàahngdākséuhngheui.

    Kéuih bàhbā yauh man kéuih: "Sìnsàang giu néi sé gódī jih néi
sésaai mei a?"   Kéuih wah: "Oh! Ngó séunghéi la! Màmā giu ngó
sihk gódī yéh, ngó juhng mei sihk, ngó yìhgā heui sihk la!."

    Yáuh yātmáan, ngoibihn lohk hóu daaih yúh, làuhseuhng yáuh géi-
go chēungmún, mei sàanhóu, kéuih màmā giu kéuih héisàn sàanmàai gódī chēungmún, kéuih wah: "Màmā! Ngó m̀sàandāk gódī chēungmún la,
ngó yìhgìng fanjeuhkjó la."

84. Resultative compound verbs: Resultative verbs (RV) are compoun
    of two members, in which the first or root verb indicates the
    kind of action involved, while the second shows the result or
    extent of the action expressed by the first.

    There are two types of resultative compounds: (a) Actual, in
    which the result or goal has been actually attained, and
    (b) Potential, in which the result or extent of the action is
    conceived of as being possible or impossible of attainment.
    The potential type is formed by inserting between the first
    and second members -dāk- for the positive and either the
    m̀-dāk- or -m̀- form is used for the negative.

    a. Actual type:

        Néi tènggin kéuih góng mātyéh ma?
        Do you hear what he says?
        Ngó tènggin.   Yes, I do.
        Ngó móu tènggin.   No, I don't.

    b. Potential type:

        Néi tèng(dākgin) m̀tèngdākgin kéuih góng mātyéh a?
        Can you hear what he says?
        Ngó tèngdākgin.   Yes, I can.
        Ngó m̀tèngdākgin.   No, I can't.
         Ngó tèngm̀gin.   No, I can't

    A Few of the Common Endings to Resultative Compound Verbs (RVE)

    -gin   indicates perception of what is seen, heard, or smelle
    -dou   indicates arrival at the goal of the action, extent of
            one's ability.

-dóu   indicates success in attaining object of the action.
-héi   indicates accomplishment of the action in time.
-hóu   indicates satisfactory accomplishment of the action.
-fàan   indicates 'back to an original or former state or
            position!
-jeuhk   indicates success in attaining object of the action.
-hòi   indicates completion of the action of opening ... or
            untying
-màai   indicates completion of the action of locking ... or
            closing.

Pattern Sentences

I. Use of Actual Type Resultative Compounds:

-gin (tái-, tèng-, màn-)

   1. Néi téigin góga hcichè ma?
      Have you seen that car?

   2. Gódouh yáuh yàhn góng syutwah néi tènggin ma?

   3. Gódī fā hóu hèung néi màngin ma?

-dou (lèih-, heui-, hàahng-, séuhng-, lohk-, sung-, jouh-, sái-,
       duhk-, gaau-, sé-, etc.)

   1. Kéuih fàandou ngùkkéi mei a?   Kéuih mei fàandou boh!
      Has he arrived home?   No, he hasn't.

   2. Néi hàahngdou gósyu jauh wúih táigin gógàan poutáu la.

   3. Kéuih wah gófùng seun yíhgìng sungdou la.

   4. Nīdī jih sédou tìngyaht jauh hóyíh séyùhn la.

   5. Kàhmyaht haih m̀haih gaaudou daihsahpbaatfo a?

-dóu (wán-, jūk-, tái-, tèng-, màn-, gin-, máai-, dá-, ló-)

   1. Néi wándóu néige bīu mei a?
      Have you found your watch?

2. Kéuih jūkdóu gógo chaahk ma?

3. Néi máaidóu góbún syù ma?

4. Néi lódóu chín ma?

-héi (jouh-, sé-, séung-, etc.)

1. Ngó gihn sāam jouhhéi mei a?
Is my coat already made? Have you finished making my coat?

2. Gófùng seun séhéi mei a?

3. Néi séunghéi kéuih haih bīngo ma? Ngó séunghéi la.

-hóu (jéng-, jeuk-, dá-, só-, etc.)

1. Néi go bīu jínghóu (or jíngfàanjóu) làh?
I suppose you had your watch fixed?

2. Ngódeih yìhgā jauh heui la, néi jeukhóu sāam mei a?

3. Néi dáhóu fùng seun mei a?

-fàan (béi-, jíng-, ló-, jeuk-, sung-, gei-, hóu-, etc.)

1. Kéuih jàang néi gódī chín béifàan néi mei a?
Has he returned the money which he borrowed from you?

2. Ngó ga chè jíngfàan la.

3. Néi lófàan dī chín mei a?

4. Ngó jeukfàan gihn sāam jauh lèih.

5. Ngó séung geifàan bún syù kéuih.

6. Kéuih hóufàan mei a? Hóufàan la, yáuh sàm!

-jeuhk (fan-, hòi-)

1. Kéuih fanjeuhk mei a?
Has he fallen asleep?

2. Mgòi néi hòijeuhk jáan dāng, dāk ma?

-hòi (gáai-, dá-, hòi-, etc.)

1. Ngó yāt gáaihòi tīuh tāai jìhauh, ngó jauh fanjeuhkjó la.
   As soon as I loosened my tie I fell asleep immediately.

2. NĪgàan fóng taai yiht (warm), dáhòi douh mùn hóu ma?

3. M̀gòi néi hòihòi douh mùn.

-màai (sàan-, só-, hahp-, etc.)

1. M̀gòi néi sàanmàai nīdouh chēungmún.
   Please close this window!

2. Néi chēutlèih gójahnsí, yáuh móu sómàai douh mùn a?

3. Chéng néideih hahpmàai bún syù.

II. Use of Potential Type Resultative Compounds:

-gin

1. Néi tái m̀táidākgin chè léuihbihn gógo yàhn haih bīngo a?
   Can you see who is the one in the car?

2. Ngó m̀tèngdākgin (or tèngm̀gin) kéuih góng mātyéh.

3. Gódī fā gam hèung néi m̀màndākgin àh?

-dou

1. Gàmmáan ngódeih heui m̀heuidākdou Hèunggóng a?
   Can we arrive in Hong Kong tonight?

2. Kéuih wah nīgihn sih kéuih m̀jouhdākdou.

3. Kéuih gàmmáan lèihdākdou nīsyu ma?

4. Hahgo láihbaai duhk m̀duhkdākdou daihyihsahpfo a?

5. NĪyihsahpmān m̀sáidākdou hahgo láihbaaiyāt jauh móu la.

-dóu

1. Ngó m̀wándākdóu néi gógo pàhngyáuh.
   I couldn't find your friend.

2. Néi táidākdóu gógo sàandéngsyu yáuh géidò gàan ngūk ma?

3. Ngànhòhng yíhgìng sàanjó mùn la, ngódeih m̀lódākdóu _ngán la.

-héi

1. (Néi) nīfùng seun géisí sédākhéi a, Chàhn sìnsàang?
   When can you finish writing this letter, Mr. Chen?

2. Néi séung m̀séungdākhéi kéuih haih bīngo a?

3. Nīgihn sāam gàmmáan m̀jouhdākhéi lo.

-hóu

1. Nīgo bīu m̀jíngdākhóu, yànwaih....
   This watch can't be fixed, because....

2. Kéuih tìuh tāai m̀dádākhóu yiu ngó tùhng kéuih dá.[1]

3. Gódouh mùn só m̀sódākhóu a?

-fàan

1. Ngó jínglaahn (or jínglaahnjó)[2] kéuihge bīu ngó m̀béidākfàan
   kéuih lo.
   I broke his watch, I can't return it to him now.

2. Néi ló m̀lódākfàan gódī chín a?

3. M̀gòi néi táiháh, nīgo biu jìng m̀jìngdākfàan a?

-jeuhk

1. M̀jì dímgáai ngó m̀fandākjeuhk.
   I don't know why I can't get to sleep.

2. Nījáan dāng m̀hòidākjeuhk boh.

1. Here 'hóu' is used as a PV to indicate satisfactory accomplishment of the action dá not as, a stative verb to describe the
   action performed as in 'kéuih dábō dádāk hóu hóu' (he plays
   ball well). The stative verb can never be used in the actual
   type; people never say 'Kéuih dáhóu bō la.'

2. In common practice, people may put verbal suffixes 'jó,' 'saai,'
   and 'gwo' after the Resultative Compound, in such cases as
   'fanjeuhkjó,' 'séhéisaai,' 'jingfàansaai,' 'táigingwo,' 'tèngging

-hòi

    1. Kéuih wah kéuih m̀gáaidākhòi tìuh tāai.
       He said he couldn't untie his tie.

    2. Dímgáai douh mùn m̀dádākhòi a?

    3. Nīdouh mùn m̀hòidākhòi.

-màai

    1. Nīdouh chēungm̲ún m̀sàandākmàai boh. (see Patt III)
       This window can't be closed.

    2. Dímgáai gódouh mùn m̀sódākmàai a?

    3. Ngó go bīu m̀hahpdākmàai, dímgáai a?

III. Final Particle 'boh' (or 'bo'), used to indicate the sense of
    a suggestion or 'so far as I can see...'

    1. Néi m̀hóu sihk boh.
       Don't eat it!

    2. Néi yātdihng yiu heui boh.

    3. Néi m̀hóu yám gamdò jau boh.

    4. Néi yiu faaidī fàanlèih boh.

    5. Néi yiu duhksīk (syù) ji hóu heui boh.

    6. Néi m̀hóu jihgēi heui boh.

    7. M̀haih boh! Ngódeih haih ǹggo yàhn boh.

    8. Ngó séung m̀hóu boh, yànwaih...

    9. Nīgihn dōu géi hóu boh.

   10. Kéuihge Gwóngdùngwá dōu géi hóu boh.

Additional Sentences

1. Néi tènggin kéuih góng mātyéh ma?
2. Néi hái gósyu tái m̀táidākgin ngó a?
3. Néi hái hahbihn táidākgin seuhngbihn ma?
4. Néi táidākdóu kéuih hái gósyu jouhgán mātyéh ma?
5. Gósyu gam hāak, néi táidākgin ma?
6. Néi hái ngoibihn tèngdākgin léuihbihn gódī yàhn góng syutwah ma?
7. Néi táidākdóu gósyu yáuh géidògo yàhn ma?
8. Nīga fèigèi gàmmàan heuidākdou Seuhnghói ma?
9. Nīgihn sih gam nàan néi jouh m̀jouhdākdou a?
10. Kéuih séuhngdou sàandéng mei a?
11. Hái bīnsyu máaidākdóu Jùnggwok bāt a?
12. Kéuih gam m̀dākhàahn, néi gindākdóu kéuih ma?
13. Ngódeih nīgo láihbaai duhkdākyùhn nīfo syù ma?
14. Gàmyaht bùndākyùhn nīdī yéh heui kéuih ngūkkéi ma?
15. Ngó ngāamngāam sàanjó jáan dāng kéuih yauh hòijeuhk(jó) kéuih.
16. Hái Méigwok máai m̀máaidākdóu Jùnggwok syù a?
17. Ngódeih hàahng yātdím jūng hàahng m̀hàahngdākdou gósyu a?
18. Néi gàmyaht hóyíh jouhdākhéi nīgihn sāam ma?
19. Kàhmmáan néi fandākjeuhk ma?
20. Néi léuhngdím jūng heui m̀heuidākdou gósyu a?
21. Nīdouh mùn sàan m̀sàandākmàai a?
22. Néi yáuh móu só(màai) mùn a? Sómàai la.
23. Nījáan dāng hòi m̀hòidākjeuhk a?
24. Ngó séung hòihòi nīdouh mùn, néi yáuh móu sósìh a?
25. Nīdouh mùn hòi m̀hòidāk(hòi) a? Ngó móu sósìh, m̀hòidākhòi.
26. Néi séhéi gófùng seun mei a?
27. Gófùng seun yiu géisí ji sédākhóu a?
28. Ngó ga heichè géisí ji jíngdākhóu a?
29. Néi nīga heichè móu géidò dihnyàuh, hàahng m̀hàahngdākdou gósyu a
30. Néi nīkdāksaai gamdò yéh ma?

Dir11 on Resultative Compounds

Néi tái mātyéh a?	Néi jouh gógihn sih àh?
Néi táigin mātyéh a?	Néi jouhhéi gógihn sih làh?
Néi yauh móu tái góbún syù a?	Néi yáuh móu jouh gógihn sih a?
Néi yáuh móu táigin góbún syù a?	Néi yáuh móu jouhhéi gógihn sih a?

Néi tèng mātyéh a?	Néi jíng góga chè àh?
Néi tènggin mātyéh a?	Néi jínghóu góga chè làh?
Néi yáuh móu tèng a?	Néi yáuh móu jíng góga chè a?
Néi yáuh móu tènggin a?	Néi yáuh móu jíng(fàan)hóu góga chè a?

Kéuih fàan ngūkkéi mei a?
Kéuih fàandou ngūkkei mei a?
Kéuih yáuh móu fàan ngūkkéi a?
Kéuih yáuh móu fàandou ngūkkéi a?

Néi béi chín kéuih àh?
Néi béifàan dī chín kéuih àh?
Néi yáuh móu béi chín kéuih a?
Néi yáuh móu béifàan dī chín kéuih a?

Néi wán góbún syù àh?
Néi wándou góbún syù làh?
Néi yáuh móu wán góbún syù a?
Néi yáuh móu wándou góbún syù a?

Néi (heui) ló góbún syù àh?
Néi heui lófàan góbún syù àh?
Néi yáuh móu heui ló góbún syù a?
Néi yáuh móu heui lófàan góbún syù a?

Néi ló chín àh?
Néi lódou chín làh?
Néi yáuh móu ló chín a?
Néi yáuh móu lódou chín a?

Néi gei góléuhngbún syù béi kéuih àh?
Néi geifàan góléuhngbún syù béi kéuih làh?
Néi yáuh móu gei góléuhngbún syù béi kéuih a?
Néi yáuh móu geifàan góléuhngbún syù béi kéuih a?

Néi máai bīu ma?
Néi máaidou bīu ma?
Néi yáuh móu máai bīu a?
Néi yáuh móu máaidou bīu a?

Translate the following sentences:

1. When did you work before?
2. Where did you live before you came here?
3. Have you ever been there before?
4. Five years ago I learned some Cantonese, afterwards I forgot it all.
5. Where were you during the war?
6. I was in China before the war. Afterwards I came back to the United States. I was in the States during the war.
7. Where do you plan to work in the future?
8. Thereafter we didn't go there (anymore).
9. Hereafter we won't go there (anymore).
10. Formerly, I couldn't speak a word of Chinese, now I can speak a little.

Below are English translations of sentences used in the vocabulary of this lesson as examples of usage. Translate these back into Chinese (numbers correspond to those in Vocabulary section.)

1. Do you have flowers for sale? Yes, I have, do you like these flowers?
2. Are these flowers expensive?
3. Where is the door? The door is at the back of the room.
4. At which gate did you come in?

5. How many windows does this room have? There are six windows.
6. Can this window be opened?
7. Does your car have gasoline? My car's gasoline is used up.
8. Is gasoline expensive here?
9. Have you been on the top of this mountain? I nave never been there, but he has.
10. Is there any house on the summit?
11. Why is there no light in this room? There were two lamps here,
12. How about that room? Hasn't it any either?
13. Do you have thieves around here? There are none left now.
14. The thief didn't take anything but two books.
15. What are you going to the bank for? I'm going there to get some money.
16. To which bank are you going? I'm going to the Bank of America.
17. Can you go with me to buy a necktie? Say! Your tie is really beautiful.
18. May I borrow twenty dollars? Could you lend me twenty dollars? I haven't got twenty dollars to lend you.
19. May I smell the flowers?
20. Don't you like to smell them?
21. Have you smelled these flowers?
22. Do you know how to repair a watch? No, I don't.
23. Has your watch ever been repaired?
24. What dishes are we going to prepare tonight?
25. Has he ever hit you? No, he never has.
26. Who hit you?
27. Have you locked your car? I already have.
28. Do you have to use a key to lock it? No, I don't have to use a key to lock it.
29. Mr. Huang, which lesson do you want us to prepare? Prepare lesson 4 and 5.
30. Do we have to prepare lesson 6?
31. What are they catching there? They are catching the thief.
32. What is that man catching? The man is catching fish.
33. Is that table broken? It was broken long ago.
34. This chair is broken, please take that one.
35. Is he very lazy? Yes, he is, he won't do anything.
36. Don't be lazy, will you?
37. Are there any fragrant flowers here? We have plenty of fragant flowers here.
38. Which ones are fragrant?
39. Is it very dark outside? Yes, it is very dark.
40. Do you like this black one?
41. Is it going to rain today? No.
42. Did it rain very hard yesterday?
43. What are these people coming here for?
44. How many classes of students do you have in your school? There are ten classes in our school.

SIMILARITY AND COMPARISON

Vocabulary

louh   SV: be old [1]

1. Kéuih yìhgā géi louh la? Kéuih yìhgā
   hóu louh la. Kéuih yìhgā m̀haih géi
   louh jē.
2. Gówái louh sìnsàang haih bīngo a?

ngái   SV: be low, be short (opp. gòu)

3. Ngó yiu yātjèung ngáige yí.
4. Gójèung ngáige yí laahnjó m̀chóhdāk la.
5. Néi jùng m̀jùngyi gójèung ngáige yí a?
6. Nījèung yí haih m̀haih taai ngái a?

fèih   SV: be fat

7. Dímgáai kéuih yìhgā gam fèih a?
8. Néi jùngyi sihk fèihge yéh ma?
9. Ngó m̀jùngyi sihk, yànwaih ngó m̀jùngyi
   taai fèih.

sau   SV: be thin

10. Kéuih haih m̀haih jùhnghaih gam sau a?
    Haih, kéuih yìhgā jùhnghaih gam sau.
11. Dímgáai kéuih sìhsìh dōu haih gam sau
    a?

1. Here louh means 'having lost the vigor of youth'; if the question
   is inquiring about the age, then one asks 'kéuih yìhgā géi dáai
   (or daaih) la?'

chèuhng   SV: be long

> 12. Gótiuh gāai géi chèuhng a? Gótiuh
>   gāai m̀haih géi chèuhng jē.
> 13. Nījì bāt taai chèuhng m̀haih géi hóu
>   sé.

fut   SV: be wide

> 14. Gótiuh gāai jànhaih fut la!
> 15. Haih m̀haih tìuhtìuh gāai dōu haih
>   gam fut ga? Haih, tìuhtìuh dōu
>   haih gam fut.

dyún   SV: be short (opp. long)

> 16. Nījì bāt taai dyún m̀sédāk.
> 17. Nījì m̀dyún, néi sái nījì lā.
> 18. Dímgáai nīgihn sāam gam dyún ga?

yiht   SV: be hot

> 19. Néi gokdāk gàmyaht yiht ma?
>   Gàmyaht m̀haih géi yiht jē. Gàmyaht
>   jànhaih yiht lo.

láahng   SV: be cold

> 20. Kàhmmáan nīsyu hóu láahng haih m̀haih
>   a?

lèuhng(sóng)   SV: be cool

> 21. Gàmyaht jànhaih lèuhngsóng la.

gányiu   SV: be important, serious

> 22. Nīgihn sih haih m̀haih hóu gányiu ga?
>   Haih, nīgihn sih hóu gányiu, m̀gòi néi
>   jīkhāak jouhjó kéuih.
>
> 23. Kéuih haih m̀haih guih dāk hóu gányiu
>   a? Haih, kéuih guih dāk hóu gányiu.

fèisèuhng   A: extraordinarily

> 24. Kéuih (nī)go yàhn fèisèuhng hóu.

25. Kéuih gógàan ngūk fèisèuhng leng.
26. Chóh fèigèi fèisèuhng jihjoih,
    yātdī dōu m̀gokdāk guih.

dougihk	P :	(suffix to SVs, indicating superlative or exaggerated degree)

27. Kéuih n̲àudougihk.
28. Ngó guihdougihk.
29. Gógàan poutàuge yéh pèhngdougihk.

-gwotàuh	P :	more than enough, (suffix to SVs indicating to a regrettable degree)

30. Gójèung yí gòugwotàuh ngó m̀jùngyi.
31. Nīgihn sāam chèuhnggwotàuh, ngo
    m̀jeukdāk.
32. Góga chè daaihgwotàuh, ngó m̀jùngyi.

-dākjaih	P :	more (or less) than enough (suffix to SVs, indicating to a regrettable degree)

33. Góga fèigèi saidākjaih, m̀chóhdāk gam-
    dò yàhn.

leihhoih		SV: severe; terrible
gàaugwàan, leihhoih, gányiu		(SV) A: seriously; terribly (when these words are used in the manner pattern; see Note 90, p. 303)

34. Dímgáai kéuih n̲àu dāk gam gàaugwàan a?
35. M̀jì dímgáai kéuih guih dāk gam gàau-
    gwàan nē!
36. Kéuih ga chè jànhaih laahn dāk gàau-
    gwàan lo.

dahkbiht		A/SV: distinctively, unusually, especially/ strange

37. Nīsyu gamdò ga chè, bīnga dahkbiht
    hóu a? Nīga dahkbiht hóu, ngó dahk-
    biht jùngyi nīga.
38. Kéuih nīgo yàhn hóu dahkbiht ge.

yáuhsìh   A: sometimes

39. Néi haih m̀haih sìhsìh sihk Tòhngchāan
    a? M̀haih, ngó yáuhsìh sihk Tòhngchāa
    yáuhsìh sihk Sāichāan.
40. Gójáan dāng yáuhsìh hòidākjeuhk, yáuh
    sìh hòim̀jeuhk.
41. Ngó jìbāt yáuhsìh hóu hóusé, yáuhsìh
    hóu nàansé.

pa   V: to be afraid of .....

42. Néi pa m̀pa hāak a? Ngó m̀pa hāak,
    kéuih pa hāak.
43. Yùhgwó néi m̀pa, néi tùhng ngó heui
    hóu ma?

chíh   V: look like, resemble

44. Kéuih chíh m̀chíh ngó a? Kéuih jàn-
    haih chíh néi lo.
45. Kéuih chíh gaausyùge.

hèimong (or mong)   N/V: hope, expect

46. Néi hèimong heui Jùnggwok yīkwaahk
    heui Faatgwok nē? Ngó hèimong heui
    Jùnggwok.
47. Juhng yáuh móu hèimong a? Yātdī
    hèimong dōu móu la.

Jùngmàn   N: Chinese (written language)

48. Néi sīk m̀sīk Jùngman a? Ngó m̀sīk,
    ngó sīk Jùnggwokwá jē.
49. Kéuihge Jùngmàn hóu hóu

yuhk (M: gauh, 'piece')N: meat

50. Néi jùngyi sihk yuhk ma? Ngó m̀jùngyi
    sihk fèige yuhk, ngó jùngyi sihk sau-
    ge yuhk.
51. Néi m̀jùngyi sihk yuhk néi jùngyi sihk
    mátyéh a?

fànbiht   N: difference

52. Nīga chè tùhng góga chè yáuh mātyéh
    fànbiht a? Yáuh hóu daaihge fànbiht,
    nīga chè gwai hóudò. (see Patt.III)
53. Nīga chè tùhng góga chè yātdī fànbiht
    dōu móu.

béi (or béigaau)   CV: than; compared with

54. Néideih léuhnggo bīngo gòu a?
    Ngó béi kéuih gòu.
55. Néi béi kéuih gòu géidò a? Ngó béi
    kéuih gòu hóudò.

béigaau   V/A: compare/ comparatively, rather, more

56. Ngó tùhng kéuih béigaau, néi jùngyi
    bīngo a? Ngó béigaau jùngyi néi.
57. Nīga chè tùhng góga béigaau, néi
    wah bīnga hóu a?

-gwo   P: used in comparison, similar to the Eng-
                               lish -er in the pattern 'X is taller
                               than Y'

58. Néi haih m̀haih gòugwo kéuih a?
    Haih, ngó gòugwo kéuih.(see Patt.
    III)
59. Néi gòugwo kéuih géidò a? Ngó gòugwo
    kéuih hóudò.

gáam   AV: dare

60. Néi gáam m̀gáam heui a? Ngó m̀gáam
    heui.
61. Néi gáam m̀gáam chóh fèigēi a?

-lóu   P: suffix means 'man' (fellow)

62. Gógo fèihlóu haih bīngo a?
63. Gógo boujílóu giu(jouh) mātyéh méng,
    néi jì m̀jì a?
64. Gógo haih Faatgwok lóu yīkwaahk haih
    Dākgwoklóu a?

-jái   P: diminutive suffix to nouns

                            65. Néi yiu gójèung tóijái yikwaahk gó-
                                jèung yíjái a? Ngó yiu gójèung yí-
                                jái.
                            66. Gósyu yáuh géidòjèung yíjái a?

yātyeuhng   SV: same (kind)

                            67. Nī léuhngga chè haih m̀haih yātyeuhng
                                ga? M̀haih yātyeuhngge, góga haih
                                Méigwokge, nīga haih Yìnggwokge.

                            68. Nī léuhngbún syù haih m̀haih yātyeuhn
                                ga?

yùhngyih (or yih)   SV/A: easy/ easily, easy to

                            69. Haih m̀haih hóu yùhngyih a? Haih,
                                hóu yùhngyih.
                            70. Nīgihn sih m̀haih géi yùhngyih boh, nè
                                wah haih m̀haih a?

yih-   P: prefixed to functive verbs, means 'easy
                                to....'

                            71. Nīgo jih néi hóu yihtáicho ge.

jeui   A: the most, -est (marker of the superlativ
                                degree)

                            72. Néideih sàamgo bīngo jeui gòu a?
                                Ngó jeui gòu.
                            73. Néi jeui gányiu sómàai douh mùn ji
                                lèih.

gamseuhnghá   Ph: about; around; approximately (comes afte
                                number-measure combinations)

                            74. Haih m̀haih léuhngmān gamseuhnghá a?
                                Haih, haih gamseuhnghá la.
                            75. Haih m̀haih seuhnggo láihbaaiyāt
                                gamseuhnghá a? Haih gamseuhnghá la.

                            Ph: about like this

                            76. Haih m̀haih gamseuhnghá a? Haih gam-
                                seuhnghá la.

Att: approximately this...

77. Haih m̀haih gamseuhnghá yéung ga?
    Haih gamseuhnghá yéung ge.

dīgamdīu   N: a tiny bit

78. Ngó yiu dīgamdēu jē.
79. Dīgamdēu jē, móuganyiu.
80. Ngó dīgamdēu dōu m̀pa.

tùhng   SV: be the same

81. Ngó tùhng kéuih tùhng yātgàan hohk-
    haauh duhksyù.
82. Ngó tùhng kéuih tùhng yātgàan poutáu
    máai ge.
83. Ngódeih tùhng (yātjek) syùhn lèih ge.

Reading

Ngó yáuh seigo pàhngyáuh. Yātgo sing Jèung, yātgo sing Léih, yātgo sing Wòhng, yātgo sing Jàu. Gógo sing Jàu ge jeui daaih, sóyíh ngódeih giu kéuih jouh Lóuh Jàu.[1] Sing Wòhng gógo haih gaau-syùge, sóyíh ngódeih giu kéuih jouh Wòhng sìnsàang. Gógo sing Jèung ge jeui sai, sojíh ngódeih giu kéuih jouh Jèung-jái. Yànwaih gógo sing Léih ge hóu ngái, sóyíh ngódeih giu kéuih jouh Ngái-jái Léih.

Jèung-jái tùhng Wòhng sìnsàang yātyeuhng gam gòu, yātyeuhng gam fèih. Ngái-jai Léih jeui ngái, ngáigwo kéuihdeih gamdògo (yàhn). Kéuih yìhkdōu jeui fèih, fèihgwo kéuihdeih gamdògo (yàhn). Lóuh

1. Lóuh (old) or A plus a surname is a familiar form of address,
   e.g. Lóuh Léih, A Wóng. Lóuh is more common in Mandarin and
   A in Cantonese. In degree of intimacy it is roughly equivalent
   to calling someone by his nickname in American English. When
   the suffix -jái is added to a surname, the resulting form is used
   for someone younger or smaller, rather like English nicknames in
   -ie (Chuckie, Jackie), although the Cantonese form is rather
   vulgar. After Lóuh or A, or before -jái, some surnames change
   their tone: high falling tone goes to high level (Jèung: A Jēung,
   Jēungjái) and low falling and low level go to high rising (Wòhng:
   Lóuh Wòng, A Wóng; Chàhn: Lóuh Chán, A Chán; Luhk: Lóuh Lúk, A
   Lúk).

Jāu jeui sau, daahnhaih kéuih jeui daaih yauh jeui gòu, sóyéih ngódeih yáuhsìh giu kéuih jouh Lóuh Jāu, yáusih yauh giu kéuih jouh
Gòulóu Jāu. Gòulóu Jāu yauh gòu yauh sau, Jèung-jái tùhng Wòhng
sìnsàang móu Gòulóu Jāu gam gòu, yihk móu kéuih gam sau, daahnhaih
kéuihdeih móu Ngái-jái Léih gam ngái, yihkdōu móu Ngái-jái Léih
gam fèih. Ngái-jái Léih jànhaih fèih, fèih dāk gányiu. Kéuih
saimānjái gójahnsí yíhgìng hóu fèih lo, daahnhaih kéuih yìhgā juhng
fèihgwo gauhsìh hóudò.

     Jèung-jái tùhng Wòhng sìnsàang pa jihgéi fèih dākjaih, sihkyéh
gójahnsí dōu hóu siusàm, fèih ge yéh, yātdī dòu m̀gáam sihk.

     Ngái-jái Léih kéuih hóu pa hahgo yuht fèihgwo nīgo yuht, chēut-
nín fèihgwo gàmnín, sìhsìh dōu (hèi)mong jihgéi yātyaht saugwo yātyaht. Daahnhaih, kéuih jeui jùngyi sihk yuhk----- jeui jùngyi sihk
féifèih ge yuhk, néideih jìdou kéuih yìhgā (yàuh) géi fèih ma?

                            Pattern Sentences

I. Description of an Object

     1. Nījèung tói hóu chèuhng.
        This table is very long.

     2. Nījèung tói dahkbiht chèuhng.
        This table is especially long.

     3. Nījèung tói jànhaih chèuhng lo!
        This table is really long.

     4. Nījèung tói fèisèuhng chèuhng.
        This table is extraordinarily long.

     5. Nījèung tói chèuhng dāk[1] gányiu.
        This table is extremely long.

     6. Nījèung tói chèuhng dougihk.

1. Here 'dāk gányiu' is a descriptive complement. In a descriptive
complement dāk will be spelled as a separate word.

7. Nījèung tói taai chèuhng, ngó m̀jùngyi.

8. Nījèung tói chèuhng (or dyún) gwotàuh.

9. Nījèung tói chèuhng (or fut) dākjaih.

10. Nījèung tói móu géi chèuhng (or m̀haih géi chèuhng).

11. Góji bāt gwai dākjaih, ngó móu gamdò chín máai.

12. Gógàan poutàuge yéh gwai dāk gányiu, daihyihchi m̀hóu heui gósyu máai lo.

13. Gógàan chāangúnge tòhngchāan dahkbiht hóu, ngó sìhsìh dōu hái gósyu sihkfaahn.

14. Góbún syù hóutái dougihk, ngó táiyùhn yātchi yauh yātchi, nīchihaih daihsàam chi lo.

15. Nīsèung faaijí chèuhng gwotàuh, m̀haih géi hóusái.

16. M̀jì dímgáai ngó gàmyaht gúiguih.

17. Ngó jùngyi chéungchèuhng gójèung.

18. Gógo bīu haih dáaidaaih ge boh, néi yiu ma?

19. Kéuih gàan ngūk leng ma? Kéuih gàan ngūk léngleng.

20. Gógo nē, gógo léngleng gógo nē!

85. The duplication of the stative verb is a common practice in Cantonese to stress the description. Tonal changes occur with the following combinations:

    middle-level becomes high-rising such as gwáigwai
    low-level   becomes high-rising such as yítyiht
    low-falling becomes high-rising such as chéungchèuhng
    low-rising   becomes high-rising such as yáaiyàaih

The high-level and high-rising keep their own tones, and the high-falling follows the rule of 'changed tones' ---- high-falling followed by another high-falling changes into high-level such as: gòugòu becomes gōugòu.

II. Similarity and Dissimilarity.

    A. Similarity (is as ... as ...):

        ... yáuh .... gam ... (pos.)

        ...tùhng ....yātyeuhng gam (pos.) ....
        ...tùhng ....yātyeuhng, (pos.) ....

     1. Nībún syù yáuh góbún syù gam hóutái ma?
        Is this book as interesting (to read) as that one?

     2. Kéuih yáuh néi gam m̀dākhàahn ma?
        Is he as busy as you are?

     3. Nīsáu gō yáuh móu gósáu gam hóutèng a?
        Is this song as good (to listen to) as that one?

     4. Gójì bāt yáuh móu nījì gam leng a?

     5. Nīfo syù tùhng gófo syù yātyeuhng, dōu haih gam nàan.

     6. Jèung sìnsàang tùhng Wòhng sìnsàang yātyeuhng gam gòu.

     7. Kéuihge jái yáuh ngóge jái gam daaih.

     8. Kéuihge bīu tùhng ngóge bīu yātyeuhng, dōu haih hái Méigwok
        máai ge.

     9. Ngóge yisi tùhng néige yisi yātyeuhng, hohk Jùngmàn yìngfah
        sìn hohk góngwá ji hohk séjih.

    10. Ngó gàan ngūk tùhng kéuih gàan ngūk yātyeuhng, dōu haih
        gauhnín máai ge.

    11. Nībún syù tùhng góbún syù yáuh māt(yéh) fànbiht a? Móu
        māt(yéh) fànbiht.

    12. Gósyu yáuh móu nīsyu gamdò yàhn a? Yātyeuhng gamdò.

    13. Kéuih yáuh kéuih gam gòu, gam daaih, yihkdōu yáuh kéuih gam
        leng.

    14. Kéuih tùhng kéuih yātyeuhng gam láahn yātyeuhng gam m̀jùngyi
        duhksyù.

    15. Nīgàan hohkhaauh tùhng gógàan hohkhaauh yātyeuhng gam daaih
        yātyeuhng gam hóu, yātyeuhng gamdò hohksāang.

B. Dissimilarity (is not so...as...):

... móu ....gam ... (neg.)

... tùhng .... m̀tùhng .... (neg.)
... m̀tuhng.... yātyeuhng gam.... (neg.)

1. Jèung sìnsàang móu Wòhng sìnsàang gam gòu.
   Mr. Chang is not as tall as Mr. Huang.

2. Chóh syùhn móu chóh fèigèi gam gwai.
   To go by ship is not as expensive as to go by airplane.

3. Léih sìnsàang móu Wòhng sìnsàang gam fèih.
   Mr. Li isn't as fat as Mr. Huang.

4. Nībún syù móu góbún syù gam hóutái.

5. Nīgo bīu tùhng gógo bīu m̀tùhng, m̀jì néi jùngyi bīngo nē?

6. Kéuih tùhng ngó yáuh dī m̀tùhng, ngóge chín hái ngósyu,
   kéuihge chín hái kéuih taaitáaisyu.

7. Néideih léuhnggo góng ge (wá) dōu haih Yìngmàn mē? Dímgáai
   néi góng ge tùhng kéuih (góng) ge m̀tùhng a?

8. Ngóge sàangyaht tùhng néige sàangyaht, tùhng yātnìn, tùhng
   yāt(go) yuht, daahnhaih m̀tùhng yātyaht.

9. Ngóge bīu tùhng néige bīu yātyeuhng gam gwai, daahnhaih
   ngóge móu néige gam hóu.

10. Chóh fóchè tùhng chóh syùhn yātyeuhng gam pèhng, daahnhaih
    chóh syùhn móu chóh fóchè gam faai.

11. Nīdī fā tùhng gódī fā yáuh māt(yéh) m̀tùhng a? Nīdī hèung,
    gódī m̀hèung.

12. Sái faaijí sihk tòhngchāan tùhng sái dōu chā sihk tòhngchāan
    yáuh māt fànbiht (or m̀tùhng) a? Oh! Yáuh hóu daaih fànbiht,
    sái dōu chā móu sái faaijí gam fòngbihn.

13. Nīgàan jáugún tùhng gógàan yáuh māt m̀tùhng a? Nīgàan gwai,
    (gó)dī choi yauh[1] móu gógàan gam hóu.

1. Yauh may sometimes be interchanged with yihk.

14. Faatgwokwá haih m̄haih móu Dākgwokwá gam nàanhohk a? Haih,
    yùhgwó néi hohk Faatgwokwá, bunnìn jauh sīk la.

15. Gósyu yáuh móu nīsyu gam láahng a? Yáuhsìh yáuh nīsyu gam
    láahng, yáuhsìh móu nīsyu gam láahng.

86. <u>Yáuh</u> (or <u>móu</u>) ...<u>gam</u> or <u>tùhng</u> (m̄tùhng) ... <u>yātyeuhng gam</u> ... are
    used to indicate similarity in the positive and dissimilarity in
    the negative.

   <u>yáuh</u> (be as much as) ... <u>gam</u> (so) ...
   <u>móu</u> (not so much as) ... <u>gam</u> (so) ...

      Nīgo yáuh gógo gam daaih. This is as big as that.
      Nīgo móu gógo gam daaih.   This one is not as big as that.

   <u>tùhng</u> (with; and) ... <u>yātyeuhng</u> (be similar) ...
   <u>tùhng</u> (with; and) ... <u>m̄tùhng</u>   (be dissimilar)

      Nīgo tùhng gógo yātyeuhng. This is the same as that.
      Jūng tùhng bīu m̄tùhng.   Clocks and watches are different.

   To indicate in what particular respect the two are similar or
   different, an appropriate SV follows <u>yātyeuhng gam</u> ...

      <u>tùhng</u> (with; and) ... <u>yātyeuhng gam</u>
      <u>m̄tùhng</u> (with; and) ...<u>yātyeuhng gam</u>

      Nīgo tùhng gógo yātyeuhng   This is the same size as that.
        gam daaih.
      Nīgo m̄tùhng gógo yātyeuhng This is not the same size as
        gam daaih.   that.

III. Degrees of Comparison, using 'gwo,' 'béi,' 'juhng,' 'jeui,'
     'dī,' and 'hóudò.'

   A.

    1. Gàmyaht hóu yiht, kàhmyaht yihtgwo gàmyaht, chìhnyaht jeui
       yiht.
       Today is (very) hot, (but) yesterday was hotter, and the
       day before yesterday was the hottest.

    2. Góbún syù hóu gwai, nībún syù béi góbún syù juhng gwai,
       góyātbún jeui gwai.
       That book is expensive, this one is even more expensive,
       but <u>that</u> one is the most expensive one.

3. Nījì bāt pèhnggwo gójì daahnhaih béi gójì housái.
   This pen is cheaper than that one, but better for writing.

4. Haih m̀haih nīgàan fóng daaihgwo gógàan a?
   Isn't this room larger than that one?

5. Haih m̀haih nīgàan fóng béi gógàan daaih a?
   Isn't this room larger than that one?

6. Kéuih tàuhsīn cheung gógéisáu gō, néi gokdāk bīnsáu jeui houtèng a?

7. Ngó jùngyi chóh syùhn, ngó gokdāk chóh syùhn jeui jihjoih.

8. Bīngo ga chè jeui leng a? Ngó m̀jì bīngo ga chè jeui leng, daahnhaih ngó jì néi ga chè lenggwo ngó ga.

9. Kéuih haih m̀haih daaihgwo[1] néi a? Haih, kéuih daaihgwo ngó.

10. Nī léuhnggo láihbaai dōu gám yiht, géisí sīnji wúih lèuhngdī a?

11. Gàmyahtge tìnhei béi kàhmyaht hóu, daahnhaih béi kàhmyaht yiht boh.

12. Gàmyaht yihtgwo kàhmyaht, daahnhaih móu chìhnyaht gam yiht, chìhnyaht jànhaih yiht lo.

13. Wòhng sìnsàang gòu, Léih sìnsàang juhng gòudī, Jèung sìnsàang jeui gòu.

14. Néi gokdāk yìhgā haih m̀haih lèuhngdī la.

15. Néi wah gàmyaht lèuhnggwo kàhmyaht àh! Ngó wah m̀haih, ngó wah gàmyaht yihtgwo kàhmyaht.

B.

1. Néideih léuhnggo bīngo daaih a? Kéuih daaihgwo ngó. Kéuih daaih(gwo) néi géidò seui a? Kéuih daaih(gwo) ngó sàamseui.
   Which of you two is older? He is older than I. How many years older (than you) is he? He is three years older.

1. Here 'daaih' means 'old in age,' i.e. A daaihgwo B, A is older than B.

2. Kéuih haih m̀haih gòugwo néi hóudò a? M̀haih, kéuih gòugwo
   ngó (yāt)dī jē.
   Is he much taller than you? No, he is only slightly taller
   than I.

3. Nībún syù haih m̀haih gwai hóudò a? M̀haih, nībún gwaigwo
   góbún (yāt)dī jē.
   Is this book much more expensive? No, it is only slightly
   more expensive than that one.

4. Wòhng sìnsàang yíhgìng hóu gòu la, daahnhaih Léih sìnsàang
   juhng gòugwo Wòhng sìnsàang (yāt)dī.

5. Néi gokdāk yìhgā haih m̀haih lèuhnggwo kàhmyaht (yāt)dī a?

6. Néideih léuhnggo ge Gwóngdùngwá bīngo hóu a? Kéuihge hóu.
   Hóugwo néi hóudò àh? Hóugwo ngó hóudò.

7. Nīfo syù dògwo gófo géidò jih a? Dògwo gófo yihbaakgéi jih

8. Nībún syù gwaigwo góbún àh? Haih. Gwai géidò a? Gwai sàam
   mān.

9. Nījèung tói pèhng léuhngmān lā, pèhng léuhngmān ngó jauh
   máai la.

10. Dímgáai nībún syù gwaigwo góbún syù gamdò ga?

C.

1. Nībún syù béi góbún nàanduhkdī.
   This book is a little bit more difficult to read than that
   book.

2. Nībún syù béi góbún yihduhk dī.
   This book is a little bit easier to study than that one.

3. Nīgihn sāam béi gógihn sāam hóutáidī.
   This coat is better-looking than that one.

4. Gámyéung wúih hóutáidī. Gámyéuhng wúih hóusihkdī, etc.
   This way it will look better. This way it will taste bette
   etc.

5. Nīsáu gō gám cheung hóu (or yih) cheungdī.
   The song will be easier to sing this way.

6. Nīgo jih gám sé hóu (or yih) sédī.

7. Nīgihn sih gám jouh hóu (or yih) jouhdī.

8. Nijèung yí gám chóh hóu (or yih) chóhdī.

9. Nibún syù gám duhk hóu (or yih) duhkdī.

10. Nitìuh yú gám jyú hóusihkdī.

87. a. -gwo or béi used in Comparison:

-gwo as a suffix is similar to the English '-er than.'

Ngó béi kéuih gòu.   I am taller than he.

When béi is used in comparison, the positive form of SV is used i.e.

Ngó béi kéuih gòu,
not Ngó béi kéuih m̀gòu, or Ngó m̀béi kéuih gòu.

The comparison form with -gwo is the more common one.

b. Juhng and jeui (or ji) are adverbs used to indicate degrees of comparison.

When it is desired to state that a person or thing is larger, for intance, than one which is already regarded as large, the adverb juhng (even more) is used:

Nīgo bīu gwai, gógo bīu   This watch is expensive, but that
   juhng gwai.   one is even more expensive.

The adverb jeui (or ji) 'the most, -est' before SV indicates the superlative degree:

Ni-sàamgo bīu bīngo   Of these three watches, which is
   (bīu) jeui gwai a?   most expensive?
Gógo jeui gwai.   That one is most expensive.

c. (yät)dī or hóudò follow the SV to indicate the comparative.

Kéuih gòudī.   He is taller.
Kéuih gòu hóudò.   He is much taller.
Kéuih gòugwo ngó dī. He is a little bit taller than I.
Kéuih gòugwo ngó hóudò. He is much taller than I.

Additional Sentences

1. Fèihlóu tùhng saulóu yáuh mātyéh fànbiht a? Fèihlóu pa yiht, saulóu móu (fèihlóu) gam pa yiht.
2. Gàmyaht yiht dākjaih, m̀sái duhksyù la, tìngyaht jìutòuhjóu sìnji duhk lā.
3. Kéuih yìngfahn sihk sau yuhk, m̀yìngfahn sihk fèih yuhk, daahn-haih kéuih wah sau yuhk móu fèih yuhk gam hóusihk, sóyìh yaht-yaht sihk fèih yuhk.
4. Ngó séung fèih daahnhaih ngó yahtyaht sihk féifèihge yuhk (ngó) dōu m̀fèih.
5. Nìgihn sāam chèuhng dākjaih, ngó m̀jeukdak, yùhgwó néi jùngyi néi lóheui jeuk lā.
6. Yùhgwó gógihn sāam m̀haih chèuhng dākjaih, ngó yìhgìng máaijó (kéuih) lo.
7. Hóu m̀hóu nìk gógihn sāam lèih béigaauháh a? Yùhgwó gógihn dyúngwo nìgihn, ngó jauh máai nìgihn.
8. Yìhga yìhgìng hāak la, lohkyúh lohkdāk gam gàaugwàan, néideih m̀hóu jáu la, hái (nì)syu jyuh yātmáan lá.
9. Ngó hèimong nìgihn sāam móu gógihn gam chèuhng, gám wúih hóu-taidì, néi wah haih m̀haih a?
10. Ngódeih gósyu yáuhsìh yítyiht, yáuhsìh léunglèuhng, yùhgwó néi pa yiht, jeui hóu sìn sé fùng seun heui manháh.
11. Kéuih ga chè tùhng ngó ga chè yātyeuhng gam gauh, yuhng hóudò dihnyàuh, yáuhsìh hàahng yātjahngāan jë, jauh yuhngjó hóudò (dihnyàuh) la.
12. Kéuih ga chè béi ngó ga sàndì, waahkjé hóyìh séuhngdāk gógo sàandéng.
13. Ngó jyuh gógàan ngūk gauh dākjaih, (gó)dī chēungmún hóu sai, sóyìh gàangàan fóng dōu hóu hāak.
14. Ngáige ngūk móu gòuge ngūk gam hóutái, daahnhaih gòuge ngūk móu ngáige ngūk gam hóujyuh.
15. Dyúnge sāam móu chèuhngge sāam gam hóutái, daahnhaih chèuhngge sāam móu dyúnge sāam gam hóujeuk.

Translate the following sentences:

1. I don't know how to fix it. Do you mind having a look at it to see whether it is still fixable?
2. Last night I closed the window, now I can't open it.
3. Last night he couldn't get to sleep because the door wouldn't lock.
4. I didn't get the money back (from the bank), so I didn't pay him back.

5. Why don't you turn on the light? Is it out of order?
6. Can we get to Hong Kong tonight? If not, how about tomorrow morning?
7. Has your child recovered? He recovered some time ago. It is kind of you to ask about it.
8. Do you recall who he is? I recall his last name, but I can't recall what his first name is.
9. Finally I found him; he said he already had spent all the money and had no money to pay me back.
10. Can't you see it?! Is it that the room is too dark or that your eyesight is not very good?
11. He said you can't lock this door without the key. (He said: if you want to lock this door, you must have the key; only then can you lock it.)
12. Can you see that boat? Can you see how many persons are on the boat? Can you tell (see) what clothing they are wearing?
13. He said he can't get to sleep without a light, so I have turned on the light.
14. The students have not arrived yet. Why did you turn on all the lights?
15. So far as I can see your car can't be repaired, Do you know which part (where it) is broken?

Below are English translations of sentences used in the vocabulary of this lesson as examples of usage. Translate these back into Chinese (numbers correspond to those in Vocabulary section.)

1. How old is he? He is very old now. He isn't very old.
2. Who is that old gentleman?
3. I want a low chair.
4. That low chair is broken, it's unusable.
5. Do you like that low chair?
6. Isn't this chair too low?
7. Why is he so fat now?
8. Do you like to eat fatty things?
9. I don't, because I don't want to be too fat.
10. Is he still so thin? Yes, he is still as thin as ever.
11. Why is he always so thin?
12. How long is that street? It isn't very long.
13. This pen is too long and not very easy to use.
14. That street is really wide!
15. Do all the streets have the same width? Yes, all the streets are the same width.
16. This pen is too short to use.

17. This one is not short, use this one.
18. Why is this coat so short?
19. Do you think it's hot today? It isn't very hot today. It is hot today.
20. Wasn't it very cold here last night?
21. It's cool today!
22. Is this a very important matter? Yes, it's a very important matter. Please do it right away.
23. Is he very tired? Yes, he is very tired.
24. He is a very nice fellow.
25. His house is extraordinarily beautiful.
26. Riding on a plane is very comfortable, you don't feel tired at all.
27. He is awfully angry.
28. I'm awfully tired.
29. The things sold in that store are all at rock bottom price.
30. The chair is too high, I don't like it.
31. The coat is too long, I can't wear it.
32. The car is too big, I don't like it.
33. The plane is too small; it can't seat so many persons.
34. Why is he so mad?
35. I don't know why he is so extremely tired!
36. His car is in terribly bad shape. (or His car is smashed.)
37. Of these cars here, which one is especially good? This one is especially good, I like this one.
38. He is a strange person.
39. Do you eat Chinese food very often? No, sometimes I do, sometimes I don't.
40. That light sometimes works and sometimes doesn't.
41. Sometimes my pen writes well, but sometimes it doesn't.
42. Are you afraid of the dark? I am not afraid but he is.
43. If you aren't afraid, how about going with me?
44. Does he look like me? He certainly does.
45. He looks like a teacher.
46. Do you expect to go to China or France? I hope to go to China.
47. Is there any hope? Not a bit.
48. Do you know Chinese? I can't read it, I can only speak it.
49. His Chinese is very good.
50. Do you like (to eat) meat? I don't like fat meat, I like lean meat.
51. If you don't like (to eat) meat, what do you like?
52. What is the difference between this car and that one? There is a big difference, this car is more expensive.
53. There isn't any difference between these two cars.
54. Which of you two is taller? I am taller.
55. How much taller are you than he? I'm much taller than he.

56. Which of us do you like better, him or me? I like you better.
57. Which of these two cars do you think is better?
58. Are you taller than he? Yes, I am.
59. How much taller are you than he? I'm much taller than he is.
60. Do you dare to go? No, I don't.
61. Do you dare to ride in a plane?
62. Who is that fat fellow?
63. Do you know what's the name of the newspaper vender?
64. Is he a Frenchman or a German?
65. Do you want the small table or the small chair? I want the
    small chair.
66. How many small chairs are there over there?
67. Are these two cars the same (kind)? No, that one is made in
    America, this one is made in English.
68. Are these two books the same?
69. Isn't it easy? Yes, it is.
70. So far as I see, this isn't very easy to do. What do you say?
71. This character is very easy to misread.
72. Which of you three is the tallest? I'm the tallest.
73. The most important thing is to lock the door before you come
    here.
74. Is it about two dollars? Yes, just about.
75. Was that around last Monday? Yes, it was about that time.
76. About like this? Yes, about like that.
77. Is it about this way? (lit. ... about this kind of appearance).
    Yes, it is about that way. (Discussing an action or the
    appearance of an object.)
78. I just want a tiny bit.
79. It's only a tiny bit, it doesn't matter!
80. I'm not a bit afraid.
81. I go to the same school with him.
82. I bought it from the same store as he did.
83. We came by the same boat.

LESSON 21

MEASURING AND DISTANCE

Vocabulary

yúhn

SV: be far

1. Yúhn myúhn a? Myúhn.
2. Nītìuh louh haih mhaih hóu yúhn a? Mhaih géi yúhn jē.
3. Bīntìuh louh yúhn a?

káhn

SV: be near

4. Nītìuh louh haih mhaih káhngwo gótìuh a? Haih, nītìuh káhn hóudò.
5. Haih mhaih hóu káhn a? Mhaih, mhaih hóu káhn.

chúhng

SV: be heavy

6. Gótìuh yú géi chúhng a?
7. Kéuih haih mhaih chúhnggwo néi a?

hèng

SV: be light (opp. heavy)

8. Kéuih haih mhaih hèngjó hóudò a? Haih, kéuih gauhnín hèngjó, yìhgā yauh chúhngfàan la.
9. Néi hèng dī yikwaahk kéuih hèng dī a?

pòhngbīn

PW: the side of, flank, beside

10. Ngó chóhhái néi pòhngbīn dāk ma? Dāk, dāk, chéng chóh, chéng chóh.
11. Gójèung tói pòhngbīn yáuh móu yí a? Gójèung tói pòhngbīn yáuh sàamjèung yí.
12. Néi pòhngbīn yáuh móu yàhn a?
13. Góbún syù(ge) pòhngbīn yáuh léuhngjī bāt, néi táigin ma?

276

jūnggāan

PW: the center

14. Néi sīk m̀sīk jūnggāan gógo jih a?
    Ngó m̀sīk jūnggāan gógo jih.
15. Kéihhái jūnggāan gógo yàhn haih
    bīngo a?

deuimin

PW: opposite

16. Haih m̀haih hái gógāan poutáu deuimin
    a? Haih, haih hái gógāan poutáu
    deuimin.
17. Deuimin gógāan haih mātyéh poutáu a?

Sàamfàahnsíh
  (or Gauhgāmsāan)

PW: San Francisco

18. Néi yáuh móu heuigwo Sàamfàahnsíh a?
    Ngó móu heuigwo Sàamfàahnsíh.
19. Sàamfàahnsíh hóuwáan ma?

Nīuyēuk

PW: New York

20. Nīuyēuk haih m̀haih hóu hóuwáan a?
    Haih, Nīuyēuk hóu hóuwáan.
21. Nīuyēuk yáuh móu Sàamfàahnsíh gam
    hóuwáan a? Niuyēuk hóuwáangwo
    Sàamfàahnsíh hóudò.

Tàahnhēungsāan

PW: Honolulu

22. Tàahnhēungsāan (deihfòng) daaih ma?
    M̀haih géi daaih jē.
23. Yáuh móu New Haven gam daaih a?
    Daaihgwo New Haven hóudò.

Yìnggwok

PW: England

24. Gójek syùhn haih m̀haih heui Yìnggwok
    ga? Gójek syùhn m̀haih heui Yìnggwok
    ge.
25. Néi yáuh móu heuigwo Yìnggwok a?

Maksāigō

PW: Mexico

26. Maksāigō yáuh móu Tàahnhēungsāan
    gam hóuwáan a? Maksāigō móu Tàahn-
    hēungsāan gam hóuwáan.

27. Néi yáuh móu heuigwo Maksāigō a?

Gànàdaaih   PW: Canada

28. Gànàdaaih haih m̀haih yáuh hóudò Faat-
    gwok yàhn a? M̀haih, kéuihdeih haih
    Gànàdaaih yàhn, daahnhaih kéuihdeih
    góng Faatgwok wá.
29. Gànàdaaih yáuh móu Jùnggwok yàhn a?

Gáulùhng   PW: Kowloon

30. Gáulùhng haih m̀haih yātdaat deihfòng-
    ge méng a?
31. Haih, haih yātdaat deihfòngge méng.

Tòihwāan   PW: Taiwan, Formosa

32. Tòihwāan haih m̀haih hái Daaihsāi-
    yèuhng a? (Atlantic Ocean)
33. M̀haih, Tòihwāan hái Taaipìhngyèuhng.
    (Pacific Ocean)

gō (or gòhgō, agō,   N: elder brother
   daaihlóu)

34. Néi yáuh géidògo gō a? Ngó yáuh
    léuhnggo gō.
35. Gógo haih m̀haih néi agō a?

gājē (or jē, jèhjē)   N: elder sister

36. Néige gājē yáuh saimānjái ma?

jímúi   N: sisters

37. Néi yáuh géidò jímúi a?

hìngdaih   N: brothers

38. Néi yáuh géi(dògo) hìngdaih a?
    Ngó yáuh sàam hìngdaih.

fùng   N: wind

39. Kàhnyaht nīsyu hóu daaih fùng haih
    m̀haih a? Haih, kàhmyaht nīsyu hóu
    daaih fùng.

síng (M: tìuh)   N: rope
  sìhng jái (M: tìuh)   N: cord, string

> 40. Nītìuh síng gau chèuhng ma? Nītìuh
>   síng m̀gau chèuhng.
> 41. Néi yiu géi chèuhng ge síng a?

sáu (M: jèk)   N: hand

> 42. Yātgo yàhn yáuh géidòjek sáu a?
>   Yātgo yàhn yáuh léuhngjek sáu.
> 43. Haih m̀haih léuhngjek sáu yātyeuhng
>   chèuhng a?

hói   N: sea

> 44. Hói seuhngbihn yáuh mātyéh a?
>   Hói seuhngbihn yáuh géijek syùhn.
> 45. Yáuh yàhn wah syùhn hái hói léuih-
>   bihn ngāam ma? M̀ngāam

hòh (M: tìuh)   N: river

> 46. Gótìuh hòh giujouh mātyéh méng a?
>   Gótìuh hòh giujouh Wòhng hòh.
> 47. Wòhng hòh haih m̀haih hóu chèuhng a?

dóu (M: go)   N: island

> 48. Gógo dóu seuhngbihn yáuh móu yàhn a?
>   Gógo dóu seuhngbihn yáuh hóudò yàhn.
> 49. Gógo dóu yáuh géi daaih a?

-chyun   M: inch

> 50. Nījì bāt géichyun chèuhng a?
>   Nījì bāt seichyun chèuhng
> 51. Gójèung tói géichyun chèuhng a?

-chek   M: a Chinese foot (14.1 English inches)
  chek (M: bá)   N: a ruler

> 52. Yātchek yáuh géidòchyun a? Jùnggwok
>   chek tùhng Méigwok chek m̀tùhng.
> 53. Yáuh mātyéh m̀tùhng a?
> 54. Jùnggwok chek sahpchyun yātchek,
>   Yìnggwok chek sahpyihchyun yātchek.

55. Néi yáuh móu Yìng(gwok) chek a?

-jeuhng   M: ten Chinese feet (141 English inches)

56. Yātjeuhng yáuh géidò chek a?
    Yātjeuhng yáuh sahpchek.
57. Yātjeuhng haih géidò Yìngchek a?
    Yātjeuhng yáuh sahpyāt Yìngchek
    lìhng gáuchyun.

-bohng   M: transliteration of pound

-ōnsí   M: transliteration of ounce

-dēun   M: transliteration of ton

bohng   V: to weigh

ching   V: to weigh with a catty stick

ching (M: bá)   N: catty stick

58. Nītìuh yú géi chúhng a?
59. Nītìuh yú léuhngbohng chúhng àh?
    Nītìuh yú móu léuhngbohng gam chúhng,
    yātbohng chúhng jē.
60. Ńgòi néi chingháh gótìuh géi chúhng?

-gàn   M: catty, pound (Chinese), (1 1/3 English
                        pound)

61. Léuhnggàn gau ńgau a? Léuhnggàn
    taai síu, ngódeih yiu baatgàn.
62. Ńgòi néi béi nggàn ngó hóu ma?

-léung   M: an ounce (1 1/16 of a catty)

63. Yātgàn yáuh géidò léung a? Yātgàn
    yáuh sahpluhkléung.
64. Nītìuh yú yáuh móu yātgàn chúhng a?

-léih(louh)   M: a Chinese mile (1/3 of an English mile)

65. Hái nīsyu heui fóchèjaahm yáuh géidò
    léih(louh) a? Ńg-luhkléih gamseuhngh
66. Haih Yìng(gwok) léih yīkwaahk haih
    Jùnggwokléih a?

-bihn (or bín)   M: -side; part

67. Néi hái bīnbihn lèih ga? Ngó hái
    góbihn lèih ge.
68. Tàuhsīn kéihhái gójèung tói góbihn
    gógo haih bīngo a? Tàuhsīn kéihhái
    gójèung tói góbihn gógo haih ngóge
    pàhngyáuh.

dùng   BF: east

69. Ngó jùngyi hái dùngbihnge fóng.
70. Dímgáai néi jùngyi hái dùngbihnge
    fóng nē? Yànwaih dùngbihnge fóng
    móu gam yiht.

sài   BF: west

71. Néi haih mhaih sàiyàhn a?
72. Haih, ngó haih sàiyàhn, dímgáai
    néideih giu ngódeih sàiyàhn nē?
73. Oh,Yànwaih néideih haih hái sàibihn
    lèihge sóyíh ngódeih giu néideih
    jouh sàiyàhn.

nàam   BF: south

74. Seuhnghói hái Hèunggóngge nàambihn,
    haih mhaih a? Mhaih, Hèunggóng hái
    Seuhnghóige nàambihn.
75. Gànàdaaih hái Méigwokge nàambihn
    haih mhaih a?

bāk   BF: north

76. Kéuih haih nàambín yàhn yīkwaahk
    haih bākbín yàhn a? Kéuih haih
    bākbín yàhn.
77. Jùnggwokge bākbín haih mhaih yáuh
    hóudò sàan a?

jó   SV: left

78. Haih mhaih jó(sáu)bihn gógàan a?
    Haih, haih jó(sáu)bihn daihyāt
    gógàan.

79. Néi jó(sáu)bihn yáuh móu yí a?

yauh   SV: right

80. Kéuih hái yauh(sáu)bihn gógàan fóng
    àh? Haih, kéuih hái yauh(sáu)bihn
    gógàan fóng duhkgán syù.
81. Tàuhsīn kéihhái néi yauh(sáu)bihn
    gógo haih bīngo a?

yuhdóu   V: to meet with; to encounter

82. Tàuhsīn ngó hái gāaisyu yuhdóu yātgo
    pàhngyáuh.
83. Néi yuhdóu bīngo a? Ngó yuhdóu gauh-
    sìh gaaugwo ngó Gwóngdùngwá ge Wòhng
    sìnsàang.

tìhng   V: ston; park

84. Néi ga chè tìhnghái bīnsyu a? Ngó
    ga chè tìhnghái gógàan poutáu hauh-
    bihn.
85. Dímgáai góga fóchè tìhngjó a?

seun   V: believe

86. Néi seun m̀seun ngó gòugwo kéuih a?
    Ngó m̀seun néi gòugwo kéuih.
87. Néi jànhaih m̀seun àh?

jyun (or jyún)   V: to turn to

88. Jyun yauhsáubihn ngāam m̀gāam a?
    M̀haih jyun yauhsáubihn, haih jyun
    jósáubihn.
89. Néi m̀hóu jyunyahp(heui) gótluh gāai
    boh!

gìnggwo   V: pass through

90. Néi yáuh móu gìnggwo kéuih jyuh ge
    gódaat deihfòng a? Yáuh, ngó gìng-
    gwo kéuih jyuh ge gódaat deihfòng
    daahnhaih ngó móu wán kéuih.
91. Néi heui Yidaaihleih gójahnsí yáuh
    móu gìnggwo Faatgwok a?

gú   V: guess, think

92. Néi gú kéuih gàmyaht wúih m̀wúih lèih
    nē? Ngó gú kéuih gàmyaht m̀wúih lèih.
93. Néi gú gàmyaht wúih m̀wúih lohkyúh nē?

heung   CV: toward (in the direction of)

94. Ngó heung bīnbihn hàahng ngāam a?
    Néi heung dùng hàahng leuhngfānjūng
    jauhhaih la.
95. Yùhgwo ngó séung heui fóchèjaahm,
    ngó heung bīnbihn hàahng ngāam a?

lèih   CV: distant from

96. Fóchèjaahm lèih nīsyu yáuh géi yúhn
    a? (see Patt. II) Móu géi yúhn jē,
    yāt lèih(louh) gamseuhnghá jē.
97. Nīsyu lèih Nīuyēuk géi yúhn a?

jauhsyun...dōu...   A: even if...still...; even if...;
                                nevertheless...

98. Jauhsyun géi pèhng ngó dōu m̀máai.
99. Jauhsyun kéuih m̀béi ngó heui ngó
    dōu yiu heui.
100. Jauhsyun kéuih chóh syùhn lèih dōu
     yìngfahn dou la.

lèihhòi   V: to leave(a place)

101. Néi géisí lèihhòi Méigwok ga?

Useful Expressions

Mātyéh wá?   What?
Gám yiu tái ....   It all depends ....

Reading

A: Néi dímyéung lèih Méigwok ga?
B: Ngó chóh syùhn lèih ge.
A: Néi chóh géidò yaht syùhn a?
B: Ngó chóhjó luhkgoyuht syùhn.
A: Mātyéh wá?
B: Néi m̀seun àh?

A: Jùnggwok lèih Méigwok yáuh géiyúhn a?
B: Yùhgwó néi wah Sàamfàahnsíh lèih Jùnggwok géiyúhn, gám ngó hóyíh
   wah: Yáuh ngchìngéiléih yúhn. Yùhgwó néi wah Nīuyēuk lèih Jùnggwok géiyúhn, gám, ngó jauh wah: Yáuh baatchìngéiléih louh yúhn.
A: Jauhsyun (haih) baatchìngéileih gam yúhn, dímgáai yiu chóh luhkgoyuht (ge syùhn) gam noi a? Jeui maan jeui maange syùhn, yātdímjūng hóyíh hàahng sahpyihléih, yātyaht yahseidímjūng hóyíh
   hàahng yihbaakbaatsahpbaatléih, sahpyaht hàahng yihchìnbaatbaak-
   baatsahpléih, sàamsahpyaht hàahng baatchìnluhkbaakgéiléih, jeui
   noi jeui noi dōu haih hàahng yātgoyuht jauh hóyíh dou la, néi
   chóh gójek haih mātyéh syùhn a? Dímgáai yiu hàahng gam noi ga?
B: Ngó chóh gójek syùhn haih housaige syùhn ...
A: Jauhsyun néi chóh jeui saige syùhn, jeui sai jeui saige syùhn
   dōu yáuh chìngéidēun chúhng, gamdáaige syùhn jauhsyun yuhdóu
   fùng, yātdī dōu m̀sái pa, ngó geidāk, ngó tàuhyātchi chóh syùhn
   lèih, gójek syùhn yihchìngéidēun jē, ngódeih hái Taaipìhngyèuhng
   yuhdóu fùng, ngódeih hái Tàahnghēungsāan tìhngjó géigo láihbaai,
   jauhsyun haih gám, ngódeih léuhnggolèhngyuht jauh dou Niuyēuk
   la. Seuhngyātchi ngo chóh syùhn lèih, ngó chóh gójek syùhn
   haih hóu daaih hóu daaihge syùhn, yáuh sàammaangéidēun chéhng,
   hàahng sahpgéiyaht jauh dou Sàamfàahnsíh la. Ngó go pàhngyáuh
   wah kéuih chóhgwo fèigēi, chóh fèigēi juhng faai houdò, chóh...
B: Haih la, haih la, ngó jì la, yùhgwó yáuh fèigēi ngó dōu chóh
   fèigēi ...
A: Haih lòh, haih lòh, dímgáai néi m̀chóh fèigēi nē? Chóh fèigēi
   jeui faai la, m̀sái sàamyaht jauh hóyíh hái Jùnggwok lèihdou
   Méigwok la ......Haih lòh, haih lòh, dímgáai néi m̀chóh fèigēi nē?
B: Néi jìdou ngó haih géisí lèih Méigwok ge ma? Ngó haih YĀTBAAT-
   BAATGÁUNÌN lèih Méigwok ge, gójahnsí yáuh fèigēi chóh mē.....?

Pattern Sentences

I. Measuring length, weight, and height.

   1. Nītìuh gāai yáuh géi chèuhng a? Yáuh léihgéi chèuhng.
      How long is this street? More than a mile long.

   2. Gógàan láu yáuh géi gòu a? Yáuh sahpgéijeuhng gòu.

1. Lòh, a sentence final. 'Haih lòh!' approximates 'Yes!' or 'That's
   it!' in English, showing sudden enlightenment or strong agreement

3. Néi (yáuh) géi gòu a? Ngchekgéi gòu. Ngchekgéi a?
   Ngchekyih(chyun).

4. Gójèung tói yáuh géi chèuhng a? Seichekyih chèuhng.

5. Nīga chè yáuh móu léuhngdēun chùhng a? Ngāamngāam léuhngdēun
   chùhng. (ngāamngaam, just, exactly)

6. Nīsyu yáuh géidò bohng a? Nīsyu yātbohng sàamgogwāt.

7. Yātbohng yáuh géidò ōnsí a? Yātbohng yáuh sahpluhk ōnsí.

8. Yātgàn yáuh géidò léung a? Yātgàn yáuh sahpluhk léung.

9. Nītìuh yú yáuh géi chùhng a? Sahpyihléung chùhng. Gótìuh
   yú nē? Gótìuh yú yáuh léuhnggàngéi chùhng.

10. Néi (yáuh) géi chùhng a? (or: Néi yáuh géidò bohng a?)
    Ngó (yáuh) yātbaakluhk-ahng bohng.

11. Yātjeuhng yáuh gcidò chck a? Yātjcuhng yáuh oahpchck.

12. Yātchek yáuh géidò chyun a? Yìnggwok chek tùhng Jùnggwok chek
     m̀tùhng, Yìnggwok chek, yātchek yáuh sahpyihchyun, Jùnggwok
    chek yātchek yáuh sahpchyun jē.

13. Nīgo chēungmún yáuh móu ngchek gòu a? Gamseuhnghá lā.

14. Gójek syùhn yáuh móu nījek gam chèuhng a? Móu, nījek syùhn
    sahpgéijeuhng chèuhng gójek m̀gau sahpjeuhng chèuhng.

15. Nītìuh síng m̀gau chèuhng, yiu sàamjeuhngsàam ji gau.

88. In measuring distance, height, age, etc. the following pattern
    is used:

    a. Question: géi   plus appropriate SV
                     yáuh géi M   plus appropriate SV
                     géi M   plus appropriate SV

    b. Answer: NU M   plus appropriate SV
                     yáuh NU M   plus appropriate SV
                     NU M   plus appropriate SV

Néi géi gòu a?   How tall are you?
Ngó luhkchek gòu.   I'm six feet tall.

Kéuih yáuh géi(dò) chek gòu a?   How tall is he?
Kéuih yáuh luhkchek gòu.   He is six feet tall.

Néige saimānjái géi seui la?   How old is your child?
Kéuih baatseui la.   He is eight years old now.

Measured description is expressed by terms of measure used
adverbially to modify the stative verb. The special verb yáuh
may precede the measure, but it is commonly omitted.

II. Distance from a given point:

1. Nīsyu lèih gósyu yáuh géi yúhn a?   Yáuh léuhng-sàam léih
   gamseuhnghá.
   How far is it from here to there?   Two or three miles, more
   or less.

2. Nīsyu lèih fóchèjaahm yúhn ma?   (or: ... yúhn m̀yúhn a?)   Hóu
   káhn jē, móu géi yúhn jē.   Gógàan ngūk hauhbihn jauhhaih la.

3. Nīsyu lèih gógàan Yìngmàn hohkhaauh yáuh géi yúhn a?   Móu
   géi yúhn jē, hàahng yātgo jih(jūng) jauh dou la.

4. Néi ngūkkéi lèih kéuih ngūkkéi yáuh géi yúhn a?   Yiu chóh
   sahpgéifānjūng ge chè ji doudāk.

5. Nīsyu lèih gósyu yúhn dākjaih, ngódeih gàmyaht m̀heuidāk la.

6. Nīsyu lèih gógàan léuihgún yáuh géi yúhn a?   M̀haih géi yúhn
   jē, néi jùngyi chóh chè heui yīkwaahk hàahngheui a?

7. Nīsyu lèih kéuihge ngūkkéi gam yúhn, ngódeih gàmyaht m̀heui
   lo, tìngyaht ji heui hóu ma?

8. Nīsyu lèih bīngàan jáugún jeui káhn a?   Lèih Sàn Gwóngjàu je
   káhn.   Gám, ngódeih jauh heui Sàn Gwóngjàu hóu ma?

9. Yìhgā lèih Hèunggóng juhng yáuh géi yúhn a?   Juhng yáuh hóu
   yúhn, juhng yáuh sà-ahgéi léih.   Haih m̀haih sà-ahgéi Yìngléi
   a?   Haih la.

10. Néigàan ngūk lèih fóchèjaahm géi yúhn a?   Lèih fóchèjaahm hó
    káhn, máanmáan dōu m̀fandāk.

89. To indicate distance between two points, the co-verb pattern
with lèih (to be distant from) is used.

III. Degrees of comparison of distance, length, weight, and height.

1. Néi ngūkkéi béi ngó ngūkkéi lèih hohkhaauh káhn, káhn géidò
a? Káhn hóudò, káhn géiléihlouh gamdò.
You say your home is a little nearer to the school than my
home. How much nearer, do you think? It's much nearer,
several miles nearer.

2. Néi gú ngódeih géigo(yàhn)ge ngūkkéi bīngoge ngūkkéi lèih
hohkhaauh jeui yúhn nē? Kéuihge ngūkkéi lèih hohkhaauh hóu
káhn, néige yihk m̀haih géi yúhn, ngóge jeui yúhn.

3. Nīsyu géijèung tói dōu m̀haih yātyeuhng gam chèuhng. Nījèung
sàamchek, jeui dyún; gójèung chèuhnggwo nījèung, gójèung
sàamcheksei. Gójèung hāakge jeui chèuhng, chèuhnggwosaai nī
léuhngjèung.

4. Ngó ngūkkéi béi néi ngūkkéi lèih fóchèjaahm juhng yúhn.
Juhng yúhn géidò a? Juhng yúhn sàamléihgéi louh.

5. Néi seun m̀seun ngó gòugwo kéuih a? Ngó m̀seun. Néi gòugwo
kéuih géidòchyun a? Néi jī ngó gòugwo kéuih géidòchyun ma?
Ngó gòugwo kéuih chyunbun.

6. Bīntiuh yú chùhngdī a? Nītiuh chùhngdī, chùhnggwo gótiuh
hóudò àh? Chùhng hóudò. Chéhng géidò a? Chùhng yātbohng
léuhngōnsí.

7. Nīga chè hóu hèng jē, m̀gau yātdēun chúhng, góga chùhnggwo
nīga hóudò, chúhng géidò a? Chúhng dēungéi.

8. Néi yáuh géidò hìngdaih jímúi a? Ngó yáuh léuhng hìngdaih
sàam jímúi, ngó jeui daaih, gàmnìn sahpbaatseui, kéuih jeui
sai, gàmnìn ngseui.

9. Néi jèhjē (or gājē) géidòseui a? Ngó daaih(gā)jē sahpluhk-
seui, yìh(gā)jē sahpngseui, ngó yihgā baatseui.

10. Néideih géigo bīngo daaih a? Ngó daaihgwo A-Chan, A-Chán
daaihgwo A-Ho, A-Chán gàmnìn sà-ahseui, A-Ho gàmnìn yah-
baatseui; ngó jeui daaih, A-Ho jeui sai.

IV. Measures and 'bín'

1. Bākgìng hái Jùnggwok bākbín (or bākbouh); Gwóngjàu hái Jùnggwok nàambín (or nàambouh).
   Peking is in the northern part of China; Canton is in the
   southern part of China.

2. Hèunggóng seibihn dōu haih hói, deuimin haih Gáulùhng, Gáulùhng hái Hèunggóng bākbín. Gwóngjàu hái Gáulùhng sàibākbín.

3. Ngó gàan ngūk sàibihn yáuh joh sàan, sóyíh máan(tàuh)hāak
   mòu gam yiht.

4. Jùnggwok bākbín móu géidò sàan, nàambín yáuh hóudò sàan.

5. Ngó gàan ngūk seibihn dōu haih sàan, dùngbihn (or dùngbín)
   sàibihn, nàambihn, bākbihn dōu haih sàan.

6. Méigwokge dùngbihn haih Daaihsàiyèuhng, sèibihn haih Taaipìhngyèuhng, nàambihn haih Maksāigō, bākbihn haih Gànàdaaih.

7. Chóhhái Léih taaitáai pòhngbīn gógo haih bīngo a? Néi góng
   jósáubihn gógo yīkwaahk yauhsáubihn gógo a? Jósáubihn gógo
   haih Jèung taaitáai, yauhsáubihn gógo haih Jèung sìnsàang.

8. Chàhn sìnsàang néi chóhhái jùnggàan lā, néi jeui daaih yauh
   jeui fèih; Wòhng síujé chóh(hái) néi yauh(sáu)bihn, Léih
   síujé chóhhái néi jó(sáu)bihn, néi taaitáai chóhhái néi
   deuimin, ngó tùhng ngó taaitáai chóhhái néi taaitáai pòhngbīn, gám hòu ma?

9. Taaipìhngyèuhng jùnggàan yáuh go dóu, giujouh Tàahnhèungsāan
   ... Mātyéh giujouh 'dóu' a? Seibihn dōu haih hói ge deihfòng ngódeih giu kéuih jouh dóu, gám, Tòihwāan haih m̀haih
   yātgo dóu a? Haih, Hèunggóng haih m̀haih yātgo dóu a? Haih.

10. Néi hái nīsyu heung dùng hàahng, hàahngdou gótìuh gāaisyu
    jyun yauhsáubihn, joi hàahng ngfānjūng, gósyu yáuh gàan
    daaih ngūk, gógàan daaih ngūk ge yauhsáubihn jauhhaih gógàan
    jáugún la.

Additional Sentences

1. Ngó yātbaakluhksahpbohng chúhng, yìngfahn yáuh géi gòu a?
2. Tòihwāan tùhng Tàahnhèungsāan bīngo daaih a?
3. Hái nīsyu heui Jùnggwok yiu gìnggwo bīngéidaat deihfòng a?
4. Néi gú Tòihwāan lèih nīsyu yáuh géi yúhn a? Tàahnhèungsāan nē?
5. Hái Hèunggóng máaiyéh, yìhgā gogo dōu m̀góng géidògàn géidòléung, gogo dōu góng géidòbohng géidòōnsí la.
6. Hái Jùnggwok fèilèih Méigwok ge fèigèi, hái Tàahnhèungsāan tìhng yātmáan, daihyihyaht sìnji fèilèih Méigwok.
7. Kéuihdeih kàhmyaht jínghéi gójek syùhnjái, (yāt)jeuhngyih chèuhng, seichek fut, hóyíh chòh seigoyàhn, yùhgwó haih fèihlóu jauh chòhdāk yātgo jē.
8. Nījek syùhn yauh(sáu)bihn taai hèng, m̀gòi néi giu gógo fèihlóu chòhgwolèih yauh(sáu)bihn hóu ma?
9. Gógàan chāangún maai tòhngchāan yihk maai sāichāan, yauhsáubihn maai tòhngchāan, jósáubihn maai sāichāan.
10. Gógàan fóng jūnggāan yáuh yātjèung tói pòhngbīn yáuh géijèung yí, seibihn yātgo chēungmún dōu móu, hóu hāak hóu hāak, ngó wah: 'Ngó m̀yahpheui la, néi yahpheui lā!'
11. Kéuih hái ngódeih deuimin gógàan ngūk jyun, kéuih tùhng kéuih léunggo agō jyuh làuhhah, kéuih léuhnggo ajē jyuh làuhseuhng.
12. Gógàan fóng m̀haih géi daaih, yáuh jeuhngsei chèuhng, gáuchek fut, yáuh sàamgo chēungmún, chēungmún ngoibihn jauhhaih gótìuh hòh.
13. Ngó séung jìdou nītìuh síng yáuh géi chèuhng, néi yáuh chek ma? M̀gòi néi jebéi ngó sáiháh dāk ma?
14. Nītìuh síng luhkchek chèuhng m̀gau chèuhng boh, jauhsyun yāt-jeuhng chèuhng juhng(haih) mei gau boh!
15. Ngódeih gàan ngūk heung nàam, sìhsìh dōu yáuh fùng yahplèih, soyíh sìhsìh dōu hóu lèuhngsóng.

Translate the following sentences:

1. His car isn't the same as mine, his is very expensive while mine is very inexpensive.
2. I hope this table is not as long as that one, then it would look prettier, don't you think so?
3. Is he taller than you? By how much?
4. He is much taller than I, but he is not as heavy as I am.
5. He isn't much shorter than I am, only a little bit.
6. That car over there is a little bit cheaper than this one.
7. That car isn't as new as this one, but this one is easier to drive.

8. This watch is different from that one; this one came from America, and that one came from Japan.
9. This window isn't as difficult to close as that one, I don't know why that one is so difficult to close.
10. This kind of gasoline isn't as good as that kind, but it is much cheaper.

Below are English translations of sentences used in the vocabulary of this lesson as examples of usage. Translate these back into Chinese (numbers correspond to those in Vocabulary section.)

1. Is it far away? No, it's not.
2. Is it very far by this road? No, it's not.
3. By which road is it farther?
4. Is it shorter by this road than by that one? Yes, it is much shorter than by that one.
5. Is it very near? No, it isn't.
6. How heavy is that fish?
7. Is he heavier than you?
8. Is he much lighter (in weight) now? Yes, last year he was, but now he's gaining weight again.
9. Are you the lighter (in weight) or is he?
10. May I sit beside you? Sure, please sit down.
11. Are there any chairs beside the table? There are three chairs beside that table.
12. Is there anyone beside you?
13. There are two pens beside the book; can you see them?
14. Do you know the word in the center? I don't know the word in the center.
15. Who is the one standing in the center?
16. Is it opposite that store? Yes, it's opposite that store.
17. What kind of store is the one opposite here?
18. Have you ever been to San Francisco? I have never been there before.
19. Is San Francisco interesting?
20. Is New York very interesting? Yes, it is.
21. Is San Francisco as interesting as New York? Oh, New York is more interesting than San Francisco.
22. Is Honolulu big? No, it's not very big.
23. Is it as big as New Haven? It's much bigger than New Haven.
24. Isn't that ship going to England? That ship isn't going to England.
25. Have you been in England?
26. Is Mexico as interesting as Honolulu. No, Mexico isn't as interesting as Honolulu.

27. Have you ever been in Mexico?
28. Are there many French people in Canada? No, they are Canadian, but they speak French.
29. Are there any Chinese in Canada?
30. Is Kowloon the name of a place?
31. Yes, it is.
32. Is Taiwan in the Atlantic Ocean?
33. No, Taiwan is in the Pacific.
34. How many elder brothers do you have? I have two elder brothers.
35. Is that man your elder brother?
36. Does your elder sister have any children?
37. How many sisters do you have?
38. How many boys in your family? We have three including me.
39. Was it very windy here yesterday? Yes, it was yesterday.
40. Is this rope long enough? No, it isn't long enough.
41. How long a rope do you want?
42. How many hands does a person have? A person has two hands.
43. Are both hands the same length?
44. What's on the sea? There are some boats on the sea.
45. Someone says the boat is in the sea, is that correct? No, it isn't.
46. What's the name of that river? That river is called the Yellow River.
47. Is the Yellow River very long?
48. Is there any human being on the island? (Is that island inhabited?) There are many people living there.
49. How big is that island?
50. How many inches long is this pen? This pen is four inches long.
51. How many inches long is that table?
52. How many inches in a foot? The Chinese foot differs from the English foot.
53. What is the difference?
54. There are ten inches in a Chinese foot, and twelve inches in an English foot.
55. Do you have an English ruler?
56. How many feet in one 'jeuhng'? There are ten feet in one 'jeuhng.'
57. How many English feet are there in a 'jeuhng'? There are 11 feet 9 inches.
58. How heavy is this fish? (What's the weight of this fish?)
59. Does this fish weigh two pounds? That fish doesn't weigh two pounds, it's only one pound.
60. Please weigh that one for me and see how heavy it is.
61. Are two catties enough? Two catties are not enough; we need eight catties.

62. Please let me have five catties.
63. How many ounces are there in one catty? There are sixteen ounces in one catty.
64. Does this fish weigh about a catty?
65. How many miles is it from here to the railroad station? It is five or six miles.
66. Is that in English miles or Chinese miles?
67. From which direction did you come? I came from that direction.
68. Who was the person standing on the other side of the table a while ago? The gentleman who was standing on the other side of the table a while ago, is my friend.
69. I like the room on the east side.
70. Why do you like the room on the east side? Because it isn't so hot.
71. Are you a Westerner?
72. Yes, I am a Westerner, but why do you call us Westerners?
73. Oh, because you come from the west, we call you Westerners.
74. Is it true that Shanghai is south of Hong Kong? No, Hong Kong is south of Shanghai.
75. Is Canada south of the United States, or isn't it?
76. Is he a southerner or a northerner? He is a northerner.
77. Are there many mountains in the northern part of China?
78. Is it the one on the left-hand side? Yes, it is the first one on the left-hand side.
79. Is there a chair to the left of you?
80. Is he in the room on the right? Yes, he is studying in the room on the right.
81. Who was standing at your right-hand a while ago?
82. I met a friend on the street a while ago.
83. Whom did you meet? I met Mr. Wong, the teacher who taught me Cantonese.
84. Where did you park your car? My car is parked behind that store.
85. Why has that train stopped?
86. Do you believe that I am taller than he? I don't.
87. You really don't believe it?
88. Is it all right to turn right? It isn't all right to turn right, turn left.
89. Don't turn into that street!
90. Did you pass through the place he lives in? Yes, I did, but I didn't call on him.
91. Did you pass through France on your way to Italy?
92. Do you think he'll come today? I guess he won't come today.
93. Do you think it'll rain today?

94. In which direction should I walk? You walk east about two
    minutes, and there it is.
95. If I want to go to the railroad station in which direction
    should I go?
96. How far is the railroad station from here? Not very far, only
    about a mile.
97. How far is it from here to New York?
98. Even if it's very inexpensive I still don't want to buy it.
99. Even if he won't let me go, I still want to go.
100. Even if he came by boat, he should have already arrived.
101. When did you leave the United States?

DESCRIBING MANNER OF ACTION WITH 'DĀK'

Vocabulary

ngáan (M: jek; sèung)   N: eye

    1. Kéuih sèung ngáan m̀haih géi hóu àh?
       M̀haih, kéuih sèung ngáan hóu hóu.
    2. Néi sèung ngáan hóyíh táidāk(gin) géi
       yúhn a?

hei (M: chēut)   N: play (dramatic), show

    3. Néi jùngyi tái hei ma? Ngó hóu jùngyi
       tái hei.
    4. Kàhmmáan góchēut hei hóutái ma?

bou (M: fūk; faai)   N: cloth, material

    5. Nīfūk bou leng ma? Nīfūk móu gófūk
       gam leng.
    6. Gófūk bou géidòchín yātchek a?

boktàuh   N: shoulder

    7. Kéuih wah kéuihge boktàuh hóu guih.
    8. Kéuih bīnbihnge boktàuh guih a?

síusyut   N: a novel

    9. Néi yáuh móu táigwo nībún síusyut a?
       Ngó móu táigwo, haih m̀haih hóu hóutái
       a?
    10. Góbún síusyut haih m̀haih néi ga?

gèihei (M: gihn)   N: a machine

11. Néi jì m̀jì nīgihn gèihei bīnsyu
    waaihjó a? Ngó m̀jì, dáng ngó tái-
    háh tìm!
12. Néi wúih m̀wúih jíng gèihei a?

yeuhk (M: jek)   N: medicine

13. Bīnsyu yáuh nījek yeuhk maai a?
    Gógàan poutáu yáuh.
14. Néi pa sihk yeuhk àh!

ngàansīk (M: jek)   N: color

15. Néi jùngyi nījek ngàansīk ma? Ngó
    m̀jùngyi nījek ngàansīk.
16. Kéuih gihn sāamge ngàansīk jànhaih
    leng lo!

syúga   N: summer vacation

17. Kéuih gàmnìn syúga dásyun heui Yìng-
    gwok wàanháh àh? M̀haih, kéuih gàm-
    nìn syúga dásyun hái nīsyu duhksyù.
18. Néi gàmnìn syúga dásyun heui bīnsyu
    wàan a?

léuihhàhng (M: chi)   N/V: a journey/ to travel

19. Néi jùngyi léuihhàhng ma? Ngó hóu
    jùngyi léuihhàhng.
20. Néi hahgoláihbaai dásyun heui bīn-
    syu léuihhàhng a?

behng (M: tíng 'kind,' N/V: sickness/ to be sick or ill
  chi 'time')1

21. Kéuih haih mātyéh behng a? Ngó
    m̀jì kéuih nītíng behng giujouh
    mātyéh behng.
22. Kéuih behngjó hóu noi làh? Kéuih
    behngjó hóu géiyaht la.

---

1. Also 'yātchèuhng behng' one'siege' of illness, but 'behnggwo
   sàamchi' was sick three times.

Tòhngyàhnfauh   PW: Chinatown (a term used among the Over-
                               seas Chinese in America)

                           23. Néi yáuh móu heuigwo Niuyēukge
                               Tòhngyàhnfauh a?
                           24. Sàamfàahnsíhge Tòhngyàhnfauh daaih
                               ma? Niuyēukge Tòhngyàhnfauh móu
                               Sàamfàahnsíhge Tòhngyàhnfauh gam
                               daaih.

Gwóngdùng   PW: Kwangtung (province)

                           25. Kéuih haih mhaih Gwóngdùng yàhn a?
                               Haih, kéuih haih Gwóngdùng yàhn.
                           26. Hèunggóng haih mhaih lèih Gwóngdùng
                               hóu yùhn a?

Lòhsáang   PW: Los Angeles

                           27. Néi heuigwo Lòhsáang ma? Ngó gauh-
                               nín heuigwo yātchi.
                           28. Néi géisí heui Lòhsáang a?

daaihgā   N: we all; all of us

                           29. Ngódeih daaihgā yātchái heui hóu ma?
                           30. Ngódeih daaihgā dōu sīk góng Gwóng-
                               dùngwá, dímgáai mgóng Gwongdùngwá nē

sàntái   N: health, body

                           31. Kéuih gahnlói sàntái hou ma? Kéuih
                               gahnlói sàntái hóu hóu.
                           32. Néige sàntái chùhnglòih dōu haih gam
                               hóu àh?

fàangáan (M: gauh)   N: soap

                           33. Nīgauh fàangáan géidò chín a? Gódī
                               léuhnghòuhbunjí yātgauh. Nīdī
                               léuhnggobun ngànchín yātgauh.
                           34. Dímgáai nīdī fàangáan gam gwai ga?
                               Waih, sìnsàang, nīdī haih Méigwok
                               fàangáan boh!

fongga

VO: to grant (someone) a holiday, have a holiday, have a vacation

    35. Tìngyaht yáuh móu ga fong a? Tìng-
        yaht móu ga fong.
    36. Néideih géisí fongga a?

héichìhng

VO: to start a journey, to set out

    37. Kéuih géisìh héichìhng heui Jùng-
        gwok a? Kéuih hahgoláihbaaiyih
        héichìhng.
    38. Néi nē, néi géisí héichìhng a?

hòihohk

VO: start   school

    39. Ngódeih haih m̀haih hahgoyuht sàam-
        houh hòihohk a? Haih, ngódeih haih
        hái hahgoyuht hòihohk daahnhaih
        m̀haih sàamhouh.
    40. Gwojó syúga jìhauh, néideih géisìh
        hòihohk a?

chēutsèng

VO: say (something), make a (vocal) sound

    41. Dímgáai kéuih m̀chēutsèng a? Kéuih
        wah kéuih m̀jùngyi chēutsèng.
    42. M̀hóu chēutsèng la!

m̀jihyìhn
jihyìhn

SV: not felling well; ill; uncomfortable
SV: comfortable

    43. Kéuih m̀jihyìhn àh? Haih, kéuih
        m̀haih géi jihyìhn.
    44. Kéuih hóu m̀jihyìhn mē?

chìngchó

SV: distinct, clear (without ambiguity
indistinctness, etc.)

    45. Kéuihge Gwóngdùngwá góng dāk hóu
        chìngchó.
    46. Ngó móu táichìngchó gógo yàhn haih
        bīngo.
    47. Ngó m̀geidāk chìngchó kéuih haih
        bīngo la.

baahk

SV: white

48. Gósyu gógàan baahk ngūk, néi táigin
    ma?
49. Néi jùngyi jeuk baahk sāam ma?

jeng

SV: be correct, accurate

50. Néige Yìngmàn góng dāk hóu jeng.
51. Kéuihge Gwóngdùngwá góng dāk jeng
    m̀jeng a?

ngàihím

SV/N: be dangerous/ danger

52. Nītluh louh haih m̀haih hóu ngàihím
    a? M̀haih, nītluh louh yātdī ngài-
    hím dōu móu.
53. Nīgihn sih gam ngàihím néi gáam
    jouh ma?

gònjehng

SV: be clean

54. Nīdaat deihfòng jànhaih gònjehng la.
55. Gósyu yáuh móu nīsyu gam gònjehng a?

fùnhéi

SV/AV: be happy; to like to, be fond of,
       be glad to

56. M̀jì dímgáai, kéuih gàmyaht m̀haih
    géi fùnhéi.
57. Néi jì m̀jì dímgáai kéuih gàmyaht
    gam m̀fùnhéi a?
58. Kéuih fùnhéi tái hei, ngó fùnhéi tái
    síusyut, néi fùnhéi (jouh) mātyéh a?

m̀sédāk

V/AV: can't bear to part with/ be grudging
      about (doing something)

59. Kéuih m̀sédāk (lèihhòi) kéuihge
    saimānjái.
60. Kéuih m̀haih móu chín, kéuih m̀sédāk
    sái jē.
61. Kéuih m̀sédāk chéng ngó sihkfaahn.

sédāk

SV/AV: to be willing to part with (something)
/to be generous (in doing something),
not be stingy (about doing something).

62. Kéuih hóu sédāk tái hei, daahnhaih
kéuih m̀sédāk máai syù.
63. Kéuih go yàhn, hóu sédāk, sìhsìh béi
hóudò chín kéuihdī pàhngyáuh sái.

sái

V: to wash

64. Néi sáijó ngó gihn sāam mei a?
Sáijó léuhngyaht lo.
65. Sáigònjehng mei a?

sái

V: drive (a car), operate a plane

66. Néi wúih sái fèigèi ma? Ngó wúih
sái.
67. Sái fèigèi nàan, yīkwaahk sái heichè
nàan a?

maakhòi
_maakdaaih

V: to open (the eyes)
V: to open (the eyes) wide

68. Néi maakhòi sèung ngáan táiháh!
69. Dímgāai ngó sèung ngáan m̄_maakdākhòi
a?

jaatjyuh

RV: to tie up

70. Dáng ngó ló tìuh síng lèih jaatjyuh
kéuih.
71. Nītìuh síng taai dyún, m̀jaatdākjyuh.

paak

V: to pat; to clap

72. Chàhn taaitáai paakgán kéuihge
saimānjái fangaau.
73. Kéuih cheungyùhn gō jìhauh, ngódeih
gogo dōu paaksáu.

daap

CV/V: go by (mode of transportation)/ ride,
take

74. Dímgáai néi mdaap syùhn a? Ngódī
saimānjái mjùngyi daap syùhn, kéuihdeih jùngyi daap fóchè.
75. Kéuih hauhyaht daap syùhn heui Hèunggóng.
76. Néi jùngyi daap syùhn yīkwaahk daap
chè a?

háng	AV:	will; to consent to

77. Néi háng mháng heui a? Ngó móu wah
mháng heui.
78. Kéuih háng mháng a?

dihngsaht	AV:	make a definite decision (to do something have decided on (doing something)

79. Néi dihngsaht bīnyaht heui a? Ngó
dihngsaht hahgoyuhtyāthouh heui.
80. Kéuih dihngsaht géisìh lèih a?

yātguhng hahmbaahnglaahng	A:	altogether, all told

81. Yātguhng géidò chín a?
82. Nīgàan fóng hahmbaahnglaahng yáuh
géidòjèung yí a?

jihnghaih	MA:	only

83. Jihnghaih kéuih tùhng ngó léuhnggo
jē.
84. Jihnghaih kéuih msīk góng Gwóngdùngw
jē.

yíhwàih	CV:	to think that, suppose

85. Kéuih yíhwàih néi haih Yìnggwok yàhn
néi haih mhaih Yìnggwok yàhn a?
86. Ngó yíhwàih ngódeih mhóu heui la.
87. Néi yíhwàih ngódeih yìngfahn jouh
nīgihn sih ma?

jyūtjì	MA:	finally

88. Kéuih jyūtjì heuijó Tàahnhēungsāan.

89. Ngódeih jyūtjì móu heui.
90. Kéuih jyūtjì máaijó góbún syù.

sèuihjì   MA: who would have thought (it) (!)

91. Sèuihjì kéuih Yātgeui Yìngmàn dōu
    m̀wúih góng!
92. Sèuihjì kéuih móu lèih!
93. Sèuihjì kéuih góng dāk hóugwo ngó-
    deih hóudò!

sèuiyìhn   MA: although

94. Sèuiyìhn ngó m̀sīk jyú, daahnhaih
    ngó sīk sihk!
95. Sèuiyìhn ngó m̀sīk kéuih, daahnhaih
    ngó jìdou kéuih haih Wòhng sìnsàangge
    pàhngyáuh.
96. Sèuiyìhn ngó móu heuigwo Jùnggwok,
    daahnhaih ngó hóu fùnhéi Jùnggwok.

Reading

Syúga Léuihhàhng

Gauhnín chātyuht hohkkhaauh fongsyúga ngó tùhng géigo pàhngyáuh
sái chè heui Gauhgāmsāan wáan. Hái nīsyu heui Gauhgāmsāan yáuh
sàamchìngéiléihlouh gam yúhn, yùhgwó chóh fóchè heui, múigo yàhn
yiu sái sàam-seibaakmān, gogo dōu m̀sédāk sái gamdò chín, seunglàih
séungheui jyūtjì dihngsaht jihgēi sái chè heui.

Ngódeih yātguhng yáuh chātgo yàhn, yātga chè m̀gau chóh, yiu
sái léuhngga chè heui. Chàhn sìnsàang ngāamngāam hohksīk sái chè,
máaijó ga sàn chè. Kéuih yātdihng yiu ngódeih chóh kéuihga sàn
chè.

Wòhng sìnsàang hóu wúih sái chè, kéuih sái chè sáijó yahgéinìn
la, kéuih yāt hohksīk sái chè jauh máaijó kéuih yìhgā sáigán nīga
chè. Doujó héichìhng góyaht, m̀jì dímgáai gogo dōu jáuheui chóh
Wòhng sìnsàangge chè, jihnghaih ngó yātgo yàhn chóh Chàhn sìnsàangge
chè.

Hái louhseuhng Chàhn sìnsàang sái kéuihga sàn chè sái dāk hóu

faai. Wòhng sìnsàang táigin Chàhn sìnsàang sáidāk gam faai, kéuih
yihk sái dāk hóu faai. Kéuih wah: "Chàhn sìnsàang ga chè sèuiyìhn
sàn, daahnhaih ngóga chè hàahng dāk faaigwo kéuih góga, néideih
m̀seun néideih táihàh!"

Chàhn sìnsàang táigín Wòhng sìnsàang sái dāk gam faai, kéuih
wah: "Wòhng sìnsàang sèuiyìhn sái chè noigwo ngó, daahnhaih kéuih
sèung ngáan móu ngó sèung (ngáan) gam hóu, kéuihga chè móu ngóga
gam sàn, néi táihàh ngó faaigwo kéuih géidò!" Ngó chòhhái Chàhn
sìnsàangge chèsyu yātgeui sèng dōu móu chēut, ngo hahpmàai sèung
ngáan yauh maakdaaih sèung ngáan, maakdaaih sèung ngáan yauh hahpmàai sèung ngáan.

Yātlouh[1] gámyéung hàahngjó chātyaht.

Ngódeih múimáan yātchái sihkfaahn gójahnsí Chàhn sìnsàang yātdihng wah: "Wòhng sìnsàang néi sái chè sái dāk jànhaih hóu lo!"
Wòhng sìnsàang wah: "Chàhn sìnsàang néi sái dāk hóu, néi sái dāk
hóu!"

Daihbaatyaht, ngódeih jauhlèih dou Gauhgāmsāan la, daaihgā dōu
hóu fùnhéi, yātgo wah: "Ngó heuidou Tòhngyàhnfauh ngó yātdihng
sìn heui sihk chāan tòhngchāan." Yātgo wah: "Ngó heuidou Tòhngyàhnfauh ngó yātdihng sìn heui tái (yāt)chēut Gwóngdùng hei."

Sèuihjì doujó Lòhsàang ngó yuhdóu yātgo pàhngyáuh, kéuih yātdihng
yiu ngó hái kéuih ngūkkéisyu jyuh géiyaht. Chóh Wòhng sìnsàang ga
chè ge géiwái pàhngyáuh yáuhdī yáuh sih, yáuhdī m̀haih géi jihyìhn,
gogo dōu yiu hái Lòhsàang jyuh géiyaht sìnji heui Gauhgāmsāan. Ngó
deih tùhng Chàhn sìnsàang Wòhng sìnsàang góng, ngódeih yāt dou
Gauhgāmsāan jauh heui Seuhnghói léuihgún wán kéuihdeih.

Chìh yātgo láihbaai, ngódeih heuidou Gauhgāmsāan, m̀gin Wòhng
sìnsàang yihk m̀gin Chàhn sìnsàang, ngódeih yíhwàih kéuihdeih yātdihng haih heuijó daihyihsyu wáan la.

Gáuyuht nghouh hohkhaauh hòihohk la, juhng m̀gin Chàhn sìnsàang
tùhng Wòhng sìnsàang fàanlèih. Yáuh yātyaht jìutàuhjóu, ngódeih
hàahngfàan hohkhaauh, táigin Chàhn sìnsàang chóh Wòhng sìnsàang ga
gauh chè fàanlàih. Chàhn sìnsàang jek jósáu yáuh tiuh baahk bou
jaatjyuh, Chàhn sìnsàang yuhng yauh sáu paakhàh Wòhng sìnsàangge
boktàuh wah: "Wòhng sìnsàang sái chè sáidāk jànhaih hóu lo! Kéuih
sái dāk hóugwo ngó hóudò!"

1. Yātlouh, all the way through

Pattern Sentences

I. Describing manner of action with 'dāk.'

1. Kéuih hàahng dāk faai. Kéuih hàahnglouh hàahng dāk faai.
   He walks fast.

2. Kéuih cheunggō cheung dāk hóu hóutèng.

3. Kéuih góng Yìngmàn góng dāk m̀haih hóu hóu.

4. Kéuih sihkfaahn sihk dāk hóu maan.

5. Ngó pàhngyáuh sé Jùnggwok jih sé dāk hóu leng.

6. Nīga fèigèi fèi dāk hóu faai.

7. Léih sìnsàang gaausyù gaau dāk hóu hóu.

8. Nī jèung yí chóh dāk hóu jihyìhn.

9. Kéuih nàu dāk hóu gányiu.

10. Kéuih taaitáai jyú tòhngchāan jyú dāk hóu hóusihk.

11. Kéuih haih m̀haih behng dāk hóu gányiu a?

12. Kéuih sái chè sái dāk hóu faai.

13. Jàu sìnsàang góng syutwah góng dāk hóu maan.

14. Ngó geidāk hóu chìngchó. Ngó geidāk m̀haih géi chìngchó.
    (or, more colloquially, Ngó m̀haih géi geidāk la.)

15. Néi gokdāk dím a? Ngó gokdāk hóu jihyìhn. Ngó gokdāk m̀jih-yìhn. Ngó gokdāk m̀haih géi jihyìhn.

90. In describing the manner in which the action of a verb is car-
    ried out the following pattern is used: V dāk SV. Note that
    the direct object is omitted or is transposed to the topic
    position.

    Kéuih (séjih) sé dāk hóu hóu. He writes well.
    Kéuih (hàahng louh) hàahng dāk hóu faai. He walks very fast.

Kéuih (cheunggō) cheung dāk hóu hóutèng. She sings extremely
well.
Gwóngdùngwá kéuih góng dāk m̀haih géi hóu. His _Cantonese_ isn't
very good. (lit. As for his speaking Cantonese, he can't
speak well.)

II. Similarity and dissimilarity of manner of action.

  1. Kéuih hàahng dāk yáuh ngó gam faai. Kéuih hàahng louh hàahng
     dāk yáuh ngó gam faai.
     He walks as fast as I do.

  2. Kéuih dá jih móu ngó dá dāk gam faai.

  3. Ngó sihk (faahn sihk) dāk móu kéuih gamdò.
     Compare with: 'Ngó móu kéuih gam sihkdāk.'

  4. Kéuih sái chè móu néi (sái dāk) gam hóu.

  5. Wòhng taaitáaige saimānjái tùhng Jèung taaitáaige saimānjái
     duhksyù duhk dāk yātyeuhng gam chùngmìng.

  6. Kàhmyaht lohk ge yúh móu gàmyaht (lohk ge yúh) lohk dāk gam
     daaih.

  7. Dímgáai ngó góng Yìngmàn móu kéuih góng dāk gam hóu nē?

  8. Ngódī Gwóngjàuwá móu kéuih góng dāk gam jeng.

  9. Ngó sái fèigèi móu ngó sái heichè (sái dāk) gam hóu.

  10. Ngó yám jáu móu kéuih yám dāk gamdò yànwaih ngó sàntái móu
      kéuih (ge sàntái) gam hóu.

III. Comparing manner of action

  1. Kéuih sái chè (sái dāk) hóu gwo ngó.
     Kéuih duhksyù duhk dāk hóu gwo ngó, _etc._

  2. Kéuih béi ngó gaau dò sàamnìn syù.
     Kéuih béi ngó sihk dò léuhngwún faahn, _etc._

  3. Néi sīk géidògo Jùnggwok pàhngyáuh a? Kéuih sīk nggo, ngó
     sīk yātgo jē, kéuih béi ngó sīk dò seigo.

4. Kéuih cheunggō móu kéuih cheung dāk gam hóu, daahnhaih
   kéuih duhksyù duhk dāk hóu gwo kéuih. <u>Or</u>: Kéuih duhksyù
   béi kéuih hóu.

5. Néi gú néi sái dāk jeui faai àh! Néi sái dāk faai dī, kéuih
   sái dāk juhng faaigwo néi, gám jauh hóu ngàihím lo!

6. Ngóge jái duhksyù móu ngóge néui gamdò, daahnhaih kéuih sīk
   jih. (sīk dāk) dò gwo kéuih, yànwaih kéuih hóu jùngyi tái
   síusyut, sóyíh kéuih sīk dò hóudò jih.

7. Nīgàan poutáuge yéh maai dāk hóu pèhng, pèhnggwo gógàan
   hóudò, dímgáai néi m̀lèih nīgàan máai a?

8. Ngó ga chè móu kéuih ga chè gam sàn, yihk móu kéuih ga chè
   gam gwai, daahnhaih ngó ga chè hàahng dāk faai gwo kéuih ga,
   dímgáai nē? Yànwaih ngó ga chège gèihei hóu.

9. Ngódeih nīsyu chùhnglòih mei lohkgwo gam daaih ge yúh, gàm-
   maan lohk ge yúh juhng daaih gwo kàhmmáan.

10. Néige Seuhnghóiwá móu kéuih góng dāk gam hóu, néige Gwóng-
    dùngwá yihk móu kéuih góng dāk gam hóu, daahnhaih néige
    Yìngmàn góng dāk hóu gwo kéuih.

IV. Degrees of comparison of manner of action by using 'dī.'

1. Sihk dò dī lā! Sihk dò dīgamdēu lā!
   Have some more! Have a little bit more!

2. Kéuih hóufàan dī mei a? Hóufàan dī lo, yáuhsàm.

3. Ngódeih duhk faaidī hahgo láihbaai jauh hóyíh duhkyùhn nībún
   syù la!

4. Wòhng sìnsàang m̀gòi néi gaau maandī lā, néi gaau dāk faai-
   dākjaih ngódeih m̀sīk.

5. Néidī yéh maai dāk gam gwai, maai pèhngdī ngó jauh máai la!

6. Ngódeih yiu hàahng faaidī ji hóyíh daapdóu gáudímléuhnggojih
   ge fóchè boh!

7. Ngó gàmyaht séung gaau dò dī daahnhaih yìhgā yíhgìng gau
   jūng la.

8. Néi yiu jài dòdī fàangáan jauh hóyíh sái dāk gònjehng.

9. Néi béi dò léuhnggo ngànchín kéuih, tái kéuih háng m̀háng?

10. M̀gòi néi dá hòidī gógo chēung hóu ma?

V. Special use of question word dím-dōu:

1. Nīdī yeuhk ngó dím sihk dōu sihkm̀lohk.
   I can't swallow this pill (medicine) no matter how hard I tr'

2. Nīfo syù ngó dím duhk dōu duhkm̀sīk.

3. Nīgo jih ngó dím sé dōu sém̀hóu.

4. Nījáan dāng ngó dím hòi dōu hòim̀jeuhk.

5. Ngó dím man kéuih (kéuih) dōu m̀háng góng.

6. Ngó dím wán dōu wánm̀dóu.

7. Nīdou mùn ngó dím sàan dōu sàanm̀màai.

8. Ngó kàhmmáan dím fan dōu fanm̀jeuhk.

9. Góbún syù ngó dím máai dōu máaim̀dóu.

10. Néi jìdou nījèung yí dímgáai néi dím chóh dōu chóhm̀lohk ma?
    Dímgáai a? Yànwaih néi fèihdākjaih.

11. Kéuih góng ngó tèng Chàhn sìnsàang hái gógàan jáugúnsyu sihk
    faahn, daahnhaih ngó dím wán dōu wánm̀dóu kéuih.

12. Kéuih jànhaih yáuhchín lo, kéuihdī chín dím sái dōu sáim̀saai

13. Nīsyu lèih gósyu gam yúhn ngódeih gàmyaht dím hàahng dōu
    hàahngm̀dou (ge) la.

14. Yìhgā yíhgìng saamdímgéi la, ngànhòhng yíhgìng sàanjó mùn la
    néidī chín gàmyaht dím ló dōu ló m̀dóu ge la.

15. Néi go bīu laahndākjaih dím jíng dōu jíngm̀fàan ge la.

VI. Final particle 'gwa' indicating probability or doubt.

1. Kéuih wúih heui gwa!
   I think he will probably go.

2. Kéuih nīgo yàhn haih hóu yàhn gwa!
   I believe he is a good man!

3. Nītìuh yú sihkdāk gwa!
   I think this fish is eatable.

4. Kéuih m̀wúih m̀béi chín néi gwa!
   I don't think he will withhold the money from you.

5. Nībún syù néige saimānjái duhkdāk gwa!
   Your child will be able to read this book, I believe.

6. Kéuih juhng sai mei duhkdāk gwa!
   He is still young, I doubt if he can read it.

7. Ngó jàang néi géidò chín a? Móu gamdò gwa!
   How much do I owe you? I don't think it's so much!

8. Kéuih haih Wòhng sìnsàangge daaihlóu mē? M̀haih gwa!
   Is he Mr. Huang's elder brother? I don't think so!

9. Kéuih m̀haih maai bīu gógo yàhn gwa!
   He isn't the man who sells watches, is he?

10. Nīgihn sih m̀hóu gám jouh gwa!
    I think we'd better not handle this matter in this way.

Additional Sentences

1. Néi sé dò léuhngchi jauh sīk la.
2. Néi sái dò léuhngchi jauh wúih sái la.
3. Néi man dò léuhnggo yàhn jauh wúih mandóu la.
4. Néi yìhgā heui ló boují àh? Ngòi néi ló dò léuhngjèung hóu ma?
5. Néi gàmyaht yiu máai dò dī sung boh, yànwaih Chàhn sìnsàang
   kéuihdeih gàmmáan wúih lèih sihkfaahn.
6. Ngó hóu séung yám dò dī, daahnhaih ngó dím yám dōu yám m̀lohk lo.
7. Ngó yíhwàih gàmyaht móu yúh lohk, sèuihjì yìhgā lohk gam daaih
   yúh.

8. Ngó yíhwàih néi m̀jùngyi sihk sāichāan, sèuihjì néi gam̀ jùngyi
   (sihk).
9. Kéuih chùhnglòih dōu m̀háng chéng yàhn sihkfaahn ge, m̀jì dímgáai
   gàmyaht gam sédēk nē?
10. Néi haih m̀haih yáuh hóudò sih yiu jouh a? M̀haih, jihnghaih
    nīdīgamdēu sih jē.
11. Néi géigihn sāam dōu laahnsaai la, jihnghaih nīgihn juhng
    hóyíh jeukdākháh.
12. Haih m̀haih tìuhtìuh louh dōu yáuh ngàihím a? M̀haih, jihnghaih
    gótìuh louh yáuh ngàihím jē.
13. Kéuih wah m̀heui, daahnhaih jyūtjì heuijó.
14. Chàhn sìnsàang wah gógo bīu taai gwai, daahnhaih kéuih jyūtjì
    máaijó.
15. Hòh taaitáai hóu jùngyi nīgihn sāam, daahnhaih kéuih m̀jùngyi
    nīgihn sāamge ngàansīk; kéuih jùngyi gógihn sāamge ngàansīk,
    daahnhaih kéuih m̀jùngyi gógihn sāamge yéung. Gógihn, kéuih
    hóu jùngyi la, daahnhaih taai gwai, jyutjì kéuih móu máai.

Translate the following sentences:

1. He is fifteen now, his height is approximately five feet but
   he isn't as tall as your child.
2. How many brothers and sisters have you? Is that tall one
   your elder brother?
3. The one sitting at the table is my sister; she is fifteen
   year old.
4. Is that hotel very far from here? Not very far, only about
   a mile from here.
5. You walk toward that hotel; when you come to it, you turn
   right. The second building on your righthand side is the
   restaurant which you are looking for.
6. This fish is too heavy; I want to buy one weighing about
   two pounds.
7. I don't think that ship is three thousand tons, at the most
   it is only two thousand tons.
8. Well, my car is heavier than yours and also longer than
   yours; mine weighs more than two tons, and is eleven feet lor
9. Your wife sits in the center, you sit beside your wife on
   the right-hand side, Mr. Huang sits on the left, I'll sit
   opposite your wife.
10. Which car is the cheapest? I want the cheapest one. Is
    that smallest one the cheapest?
11. Of those three ships over there, the largest one is sailing
    to France, the smallest one is bound for China; I don't know
    where the one in between is bound for.

12. My home is two miles farther from school than yours, so I have
    to get up at 6:30 every morning. If there is some place nearer
    to the school please let me know, I'll certainly have a look at
    it.

Below are English translations of sentences used in the vocabulary
of this lesson as examples of usage. Translate these back into
Chinese (numbers correspond to those in Vocabulary section.)

1. Is it true that his eyesight is not very good? No, his eyesight is very good.
2. How far can you (your eyes) see?
3. Do you like seeing plays? Yes, I like seeing them very much.
4. Was the show you saw last night amusing?
5. Is this cloth pretty? This piece isn't as pretty as that one.
6. How much per foot for that material?
7. He said his shoulder is tired.
8. Which of his shoulders is tired? He said it is the left shoulder.
9. Have you read this novel? I haven't, is it interesting?
10. Does the novel belong to you?
11. Do you know what is wrong with this machine? I don't know,
    let me see it once more.
12. Do you know how to fix the machine?
13. Where is this medicine sold? At that store.
14. Are you afraid to take medicines?
15. Do you like this color? I don't like this color.
16. The color of her dress is really beautiful.
17. Is he planning to spend his summer vacation in England? No, he
    plans to study here this summer vacation.
18. Where are you going to spend your summer vacation?
19. Do you like travelling? I like it very much.
20. Where do you plan to travel next week?
21. What kind of sickness has he? I don't know what it is called.
22. Has he been sick for a long time? He has been sick for several
    days.
23. Have you ever been to Chinatown in New York?
24. Is Chinatown in San Francisco extensive? The Chinatown in New
    York isn't as big as the one in San Francisco.
25. Is he a Cantonese? (Lit. Is he a native of Kwangtung province?)
    Yes, he is.
26. Is Hong Kong very far from Kwangtung province?
27. Have you been to Los Angeles? I have been there once.
28. When will you go to Los Angeles?
29. How about all of us going together?
30. All of us can speak Cantonese; why don't we speak it?

31. How has his health been recently? He has been in very good
    health recently.
32. Are you always so healthy?
33. How much is this cake of soap? Those are twenty-five cents a
    cake. These are two dollars and a half.
34. Why is it so expensive? Well, sir, this is made in the U.S.A.
35. Is there a holiday tomorrow? No, there isn't any.
36. When will you have a holiday?
37. When will he start his journey to China? He'll start next week
    Tuesday.
38. How about you? When'll you start?
39. Will our school start on the third of next month? Our school
    is going to start next month, but not on the third.
40. When will your school start after the summer vacation is over?
41. Why doesn't he say something? He said he didn't care to speak.
42. Don't say anything!
43. Is he sick? Yes, he doesn't feel very well.
44. Is he very sick?
45. He speaks Cantonese very distinctly.
46. I didn't see clearly who that man was.
47. I can't remenber clearly who he is.
48. Can you see that white house over there?
49. Do you like to wear white clothing?
50. Your English is quite correct.
51. Does he speak Cantonese accurately?
52. Is this road very dangerous? No, there isn't any danger on
    this road.
53. This is so dangerous, do you dare to do it?
54. This place certainly is very clean.
55. Is that place as clean as this one?
56. I don't know why he isn't very happy today.
57. Do you know why he is so unhappy today?
58. She likes to see a show, I like to read a novel, what do you
    like to do?
59. She can't bear to part with her child.
60. He isn't poor, he merely is loth to spend the money.
61. He is reluctant to invite me to dinner.
62. He likes to spend his money on seeing show, but he hates to
    spend a dime on books.
63. He is a very generous fellow, he always gives a lot of money
    to his friends.
64. Have you had my coat washed? I had it washed two days ago.
65. Have you washed it clean?

66. Do you know how to fly (a plane)? Yes, I do.
67. Is flying or driving more difficult?
68. Open your eyes and look!
69. Why can't I open my eyes?
70. Let me get a rope and tie it up.
71. This rope is too short, I can't tie it up.
72. Mrs. Chen is patting her child to make it go to sleep.
73. After she finished singing, we all clapped our hands.
74. Why don't you go by boat? My children don't like to go by boat, they prefer to go by train.
75. He'll go by boat to Hong Kong tomorrow.
76. Do you like to go by boat or by train?
77. Are you willing to go? I didn't say I wouldn't go.
78. Has he consented?
79. On which day have you decided to go? I've decided that I'll go on the first of next month.
80. Has he decided when he'll come?
81. How much altogether?
82. All told how many chairs in this room?
83. It's only he and I, that's all.
84. He is the only one who doesn't know how to speak Cantonese.
85. He thought you were British, are you or aren't you?
86. I think we'd better not go.
87. Do you think we ought to do this thing?
88. He finally went to Honolulu.
89. Finally we didn't go.
90. He finally bought that book.
91. Who would have thought it — he doesn't even speak a word of English!
92. Who would have thought it — he didn't come!
93. Who would have thought it — he could speak much better than we.
94. Although I don't know how to cook, I do know how to eat!
95. Although I don't know who he is, I do know he is Mr. Huang's friend.
96. Although I haven't been to China, I like China very much.

LESSON 23

INCLUSIVE AND EXCLUSIVE PHRASES

Vocabulary

daaihhohk   PW: university, college

1. Gógàan daaihhohk yáuh géidò hohksāang a?
2. Néi yìhgā hái bīngàan daaihhohk duhk-gán a?

fuhmóu   N: parents

3. Kéuihge fuhmóu hái bīnsyu a? Kéuih fuhmóu hái Hèunggóng.
4. Néi fuhmóu hái bīnsyu a?

a-baak, baakfuh   N: father's elder brothers, uncles,
-baak   a familiar title applied to any elderly man.

5. Néi yáuh géidògo a-baak a? Ngó yáuh sàamgo a-baak.
6. Chàhn-baak gàmnìn géidòseui la?

hauhsāangjái   N: young fellows, youths

7. Gógo hauhsāangjái haih bīngo a? Gógo hauhsāangjái haih Hòh sìnsàangge jái.
8. Chòhhái nei pòhngbīn gógo hauhsāangjá haih bīngo a?

Gwokyúh   N: Chinese Mandarin (language)

9. Kéuih sīk góng Gwokyúh ma? Kéuih m̀sīk góng Gwokyúh, jihnghaih sīk góng Gwóngdùngwá jē.
10. Néi yáuh móu hohkgwo Gwokyúh a?

312

yàhndeih   N: other people

> 11. Yàhndeih góng ge yéh, m̀hóu seunsaai,
>   néi seun dī jauh hóu la.
> 12. Yàhndeih móu, kéuih yihk móu, móu-
>   gányiu, jeui pa yàhndeih yáuh kéuih
>   móu.

cho   N/SV (RVE): error, mistake; fault/ be wrong,
                                        to be wrong

> 13. Kéuih sé gógéigo jih yātdī cho dōu
>   móu.
> 14. Nīsyu chojó yātgo jih, nīgo jih gám-
>   yéung sé ji ngāam.
> 15. Móu cho la, gámyéung sé ngāam la.
> 16. Nījèung boují cho jih taai dò.
> 17. Góngcho móu gányiu, jeui pa jouhcho
>   jē.

sìmàn   SV: be cultured

> 18. Gógo saimānjái jànhaih sìmàn la.
> 19. Kéuih haih sìmàn yàhn.
> 20. Kéuih móu kéuih gam sìmàn.

ngáanfan   SV: be sleep

> 21. Kéuih yāt duhksyù jauh ngáanfan.
> 22. M̀jì dímgáai gàmyaht ngó gam ngáanfan
>   nē?

tèngwah   SV: be obedient

> 23. Gamdògo saimānjái bīngo jeui tèngwah
>   a? Gogo dōu m̀haih géi tèngwah.
> 24. Néi saimānjái gójahnsí tèngwah ma?

kàhnlihk   SV: be industrious, dilligent

> 25. Kéuih jouhsih hóu kàhnlihk.
> 26. Kéuih duhksyù hóu kàhnlihk daahnhaih
>   kéuih m̀haih géi tèngwah.

tóuhngo (or ngo)   SV: be hungry

27. Néi tóuhngo mei a? Ngó mei tóuhngo.
28. Ngó ngo dāk hóu gányiu, yáuh móu yéh
    sihk a?

génghot   SV: be thirsty

29. Néi génghot ma? Ngó yātdī dōu
    ṁgénghot.

báu   SV (RVE): have eaten one's fill, be satisfied

30. Néi (sihk)báu mei a? Ngó yíhgìng
    hóu báu la, ṁsihkdāklohk la.
31. Néi mèi báu ge, sihk dī tìm lā!

waaih   SV: bad (in character); (things) out of
                               order

32. Kéuih go yàhn haih ṁhaih hóu waaih
    a? Kéuih go yàhn ṁhaih hóu waaih
    gwa!
33. Yànwaih gèihei waaihjó sóyíh ṁhàahng-
    dāk.
34. Ngó ga chè waaihjó, néi wúih jéng ma?

pìhngsèuhng   SV/MA: be ordinary/ ordinarily

35. Nīgihn sih hóu pihngsèuhng jē!
36. Nīgo bīu hóu pìhngsèung jē, dímgáai
    maai dāk gam gwai a?

faisih   SV: laborious, troublesome

37. Dímgáai gam faisih ga?[1] Yùhgwó taai
    faisih jauh ṁhóu lo.

leuhnjeuhn   SV: awkward (unskillful, clumsy)

38. Dímgáai gam leuhnjeuhn a?
39. Daihyihchi ṁhou gam leuhnjeuhn lo.
40. Kéuih haih ṁhaih sìhsìh dōu haih gam
    leuhnjeuhn ga?

1. 'Ga' is a fusion of 'ge ╪ a.' See Patt. V.

cheutkeih   SV: strange (unnatural; inexplicable;
                                puzzling)

                            41. Jànhaih chēutkèih la, gàmyaht móu
                                lohkyúh.
                            42. Dímgáai gam chēutkèih, kéuih gàmyaht
                                móu fàanlèih sihkfaahn a?

tyut   V: to undress; to take off

                            43. Gàmyaht gam yiht, dímgáai néi m̀tyut-
                                jó gihn sāam a?
                            44. Dímgáai tyutjó gihn sāam juhnghaih
                                gam yiht a?
                            45. Dímgáai néi m̀tùhng néige saimānjái
                                tyutjó gihn sāam a?

gwajyuh   V: to be concerned with; to worry; to be
                               anxious about

                            46. Néi gwajyuh mātyéh a? Dímgáai ngó
                                tùhng néi góngwá néi dōu tèngm̀gin a?
                            47. Ngó gwajyuh kéuih wán m̀dou sih jouh.

gwasàm   SV: worry, be worried

                            48. Néi m̀sái gwasàm la! Kéuih yìhgìng
                                doujó la.

tái-mùnháu   V: to take care of a house

                            49. Móu yàhn tùhng ngó tái-mùnháu, ngó
                                m̀lèihdāk.
                            50. Bīngo hái ngūkkéi tái-mùnháu a?

yihngdāk   V: to recognize

                            51. Néi juhng yihngdāk kéuih ma? Ngó
                                m̀yihngdāk kéuih.
                            52. Néi yìhngdāk gógo yàhn haih bīngo ma?

siu   V : to laugh
    hóusiu   SV: funny, ridiculous

                            53. Kéuih siu mātyéh a? Kéuih siu kéuih

m̀sīk sái faaijí.
54. Māt(yéh) gam hóusiu a?
55. Néi gú mātyéh gam hóusiu nē?

hàan   V/SV: to save[1] / be thrifty

56. Gám hàan hóudò chín.
57. Kéuih hóu sīk hàan.
58. Kéuih hóu hàan ge.

gú   V/N: to make a guess/ riddle
   gúdóu   RV: guess (an answer) correctly

59. Néi gú ngó yáuh géidò chín? Ngó
    gú nei yauh ngsahpmān.
60. Néi gú m̀gúdākdóu kéuih yáuh géidò
    chín a?

sihkyīn   VO: smoke
   yīn(jái) (M: háu-individual cigarette; jek-brand)
                        N: cigarette

61. Néi sihkyīn ma? Ngó m̀sihkyīn.
62. Sihk (yāt) háu lā!
63. Nījek haih m̀haih Yìnggwok yīn a?

hóujoih   MA: fortunately

64. Hóujoih gàmyaht móu lohkyúh.
65. Hóujoih néi móu heui.
66. Hóujoih ngó móu sihk.

sàuh   V: worry

67. Néi sàuh mātyéh a?
68. Néi m̀sái sàuh kéuih m̀làih.

yeuhkm̀haih   MA: otherwise

69. Hóujoih móu lohkyúh, yeuhkm̀haih jauh
    hóu leuhnjeuhn la.
70. Hóujoih néi lèihjó, yeuhkm̀haih ngó
    m̀jì dím syun la.

1. i.e. To save money by getting a bargain, etc.; but hàan does not
   mean "save up (money)"

ṁjí

MA: not merely...; not only...; not as little as you say

71. Kéuih ṁjí sīk góng Jùnggwok wá, juhng sīk sé Jùnggwok jih tìm.
72. Kéuih ṁjí yáuh leuhnggo jái, juhng yáuh sàamgo néui tìm.
73. Ṁjí, ngó jìdou kéuih yáuh luhkgo jái baatgo néui.

chìhngyún

A: rather; prefer

74. Ngó chìhngyún hohk góng Jùnggwok wá, ṁchìhngyún hohk sé Jùnggwok jih.
75. Ngó chìhngyún duhksyù, ṁchìhngyún jouhsih.
76. Néi chìhngyún heui Hèunggóng yīkwaahk heui Tàahnhēungsāan a?

sèhng-

NU: a whole, entire

77. Dímgáai sèhnggàan ngūk dōu móu dāng a?
78. Gàmyaht sèhngyaht dōu haih gam yiht.
79. Kéuih sèhnggoyuht móu lèihgwo la.

kàuhkèih

MA: at one's convenience, pleasure; any (whatever)

80. Kàuhkèih néi géisìh lèih dōu dāk.
81. Néi kàuhkèih jùngyi bīngo jauh ló bīngo.
82. Kàuhkèih yātgo dōu dāk.

joi

A: again

83. Nīgo jih yiu joi ségwo. Kéuih yáuh móu joi lèihgwo a?
84. Joi duhk leuhngchi tìm jauh sīk la.

jouh

V: be, act as

85. Kéuih haih jouh mātyéh ga? Kéuih haih jouh sàangyi ge.
86. Néi hái gósyu jouh sìnsàang àh?
87. Ṁhaih, ngó hái gósyu jouh hohksāang jē.

Useful Expressions

juhkyúh wah	there is a saying
hóusēng boh!	be careful!
fongsām lā!	don't worry (lit. be free from an anxiety)
Móu cho la!	That's right!
Móusówaih!	It doesn't matter!

Reading

Léih sìnsàang Léih taaitáai chìhn-léuhngyaht hái Méigwok geijó fûng seun béi ngó, yiu ngó heui Hèunggóng daaihhohk taamháh kéuih-deihdī saimānjái, fuhmóu gwasàm jái-néui, gogo dōu haih yātyeuhng ge lo!

Ngó sahpgéinìn móu gingwo kéuihdeihdī saimānjái lo!

Góyaht, ngó heuidou Hèunggóng daaihhohk wán kéuihdeih, ngó wah ngó wán Léih Gwok-Lèuhng tùhng Léih Gwok-Jān, táimùnháu gógo yàhn wah: "Ngódeih nīsyu móu gám(yéuhng) ge yàhn." Ngó wah: "Gám jauh chēutkèih la! Néideih nīsyu jànhaih móu nī-léuhnggo yàhn àh!?" Gógo yàhn séungjó yātjahngāan, kéuih béi géigo méng ngó tái, man ngó haih mhaih nīgéigo méng, ngó wah: "Mhaih nīgo yihk mhaih gógo, dáng ngó séunghàh ..., kéuihdeih mhaih giujouh Gwok-Lèuhng, Gwok-Jān jauhhaih giujouh Gok-Lèuhng, Gok-Jān la. Néideih nīsyu yáuh móu nī léuhnggo hohksāang a?" Gógo yàhn wah: "Móu cho la! Kéuihdeih léuhnggo haih hái Méigwok fàanlàih duhksyù ge, haih mhaih a?" Ngó wah: "Haih la!"

Yātjahngāan, yáuh géigo yàhn hái làuhseuhng jáu lohklèih, gógo yàhn wah: "Kéuihdeih lohkgánlàih la." Ngó wah: "Bīngo haih Léih Gok-Lèuhng, bīngo haih Léih Gok-Jān a?" Gógo yàhn wah: "Néi msīk kéuihdeih mē?" Ngó wah: "Ngó myihngdāk kéuihdeih lo!"

Yáuh go néuijái hàahngmàailèih wah: "Néi haih Chàhn-baak àh?" Ngó wah: "Haih la! Néi jauhhaih Gok-Jān làh!" Kéuih wah: "Haih la! Ngó jauh haih Gok-Jān, Gok-Lèuhng haih ngó a-gō, néi juhng yihngdāk kéuih ma? Nīgo jauhhaih Gok-Lèuhng la!" Ngó táigin Gok-Lèuhng yauh gòu yauh daaih, Gok-Jān yauh leng yauh sìmàn, ngó wah: "Gok-Jān, néi jànhaih yuht daaih yuht leng lo! Néi bàhbā-màmā tái-gin néi jauh hòisàm lo, kéuihdeih yáuh móu (sé) seun béi néideih a?"

Kéuih wah: "M̀jí yáuh seun lèih juhng geijó hóudò chín béi ngódeih tìm!" Ngó wah: "Kéuihdeih hóu gwasàm néideih boh, dímgáai néideih m̀sé seun béi kéuihdeih a?" Gok-Jān siuháh wah: "Juhkyúh wah: "Móu seun jīk pìhngngòn"[1] lā má, Chàhn-baak! Ngó wah: "Néideihdī hauhsāangjái jìhnghaih m̀jì jouh fuhmóuge gwasàm néideih ge."[2]

Pattern Sentences

I. Cumulative expressions

A. 'Yauh...yauh' (Both...and)

1. Nījèung tói yauh pèhng yauh leng.
   This table is both good-looking and inexpensive.

2. Nījī bāt yauh gwai yauh m̀hóu.

3. Gógo yàhn yauh gòu yauh daaih.

4. Gógo saimānjái yauh chùngmìng yauh tèngwah.

5. Ngó yauh guih yauh ngáanfan.

6. Nīgo chāan yauh gwai yauh m̀hóu sihk.

7. Kéuih ga chè yauh faai yauh hóusái.

8. Gàmyahtge tìnhei yauh lohkyúh yauh láahng.

9. Ngó jyuh gógàan ngūk yauh yúhn yauh m̀hóu.

10. Kéuih sé ge jih yauh daaih yauh cháuyéung.

B. 'Yuht...yuht...' used as 'The more...the more...,' 'yuht lèih...yuht...' used as 'getting more and more... .'

1. Kéuih yuht daaih yuht leng.
   The older she gets the handsomer she is.

2. Gógo saimānjái yuht lèih yuht tèngwah.

1. "Móu (Lit. 'móu') seun jīk pìhngngòn" "No news is good news."
2. Jìhnghaih...ge., always....

3. Néidī Gwóngdùngwá góngdāk yuht lèih yuht hóu boh!

4. Yìhgā nī géifo syù yuht lèih yuht nàanduhk la!

5. Gógàan chāangúnge chāan ngó yuht sihk yuht jùngyi sihk.

6. Nīgihn sih yuht jouh yuht nàan m̀jī dím(yéung) jouh sìnji hóu.

7. Kéuihge chín yuht lèih yuht dò m̀jī dím(yéung) ji sáidāksaai

8. Nīfo syù jànhaih nàan lo! Ngó yuht duhk yuht m̀sīk.

9. Kéuih wah yāt yám jáu jauh m̀génghot, ngó wah yuht yám jáu yuht génghot.

10. Kéuih wah chín m̀pa dò, chín yuht dò yuht hóu, ngó wah chín yuht dò jauh yuht sàuh dī chín wúih síujó.

C. 'M̀jī (wah)...juhng...(tìm)' (Not only...but also)
   'M̀jī...   yihkdōu...   ' (Not only...but also)

1. Kéuih m̀jī sīk Yìngmàn juhng sīk Faatmàn tìm.
   He knows not only English but also French.

2. Kéuih m̀jī sīk (góng) Gwóngdùngwá juhng sīk Gwokyúh tìm.

3. Ngó m̀jī jùngyi yám Jùnggwok chàh, juhng jùngyi yám Jùngwok jáu tìm.

4. Ngó m̀jī tùhng ngó taaitáai heui juhng tùhngmàai ngódeihdī saimànjái heui tìm.

5. Kéuih m̀jī (wah) jihgéi m̀heui juhng sái kéuihdī pàhngyáuh dōu m̀hóu heui.

6. Ngó m̀jī séung hohk Gwóngdùngwá juhng séung hohk Gwokyúh tìm

7. Gógàan poutáu m̀jī maai Yìngmàn syù juhng maai Jùngmàn syù t

8. Gógàan hohkhaauh m̀jī yáuh hóudò Jùnggwok sìnsàang juhng yáu
   hóudò Méigwok sìnsàang tìm.

9. Ngó m̀jī sīk Yìngmàn yihkdōu sīk Faatmàn.

10. Kéuih m̀jī sihk yīn yihkdōu yám jáu.

91. There are very few true conjunctions in Cantonese. Adverbs
    function as connectives between verbs and clauses.

    D. 'Lìhn...dōu' (Even including, even)

        1. Lìhn néi dōu m̀seun ngó àh?
           Won't even you trust me?

        2. Lìhn jeui nàange ngó dōu sīk la.

        3. Lìhn néi dōu m̀heui àh?

        4. Lìhn ngó dōu m̀jì kéuih sing māt.

        5. Lìhn faahn dōu m̀séung sihk.

        6. Lìhn yātgo sīn dōu móu.

        7. Lìhn góléuhngbún syù giujouh mātyéh <u>méng</u> ngó dōu m̀jì.

        8. Lìhn jì makséuibāt dōu m̀giujó.

        9. Kéuih góng gódī wá haih mātyéh wá a? Dímgáai ngó lìhn
           yātgeui dōu m̀sīk a?

       10. Dím syun a? Ngó lìhn kéuihge mùnpàaih dōu m̀geidākjó!

92. <u>Lìhn</u> is a co-verb whose object may be either nominal or verbal.
    The main verb of the sentence, which is modified by the <u>lìhn-O</u> [1]
    phrase, must be preceded by <u>dōu</u>.

II. Alterntive expressions, double denial

    A. 'M̀haih...jauhhaih' (Either...or)

        1. M̀haih nīgo yàhn jauhhaih gógo yàhn.
           It is either this man or that man.

        2. Kéuih géisí lèihgwo a? M̀haih kàhmyaht jauhhaih chìhnyaht.

        3. Kéuih ngūkkéige mùnpàaih m̀haih 231 houh jauhhaih 321 houh.

        4. Kéuih m̀haih duhksyù jauhhaih séjih jànhaih kàhnlihk la.

1. O, i.e. object.

5. M̀haih nītìuh sósìh jauhhaih gótìuh sósìh, kàuhkèih yāttìuh dōu hóyìh hòi(dāk) gódouh mǜn ge la.

6. M̀haih nīgàan poutáu jauhhaih gógàan poutáu néi yātdihng hóyìh máaidóu góbún syù ge la.

7. Góga fèigèi m̀haih hái Nīuyēuk lèih jauhhaih hái Gauhgām-sāan lèih ge la.

8. Kéuih m̀haih chóh nīga chè jauhhaih chóh góga chè heui ga la.

9. Ngó geidāk kéuih m̀haih gaau Yìngmàn ge jauhhaih gaau cheung-gō ge la.

10. Nīgihn sāam m̀haih chìhnnín máai ge jauhhaih gauhnín máai ge la.

B. 'M̀haih...yihkm̀haih'   (Neither...nor).
    'M̀...yihk m̀....'   (Neither...nor).
    'Móu...yihkmóu....'   (Neither...nor).
    'M̀jí...yihkdōu m̀...'   (Neither...nor).

1. M̀haih nīgo yihk m̀haih gógo, m̀jí haih m̀haih gógo nē?
   It is neither this one nor that one, it might be that one?

2. Kéuih jeui jùngyi ge m̀haih chín yihkm̀haih méng, néi gú haih mātyéh nē?

3. Kéuih m̀jí m̀yám jáu yihkdōu m̀sihk yīn jànhaih sīk hàan lo.

4. Kéuih m̀duhksyù yihk m̀jouhsih m̀jí kéuih yahtyaht chóhhái ngūkkéisyu jouh mātyéh nē?

5. Kéuih góng gódī wá m̀haih Gwóngdùngwá yihkm̀haih Gwokyúh, néi jì m̀jí haih mātyéh wá a?

6. Néi wah nīgihn sih m̀haih néi jouhchojó yihkm̀haih kéuih jouhchojó, gám bīngo jouhchojó a?

7. Ngó yiu ge m̀haih nībún syù yihkm̀haih góbún syù haih yātbún gaau yàhn hohk Gwóngdùngwá ge syù.

8. Néi jyuhhái nītìuh gāai àh? M̀haih, m̀haih nītìuh yihkm̀haih gótìuh haih hái gógàan daaih ngūk hauhbihn gótìuh.

9. Néi wah kéuih m̀haih chóh fèigèi yihkm̀haih chóh fòchè lèih
   kéuih chóh mātyéh lèih ga?

10. Ngó m̀jùngyi táisyù yihk m̀jùngyi táiboují, ngó jùngyi tái-
    siusyut.

11. Nībún syù móu góbún syù gam gauh yihkmóu góbún syù gam
    gwai, m̀jì néi jùngyi m̀(jùngyi) nē?

12. Ngóge Gwóngdùngwá góng dāk móu kéuih gam hóu yihkmóu kéuih
    (góng dāk) gam faai.

13. Yìngmàn jih móu Jùnggwok jih gam nàan sé, yihkmóu Jùnggwok
    jih gam nàanduhk.

14. Gàmyaht móu kàhmyaht gam láahng yihkmóu kàhmyaht gam daaih
    fùng.

15. Nīgihn sāam móu gógihn sāam gam leng yihkmóu gógihn sāam
    gam hóujeuk.

III. The uses of béi:

A. Co-verb of agent 'béi' indicates 'by'

1. Gójèung yí béi gógo saimānjái jínglaahnjó.
   The chair was broken by that boy.

2. Góga chè béi kéuih sáigwo jìhauh jauh m̀hàahng la.

3. Ngó gihn sāam béi kéuih jeuklaahnjó.

4. Gogàan ngūk béi kéuih jyuhjó la.

5. Gódī chàh béi ngódeih yámsaai la.

B. Co-verb 'béi' indicates 'let,' 'allow'

1. Kéuihdeih m̀béi ngó jáu, yātdihng giu ngó hái kéuihdeihsyu
   sihkfaahn.

2. Néi béi nīdī chín kéuih daahnhaih m̀hóu béi kéuih sáisaai
   kéuih.

3. Kéuih màmā m̀béi kéuih heui boh, dímgáai néi béi kéuih heui
   a?

4. Kéuih gam jùngyi tùhng gódī saimānjái wáan, béi kéuih heui
   lā.

5. Yùhgwó néi béi kéuih sái góga chè hóu faaicheui jauh laahn
   la.

C. Béi used as a suffix of verb.

   1. Dímgáai kéuih m̀maaibéi néi nē?
      Why didn't he sell it to you?

   2. Kéuih wah kéuih yíhgìng m̄aaijóbéi Chàhn sìnsàang la.

   3. Nībún syù haih bīngo jebéi néi ga?

   4. Chéng néi jouhbéi ngó táiháh.

   5. Nījì bāt haih ngó go pàhngyáuh sungbéi ngó ge.

D. Béi used as 'to'.

   1. Ngó sungjó ga chè béi gógàan hohkhaauh.
      I presented a car to that school.

   2. Ngó máaijó léuhngbún syù béi ngóge saimānjái.

   3. Kéuih wah kéuih yāt dou Jùnggwok jauh sé seun béi néi, kéuih
      móu sébéi néi mē?

   4. Dímgáai néi m̀góng(béi) ngó tèng néi sungjó dī mātyéh béi
      kéuìh a?

   5. M̀gòi néi nīk nī-léuhngbún syù heui béi kéuih.

E. Béi used as 'for (someone to do something)':

   1. Dáng ngó heui ló jèung yí lèih béi Jèung sìnsàang chóh.
      Let me go and get a chair for Mr. Chang to sit down.

   2. M̀gòi néi dáng yātjahngāan, ngó heui ló dī yéh lèih béi dī
      saimānjái wáan.

   3. Ngó heui ló bùi jáu lèih béi néi yám néi jauh móu gam guih

   4. M̀gòi néi heui ló jèung boují lèih béi ngó táiháh tīngyaht
      yáuh móu fèigèi heui Méigwok.

5. Yáuh mātyéh sih béi ngó jouh ma?

F. Béi used as 'with' (using)

1. Béi Jùnggwok bāt sé Yìngmàn hóu nàansé.
   It's very difficult to write English with a Chinese brush.

2. Béi dī bou jaatjyuh kéuih jauh dāk la.

3. Nīdī yéh yiu béi chìhgāng sihk.

4. Béi go bohng bohnghâh kéuih jauh jìdou géi chúhng la.

5. Néi yiu béi yauhsáu nīk mhóu béi jósáu nīk.

IV. Final particle 'wóh' shows quotation from other's speech:

1. Kéuih mheui wóh. (Kéuih wah kéuih mheui wóh).
   He said that he wouldn't go.

2. Kéuih wah kéuih hóu jùngyi sihk tòhngchāan wóh.

3. Kéuih wah kéuih haih Jùnggwok yàhn daahnhaih kéuih msīk góng
   Jùnggwok wá wóh.

4. Kéuih wah sihk mātyéh dōu móusówaih wóh.

5. Kéuih wah néi chùhnglòih dōu mei chénggwo kéuih yám chàh wóh.

6. Kéuih wah kéuih chùhnglòih (dōu) mei hohkgwo Jùnggwokwá (wóh),
   daahnhaih kéuih góng dāk gam hóu néi seun ma?

7. Kéuih wah géidím jūng lèih a? Léuhngdím wóh.

8. Kéuih yiu myiu nījèung tói a? Kéuih myiu nījèung yiu gójèung
   wóh.

9. Bīngo wah ngó máai yéh móu béi chín a? Gógo wóh.

10. Gógàan poutáu lèihjó hóudò sàn syù wóh, ngó séung heui máai
    sàamléuhngbún.

93. Final particle 'ge' (situational'ge'), 'such is the case':

Ge is used at the end of a sentence to assert that the situation
described is the case:

Nīgihn sih néi yiu manháh kéuih sìnji dāk ge.
    You'd better ask him about this first. (That's what you'd
    better do.)

The (haih)... V ge construction stressing attendant circumstance
(Les. 14, Patt. II, pp. 162-163) is a special usage of the struc
tural ge:

Kéuih kàhmyaht lèih ge.
    He came yesterday. (That's when it was.)
Ngó chóh syùhn fàanlèih ge.
    I returned by boat. (That's how I returned.)

In some situations the 'ge' may be changed to 'ga' by the addition of a final particle 'a' (different from the question particle 'a') which imparts a warning tone to the sentence:

Nīgihn sih néi yiu manháh kéuih sìnji dāk ga.
    You'd better ask him about this first. (I'm warning you
    that's what you'd better do.)
Yùhgwó góng kéuih tèng, kéuih wúih nàu ga.
    If you tell him, he's going to be angry. (I warn you that's
    how it's going to be.)

The question particle 'a' also contracts with 'ge' to form 'ga':

Dímgáai gam faisih ga?
    Why is it so troublesome? (Why does it have to be this way?

Additional Sentences

1. Kéuih wah nīgihn sih haih hóu pìhnsèuhng ge sih, chéng néi m̀hóu
   gwasàm.
2. Kéuih pìhngsèuhng lìhn yātgeui wá dōu m̀góng, m̀jì dímgáai kéuih
   gàmyaht góng gamdò wá.
3. Ngó m̀jì Dākgwok wá haih gam nàan ge, yùhgwó ngó jì Dākgwok wá
   haih gam nàan ge ngó chìhngyùn hohk Faatgwok wá la.
4. Jyú tòhngchāan gam faisih, ngó chìhngyùn sihk sāichāan lo.
5. Góga sànge gam gwai, ngó chìhngyùn máai góga gauhge la.
6. Ngó máai nījáan dāng móu yuhng, ngó chìhngyùn máai gójáan la.
7. Néi yiu kàhnlihk duhksyù yeuhkm̀haih yàhndeih jauh wúih wah néi
   m̀haih hóu hohksāang la.
8. Nīga chè néi yiu gam sái jì dāk, yeuhkm̀haih jauh hóu yihlaahn la.

9. Nīdī yéh sihk m̀báu ge, ngó chìhngyún sihkfaahn la.
10. Ngó yìhgā yauh tóuhngo yauh ngáanfan, yeuhkm̀haih ngó jauh bòng nei la.
11. Pìhngsèuhng yuhng nīgo faatjí jauh jouhdāk la, m̀jì dímgáai gàmyaht m̀jouhdāk nē?
12. Kéuih wah gósyu hóu ngàihhím, m̀hóu heui gósyu, yeuhkm̀haih ngó yìhgìng heuijó gósyu lo.
13. Pìhngsèuhng kéuih tùhngmàai kéuihdī pàhngyáuh yātchái heui, sóyíh ngó hóu fongsàm.
14. Haih m̀haih hóu faisih a? Yùhgwó taai faisih jauh m̀hóu lo.
15. Pìhngsèuhng ngó giu kéuih jouhsih, yeuhngyeuhng dōu jouh dāk ngāam ge, m̀jì dímgáai gàmyaht jouh m̀ātyéh nē?

Translate the following sentences:

1. I had my car fixed just yesterday, I don't know why it's still going so slowly.
2. Although he talks very slowly, I don't know what he is talking about.
3. I can't drive as fast as he does.
4. They don't charge as much for it as you do.
5. Oh, no! We sell it much more cheaply than they do.
6. Which of you two types faster?
7. He types a little faster than I do.
8. Please give me a tiny bit more!
9. No matter how I say this word I can't say it correctly.
10. I don't think that car will go so fast.
11. I thought that he talked very slowly, who would have thought that he talked faster than I do.
12. Although I can't write as fast as he can, nevertheless I can read as fast as he can.
13. No matter how I try, I can't wash it clean.
14. He is very fond of reading novels, he reads much more than I do.

Below are English translations of sentences used in the vocabulary of this lesson as examples of usage. Translate these back into Chinese (numbers correspond to those in Vocabulary section.)

1. How many students does that college have?
2. At which university are you studying now?
3. Where are his parents? His parents are in Hong Kong.
4. Where are your parents?
5. How many uncles do you have? I have three uncles.

6. How old is uncle Chan?
7. Who is that young fellow? He is Mr. Ho's son.
8. Who is the young fellow sitting beside you?
9. Does he know how to speak Mandarin? He doesn't know how to speak Mandarin, he speaks only Cantonese.
10. Have you ever studied Mandarin before?
11. Don't believe all that other people say, believe only some of it.
12. If other people don't have what she doesn't have that's all right; but if other people have what she doesn't have — beware!
13. There isn't a single error in the characters he wrote.
14. Here is a mistake, this character should be written this way.
15. That's right, that's the way to write it.
16. There are many errors in this newspaper.
17. There's no harm in saying it wrong, but beware of doing it wrong.
18. That child is really very gentle.
19. He is a cultured gentleman.
20. He isn't as cultured as she is.
21. Whenever he studies, he feels sleepy.
22. I don't know why I'm so sleepy today!
23. Which is the most obedient of all the children? None of them is very obedient.
24. Were you obedient when you were a child?
25. He is a very industrious worker.
26. He is very studious, but he isn't very obedient.
27. Aren't you hungry yet? Not yet.
28. I'm terribly hungry, is there anything to eat?
29. Are you thirsty? I'm not a bit thirsty.
30. Have you had enough (to eat)? I'm so full that I can't eat any more.
31. I know that you haven't had enough yet, come on, have some more!
32. Is he a very bad man? I don't think that he is a very bad man.
33. Because the engine is out of order, it won't run.
34. My car is out of order, do you know how to fix it?
35. It is a very trifling matter.
36. This is a very ordinary watch, how come it sells for so much?
37. How come it is so troublesome? If it's too troublesome, please don't bother.
38. Why is it that it is so awkward?
39. Next time don't be so clumsy!
40. Does he always behave so awkwardly?
41. It is strange that it didn't rain today.
42. How strange that he hasn't come home to eat today!
43. The weather is so hot, why don't you take off your coat?
44. How come it is so hot even after I have taken off my coat?
45. Why don't you take off your child's coat?
46. What are you worried about, why don't you pay any attention to what I say?

47. I'm worried he might not be able to find a job.
48. You don't have to worry now, she has already arrived.
49. There is no one to take care of my house for me, I can't come.
50. Who is going to mind the house? That man is sitting there to watch the door.
51. Do you still recognize him? I can't recognize him at all.
52. Do you recognize that man?
53. What is he laughing at? He is laughing because he doesn't know how to use chopsticks.
54. What is so funny about it?
55. Can you guess what's so funny about it?
56. That way will save a lot of money.
57. She really knows how to be thrifty.
58. She is very saving.
59. (You) guess how much money I have? I guess you have fifty dollars.
60. Can you guess how much money he has?
61. Do you smoke? No, don't.
62. Please have one!
63. Is it an English brand?
64. Fortunately it hasn't rained today.
65. It was lucky you weren't there. (or you didn't go)
66. It was lucky that I didn't eat it.
67. What are you worrying about?
68. You don't need to worry that he won't come.
69. It's lucky that it isn't raining, otherwise it will be very awkward.
70. It's lucky that you are here, otherwise I wouldn't know what to do.
71. He not only knows how to speak Chinese, but can also write Chinese characters.
72. He not only has two sons but also three daughters.
73. No, there aren't as few as you say, I know he has six sons and eight daughters.
74. I would rather learn to speak Chinese than learn to write Chinese characters.
75. I prefer studying to working.
76. Would you prefer to go to Hong Kong or to Honolulu?
77. How is it that there isn't a light in the entire house?
78. It was hot the whole day long today.
79. He hasn't been here for a whole month.
80. It's O.K. for you to come anytime.
81. You may take anyone you like at your pleasure.
82. Anyone will do.
83. You have to write this character again. Has he come again?
84. You'll know it by reading it over two more times.
85. What is his profession? He is a business man.
86. Are you a teacher there?
87. No, I am only a student.

LESSON 24

PAIRED CLAUSES

Vocabulary

yèuhnghóng	N:	foreign firm

1. Kéuih hái yèuhnghóng jouhsih.
2. Gógàan yèuhnghóng giujouh mātyéh méng a?

Singdaanjit	N:	Christmas

3. Singdaanjit fong m̀fongga a?
4. Singdaanjit néi dasyun heui bīnsyu wáan a?

chèngchoi	N:	green vegetables

5. Nīdī chèngchoi géi(dò)chín bohng a?
6. Nīdī chèngchoi hái bīnsyu lèih ga?
   Nīdī chèngchoi haih hái Gwóngjàu lèih ge.

yīsāng	N:	physician

7. Ngó go pàhngyáuh behngjó, ngó yiu wán go yīsāng heui tái kéuih.
8. Yīsāng lèihgán mei a? Yīsāng lèihgán la.

gújái	N:	story

9. Nīgo gújái haih góng gauhsìh yātgo hó wúih cheunggō ge yàhn ge.
10. Ngó jùngyi tèng gújái, ngó m̀wúih góng gújái.
11. (Néi) góng go gújái béi ngódeih tèng hóu ma?

330

siuwá   N: joke

                                  12. Yáuh yātgo siuwá, ...
                                  13. Gógo siuwá wah ...
                                  14. Gógo siuwá jàn(haih) hóusiu la.

séui   N: water

                                  15. Ngó séung yám séui, néi yám ma?
                                  16. Gódī séui yámdāk ma?

hèunghá   N: the country; (rural) one's native place

                                  17. Gahnlói néi yáuh móu fàan hèunghá a?
                                  18. Néi haih bīnsyu hèunghá ga?

sáangsèhng   N: capital city of a province; it also means
                                  Canton

                                  19. Kéuih haih sáangsèhngjái m̀haih hèung-
                                      hájái.
                                  20. Gwóngjàu haih Gwóngdùngge sáangsèhng.

chìhngyìhng   N: circumstances; condition; situation

                                  21. Yìhgā Jùnggwokge chìhngyìhng dím-
                                      yéung a?
                                  22. Hèunggóngge chìhngyìhng wúih m̀wúih
                                      béi sáangsèhng hóudī a?
                                  23. Gósyuge chìhngyìhng dímyéung a?
                                      Yáuh móu ngàihhím a?

sāmgāp   SV: be impatient

                                  24. Kéuih go yàhn hóu sāmgāp ge, néi
                                      faaidī heui lā.
                                  25. M̀sái gam sāmgāp, kéuih jauh fàanlèih
                                      ge la.
                                  26. M̀sái gam sāmgāp, néidī Gwóngjàuwá
                                      jauh lèih góng dāk hóu hóu la.

yáih   SV: be bad or poor (in quality)

                                  27. Nīgihn sāam gam yáih, yāt jeuk jauh
                                      laahn la.
                                  28. Dímgáai néi máai go gam yáih ga?

29. Gógo saimānjái hóu yáih, hóu m̀tèngwah

bahn   SV: be stupid

30. Kéuih jànhaih bahn lo, lìhn nīgo jih
    dōu m̀sīk.
31. M̀pa bahn, jeui pa mātyéh dōu m̀man.
32. Daihyihchi m̀hóu gam bahn lo.

dākyi   SV: be interesting, cute, strange

33. Góchēut hei jànhaih dākyi la.
34. Néige saimānjái jànhaih dākyi la.
35. Dímgáai kéuih gam dākyi ga, kéuih wah
    lèih dímgáai yìhgā juhng mei lèih a?

hùhngsīk   N: red color
  hùhng   SV: be red

36. Hùhngsīkge hóutái.
37. Ngó ga chè haih hùhngsīk ge.

wòhngsīk   N: yellow color
  wòhng   SV: be yellow

38. Wòhng hòh hái bīnsyu a? Wòhng hoh
    hái Jùnggwok.
39. Góga wòhngsīkge chè haih bīngo ga?

làahmsīk   N: blue color
  làahm   SV: be blue

40. Kéuih m̀jùngyi làahmsīkge, kéuih jùng-
    yi hùhngsīkge.
41. Ngó jùngyi hái hóibīn tái gódī làahm-
    sīkge hóiséui.

luhksīk   N: green color
  luhk   SV: be green

42. Yìhgā haih luhk dāng la, m̀haih hùhng
    dāng la.
43. Chàhn síujé hóu jùngyi jeuk luhksīkge
    sāam.

fūisīk   N: gray color

                                      44. Ngó ga chè haih fūisīk ge, néi ga nē?
                                      45. Ngó fùnhéi fūksīk gójèung tói, ngó
                                               mjùngyi gójèung luhksīkge.
                                      46. Gójek fūisīkge syùhn haih mātyéh
                                             syùhn a?

sànfú   SV: be taxing, exhausting; causing suffering

                                      47. Nīgihn sih gam sànfú mhóu jouh lo.
                                      48. Kéuih haih mhaih behng dāk hóu sànfú
                                             a?
                                      49. Gàmyaht jànhaih yiht dāk sànfú lo.

mhóuyisi   SV: embarassed; embarassing
                                AV: ashamed to

                                      50. Mhóuyisi gwa! (Mhaih gei hóu yisi gwa!)
                                      51. Jànhaih mhóu yisi lo!
                                      52. Msái mhóuyisi, néi heui man kéuih la.
                                      53. Mhóuyisi!

Gwai-   SV: your honorable — as to school, store,
                                factory, etc.

                                      54. Gwai-hohkhaauh yáuh géidò yàhn a?
                                      55. Gwai-léuihgún yáuh géidògàan fóng a?
                                      56. Gwai-yèuhnghóng yáuh géidò yàhn jouh-
                                             sih a?

wìhnghahng   SV: be privileged (to do something), feel
                                privileged (that ...)

                                      57. Ngó gokdāk fèisèuhng wìhnghahng,
                                             gàmyaht hóyíh lèih Gwaihaauh chàahmgùn.
                                      58. Ngó gokdāk hóu wìhnghahng ngó hóyíh
                                               lèihdou Gwaigwok chàahmgùn.
                                      59. Ngó gokdāk fèisèuhng wìhnghahng gàm-
                                             yaht lèih nīsyu tùhng gokwái kìngháh.

gok   SP: each, every

                                      60. Gokyàhn yáuh gokyàhnge sih.
                                      61. Gokwái chéngchóh.
                                      62. 'Gokwái pàhngyáuh ...'

manhauh   V: to ask after the health of (someone);
                                     to send kind regards to ...

                                     63. Kéuih giu ngó manhauh néi.
                                     64. Néi yauh móu tùhng ngó manhauh kéuih
                                         a?
                                     65. Ṁgòi néi tùhng ngó manhauh kéuih.

wùihseun (béi ...)   VO: to send a letter in return (to ...)

                                     66. Néi wùihjó fùng seun béi kéuih mei a?
                                     67. Kéuih yáuh móu wùihseun béi néi a?

gwo   V: to pass; to cross

                                     68. Gwojó gàmnín kéuih jauh chātseui la.
                                     69. Yìhgìng gwojó léuhnggo láihbaai la,
                                         kéuih juhng mei lèih.
                                     70. Gwojó gógàan poutáu jauhhaih la.

jàm   V: to pour

                                     71. Ṁgòi néi jàm bùi chàh béi ngó.
                                     72. Ṁgòi néi jàm dò dī.
                                     73. Dímgáai ṁjàmdākchēut a?

yùhnleuhng   V: to excuse
  (or gìnleuhng)

                                     74. Chéng néi yùhnleuhng ngó! Ngó gàm-
                                         yaht ṁdākhàahn.
                                     75. Chéng néi gìnleuhng ngó, ngó móufaat
                                         tùhng néi heui.
                                     76. Néi gìnleuhng kéuih nī yātchi la,
                                         daihyihchi kéuih ṁgáam la.

mìngbaahk   V/SV: to understand; be clear (lit. under-
                                        standable)

                                     77. Néi mìngbaahk ngóge yisi ma?
                                     78. Néi yìhgā mìngbaahk mei a? Kéuih
                                         góng dāk ṁhaih géi mìngbaahk
                                     79. Ṁgòi néi góng mìngbaahk dī dāk ma?

binsèhng   V: to become; to change into

                                     80. Kéuih yìhgā binsèhng ngóge hóu
                                         pàhngyáuh la.

81. Baahksīkge hóyíh binsèhng hāaksīkge,
daahnhaïh hāaksīkge móu faatjí binsèhng baahksīkge.
82. Kéuih búnlòih haih yātgo fèihlóu,
yìhgā kéuih binsèhng saulóu la.

dádihnwá   VO: to make a phone call

83. Néi dádihnwá béi bīngo a? Ngó dá
(dihnwá) béi ngóge sìnsàang.
84. Néi dábéi kéuih jouh mātyéh a?
85. Ṁgòi néi tùhng ngó dá yātgo dihnwá
dāk ma?

chàamgùn   V: to pay a visit to (a school, factory, etc.)

86. Yáuh yàhn chéng ngó heui chàahmgùn
Héunggóng daaihhohk.
87. Ngó séung heui chàahmgùn néideihge
hohkhaauh, dāk ṁdāk a?
88. Ngó kàhmyaht chàahmgùn géigàan hohkhaauh, gàangàan dōu hóu hóu.

lihng(dou)   CV: to cause

89. Góchi lihng ngó hóu ṁhóuyisi.
90. Gám ge tìnghei lihng yàhn gokdāk hóu
ṁjihyìhn.
91. Nīgihn sih lihng ngó hóu nàanjouh.

yíngóng   V/N: to give a speech/ a speech

92. Kéuih yíngóng dāk hóu hóu.
93. Yáuh yàhn chéng kéuih heui yíngóng.
94. Néi yáuh móu hohkgwo yíngóng a?

jihchùhng   MA: ever since; since

95. Jihchùhng kéuih hohksīk Gwóngdùngwá
jìhauh, kéuih jauh sìhsìh dōu góng
Gwóngdùngwá la.
96. Jihchùhng néi jáujó jìhauh, kéuih
móu lèihgwo.
97. Jihchùhng kéuih máaijó ga chè kéuih
jauh móu chín la.

| chénghaak | VO: to give a party (lit. to invite a guest) |

98. Gàmyaht yáuh móu yàhn chénghaak a?
99. Haih m̀haih néi chénghaak a?
100. Kéuih hóu jùngyi chénghaak.

| góngsíu | VO: to crack a joke |

101. Haih m̀haih góngsíu a? M̀haih góngsíu haih jànge.
102. Kéuih tùhng néi góngsíu jē, néi m̀hóu nàu.

| góngm̀chēut | RV: can't say |
| góngm̀chēut gam ... | A: indescribably |

103. Nīgeui wá ngó góngm̀chēut.
104. Kéuih nàudou yātgeui wá dōu góngm̀chēut.
105. Gógo néuijái góngm̀chēut gam leng.

| yùhnlòih | MA: so ... after all ... (used in exclamatio on discovering the true facts of a situa tion) |

106. Yùhnlòih kéuih haih ngóge néui pàhngyáuh.
107. Yùhnlòih néi haih Yìnggwok yàhn.
108. Kéuih wah kéuih hóu yauhchín, yùhnlò kéuih yātgo sīn dōu móu.

| dā | M: a dozen |

109. Géi(dò) chín yātdā a? Yihsahpmān yātdā.
110. Néi yiu géidòdā a?

| bātyùh | IE: it's better to; might as well |
| | V: not as good as, not up to |

111. Bātyùh máai nīgo lā!
112. Bātyùh m̀hóu heui lo.
113. Nīgo bātyùh gógo.

| héisáu | V: start, begin |

114. Néideih géisí héisáu a?

Introductory Expressions

peiyùh, ...   for instance
Peiyùh ...   if; suppose

   Peiyùh néi m̀sīk góng Yìngmàn, néi hóyíh heui gógàan hohkhaauhsyu
    hohk.
   Peiyùh néi m̀sīk góng Yìngmàn néi hóyíh tùhng kéuih góng Faatmàn.
   Peiyùh néi m̀sihk tòhngchāan, néi hóyíh sihk sāichāan.

hóuchíh ... gám   take ... as an example

   Hóuchíh Jùnggwok gám, deihfòng yauh daaih, yàhn yauh dò, yìngfahn
    yáuh hóudò hóu hóu ge louh.
   Hóuchíh kéuih gám, kéuihge saimānjái gogo dōu daaih lo, kéuih
    yìhgā jànhaih ngònlohk lo.
   Hóuchíh kéuihdeih ngūkkéi gám, gam dò saimānjái móu gam dò gàan
   fóng dím gau jyuh a?

gánghaih lā, ...   of course ...

   Gánghaih lā, hái nīsyu heui Jùnggwok yáuh sàamchìngéiléih gam yúhn,
    léuhngyaht dím doudák a?
   Gánghaih lā, nītyut sāam gwaigwo gótyut hóudò boh!
   Gánghaih lā, néi gam gòu gam daaih, néi m̀sihk dògwo kéuih dím dāk a?

gámge chìhngyìhng (jìhah)   under such circumstances

   Gámge chìhngyìhng néi m̀hóu heui la.
   Gámge chìhngyìhng ngó móu faatjí jouh ge boh.
   Gamge chìhngyìhng jeui hóu heui góng (béi) kéuihge sìnsàang jì la.

yùhgwó haih gám, ...   if this is the case, ...

   yùhgwó haih gám, néi jauh m̀hóu máai la.
   yùhgwó haih gám, néi tìngyaht m̀sái lèih la.
   yùhgwó haih gám, dím syun nē?

Reading

Jihchùhng Hòh síujé heuijó Bākgìng jìhauh, Jèung sìnsàang sìhsìh dōu hóu gwajyuh kéuih. Heisáu, léuhnggo láihbaai sé yātfùng
seun béi Hòh síujé, sāuméi yuht sé yuht dò, yáuhsìh yātgo láihbaai
sé sàam-seifùng. Jèung sìnsàang yahttáu hái yātgàan yèuhnghóngsyu
jouhsih, máanhāak heui yātgàan hohkhaauhsyu hohk Jùngmàn.

Gógàan hohkhaauh gaau Jùngmàn ge faatjí, haih yuhng Gwokyúh
làih gaau, Jèung sìnsàang yáuh yātwái sīk Yìngmàn ge sìnsàang hái
ngūkkéisyu gaau kéuih Gwokyúh. Kéuih yātmin duhksyù yātmin jouhsih
fèisèuhng sànfú, yáuhsìh máantáu duhksyù gójahnsí, yauh tóuhngo
yauh ngáanfan, daahnhaih kéuih yāt séunghéi Hòh síujé góng gógeui
wá kéuih jauh m̀geidāk tóuhngo tùhng ngáanfan la!

Jèung sìngsàang hohkjó léuhnggo yuht ge Jùngmàn tùhng Gwokyúh
jìhauh, kéuih wah: "Māt(yéh) gam nàan ga?[1] Ngó m̀hohk lo!" Góyaht,
kéuih jipdóu Hòh síujé yātfùngseun, chèuihjó manhauh kéuih, juhng
man kéuih yìhgā sīk góng Jùngwok wá mei a? Jèung sìnsàang wùih
fùng seun béi Hòh síujé wah: "Ngó yìhgìng hohkjó léuhnggo yuht ge
Jùnggwok wá la, ngó yìhgā juhng hohkgán ..."

Yauh gwojó sàamgoyuht, Jèung sìnsàang yànwaih bùnjó heui yātwái
pàhngyáuhge ngūkkéisyu jyuh, kéuih tùhng kéuih pàhngyáuh ngūkkéidī
yàhn yātchái sihkfaahn, yātchái kìnggái, maanmáan kéuih hohksīk hóu
géi geui Gwóngdùngwá. Yáuh yātyaht, kéuih man gógo gaau kéuih Gwokyúh ge sìnsàang wah: " Léih sìnsàang ngó hohklàihhohkheui ngódī
Gwokyúh juhng haih gam yáih, ngó jànhaih bahn lo, ngó juhng yiu
hohk géinói sìnji hohkdāksīk a?" Léih sìnsàang wah: "Jèung sìnsàang néi m̀hóu gam sāmgāp, néi joi hohk yātnìn tìm, néi jauh hóyìh
góng dāk hóu hóu la!"

Chìh géigoyuht, Jèung sìnsàang hái hohkhaauh m̀jí sīktèng gaau
Jùngmàn ge sìnsàang góng ge haih mātyéh, juhng hóyìh yuhng Gwokyúh
làih tùhng gówái sìnsàang kìnggái tìm, kéuih jihgéi hóu fùnhéi.

Jauh(lèih) dou Sìngdaanjit la, Jèung sìnsàang jipdóu Hòh síujé
yātfùng seun, Hòh síujé fùng seun wah: "Méisāng! Ngó jipdou néi
fùng Jùngmàn seun, ngó jànhaih góngm̀chēut gam fùnhéi, chéng néi
yùhnleuhng ngó gam m̀haakhei[2] (lèih) man néi, nīfùng seun haih m̀haih
néi jihgéi sé ga? Yùhgwó haih néi jihgéi sé ge, nei jànhaih...."

1. Mātyéh gam nàan ga? why in the world is it so difficult!
2. Mhaakhei, impolitely.

Gwojó nìn, Hòh sìujé tùhng kéuih màmā hái Bākgìng bùn lohklèih Hèunggóng jyuh, Hòh sìujé jihgéi heui wán ngūk, moufaatjí wándākdóu, kéuih góng Gwokyúh móu yàhn sīk tèng, kéuih chéng Jèung sìnsàang tùhngmàai kéuih yātchái heui.

Daihyihyaht, Jèung sìnsàang wah: "Hòh sìujé néi yiu ngó gaai-siuh yātwái sīk góng Gwokyúh yauh sīk góng Yìngmàn ge sìnsàang lèih gaau néi Gwóngdùngwá ma?" Hòh sìujé wah: "Hóu aak, hóu aak!"[1]

Gómáan, Jèung sìnsàang dájó go dihnwá béi Hòh sìujé, wah: "Ngó yìhgā tùhng gówái sìnsàang lèih la hóu ma!" Hòh sìujé wah: "Chéng lèih chóh lā!"

Yātjahngāan, Jèung sìnsàang yātgo yàn (changed tone of yàhn) heuidou Hòh sìujésyu. Hòhsìujé wah: "Gówái gaau Gwóngdùngwá ge sìnsàang nē?" Jèung sìnsàang wah: "Ngó jauhhaih la! M̀ .... Hohk Gwóngdùngwá yiu maanmáan hohk ji dāk, gàmyaht hohk dī, tìng-yaht hohk dī, yahtyaht dōu hohk dòdī. Gàmyaht góng dāk m̀hóu, tìng-yaht góng dāk hóu dī, yātyaht hóugwo yātyaht, hohk dāk léuhng-sàam-nìn jìhauh, gám jauh yuht sīk yuht dò yuht góng yuht hóu lo ...."

Pattern Sentences

I. Sèuiyìhn ... daahnhaih ...   Used as 'Although ...'

1. Sèuiyìhn Gwóngdùngwá hou nàan hohk, daahnhaih ngó hóu jùngyi hohk.
   Although Cantonese is very difficult to learn I enjoy studying it very much.

2. Sèuiyìhn kéuih chéng ngó sihkfaahn, daahnhaih ngó m̀séung heui, yànwaih ngó yáuh hóudò sih yiu jouh, ngó m̀dākhàahn heui.

3. Sèuiyìhn ngó m̀sīk kéuih daahnhaih ngó jì kéuih haih Chàhn sìn-sàangge pàhngyáuh Léih sìnsàang.

4. Sèuiyìhn kéuih hóu séung duhksyù, daahnhaih kéuih móu chín, sóyíh moufaatjí duhksyù.

1. Aak, a sentence final

5. Sèuiyìhn ngó tùhng kéuih haih hóu pàhngyáuh, daahnhaih nīgihn sih ngó m̀bòngdāk kéuih.

6. Kéuih sèuiyìhn m̀haih géi chùngmìng daahnhaih hóu kàhnlihk.

7. Sèuiyìhn kéuih móu lèih wángwo ngó daahnhaih ngó jì kéuih yìhgìng lèihjó Hèunggóng la.

8. Sèuiyìhn nīgihn sih m̀haih géi nàan jouh, daahnhaih ngó gú kéuih yātgo yàhn m̀jouhdāk, yātdihng yiu yāt-lèuhnggo yàhn bòng kéuih jidāk.

9. Sèuiyìhn ngó sīk kéuih móu géinói, daahnhaih ngó jì kéuih nīg(yàhn hóu hóu.

10. Kéuih sèuiyìhn haih gám góng, daahnhaih ngó gú kéuih m̀wúih gái jouh.

II. Héisáu (or héisìn) ... sāumēi ... Used as
   '... at first, and then (or later) ...'

1. Héisáu (or chùhnglòih) ngó yātdī dōu m̀sīk, sāumēi ngó hohkjó lèuhngnìn sìnji sīk.
   At the beginning I didn't know anything about it, after study-
   ing two years I learned it.

2. Héisáu kéuih yātdī dōu m̀yám, sāumēi kéuih yámháh, yámháh, yuh yám yuht jùngyi yám.

3. Héisáu kéuih wah m̀lèih, sāumēi kéuih wah yùhgwó Wòhng sìnsàan, lèih kéuih yihkdōu lèih.

4. Héisáu ngó móu man kéuih sing mātyéh, sāumēi kéuih jihgéi wah kéuih sing Chàhn, ngāamngāam hái Méigwok fàanlèih.

5. Héisáu ngó m̀seun kéuih, sāumēi kéuih wah kéuih haih néige hóu pàhngyáuh, sóyíh ngó béijó yihsahp mān kéuih.

6. Héisáu kéuih wah kéuih m̀sīk ngó, sāumēi kéuih wah: "Oh! Néi jauhhaih Wòhng sìnsàang làh!!"

7. Héisáu ngódeih móu dásyun heui Faatgwok ge, sāumēi yáuh go pàhngyáuh wah: "Faatgwok gam hóuwáan, dímgáai néideih m̀heui wáanháh nē?" Ngódeih tènggin kéuih gám wah, sóyíh hái Faat-gwok juyhjó lèuhnggo láihbaai.

8. Héisáu kéuih mhǎng maai, sāuméi ngó béi ngmǎn kéuih, kéuih
wah: "Sīnsàang chéng (néi) fàanlèih lā! Nggoyíh hóu ma?

9. Héisáu ngó msīk sái faaijí, yáuh yàhn góng ngó tèng: "Néi
maanmǎan hohkháhhohkháh jauh sīk la! Sāuméi, ngó jànhaih
hohkháhhohkháh jauh sīk la!"

10. Héisáu kéuih mjí (wah) msīk Jùnggwok jih, kéuih lìhn yātgeui
Jùnggwokwá dōu msīk tèng, sāuméi kéuih mjí (wah) sīk tèng
Jùnggwokwá, sīk góng Jùnggwokwá, juhng sīk sé Jùnggwok jih
tìm!

III. Yātmin ... yātmin (Yātbihn ... yātbihn)   Used as
'While ... ',
'Meanwhile, at the same time',
'On the one hand ..., on the other hand ...'

1. Kéuih yātmin sé jih yātmin cheunggō.
He sings and writes at the same time.

2. Kéuih yātmin giu yàhn mhóu yám jáu, kéuih yātmin jihgēi sèhng-
yahl yám jáu.

3. Ngó yātmin heui máai sung, néi yātmin fàan ngūkkéi jyúfaahn lā.

4. Kéuih yātmin chéng ngódeih chóh, yātmin jàm chàh béi ngódeih
yám.

5. Kéuih yātmin hàahng yātmin séung, nīgihn sih jànhaih jouh cho
lo.

6. Ngó yātmin hohk góng Jùnggwokwá, yātmin hohk sé Jùnggwok jih.

7. Kéuih yātmin wah: "Gau la! Gau la! Ngó myám la!" Kéuih yātmin yauh jàmjó léuhngbùi.

8. Gàmyahtge tìnhei jànhaih dākyi la, yātmin lohkyúh yātmin chēut
yahttáu.

9. Kéuih yātmin duhksyù yātmin jouhsih, jànhaih sànfu lo.

10. Kéuih yātmin wah móu chín yātmin yauh sèhngyaht chénghaak,
ngó jànhaih mjì dímgáai lo.

IV. Chèuihjó ... jì'ngoi, jauh ....
    Chèuihjó ... jì'ngoi, juhng ....   Used as
    'Besides; in addition to'

1. Chèuihjó nīgéigihn jì'ngoi, juhng yáuh móu daaiyihgihn a?
   Are there others besides these?

2. Chèuihjó Wòhng sìnsàang jì'ngoi, ngó jauh yātgo dōu m̀sīk la.

3. Néi chèuihjó wúih góng Gwóngdùngwá jì'ngoi, néi juhng wúih
   góng mātyéh wá a?

4. Nīsyu gamdògo yàhn chèuihjó kéuih jì'ngoi, gogo dōu m̀heui.

5. Chèuihjó nīgéisáu gō jì'ngoi, néi juhng wúih cheung bīnsáu a?

6. Chèuihjó néi gaaugwo ngó jì'ngoi, jauh móu yàhn gaaugwo ngó lo

7. Chèuihjó néi jì'ngoi juhng yáuh móu bīngo wúih góng Yìngmàn ga

8. Ngó yahtyaht chèuihjó séuhngfo jì'ngoi, jauh hái ngūkkéi duhks
   hóu noi móu chēutheui wáan lo.

9. Néi chèuihjó máai syù jì'ngoi, juhng séung máai dī mātyéh a?

10. Chèuihjó Chàhn sìnsàang jì'ngoi, juhng yauh móu yàhn (lèih)
    taamgwo ngó a?

V. Double finals:

A. 'La,' 'lo,' 'lā' or 'tìm' plus 'woh,' 'boh,' 'bo,' 'gwa,' 'mē,
   'ma,' or 'má.'

1. Kéuih m̀heui la woh.
   It is said he wouldn't go anymore.

2. Jèung sìnsàang yíhgìng heuijó Méigwok lo woh.

3. Néideih hóu heui la bo(boh), dímgáai juhng m̀heui a?

4. Nī-léuhngyahtge tìnhei móu chìhn-géiyaht gam láahng lo boh.

5. Kéuih heuijó la gwa! Kéuih juhng mei heui mē?

6. Yìhgā dī chèngchoi móu chìhngéiyaht gam gwai lo boh.

7. Kéuih m̀heui la mē? Dímgáai kéuih m̀jóu dī góng ngódeih jì
   nē?

8. Kéuih yìhgā yauh heui la mē? Ngó jàn(haih) m̀mìngbaak
   kéuih mātyéh yisi la.

9. Kéuih wah kéuih heui lā ma (or má), ngó m̀jì kéuih m̀heui
   boh!

10. Haih yātgo yàhn lā ma (or má)? M̀haih léuhnggo lā ma (or má)?

B. Tìm lā: '... more,' plus the particle of gentle urging (see
   Les. 11, Note 62).
   Jīmá: 'only ....' Suggests that the situation is not as
      extreme as one might think: Léuhnggo ngànchìn jīmá,
      'It's only two dollars ... (and that's not much).'
   Jemē: 'only ...??' (jēmē becomes jemē).
   Ge la: Situational ge (Les. 23, Note 93) and change of status
      la, indicating that the speaker has come to a very
      definite decision about a situation or course of action.

1. Sihk dī tìm lā! Dímgáai néi m̀sihk a?
   Have some more, why do you stop eating?

2. Duhk dò léuhngtong (or chi) tìm lā (or là) duhk dò léuhngtong néi jauh sīk la.

3. Dáng ngó heui máai dī tìm lā, joi máai bundā gau mei a?

4. Pèhng dī tìm lā! Seimān néi máai ma?

5. Béi dò yātmān tìm lā!

6. Ńg mān jīmá, máaijó kéuih lā!

7. Kéuih m̀haih m̀sīk (cheung) kéuih m̀jùngyi cheung jīmá!

8. Nīsyu yáuh nggo yàhn jīmá! Bīnsyu yáuh géisahp(go) yàhn
   gamdò nē!

9. Yīsāng sái kéuih yātdī jáu dōu m̀hóu yám, kéuih wah: 'Yīsāng sái ngó yám síu dī jīmá, m̀haih sái ngó yātdī dōu m̀yám.'

10. Ngó m̀haih hohkjó léuhngnìn, ngó hohkjó léuhnggoyuht jīmá!

11. Jihnghaih nījek ngàansīk jemē?

12. Ngó móu faatji hòi nīdouh chēungmún, néi yáuh faatjí hòi
    ma? Móu faatjí ge la, haih gám ge la.

Additional Sentences

1. Kéuih sèuiyìhn hóu jùngyi góngsíu daahnhaih kéuih jouhgán sih
   gójahnsí yātgeui sèng dōu mchēut ge.
2. Hèisáu ngó yìhwàih Gwóngdùngwá tùhng Sáangsèhngwá mtùhng, yìhgā
   ngó sìnji jì Sáangsèhngwá (or Sáangwá) jīkhaih Gwóngdùngwá.
3. Hèisáu ngó yìhwàih Gwóngjàu jīkhaih Gwóngdùng, yùhnlòih Gwóngjàu
   haih Gwóngdùngge sàangsèhng.
4. Chèuihjó hùhng sīk, wòhng sīk, làahm sīk, luhk sīk jì'ngoi, ngódeih juhng yáuh fūi sīk ge mjì néi jùng mjùngyi nē?
5. Yùhgwó nīgihn sāam haih làahm sīk ge gám jauh hóutái hóudò la.
6. Chèuihjó manhauh kéuih jì'ngoi, mgòi néi tùhng ngó béi nīléuhngbún syù kéuih.
7. Kéuih nīgo yàhn jànhaih dākyi la, yātmin hái ngàanhòng je chín
   yātmin yahtyaht chènghaak.
8. Gánghaih lā, yìhgā nīsyudī yéh gam gwai, bātyùh fàan hèunghá
   jyuh lo.
9. Gósyuge chìhngyìhng dím a? Yáuh móu ngàihím a? Chèuihjó yātdaat deihfòng jì'ngoi, syusyu dōu móu sih la.
10. Sèuiyìhn kéuih yùhnleuhng ngó, daahnhaih ngó juhnghaih gokdāk
    mhóuyisi.
11. Hóuchíh Hèunggóng gám, deihfòng yauh sai yàhn yauh dò, séung
    wán yātgàan hóu hóujyuh ge ngūk mhaih géi yih boh.
12. Sèuiyìhn yīsāng wah kéuih yìhgìng hóufàan lo, daahnhaih kéuih
    wah keuih jek sáu juhnghaih mhaih géi jihyìhn.
13. Hèisáu kéuih mgokdāk dím, sāumēi kéuih yuht lèih yuht sāmgāp,
    kéuih giu yàhn dádihnwá béi yīsāng, giu yīsāng jīkhāak lèih.
14. Mhaih ngó góng mmìngbaahk, jauhhaih kéuih tèng mmìngbaahk la,
    ngó góonglèihgongheui, kéuih juhng mei mìngbaahk ngóge yisi.
15. Gánghaih lā, néi góng ge Gwóngdùngwá mhaih géi chìhngchó, kéuih
    góngge Yìngmàn mhaih géi jeng, néi yuhng Gwóngdùngwá man kéuih,
    kéuih yuhng Yìngmàn daap néi, néi mmìngbaahk kéuih man mātyéh,
    kéuih yihk mmìngbaahk néi góng mātyéh, kéuih gánghaih móu faatjí
    mìngbaahk néi ge yisi ge la.
16. Gàmyaht néi chèuihjó heui chàamgùn gógàan daaihhohk jì'ngoi
    juhng yáuh bīnsyu yiu heui ge ma?
17. Gám ge chìhngyìhng chèuihjó hàahngsèuhngheui móu daihyihyéung
    faatjí sèuhngdākheui boh.

18. Gám ge chìhngyìhng, lìhng ngó mjì dím syun hóu, ngó yìngfahn
    heui gógaan Yìngmàn hohkhaauh chàamgùn nē, yīkwaahk heuih gógaan
    Jùngmàn hohkhaauh yíngóng nē?
19. Ngódeih gàmyaht hóyìh lèihdou Gwaigwok bòng néideih gówái jouhsih,
    ngódeih gokdāk fèisèuhng wìhnghahng ....
20. Ngó táigin néideih gówái jouhsih gam kàhnlihk, gihngihn sih dōu
    jouhdāk gam hóu, lìhng ngó gokdāk ngó yíhhauh tùhngmàai néideih
    gówái yātchái jouhsih, yātdihng hóyìh hohkdóu hóudò yéh ....

Translate the following sentences:

1. Forty years ago, the ship in which I went to China was both
   small and slow.
2. He is both clever and diligent, everybody likes him.
3. Your method is very good, it saves time and money. (also use
   the pattern 1.B. Les. 23, for translating the above sentences)
4. Your children are not only clever, but also industrious, you
   have really taught them well.
5. He worries not only about his children but also about his
   parents, so he sometimes doesn't even eat his meals.
6. I haven't been in either China or Japan, I'm only joking.
7. I'm neither sleepy nor hungry, I don't know why.
8. Because he hasn't heard from his parents for about a year,
   he is getting anxious about them.
9. He won't let either me or his elder brother drive his car.
10. Not only have he and his son studied in that university, even
    his parents have.
11. He won't let anyone else teach him how to do it, nor will be
    let other people tell him he is wrong.
12. The more he thinks about it, the happier he feels.
13. Young people nowadays are getting lazier and lazier.
14. This method is becoming more laborious, we'd better not use
    it again.
15. She said that the older you get the prettier you are. She
    actually couldn't recognize you.

Below are English translations of sentences used in the vocabulary
of this lesson as examples of usage. Translate these back into
Chinese (numbers correspond to those in Vocabulary section.)

1. He is working with a foreign firm.
2. What's the name of that firm?
3. Do we have a vacation at Christmas?

4. Where do you plan to spend your Christmas?
5. How much a pound for these green vegetables?
6. Where do these green vegetables come from? These green vegetables are shipped in from Canton.
7. My friend is sick, I have to find a doctor to see him.
8. Is the doctor coming? Yes, he is already on the way.
9. This is a story telling about a famous singer (who lived) a long time ago.
10. I'm fond of listening to stories but I don't know how tell them.
11. How about telling us a story?
12. There is a joke, ...
13. That joke runs as follows ....
14. The joke is very funny!
15. I want a drink of water, how about you?
16. Is the water drinkable?
17. Have you been back to your native place recently?
18. From which rural area do you come?
19. He is Canton-born, not country-born.
20. Canton is the capital city of Kwangtung province.
21. How is the situation in China now?
22. Are the conditions in Hong Kong a little better than in Canton?
23. How is the situation there, is there any danger?
24. He is very impatient, you had better hurry up.
25. Don't be so impatient, he'll be back pretty soon.
26. Don't be impatient, you'll speak very good Cantonese pretty soo
27. The material of this garment is so poor, it'll tear as soon as you wear it.
28. How did it happen that you bought such a bad one?
29. That child is very naughty and disobedient.
30. He's really stupid, he doesn't even know this word.
31. Don't fear ignorance, but beware of failure to ask questions.
32. Next time don't be such a fool.
33. That show is very interesting.
34. Your child is very cute.
35. How come he acts so strangely? He said he would come but hasn't turned up yet.
36. The red one is good-looking.
37. My car is red.
38. Where is the Yellow River? The Yellow River is in China.
39. To whom does that yellow car belong?
40. She doesn't like the blue one, she likes the red one.
41. I like to watch the blue color of the sea.
42. Now there is a green light, there isn't a red light anymore.
43. Miss Chen is very fond of wearing green clothes.
44. My car is gray, how about yours?
45. I like that gray table, I don't like the green one.

46. What kind of boat is that gray one?
47. It's such a taxing job, you better quit.
48. Is he suffering much from his sickness?
49. Today's heat is torturing.
50. Isn't it embarassing!
51. I'm awfully sorry to cause you so much trouble.
52. Don't feel ashamed to go and ask him.
53. Sorry to bother you!
54. How many students does your (honorable) school have?
55. How many rooms has your (honorable) hotel?
56. How many people are working in your (honorable) firm?
57. I feel very much privileged that I can come here to visit your (honorabe) school.
58. I feel very much privileged at being able to come to vist your (honorable) country.
59. It is a privilege for me to come here and talk with you.
60. Each has his own affairs.
61. Please sit down, everyone.
62. 'Ladies and gentlemen ...'
63. He sends his best regards to you.
64. Did you ask after his health for me?
65. Please give my best regards to him.
66. Have you replied to his letter?
67. Has he replied to you?
68. Next year (after this year is passed) he'll be seven.
69. It has already been two weeks, and he hasn't come yet.
70. As soon as you pass that store, there it is.
71. Please pour a cup of tea for me.
72. Please pour a little more.
73. Why doesn't it pour out?
74. Please excuse me! I have no time today.
75. Please excuse me, I can't go with you.
76. Excuse him this time, he won't dare do it again.
77. Do you understand what I mean? I don't quite understand.
78. Do you understand it now? He didn't explain it very clearly.
79. Can you explain it a bit more clearly?
80. He has become my good friend now.
81. The white one can be changed into black, but not vice versa.
82. He used to be quite a fat man, now he has become thin.
83. Whom are you calling (on the phone?) I am calling my teacher.
84. What are you calling him for?
85. Can you make a phone call for me?
86. Someone has invited me to visit Hong Kong University.
87. I wish to visit your school, is that all right?
88. I visited a few schools yesterday, they are all very good.
89. It very much embarassed me that time.

90. Such weather makes people feel very uncomfortable.
91. This affair puts me in a very difficult position.
92. He spoke well.
93. Someone invited him to give a speech.
94. Have you ever studied public speaking?
95. Ever since he learned to speak Cantonese he always speaks in Cantonese.
96. He hasn't been here since you left.
97. Since he bought that car, he has no money left.
98. Is there anyone giving a party today?
99. Are you going to give a party? (Are you going to give us a treat?)
100. He is very fond of giving parties.
101. Are you joking? No, it's something serious.
102. He's only joking with you, don't take it too seriously.
103. I can't say such a thing.
104. He is so angry that he's speechless.
105. That girl is beautiful beyond description.
106. Oh, so she is your girl friend!
107. Oh, you're British!
108. He said he has a lot of money, now it turns out that he has not even a penny.
109. How much for a dozen? Twenty dollars.
110. How many dozen do you want?
111. Might as well buy this one.
112. Better not go!
113. This one is not as good as that one.
114. When are you going to start?

REVIEW LESSON 19 - 24

I. Reading

Yáuh yātyaht ngó heui sáangsèhng yātgàan chēutméngge daaihhohk chàam-gùn, chàamgùnyuhn jíhauh, gógàan hohkhaauhge sīnsàang, tùhng hohksāang chéng ngó sihkfaahn. Sihhkyùhn faahn jíhauh, yáuh yātwái sīnsàang giu ngó yíngóng. Ngó wah: "Ngáamdòng, Ngó mwúih yíngóng." Kéuih wah: "Msái haakhei, néi chèuihbín góng géigeui lā!" Ngó kéihhéisàn deui gokwái sīnsàang gokwái hohksāang wah: "Ladies and gentlemen: ....." Yáuh go hohksāang wah: "Néige Gwóngdùngwá góng dāk gam hóu, dímgáai néi myuhng Gwóngdùngwá góng a?" Ngó wah: "Mātyéh wa!?" Daihyihdī hohksāang wah: "Haih lóh!" Haih lóh! Yātdihng yiu yuhng Gwóngdùng-wá góng!" Ngó séungjó yātjahngāan, ngó wah: "Néideih gokwái yātdihng yiu ngó yuhng Gwóngdùngwá góng, hóu lā, ngó yuhng Gwóngdùngwá góng, daahnhaih ngó góng dāk mhóu, néideih gokwai mhóu siu ngó boh!"

"Gokwái sīnsàang gokwái hóu pàhngyáuh: Gàmyaht ngó lèihdou gwai(hohk) haauh chàamgùn, ngó táigin houdò ngó yíhchìhn mei táigingwo ge yéh, ngó sīk dò hóudò yíhchihn mei sīk ge yéh, ngó yihk sihkjó hóudò ngó chùhnglòih mei sihkgwo gam hóusihk ge yéh, ngó gokdāk fèisèuhng ge fùnhéi fèisèuhng ge wíhnghahng.

"Ngó lèihdou nīsyu táigin gokwái duhksyù gam kahnlihk, gokwái sīnsàang gaausyù gaau dāk gam hóu, lihng ngó séunghéi ngó saimānjái gójahnsí duhksyù ge chìhngyìhng. Ngó séunghéi ngóge sīnsàang, ngó séunghéi kéuih gaaugwo ngó dímyéung yíngóng, ngó séunghéi kéuih wahgwo: 'Hóuge yíngóng msái góng dāk hóu chèuhng, yáuhsìh yuht dyún yuht hóu, ..., sóyíh, ngó ... ngó ... ngó yìhgā góngyùhn la, dòjeh gokwái, dòjeih gokwái.'."

Ngó góngyùhn jíhauh gódī hohksāang wah: "Mdāk, mdāk, juhng yiu góng! Juhng yiu góng!" Ngó wah: "Deuimjyuh, ngó msīk góng lā, ngó msīk góng lā, ngó haih sīk góng gamdò jē!" Yáuh yātgo hohksāang wah: " Néidī Gwóngdùngwá dím(yeung) hohk ga?"

Ngó wah: "Ngó hái yèh-lóuh (Yale) daaihhohk hohk ge, ngó hái gósyu hohkjó luhkgo yuht, héisáu ngó mgáam hohk, yànwaih ngó tèngginwah Gwóngdùngwá hóu nàanhohk, sāuméi ngó man yātwái hái gósyu gaau Gwóng-dùngwá ge sīnsàang: 'Gwóngdùngwá haih mhaih hóu nàanhohk a?' Kéuih wah: 'Hohk Gwóngdùngwá mnàan, hohk Gwóngdùngwá hóuchìh hohk cheunggō gám, néi wúih cheunggō ma?' Ngó wah: 'Ngó wúih.' Kéuih wah: 'Oh! Gám jauh dāk la!' "

349

II. Drill

Drill on the use of the Resultative Compounds:

a. Ngó máaijó góbún syù la.   Ngó jínggwo go bīu la.
   Ngó máaidóu góbún syù la.   Ngó jínghéi go bīu la.

   Ngó duhkgwo góbún syù la.   Kéuih heuijó Jùnggwok la.
   Ngó duhksīk góbún syù la.   Kéuih heuidou Jùnggwok la.

   Ngó béijó dī chín kéuih la.   Kéuih jouhgwo gógihn sih la.
   Ngó béifàan dī chín kéuih la.   Kéuih jouhhéi gógihn sih la.

b. Bīngo sáigwo nīga chè a?   Bīngo sihkjó nīdī yéh a?
   Bīngo sáilaahnjó nīga chè a?   Bīngo sihksaaijó nīdī yéh a?

   Bīngo chóhgwo nījèuhng yí a?   Bīngo jeukjó ngó gihn sāam a?
   Bīngo chóhlaahnjó nījèung yí a?   Bīngo jeuklaahnjó ngó gihn sāam a

   Bīngo lèihjó a?   Bīngo sàangwo douh mùn a?
   Bīngo lèihchìhjó a?   Bīngo sàanmàai douh mùn a?

c. Ngó hòigwo douh mùn la, daahnhaih douh mùn m̀hòidākhòi.
   Ngó jínggwo ga chè la, daahnhaih mei jíngdākhéi.
   Ngó wánjo sèhngyaht la, juhng mei wándóu.
   Ngó duhkjó sèhngyaht la, juhng mei duhksīk.
   Ngó ga chè jíngjó lèuhngyaht la, juhng mei jínghéi.
   Ngó fanjó lèuhngdímjūng la, daahnhaih juhng mei fanjeuhk.
   Ngó heui ngànhòhng jegwo chín la, daahnhaih m̀jedākdou (or jèm̀dóu)
   Ngó séunggwo la, daahnhaih m̀séungdākhéi.
   Ngó hòigwo gójáan dāng la, daahnhaih hòi m̀jeuhk.

d. Gófùng seun ngó séjó lèuhngdímjūng juhng mei séhéi.
   Gófùng seun ngó séhéijó lèuhngdímjūng la.

   Gógihn sih ngó jouhjó lèuhngyaht juhng mei jouhyùhn.
   Gógihn sih ngó jouhyùhnjó lèuhngyaht la.

   Nīfo syù ngó duhkjó lèuhngyaht la, juhng mei duhksīk.
   Nīfo syù ngó duhksīkjó hóu noi la.

   Ngó ga chè kéuih jíngjó lèuhngyaht la, juhng mei jínghóu.
   Ngó ga chè yìhgìng jínghóu lèuhngyaht la.

   Gó yātchìn mān ngó yìhgìng sáijó hóu nói la, juhng mei sáisaai.
   Gó yātchìn mān ngó yìhgìng sáisaai hóu noi la.

e. Kéuih fan mei a?
   Kéuih fangán la.
   Kéuih fanjó mei a?
   Kéuih fanjó la.
   Kéuih fanjeuhk mei a?
   Kéuih fanjeuhk la.
   Kéuih fan m̀fandākjeuhk a?
   Kéuih fandākjeuhk.
   Kéuih m̀fandākjeuhk.
   Kéuih fanjó géi noi a?
   Kéuih fanjó hóu noi la.
   Kéuih fanjeuhkjó géi noi la?
   Kéuih fanjeuhkjó hóu noi la.
   Kéuih yáuh móu fangwo a?
   Kéuih fangwo léuhngchi la.

   Kéuih wán mātyéh a?
   Kéuih wángán yātbún syù.
   Kéuih wángwo góbún syù mei a?
   Kéuih wángwo la.
   Kéuih wándóu mei a?
   Kéuih wándóu la.
   Kéuih wán m̀wándākdóu a?
   Kéuih wándākdóu.
   Kéuih m̀wándākdóu.
   Kéuih wánjó géi noi la?
   Kéuih wánjó hóu noi la.
   Kéuih wándóu géi noi la?
   Kéuih wándóu hóu noi la.

Kéuih gáai mātyéh a?
   Kéuih gáai gotluh sing.
   Kéuih gáaijó mei a?
   Kéuih gáaijó la.
   Kéuih gáaihòi mei a?
   Kéuih gáaihòi la.
   Kéuih gáai m̀gáaidākhòi a?
   Kéuih gáaidākhòi.
   Kéuih mgaaidākhòi.
   Kéuih gáaijó géi noi a?
   Kéuih gáaijó hóu noi la.
   Kéuih gáaihòijó géi noi la?
   Kéuih gáaihòijó hóu noi la.
   Kéuih yáuh móu gáaigwo a?
   Kéuih gáaigwo léuhngchi la.

Kéuih jíng mātyéh a?
   Kéuih jínggán kéuih ga chè.
   Kéuih jíngjó kéuih ga chè mei a?
   Kéuih jíngjó kéuih ga chè la.
   Kéuih jíngnei mei a?
   Kéuih jínghéi la.
   Kéuih jíng m̀jíngdākhéi a?
   Kéuih jíngdākhéi.
   Kéuih jíngm̀héi.
   Kéuih jíngjó géi nói la?
   Kéuih jíngjó hóu noi la.
   Kéuih jínghéi géi noi la?
   Kéuih jínghéi hóu noi la.

f. Héisáu ngó jem̀dóu sāumēi ngó jedóu la.
Héisáu ngó seungm̀héi sāumēi ngó seunghéi la.
Héisáu ngó lóm̀dóu sāumēi ngó lódóu la.
Héisáu ngó táimgin sāumēi ngó táigin la.
Héisáu ngó wánm̀dóu sāumēi ngó wándóu la.
Héisáu ngó hòim̀hòi sāumēi ngó hòihòi la.
Héisáu ngó fanm̀jeuhk sāumēi ngó fanjeuhk la.
Héisáu ngó máaim̀dóu sāumēi ngó máaidóu la.

Héisáu ngó yíhwàih m̀lódākfàan, sāumēi ngó lófàan la.
Héisáu ngó yíhwàih m̀jíngdākfàan, sāumēi ngó jíngfàan la.
Héisáu ngó yíhwàih m̀jouhdākhéi, sāumēi ngó jouhhéijó la.
Héisáu ngó yíhwàih m̀hòidākjeuhk, sāumēi ngó hòijeuhkjó la.
Héisáu ngó yíhwàih m̀heuidākdou gósyu, sāumēi ngódeih heuidou la.
Héisáu ngó yíhwàih m̀wándākdóu, sāumēi ngó wándóu la.
Héisáu ngó yíhwàih m̀hohkdāksīk, sāumēi ngó hohksīk la.
Héisáu ngó yíhwàih m̀gáaidākhòi, sāumēi ngó gáaihòi la.

Sèuiyìhn ngó wándóu ngóge bīu, daahnhaih yíhgìng laahnjó la.
Sèuiyìhn ngó gindóu kéuih daahnhaih ngó móu tùhng kéuih kìnggái.
Sèuiyìhn ngó táigingwo gójek syùhn daahnhaih ngó m̀jì gójek haih
bīngwokge syùhn.
Sèuiyìhn ngó tènggingwo kéuih gám góng, daahnhaih ngó m̀jì kéuih
jànhaih yiu heui.
Sèuiyìhn ngó séhéi fùng seun la, daahnhaih ngó m̀geidāk kéuih jyuh-
hái bīnsyu la.
Sèuiyìhn ngó sàanmàai gódouh chēungmún, daahnhaih juhnghaih yáuh
fùng yahplèih.
Sèuiyìhn ngó hòijeuhk jáan dāng daahnhaih juhnghaih taai hāak.
Sèuiyìhn gogo chaahk yíhgìng jūkdóu la, daahnhaih ngódì chín yíh-
gìng béi kéuih sáisaai la.

Drill on Comparison:

a. Nīsyu tùhng gósyu bīnsyu lèih fóchèjaahm yúhn dī a?
   Nīsyu yúhn dī. Gósyu lèih fóchèjaahm móu nīsyu gam yúhn.

   Nīgihn sih tùhng gógihn sih bīngihn sih yihjouh dī a?
   Nīgihn yihjouh dī. Gógihn sih móu nīgihn gam yihjouh.

   Nīgo saimānjái tùhng gógo saimānjái bīngo tèngwah dī a?
   Nīgo tèngwah dī. Gogo móu nīgo gam tèngwah.

   Néi ga chè tùhng kéuih ga chè bīnga hóusái dī a?
   Kéuih ga hóusái dī. Ngó ga móu kéuih ga gam hóusái.

   Néideih léuhnggo góng Yìngmàn bīngo góng dāk hóudī a?
   Kéuih góng dāk hóudī. Ngó góng dāk móu kéuih gam hóu.

   Kéuihdeih léuhnggo bīngo dájih dá dāk faaidī a?
   Kéuih dá dāk faaidī. Ngó dá dāk móu kéuih gam faai.

   Néideih   léuhnggo bīngo gòudī a?
   Kéuih gòugwo ngó léuhngchyun. Ngó ngáigwo kéuih léuhngchyun.

   Gójek syùhn tùhng nījek syùhn bīnjek chúhng dī a?
   Gójek chúhng sàambaakdēun. Nījek móu gójek gam chúhng.

   Nīsyu gamdò ga chè bīnga jeui pèhng a?
   Nīga yihchìn mān, góga pèhnggwo nīga yihbaak mān, góga fūisīkge
   jeui pèhng, chìnluhk mān jē.

Gósyu gamdòjek syùhn bīnjek jeui chúhng a?
Gójek hùhngsīkge chìnyihdēun chúhng, gójek luhksīkge chúhnggwo
nījek hùhngsīkge, gójek haaksīkge jeui chúhng.

b. Kéuih yáuh kéuih gam gòu, daahnhaih móu kéuih gam sau.
Kéuih tùhng kéuih yātyeuhng gam gòu, daahnhaih móu kéuih gam sau.
Kéuih móu kéuih gam gòu, yihkmóu kéuih gam sau.
Kéuih gòugwo kéuih daahnhaih móu kéuih gam sau.
Kéuih gòugwo kéuih hóudò, daahnhaih móu kéuih gam sau.

Ngó   ga chè yáuh kéuih ga chè gam sàn, daahnhaih móu kéuih ga
    gam hóusái.
Ngó ga chè tùhng kéuih ga chè yātyeuhng gam sàn, daahnhaih móu
    kéuih ga chè gam hóusái.
Ngó ga chè móu kéuih ga gam sàn, yihkmóu kéuih ga gam hóusái.
Ngó ga chè sàngwo kéuih ga chè, daahnhaih móu kéuih ga chè gam
    hóusái.
Ngó ga chè sàngwo kéuih ga chè hóudò, daahnhaih móu kéuih ga chè
    gam hóusái.

Ngó gàan ngūk yáuh kéuih gàan ngūk gam hóu, daahnhaih móu kéuih
    gàan ngūk gam káhn.
Ngó gàan ngūk tùhng kéuih gàan yātyeuhng gam hóu, daahnhaih móu
    kéuih gàan ngūk gam káhn.
Ngó gàan ngūk móu kéuih gàan gam hóu, yihkmóu kéuih gàan ngūk gam
    káhn.
Ngó gàan ngūk hóugwo kéuih gàan ngūk, daahnhaih móu kéuih gàan
    ngūk gam káhn.
Ngó gàan ngūk hóugwo kéuih gàan ngūk hóudò, daahnhaih móu kéuih
    gàan ngūk gam káhn.

Gójek syùhn yáuh nījek syùhn gam daaih, daahnhaih móu nījek syùhn
    gam faai.
Gójek syùhn tùhng nījek syùhn yātyeuhng gam daaih, daahnhaih móu
    nījek syùhn gam faai.
Gójek syùhn móu nījek syùhn gam daaih, yihkmóu nījek syùhn gam
    faai.
Gójek syùhn daaihgwo nījek syùhn, daahnhaih móu nījek syùhn gam
    faai.
Gójek syùhn daaihgwo nījek syùhn hóudò, daahnhaih móu nījek syùhn
    gam faai.

Tàahnhèungsàan yáuh Hèunggóng gam hóuwáan, daahnhaih móu Hèung-
    góng gam daaih.
Tàahnhèungsàan tùhng Hèunggóng yātyeuhng gam hóuwáan, daahnhaih
    móu Hèunggóng gam daaih.

Tàahnhèungsàan móu Hèunggóng gam hóuwáan, yihkmóu Hèunggóng gam
daaih.
Tàahnhèungsàan hóuwáangwo Hèunggòng, daahnhaih móu Hèunggóng gam
daaih.
Tàahnhèungsàan hóuwáangwo Hèunggóng hóudò, daahnhaih móu Hèunggóng gam daaih.

Drill on Comparing the Actions:

Kéuih sé jih yáuh ngó gam faai, daahnhaih móu ngó sé dāk gam leng.
Kéuih sé jih tùhng ngó yātyeuhng gam faai, daahnhaih móu ngó sé
dāk gam leng.
Kéuih sé jih móu ngó gam faai, yihkmóu ngó sé dāk gam leng.
Kéuih sé jih faaigwo ngó daahnhaih sé dāk móu ngó gam leng.
Kéuih sé jih faaigwo ngó hóudò, daahnhaih móu ngó sé dāk gam leng.

Kéuih hàahng dāk yáuh ngó gam faai, daahnhaih kéuih móu ngó hàahng
dāk gam yùhn.
Kéuih hàahng dāk tùhng ngó yātyeuhng gam faai, daahnhaih kéuih móu
ngó hàahng dāk gam yùhn.
Kéuih hàahng dāk móu ngó gam faai, yihkmóu ngó hàahng dāk gam yùhn.
Kéuih hàahng dāk faaigwo ngo, daahnhaih móu ngó hàahng dāk gam yùhn.
Kéuih hàahng dāk faaigwo ngó hóudò, daahnhaih móu ngó hàahng dāk
gam yùhn.

Ngó sái chè yáuh kéuih gam hóu, daahnhaih móu kéuih sái dāk gam
faai.
Ngó sái chè tùhng kéuih yātyeuhng gam hóu, daahnhaih móu kéuih
sái dāk gam faai.
Ngó sái chè móu kéuih gam hóu, yihkmóu kéuih sái dāk gam faai.
Ngó sái chè hóugwo kéuih, daahnhaih móu kéuih sái dāk gam faai.
Ngó sái chè hóugwo kéuih hóudò, daahnhaih móu kéuih sái dāk gam
faai.

Kéuihge Gwóngdùngwá góng dāk yáuh néi gam hóu, daahnhaih móu néi
gam jeng.
Kéuihge Gwóngdùngwá góng dāk tùhng néi yātyeuhng gam hóu, daahnhaih móu néi góng dāk gam jeng.
Kéuihge Gwóngdùngwá góng dāk móu néi gam hóu, yihkmóu néi góng dāk
gam jeng.
Kéuihge Gwóngdùngwá góng dāk faaigwo néi, daahnhaih móu néi góng
dāk gam jeng.
Kéuihge Gwóngdùngwá góng dāk faaigwo néi hóudò, daahnhaih móu néi
góng dāk gam jeng.

Kàhmyaht lohk ge yúh yáuh gàmyaht gam daaih, daahnhaih móu gàmyaht
  lohk dāk gam noi.
Kàhmyaht lohk ge yúh tùhng gàmyaht yātyeuhng gam daaih, daahnhaih
  móu gàmyaht lohk dāk gam noi.
Kàhmyaht lohk ge yúh móu gàmyaht gam daaih, yihkmóu gàmyaht gam
  noi.
Kàhmyaht lohk ge yúh daaihgwo gàmyaht, daahnhaih móu gàmyaht lohk
  dāk gam noi.
Kàhmyaht lohk ge yúh daaihgwo gàmyaht ge hóudò, daahnhaih móu gàmyaht lohk dāk gam noi.

<u>Drill on Final Particle (boh, gwa, and woh)</u>

a. Translate the following conversation into English:

A: Haih m̀haih nīgo a?
B: M̀haih.
A: Haih m̀haih gógo a?
B: Yihkm̀haih.
A: M̀haih nīgo yihkm̀haih gógo haih bīngo a?
B: Gógo!? M̀haih gwa! Gógo gam sìmàn, m̀haih gwa!
A: Haih nīgo m̀haih!
B: M̀haih nīgo boh! Gógo móu nīgo gam fèih boh.
A: Kéuih wah haih kéuih la wóh.
B: Gám waahkjé ngó sèung ngáan m̀haih géi hóu, máantàuhhāak ngó
  tàimchìngchó la.

b. Fill in the following blanks with appropriate final particles:

1. Néi ga chè yauh waaihjó!? M̀haih _____.
2. Gam daaih yúh néi m̀hóu heui la _____.
3. Kéuih sīk la _____.
4. Kéuih lèih la _____.
5. Kéuih jauh lèih la _____.
6. Kéuih máaijó la _____.
7. Kéuih móu chín _____.
8. Kéuih m̀wúih m̀gaau néi _____.
9. Kéuih wúih heui _____.
10. Kéuih heuijó lo _____

III. Translation

1. He didn't feel very well last month so the doctor told him not to eat anything but vegetables.
2. Although the doctor told him not to, he still ate a lot of meat and fish.
3. At first, he didn't feel anything (wrong) later he said he suffered very much.
4. His wife was very worried, She gave him some medicine, meanwhile she called the doctor on the phone.
5. The doctor told his wife not to worry, although his condition seemed pretty serious. The best thing to do was to give him a lot of water to drink, meanwhile he would come to see him.
6. After the doctor came and gave him some medicine, he opened his eyes and asked his wife what day it was.
7. When he realized that it was Christmas day, he said: "Doctor! I feel so embarrassed bothering you. I know my wife has prepared many good dishes today, we not only have meat and fish, but also some fine wine, how about having a drink with me!"
8. When his wife heard what he said she was puzzled that he had recovered so quickly. She said: "Doctor! He looks like he is recovering, can we give him something to eat?"
9. The doctor said: "Mrs. Lee! Suppose you were the doctor, under such circumstances, would you let him eat anything?"
10. The man didn't wait for his wife to answer the doctor, he said happily: "In that case, hurry up, let's eat."

VOCABULARY

Lesson

A

a	呀	P: sentence particle to choice type questions and question made with interrogative words	1
a-baak	阿伯	N: father's elder brothers, uncles, a familiar title applied to an elderly man	23
a-go	阿哥	N: elder brother	21
àh(!?)	吖	P: sentence particle making statement into yes-no question; expresses surprise or disbelief, ask for confirmation of surprising statement	1

B

-bá	把	M: measure for knife, catty stick, etc.	15
baahk	白	SV: white	22
-baak	百	NU/M: hundred	6
-baak	伯	BF: father's elder brother, uncles, a familiar title applied to an elderly man	23
baakfuh	伯父	N: father's elder brother, uncles	23
-bàan (or bāan)	班	M: measure for a group of persons	19
baat	八	NU: eight	3
Baatyuht	八月	TW: August	13
bàhbā	爸爸	N: daddy, father	16

357

bahn	笨	SV: be stupid	24
bāk	北	BF: north	21
Bākgìng	北京	PW: Peking	13
Bàlàih	巴黎	PW: Paris	14
bāt	筆	N: pen, pencil, writing brush	3
bātyùh	不如	V/IE: not as good as, not up to/ it's better to; might as well	24
báu	飽	SV/(RVE): have eaten to one's full, be satisfied	23
behng	病	N/V: sickness/ to be sick, ill	22
béichín	俾錢	VO: pay	7
béigaau	比較	V/A: compare/ comparatively, rather	20
-bihn (or bín)	邊	M: -side; part	21
bīn-	邊	SP: which, who; whom	4
bīndī(?)	邊的	N: which? (plural)	6
béi	畀	V: to give	4
béi	比	CV: than; compared with	20
binsèhng	變成	V: to become, to change into	24
bīu	錶	N: watch	3
bohng	磅	V: to weigh	21
-bohng	磅	M: a pound	21
boktàuh	膊頭	N: shoulder	22
bòhng	帮	V/CV: help	16
bou	布	N: cloth, material	22

boují	報紙	N: newspaper	2
būi	杯	N/M: glass, cup	15
-bún	本	M: (for books)	3
bùn	搬	V: move	13
bùngūk	搬屋	VO: to move from one dwelling to another	13
bun--bun	半	NU/M: half uses of bun: bungo(1/2), (yāt)gobun (1 1/2) sàamgo bungo(3 halves)	6
búnlòih	本來	MA: originally	18

<h2 style="text-align:center">C</h2>

chā	叉	N: fork	15
chaahk	賊	N: thief, bandit	19
chàamgùn	參觀	V: to pay a visit to school, factory, museum, etc.	24
chāan	餐	N: food, meal	7
chàan	餐	M: measure of 'faahn' - meal	7
chàh	茶	N: tea	15
chàhmmáan	尋晚	TW: last night	12
chàhmyaht	尋日	TW: yesterday	13
chàhmyahtjìu	尋日朝	TW: yesterday morning	12
Chàhn	陳	N: Chen (surname)	5
chāt	七	NU: seven	3
chātyuht	七月	TW: July	13
chàu	呐抽	M: measure for 'sósìh' - keys	11

cháuyéung	醜樣	SV: ugly	13
chek	尺	N: a ruler	
-chek		M: a Chinese foot	21
chéng	請	CV/V: invite, please; (invitational sense), request	4

Chéng chóh la 請坐啦 IE: Pleas sit down!   12

Chéng néi joi góng yātchi

請你再講一次 IE: Please say it again.   5

Chéng néi tùhng ngó manhauh...

請你同我問候… IE Please give my regards to...   18

chèngchoi	青菜	N: green vegetables	24
chénghaak	請客·	VO: to give a party	24
chéngman	請問	IE: may I ask ...; Would you please tell me....	9

Chéng wùih 請回 IE: Please return. Don't escort me further. (said to a host accompanying his departing guest)   18

chèuhng	長	SV: be long	20
chèuihbín	隨便	MA: as one pleases, at random	15
cheung	唱	V: sing	
cheunggō	唱歌	VO: sing (intransitive)	7
chēung, chēungmún	窗門	N: window	19
chēut-	出	BF: out	
chēutlàih	出嚟	V: come out (here)	
chēutheui	出去	V: go out (there)	11
-chēut	齣	M: measure for show or play	22
chēutkèih	出奇	SV: strange (unnatural; inexplicable, puzzling)	23

chēutméng	出名	SV: famous	18
chēutnìn	出年	TW: next year	13
chēutsai	出世	VO: be born	13
chēutsèng	出聲	VO: say (something), make a (vocal) sound	22
chi	次	M: a time or occasion, for sickness	16
chìh	遲	SV: late; later·	17
chíh	似	V: look like, resemble	20
chìhgāng	匙羹	N/M: spoon, spoonful	16

chìhn-	前	TW: ago	13
chìhngéinìn		several years ago	
chìhngéiyaht		several days ago	
chìhngéigoláihbaai		several weeks ago	
chìhngéigoyuht		several months ago	
chìhngoláihbaai		week before last or last week	
chìhngoyuht		month before last month	

chìhnbihn	前邊	PW: front, in front of, before	9
chìhngyìhng	情形	N: circumstance, condition, situation	24
chìhngyún	情願	A: rather; prefer	23
chìhnnìn	前年	TW: year before last	13
chìhnyaht	前日	TW: day before yesterday	13
chín	錢	N: money	6
-chìn	千	NU/M: thousand	6
ching	秤	V: to weigh with a catty stick	21
ching	秤	N: catty stick	21
chìngchó	清楚	SV: distinct, clear	22

| cho | 錯 | N/SV(RVE): | error, mistake; fault/ be wrong to be wrong | 23 |

| chóh | 坐 | V: | sit, drop in (for a vist); take a seat | 10 |

| chóh | 坐 | CV: | ride on, take, by (bus, train, ship, plane) | 10 |

| choi | 菜 | N: | vegetable; dish of food as those served in restaurants | 15 |

| chúhng | 重 | SV: | be heavy | 21 |

| chùhngchìhn | 從前 | MA: | formerly, in the past | 18 |

| chùhnglòih dōu... 從來都… | | Ph: | all along, have always... | 18 |

| chùhnglòih mei (or m̀, móu) 從來未 | | Ph: | never have (done something) | 18 |

| chùngmìng | 聰明 | SV: | be clever, mentally bright, smart | 8 |

| -chyun | 寸 | M: | inch | 21 |

D

| dá | 打 | V: | to hit | 19 |

| dā | 打 | M: | a dozen | 24 |

| daahnhaih | 但係 | MA: | but, however | 4 |

| daai | 帶 | V: | take or bring along | 13 |

| daaih | 大 | SV: | be large, big | 4 |

| daaihchìhnyaht 大前日 | | TW: | the day before the day before yesterday (three days ago) | 13 |

| daaihgā | 大家 | N: | we all; all of us | 22 |

| daaihhauhyaht 大後日 | | TW: | the day after the day after tomorrow | 13 |

| daaihhohk | 大學 | PW: | university, college | 23 |

daaihlóu	大佬	N:	elder brother	21
Daaihsàiyèuhng	大西洋	PW:	Atlantic	21
daaihyàhn	大人	N:	adult	8
dàan	單	M:	measure for 'sàangyi' - business, an item of business	7
daap	搭	CV/V:	go by (mode of transportation)/ ride, take	22
daap	答	V:	to answer	18
-daat	笪	M:	measure for place	15
dádihnwá	打電話	VO:	to make a phone call	24
dahkbiht	特別	A/SV:	distinctively, unusually, especially/ strange	20
dáhòi	打開	RV:	open	19
daih-	第	P:	prefix to make cardinal numbers ordinal	5
daih (plus M)	第	SP:	other, another	5
dájeung	打仗	VO:	make war, fight	18
dájih	打字	VO:	to type	19
-dāk	得	P:	can (be possible), may	7
Dāk mei a?	得未呀？	IE:	Is it ready? It is done yet? Is that all right now?	12
Dākgwok	德國	PW:	Germany	14
dākhàahn	得閒	SV:	having leisure time	11
-dākjaih	得滯	A:	more (or less) than enough; (suffix to SV indicating a regrettable degree)	20
dākyi	得意	SV:	be interesting, cute; strange	24

dáng	等	V: wait	11
dāng	燈	N: lamp, light	19
dáng ngó táiháh 等我睇吓		IE: let me see	13
dásyun	打算	V/N: plan to, plan	18
deihfòng	地方	N: place	15
deihjí	地址	N: address	17
deui	對	CV: to, towards (Lit. facing)	18
deuimin	對面	PW: opposite	21
deuimjyuh	對唔住	IE: I'm sorry.	9
-dēun	噸	M: a ton	21
-dī	啲	M: indicates that the noun following is plural)	6
(yāt)dī	（一）啲	N: a little, a few	6
dīgamdēu	啲咁嗲	N: a tiny bit	20
dihng(haih)	定係	MA: or (as in 'whether...or...')	17
dihngsaht	定實	AV: make a definite decision (to do something); have decided on (do something)	22
dihnyàuh	電油	N: gasoline	19
dihp	碟	M: measure for dish of food	15
Dím syun a?	點算呀	IE: what can be done about it?	10
dímgáai	點解	MA: why? How is it that...?	10
dím(jūng) dímjūng	點鐘	M: o'clock M: hour	17
dím(yéung)	點（樣）	MA: how?	10
Dím(yéung) a?	點樣呀	IE: How's everything? How's it coming.	10

dò	多	SV: be much, many; more	6
doihmaansaai	待慢哂	IE: I have treated you shabbily	18
dòjeh(néi)	多謝 (你)	IE: thank you (for a gift)	4
dòjehsaai	多謝哂	IE: thanks for everything; thank you very much	4
dóu	島	N: island	21
-dóu	到	RVE: ending of RV	19
dou	到	V: arrive(at), reach	12
-dou	到	RVE: ending of RV	19
dōu	都	A: also; too, likewise; in all cases; in either case; both	2
dōu	刀	N: knife	15
-dougihk	到極	A: suffix to SV, indicating superlative or exaggerated degree	20
-douh	度	P: a place	9
-douh	道	M: measure for door, gate, window	19
dōujái	刀仔	N: pocket knife	15
duhk	讀	V: study; read (aloud)	7
duhksyù	讀書	VO: study (intransitive); go to school	7
dùng	東	BF: east ·	21
dyún	短	SV: be short (opp. long)	20

F

fā	花	N: flower	19
faahn	飯	N: cooked rice, meal	7

faaichè	快車	N: express	18
faai(cheui)	快（趣）	SV: fast	16
faaiíí	筷子	N: chopstick	15
-fàan	返	P: indicates 'return to'	13
-fàan	返	RVE: ending of RV	19
fàangáan	番梘	N: soap	22
fàangùng	返工	VO: go to work	17
fàanhohk	返學	VO: go to school	17
fàanlèih	返來	V: return (to)	11
Faatgwok	法國	PW: France	14
faatjí	法子	N: method, way, device	14
faisih	費事	SV: laborious, troublesome	23
fān(jūng)	分（鐘）	M: minute	17
fan	瞓	V: sleep	17
fànbiht	分別	N: difference	20
fangaau	瞓覺	VO: sleep	17
fanséng	瞓醒	SV: awake	17
fèigèi	飛機	N: airplane	10
fèih	肥	SV: be fat	20
fèisèuhng	非常	A: extraordinarily	20
-fo	課	M: lesson	12
fóchè	火車	N: train	10
(fó)chèjaahm	火車站	PW: railroad station	10

fòngbihn (or bihn) 方便		SV: convenient	18
fongga 放假		VO: to grant (someone) a holiday, have a holiday, have a vacation	22
fongsàm lā 放心		IE: don't worry(lit. be free from an anxiety)	23
fuhmóu 父母		N: parents	23
fūisīk 灰色		N: gray color	24
-fūk 幅		M: measure for cloth	22
fùng 風		N: wind	21
fóng 房		N: room	9
fonggùng 放工		VO: stop work (at the end of the day)	17
fonghohk 放學		VO: get out of school (at the end of the day)	17
-fu 付		M: set(measure for set of fork and knife, etc.)	15
fuhchàn 父親		N: daddy, father	16
fùnhei 歡喜		SV/AV: be happy/ to like to, be fond of, be glad to	22
fut 濶		SV: be wide	20

G

-ga 架		M: measure for car, airplane	10
gáai 解		V: to untie	19
gāai 街		PW: street	10
gaaisiuh 介紹		V: introduce	18
gàan 間		M: measure for 'ngūk' - building, house, room, school, etc.	9

gáam	敢	AV: dare	20
gaau	教	V: teach	8
gàaugwàan	交關	SV/A: seriously; terribly	20
gaausyù	教書	V/VO: teach/teach(intransitive)	8
gahnlói	近來	MA: recently	18
gājē (or jē, jèhjē)	家姊	N: elder sister	21
gám	嗽	A: in this (or that) way; in that case; then...; well...	11
gam	咁	A: so, such	6
Gám yiu tái....	咁要睇	IE: It all depends....	21
gàmjíu, gàmjùjou	今朝早	TW: this morning	11
gàmmáan	今晚.	TW: tonight	11
gàmnín, gàmnìn	今年	TW: this year	13
gamseuhnghá	柑上下	Ph: about; around, approximately	20
gàmyaht	今日	TW: today	10
-gàn	斤	M: a catty, pound(1 1/3 English pound)	21
gán	緊	P: indicating continuance of action	11
Gànàdaaih	加拿大	PW: Canada	21
gāng	匙	M: spoonful	16
gányiu	緊要	SV: important, serious	20
gàyàhn	家人	N: the family(members)	14
gáu	九	NU: nine	3
gau	够	SV: be enough, sufficient	6
gau chín	够錢	Ph: have enough money	6

Gau mei a?	够未呀	IE: Is that enough?	12
gauh	舊	SV: be old (opp. of new)	6
-gauh	嚿	M: piece (lit. lump) measure for soap, meat, etc.	22
Gauhgāmsāan	舊金山	PW: San Francisco	24
gauhnín	舊年	TW: last year	13
gauhsìh, gauhsí	舊時	MA: formerly, in the past	18
Gáulùhng	九龍	PW: Kowloon	21
Gáuyuht	九月	TW: September	13
-ge	嘅	P: particle indicating modification	6
géi	幾	A: fairly, quite, rather	1
géi	幾	NU: several, some, a few	4
géi(dò)	幾(多)	NU: how many, how much	3
géi	幾	A/NU: how/ few, several; odd, more than; which(of a series)	13
gei	寄	V: send (something by mail), mail	13
geidāk	記得	V: remember	16
gèihei	機器	N: a machine	22
géisí, géisìh	幾時	TW: when(?), at what time?	12
génghot	頸渴	SV: thirsty	23
geu	句	M: measure for 'syutwah' or 'wá' - spoken language	7
-gihn	件	M: task, undertaking; article, piece, item(measure for 'sihgon' -affair, or 'yéh' -thing)	7
gin	見	V: meet (somebody by prior arrangement); pay a visit to(rather formally)	12

-gin	見	RVE: ending of RV	19
ginggwo	經過	V: pass through	21
ginleuhng	見諒	V: to excuse	24
giu	叫	V/CV: call; order (dishes)/ call; tell, order	14
giu(jouh)	叫（做）	EV: named, is called; considered as	16
giuséng	叫醒	RV: to wake (somebody) up	17
gó	嗰	SP: that (there)	4
-go	個	M: for persons or things	3
go	個	M: measure for 'jih' - word	7
gō	歌	N: song	7
gō	哥	N: elder brother	21
gódī	嗰的	N: those	6
gójahnsí	嗰陣時	TW: at the time of...; meanwhile	12
...gójahnsí		TW: when (while)...; at the time of...	12
gokdāk	覺得	V: feel	18
góng	講	V: say; talk, speak; tell	7
góng...jī 講…知 góng...tèng 講…聽		Ph: tell (someone something)	7
góngm̄chēut	講唔出	RV: can't say	24
góngm̄chēut gam... 講唔出咁		A: indescribably	24
góngsíu	講笑	VO: to crack a joke	24
góngsyutwah	講說話	VO: talk, speak (intransitive)	7
gònjehng	乾淨	SV: be clean	22

gok-	各	SP: each, every	24
gòu	高	SV: be tall, high	1
gú	估	V/N: to make a guess; riddle	21,23
gúdóu	估到	RV: guess (an answer) correctly	23
guih	瘸	SV: be tired	1
gújái	古仔	N: story	24
gwai	貴	SV: be expensive	2
gwai-	貴	SV: you honorable - as to school, store, factory, etc.	24
Gwai sing a?	貴姓呀	IE: What is your surname? (Lit. What is your honorable name?)	2
gwajyuh	掛住	V: to be concerned with; to worry; to be anxious about	23
gwasàm	掛心	SV: worry, be worried	23
gwo	過	V: pass, exceed, to cross	17,24
-gwo	過	P: verb suffix, indicating experience	12
-gwo	過	P: used in comparison, similar to the English '-er than' in the pattern 'X is taller than Y'	20
gwok	國	N: country	6
Gwokyúh	國語	N: Chinese Mandarin (language)	23
-gwolèih -gwoheui	過來 過去	P: over, over to, across, across to	13
Gwóngdùng	廣東	PW: Kwangtung (Province)	7,22
Gwongdùngwá	廣東話	N: Cantonese (dialect)	7
Gwóngjàu	廣州	PW: Canton	7

Gwóngjàuwá　廣州話　　N: Cantonese (dialect)

-gwotàuh　　過頭　　A: more than enough; (suffix to SV
　　　　　　　　　　　　indicating to a regrettable degree) 20

<u>H</u>

hàahng　　行　　V: walk, go or run (of watch, cars, etc.)11

hàahnglèih hàahngheui Ph: walk back and forth　　　　11
　　行嚟黎行去

hāak (hāk)　黑　SV: black; dark　　　　　　　　　19

hàan　　慳　V/SV: to save/ be thrifty　　　　　23

-háh　　吓　P: (do something) once, a little　15

hahbihn　　下邊　PW: bottom, below, underneath, under　9

hahgo láihbaai 下個禮拜 Ph: next week　　　　　　13

hahgo yuht　下個月　Ph: next month　　　　　　13

hahjau　　下晝　TW: afternoon　　　　　　　　17

hahmbaahnglaahng喊嚸吟A: altogether, all told　　22

hahp　　合　V: to close (book, eye, box, etc.)　19

hái　　嚡　V: be located at, in, on　　9
hái　　　　　CV: from
-hái　　　　　P: at

haih　　係　EV: to be; equal; it is　　　5

háng　　肯　AV: will; to consent to　　22

háu　　口　M: measure for cigarette　　23

hauhbihn　後邊　PW: rear, in back of, behind　9

hauhlòih　後來　MA: afterwards, later on　18

hauhnín　後年　TW: year after next　　13

hauhsāangjái	後生仔	N: young fellows, youths	23
hauhyaht	後日	TW: day after next	13
hei	戲	N: play (dramatic), show	22
-héi	起	RVE: ending of RV	19
heichè	汽車	N: automobile, car	10
héichìhng	起程	V: to start a journey, to set out	22
hèimong	希望	N/V: hope/ expect, hope	20
héisàn	起身	VO: get up	17
héisáu	起首	V: start, begin	24
hèng	輕	SV: be light (opp. heavy)	21
heui	去	V: go,go away, go to	10
heuigāai	去街	VO: go out (onto the street)	10
hèung	香	SV: fragrant	19
heung	向	CV: towards (in the direction of)	21
Hèunggóng	香港	PW: Hongkong	10
hèunghá	鄉下	N: the country (rural); one's native place	24
hìngdaih	兄弟	N: brothers	21
Hòh	何	N: Ho (surname)	10
hòh	河	N: river	21
hohk	學	V/AV: learn; study/ learn to, study how to	10
hohkhaauh	學校	N/PW: school	9
hohksāang	學生	N: student	8
hòi	開	V: open; start away (train, bus, ship)	16

-hòi	開	P: away from, away	13
		RVE: ending of RV	19
hói	海	N: sea	21
hòihohk	開學	VO: start of school	22
hòisàm	開心	SV: amused, happy, contented	18
hóu	好	SV: be good, well, O.K., fine	1
		A: very, quite	1
		AV: may, should (used only in questions)	11
		RVE: ending of RV	19
...hóu ma?	好嗎	IE: ...all right? Would you...?	4
Hóu noi m̀gin	好耐唔見	IE: Haven't seen you for a long time	10
hóugéinìn	好幾年	TW: a good many year	13
houh	號	M: day (of month); number (house, room etc.)	17
hòuhjí, hòuh hòuhjí	毫子	M: ten-cent unit	6
		N: dime, ten-cent piece	6
hóujoih	好在	MA: fortunately	23
hóusēng boh	好聲啲播	IE: be careful	23
hóusiu	好笑	SV: funny, ridiculous	23
hóuwáan	好玩	SV: amusing, interesting	14
hóuwah	好話	IE: you are welcome; kind of you to say so	4
hóuyéung	好樣	SV: good-looking	13
hóyíh	可以	AV: can (be permitted), may	7
hùhng	紅	SV: be red	24
hùhngsīk	紅色	N: red color	24

J

-jáan	盞	M: measure for lamp, light	19
jàang	掙	V: lack, be short; differ by; owe	17
jaatjyuh	紮住	RV: to tie up	22
jái	仔	N: son	8
-jái	仔	P: diminutive suffix to nouns	20
jài	擠	V: put	14
jàihái		V: put at	
jài...hái	擠喺	Ph: put something at	
jàm	斟	V: pour	24
jànhaih	眞係	A: certainly, really	10,16
Jàu	周	N: Chou, chow (surname)	8
jáu	走	V: run; leave (to depart)	.11
jáu	酒	N: wine	15
jáudim	酒店	N: hotel	12
jáugā	酒家	N: restaurant	15
jáugún	酒館	N: restaurant	15
jauh	就	A: then (introducing subsequent action), at once; only, just	15
Jauh gám lā!	就咁喇	IE: Good, let's do it that way	13
jauhhaih	就係	EV: is (more emphatic)	16
jáulèih jáuheui	走來走去	Ph: run back and forth	11
jauhsyun...dōu...	就算…都	A: even if...still...; even if...; nevertheless	21
je	借	V: to borrow	19
je...béi	借俾	V: to lend	19

jē	啫	P: that's all, only; not at all (negative)	7
jek	隻	M: measure for ship, boat; hand, foot; domestic animals, etc.	10
		M: kind, brand (for gasoline, cigarette, medicine, etc.)	19
		M: measure for fork, spoon	15
jeng	正	SV: accurate, correct	22
-jeuhk	着	RVE: ending of RV	19
-jeuhng	丈	M: ten Chinese feet (1.41 in English inches)	21
jeui	最	A: the most, -est	20,23
jeuk	着	V: wear	14
Jèung	張	N: Chang, cheung (surname)	5
-jèung	張	M: measure for table, chair, paper, etc.	3
jèunglòih	將來	MA: in the future	18
ji	至	A: 'not...until', 'must...','then and only then'; only	18
-jì	枝	M: measure for writing instruments, etc.	3
jìchìhn	之前	MA: ...before...;...ago	18
jì(dou)	知道	V: know about, know	5
jih	字	N: word, character (written word)	7
jìhauh	之後	MA: after...	18
jihchùhng	自從	MA: ever since; since	24
jihgéi, jihgēi	自己	N: self, oneself	14
jihjoih	自在	SV: comfortable	18,20
jihmjím	漸漸	MA: gradually	18

jihnghaih	淨係	MA: only	22
jihyìhn	自然	SV: comfortable	22
jīkhāak	卽刻	A: immediately, at once	14
jīkhaih	卽係	A: is precisely, is (emphatic), is none other than	16
jímúi	姊妹	N: sisters	21
jíng	整	V: to repair, to fix, to prepare(dishes)	19
jingwah	正話	MA: just a while ago	17
Jìngyuht	正月	TW: the first month of the Lunar year	13
jip	接	V: meet; receive (a letter)	10
jìu	朝	M: morning	17
jìu(tàuh)jóu	朝頭早	TW: morning	17
jó	左	SV: left	21
-jó	咗	P: verb suffix, indicating completed action	12
-joh	座	M: measure for storied building - 'láu'	9
johkmáan	昨晚	TW: last night	12
johkyaht	昨日	TW: yesterday	13
johkyahtjìu	昨日朝	TW: yesterday morning	12
joi	再	A: once more, ...more, again	16,23
joigin	再見	IE: goodbye	2
jóu	早	SV: early	17
jóuchāan	早餐	N: breakfast	17
jouh	做	V: do, be, act as	7/23

jouh mātyéh a?   IE: What is the matter?   9
　　做乜嘢呀？
jouh māt(yeh) sihgon a?IE: what happened?   9
　　做乜嘢事幹呀？
jouhmātyéh 做乜嘢   MA: why   18

jouhsàangyi 做生意   VO: do business, be in business   7

jouhsih   做事   VO: do (deeds, work), work (intransitive) 7

jóusàhn   早晨   IE: good morning   2

juhkyúhwah 俗語話   IE: there is a saying   23

juhng   重   A: still, yet   8

juhnghaih   重係   A: still, as before, as usual   16

jūk   捉   V: to catch, to net   19

jūng   鐘   N: clock, bell   3

jūngdím   鐘點   N: hour   17

jūnggāan   中間   PW: the center   21

Jùnggwok   中國   N: China   2

Jùngmàn, Jùngmán 中文   N: Chinese (language)   20

jùngyi   鍾意   V: to like, be fond of   4

jyú   煮   V: to cook   8

jyúfaahn   煮飯   VO: cook (intransitive)   8

jyuh   住   V: stay, live (at a place)   11

jyuhjí   住址   N: address   17

jyun or jyún 轉   V: to turn to   21

jyūtjì   卒之   MA: finally   22

K

kàhmmáan	噙晚	TW: last night	12
kàhmyaht	噙日	TW: yesterday	12
kàhmyahtjìu	噙日朝	TW: yesterday morning	12
káhn	近	SV: be near	21
kàhnlihk	勤力	SV: industrious, diligent	23
kàuhkèih	求其	MA: at one's convenience, pleasure; any (whatever)	23
kéi	企	PW: house of family (cannot use as a true noun)	9
kéih	企	V: stand	11
kéuih	佢	PN: he, she, him, her	1
kéuihdeih	佢哋	PN: they, them	1
kìnggái	傾偈	VO: chat, converse	14

L

la	喇	P: indicating changed status	8
lā	啦	P: sentence final, used with mild commands, suggestions, request; or to express final decision	11
làahm	藍	SV: be blue	24
làahmsīk	藍色	N: blue color	24
láahn	懶	SV: lazy	19
laahn	爛	SV: be broken; rotten; overripe	19
láahng	冷	SV: be cold	20
làh	嗱	P: fusion of 'la' and 'àh'	8

làih	來	V: come	10
làihbaai	禮拜	N: week	13
Làihbaaigéi a? 禮拜幾呀？		Ph: Which day in the week?	13
Làihbaailuhk	禮拜六	TW: Saturday	13
Làihbaaing	禮拜五	TW: Friday	13
Làihbaaisàam	禮拜三	TW: Wednesday	13
Làihbaaisei	禮拜四	TW: Thursday	13
Làihbaaiyāt	禮拜一	TW: Monday	13
Làihbaaiyih	禮拜二	TW: Tuesday	13
Làihbaaiyaht	禮拜日	TW: Sunday	13
láu	樓	N: building with two or more floors; storey, floor	9
làuhhah	樓下	PW: downstairs; the main floor	9
làuhseuhng	樓上	PW: upstairs; second floor	9
léhngdáai	領帶	N: necktie	19
lèih	來	V: come	10
lèih	離	CV: distant from	21
Léih	李	N: Li, Lee (surname)	5
-léih	里	M: a Chinese mile (1/3 of an English mile)	21
lèihhòi	離開	V: to leave (a place)	21
leihhoih	利害	SV: severe; terrible	20
leng	靚	SV: be pretty, handsome, good looking	1
léuhng	兩	NU: two or couple	3
léuhng-sàamchi 兩三次		Ph: a couple of time	16

lèuhng(song)	涼爽	SV: cool	20
leuhnjeuhn 〔論盡〕		SV: awkward (unskillful, clumsy)	23
léuihbihn	裡邊	PW: inside, in, within	9
léuihgún	旅館	N: hotel	12
léuihhàhng	旅行	N/V: journey/ to travel	22
-léung	兩	M: an ounce (1/16 of a catty)	21
-lìhng (lèhng)	零	NU: zero (where one or more digits in the middle of a number are zeros, 'lìhng' is inserted)	6
lihng(dou)	令	CV: to cause	24
lo	囉	P: indicating changed status	8
ló	攞	V: get, fetch	13
lòhkleih (or--heui)	落來	V: down	11
lohktòhng	落堂	VO: finish class	16
lohkyúh	落雨	VO: raining	14,19
Lohsáang	羅省	PW: Los Angeles	22
-lóu	佬	P: suffix means 'man' (fellow)	20
lóuh	老	SV: old	20
louh	路	N: road	17
lóuhdauh	老〔竇〕	N: daddy, father	16
lóuhmóu	老母	N: mother	16
luhk	六	NU: six	3
luhk	綠	SV: be green	24
luhksīk	綠色	N: green color	24
Luhkyuht	六月	TW: June	13

<u>M</u>

m̀	唔	P: negative prefix to unmodified verb	1
ma	嗎	P: sentence particle; make a statement into a yes-no question	1
Má	馬	N: (surname)	12
máai	買	V: buy	2
maai	賣	V: sell, sell for, for sell	6
-màai	埋	P: up to, over to, against; near (only with verb of motion)	13
-màai	埋	P: indicating 'with' 'along with', 'also with'	14
-màai	埋	RVE: ending of RV	19
máai yéh	買啲野	V: shop	7
maakdaaih	擘大	V: to open (the eye, etc.) wide	22
maakhòi	擘開	V: to open (the eye, etc.)	22
máan	晚	M: night	17
maan	萬	NU/ M: ten thousand	6
maan	慢	SV: slow	16
máancháan	晚餐	N: super	17
maanmáan	慢慢	A: slowly, gradually	18
maanmāan hàahng	慢慢行	IE: depart slowly	18
máanhāak	晚黑	TW: night, evening, nighttime	17
máantáu	晚頭	TW: night, evening, nighttime	17
máantàuhhāk	晚頭黑	TW: night, evening, nighttime	17
Maksāigō	墨西哥	PW: Mexico	21

makséuibāt	墨水筆	N: fountain pen	16
màmā	媽媽	N: mother	16
màn	聞	V: to smell	19
man	問	V: to ask	9
-mān	文	M: dollar unit (used for whole dollars)	6
manhauh	問候	V: to ask after the health of (someone); to send kind regards to...	24
māt(yéh)	乜嘢	N: what (mātyéh is sometime contracted to mē'éh or mè)	5
Mātyéh wá	嘢話	IE: What	21
m̀dākhàahn	唔得閒	SV: busy	11
mē	咩	P: question ending expressing surprise, doubt, etc.	10
mei (or meichàhng)	未	P: negative indicating, that action has not yet been performed	12
mei	味	M: measure for dish of food	15
Mei dāk	未得	IE: not yet	12
Mei gau; gau la!	未夠 夠喇	IE: not yet; it's enough!	12
Méigwok	美國	N: America (U.S.A.)	2
méng	名	N: name	16
m̀gáamdòng	唔敢當	IE: you are flattering me! (lit. I am not entitled to...)	11
m̀gányiu	唔緊要	IE: never mind, it doesn't matter	15
m̀geidāk	唔記得	V: unable to remember - forget	16
m̀ginjó	唔見咗	V: lost; be lost, become lost	12
M̀gòi	唔該	Ph: Please, thank you (for a favor); sorry; excuse me	4

m̀gòi néi dánghah 唔該你等吓		IE: please wait a minute	11
m̀gòisaai 唔該哂		IE: thank you for everything; thank you very much	4
m̀haih 唔係		Ph: negative used instead of 'm̀' when verb is precede by an adverb, e.g. m̀haih géi..., is not very...	1
m̀hóu 唔好		AV: better not; don't (imperative), should not	11
m̀hóuyisi 唔好意思		IE: I'm sorry	13
m̀hóuyisi 唔好意思		SV: embarassed; embarassing, ashamed to	24
mìngbaahk 明白		V/SV: to understand; be clear (lit. understandable)	16,24
m̀jí 唔止		MA: not merely...; not only...; not as little as you say	23
m̀jihyìhn 唔自然		SV: not feeling well; ill, uncomfortable	22
m̀ngāam 唔啱		IE: it is not correct	5
mong 望		V: hope, expect	20
móu 冇		V: have not	3
móucho la 冇錯喇		IE: that's right	23
móu mantàih 冇問題		IE: no problem at all	13
móuchàn 母親		N: mother	16
móugányiu 冇緊要		IE: never mind; it doesn't matter	15
móugéinói 冇幾耐		IE: after a while (lit. not very long)	11
móusówaih 冇所謂		IE: it doesn't matter	23
mòuleuhn 無論		MA: no matter..., whether... or not	16
móuyuhng 冇用		SV: useless	16

m̀sái haakhei	唔使客氣	IE: don't mention it; please don't bother	4
m̀sáim̀gòi	唔使唔該	IE: don't mention it; you are welcome	4
m̀sédāk	唔捨得	V/AV: can't bear to part with/ be grudging about doing something	22
múi	妹	N: younger sister	16
múi	每	SP: each, every	13
mùn	門	N: door, gate	19
mùnpàaih	門牌	N: number of house	17

N

nàam	南	BF: south	21
Nàamgìng	南京	PW: Nanking	18
nàan	難	SV: be difficult	7
nāp	粒	M: measure for 'faahn' - grain	7
nàu	嬲	SV: angry, getting angry	16
nē	呢	P: a question particle	4
néi	你	PN: you (singular)	1
néi wah...	你話	Ph: Do you think...? Don't you think...	16
néideih	你哋	Ph: you (plural)	1
néui	女	N: daughter	8
néui	女	BF: woman, girl-	8
Ǹg	吳	N: Wu (surname)	10
ńg	五	NU: five	3
ngāam	啱	SV: be right; fit	5,17

ngāam la	啱喇	IE: yes, that is right	5
ngāam ma?	啱嗎	IE: is this correct?	5
ngāamŋgāam	啱啱	MA: just (a moment ago), luckily	17
ngaan	晏	SV: late (in the day)	17
ngáan	眼	N: eye	22
ngáanfan	眼瞓	SV: sleepy	23
ngaangaau	晏覺	N: a nap	17
ngaanjau	晏晝	TW/N: noontime/ lunch	17
ngàansīk	顏色	N: color	22
ngái	矮	SV: be low, be short (opp. gòu)	20
ngàihím	危險	SV/N: be dangerous/ danger	22
ngán	銀	N: money (vernacular)	6
ngànchín	銀錢	N: dollar	6
ngànhòhng	銀行	N: bank	19
ngó	我	PN: I, me	1
ngo	餓	SV: hungry	15
ngódeih	我哋	PN: we, us	1
ngoi	愛	V: want	2
ngoibihn	外邊	PW: outside	9
ngoilèih	愛來	CV: used (or needed) for	16
ngònlohk	安樂	SV: contented, comfortable	18
ngūk	屋	N: house	9
ngūkkéi	屋企	PW: house of family	9
Ngyuht	五月	TW: May	13

nī	呢	SP: this (here)	4
nīdī	呢啲	N: these	6
nīk	(搦)	V: hold (in one hand); hold (in general); bring or take	13
-nìn (or nín)	年	M: year	13
nìng	搦	V: hold; bring or take	13
nìnnìn	年年	TW: every year	13
Nīuyēuk	紐約	PW: New York	21
noi (or nói)	耐	SV: a long time	13

O

-ōnsí	安士	M: ounce	21

P

pa	怕	V: to be afraid of...	20
paak	拍	V: to pat; to clap	22
pàhngyáuh	朋友	N: friend	4
pèhng	平	SV: inexpensive, cheap	18
peiyùh(wah)	譬如	MA: for instance, if, in case	16
pìhngngòn	平安	SV: peaceful, safe	21
pìhngsèuhng	平常	SV/MA: be ordinary/ ordinarily	23
pìhngsìh	平時	MA: usually, ordinarily	18
pòhngbīn	旁邊	PW: the side of, flank, beside	21
poutáu	舖頭	N/PW: store, shop	9

S

sà'ah	卅	NU: thirty (abbr. form)	3
-saai	晒	P: verb sufix, used as 'all' or 'whole'	12
sàam	三	NU: three	3
sāam	衫	N: clothes, dress, gown, coat, suit	14
Sàamfàahnsíh	三藩市	PW: San Francisco	21
sàamgogwāt	三個骨	Ph: three quarters	17
Sàamyuht	三月	TW: Marth	13
sàan	閂	V: to close (door, gate)	19
sàandéng	山頂	N: summit	19
sáangsèhng	省城	N: capital city of a province; it also means Canton	24
sàangyaht	生日	N: birthday	13
sàangyi	生意	N: business of buying and selling	7
sahp	十	NU: ten	3
Sahpyātyuht	十一月	TW: November	13
Sahpyihyuht	十二月	TW: December	13
Sahpyuht	十月	TW: October	13
sài	西	BF: west	21
sái	使	V: use, spend CV: to send; tell (someone to do something) AV: need to, have to	15
sái	洗	V: to wash	22
sái	駛	V: drive (a car), operate a plane	22
sai	細	SV: be small, little	4
sàichāan	西餐	N: Western food	7

saimānjái	細蚊仔	N: child, children	5
sāmgāp	心急	SV: be impatient	24
sàn	新	SV: be new	6
sànfú	辛苦	SV: be taxing, exhausting; causing suffering	24
sàntái	身體	N: health, body	22
sáu	手	N: hand	21
sau	瘦	SV: be thin	20
-sáu	首	M: measure for 'gō' - song	7
sàuh	愁	V: worry	23
sāumēi	收尾	A/MA: afterwards, later on	18
sé	寫	V: to write	7
sédāk	捨得	SV/AV: to be willing to part with (something)/ to be generous (in doing something), not be stingy (about doing something)	22
sèhng	城	N: wall city, city, town	9
sèhng-	成	NU: a whole, entire	23
sei	四	NU: four	3
Seiyuht	四月	TW: April	13
séjih	寫字	VO: to write	7
séng	醒	SV: awake	17
seuhngbihn	上邊	PW: top, above, on	9
seuhnggo láihbaai	上個禮拜	Ph: last week	13
seuhnggo yuht	上個月	Ph: last month	13
Seuhnghói	上海	PW: Shanghai	10

seuhngjau	上晝	TW: forenoon	17
séuhnglèih (or -heui) 上來		V: up	11
séuhngtòhng	上堂	VO: go to class	16
séui	水	N: water	24
seui	歲	N: years (old)	16
sèuihjì	誰知	MA: who would have thought (it) ?	22
sèuiyìhn	雖然	MA: although	22
seun	信	N: letter (M: fùng)	13
seun	信	V: believe	21
séung	想	V: think of, think about	6
séung	想	AV: consider (doing something); plan to, want to, wish to, would like to	6
sèung	雙	M: measure for chopsticks	15
sih, sihgon, sihchìhng 事, 事幹, 事情		N: task, undertaking, project, job	7
sihk	食	V: eat	7
sihkfaahn	食飯	VO: eat (intransitive)	7
sihkyīn	食烟	VO: smoke (intransitive)	23
sìhngjái	繩仔	N: cord, string	21
sìhsìh	時時	A: often, always, frequently	18
sīk	識	V/AV: know (a person, subject, etc.); recognize; become acquainted with/ know how to	12
sìmàn	斯文	SV: be cultured	23
sìn	先	A: first (in Cantonese sìn as an adverb can be used after the verb)	14

sīn	仙	N: cent	6
síng	繩	N: rope	21
sing	姓	EV/N: be surnamed/ surname	5
singdaanjit	聖誕節	N: Christmas	24
sìnji	先至	A: then, and only, then	18
sìnsàang	先生	N: Mr., sir, gentleman; teacher; husband (polite)	5
síu	少	SV: be little, few; less	6
siu	笑	V: to laugh	23
síujé	小姐	N: miss, daughter (polite); lady (unmarried)	5
síusyut	小說	N: novel	22
siuwá	笑話	N: joke	24
só	鎖	V/N: lock	19
sósìh	鎖匙	N: key	11
sóyíh	所以	MA: therefore, so	8
sung	送	V: deliver (a things), escort, send off, take (a person somewhere); present (a gift)	13
sung	餸	N: dish of food	15
syù	書	N: book	2
-syu	處	P: a place	9
syúga	暑假	N: summer vacation	22
syùhn	船	N: ship, boat, steamship	10
syutwah	說話	N: spoken words	7

T

Tàahnhèungsàan	檀香山	PW: Honolulu	21
taai	太	A: too	1
tāai	呔	N: necktie	19
Taaipìhngyèuhng	太平洋	PW: Pacific Ocean	21
taaitáai	太太	N: Mrs., madam; wife (polite); lady (married)	5
taam	探	V: vist	10
tái	睇	V: look, look at, read	2
táigin	睇見	RV: see	12
tái-mùnháu	睇門口	V: to take care of a house	23
táu	唞	V: rest	13
tàuh-	頭	BF: first (ordinalizing prefix denotes the first one or more persons or things)	16
tàuhsīn	頭先	MA: just a while ago	18
tèng	聽	V: listen to	8
tèngginwah	聽見話	IE: hear(d) it said that	15
tèngwah	聽話	SV: obedient	23
tìhng	停	V: stop; park	21
tìm	添	P: a sentence final meaning 'more' or 'also'	16
tíng	挺	M: kind (for sickness)	22
tíng	挺	M: kind, sort of (measure for 'sàangyi' - business, a kind of business	7
tìngjìu, tìngjìujóu	嚟朝 嚟朝早	TW: tomorrow morning	11

tìngmáan	聽晚	TW: tomorrow night	11
tìngyaht	聽日	TW: tomorrow	10
tìnhei	天氣	N: weather	10
Tìnjèun	天津	PW: Tientsin	18
-tìuh .	條	M: measure for 'gāai' - street, 'sósìh' - key,; necktie, rope, road, etc.	10
tòhngchāan	唐餐	N: Chinese food	7
Tòhngyàhnfauh	唐人埠	PW: Chinatown	22
tói (or tòih)	枱	N: table, desk	3
Tòihwāan	台灣	PW: Formosa	21
tòng	湯	N: soup	15
tong	趟	M: a time or occasion	16
tóuhngo, ngo	肚餓	SV: hungry	15,23
tùhng	同	SV: be the same	20
tùhng(màai)	同 (埋)	CV: with, and, for	14
tyut	脫	M: suit for clothes	14
tyut	脫	V: to undress; to take off	23

<u>W</u>

wá	話	N: spoken language or dialect	7
waahkhaih	或係	MA: or (as in whether...or...)	17
waahkjé	或者	MA: may, maybe; perhaps; or (only used in answer)	17
waaih	壞	SV: bad (in character); (things) out of order	23

wáan	玩	V: play, enjoy or amuse oneself, play (musical instruments)	14
wah	話	V: say (usually used in indirect speech), think (expressing opinion)	7
wái	位	M: for person (polite form)	8
waih, wái	喂	P: hello! (on the telephone) Hey! (only 'waih' can be used in this sense)	11
wán	搵	V: look for; find	9
wìhnghahng	榮幸	SV: be privileged (to do something), feel privileged (that...)	24
Wòhng	黃	N: Wong, Huang, (surname)	5
wòhng	黃	SV: be yellow	24
wóhngsí	往時	MA: formerly, in the past	18
wòhngsīk	黃色	N: yellow color	24
wúih	會	AV: can (know how to), be able to; may, would, likely	7,18
wùihseun (béi...)	回信畀	VO: to send a letter in return (to...)	24
wún	碗	N/M: bowl	15

Y

yah	廿	NU: twenty (abbr. form)	3
yàhn	人	N: man, person	4
yàhndeih	人哋	N: other peoples	23
yàhplèih	入來	V: in	11
-yaht	日	M: day	13
Yahtbún	日本	PW: Japan	18

yahttáu	日頭	TW/N:	daytime/ sunshine	17
yahtyaht	日日	Ph:	every day	13
yáih	吟	SV:	be bad or poor (in quality)	24
yám	飲	V:	drink	15
Yandouh	印度	PW:	India	18
yànwaih	因爲	MA:	because	8
yāt	一	NU:	one	3
yāt (plus M) 一		N:	each (e.g. 'Sàammān yātgo' - Three dollars each. 'yāt' may be omitted)	6
yātbun	一牛	N:	a half	6
yātchái (or yātchàih) 一齊		A:	together	14
yātdihng	一定	A:	definitely, certainly, sure	11
yātgogwāt	一個 (骨)	Ph:	one quarter	17
yātguhng	一共	A:	altogether, all told	22
yātheung dōu... 一向都 …		Ph:	all along; have always...	18
yātheung m̀ (or Móu) 一向唔		Ph:	never have (done something)	18
yātjahngāan 一陣間		TW:	(in) a moment, (after) a short while	11
yātlouh seuhnfùng 一路順風		IE:	a pleasant journey (to you)	18
yātyeuhng 一樣		SV:	same (kind)	20
Yatyuht	一月	TW:	January	13
yáuh	有	V:	have	3
yauh	右	SV:	right	21
yauh	又	A:	again	11
Yáuh māt jígaau a? 有乜指敎		IE:	Is there anything I can do for you? (Lit. Any instructions?)	11

yáuhchín	有錢	SV: be rich, wealthy	6
yáuh(yāt)dī	有(一)啲	N: some, a little (Lit. there are some) there is a little)	6
yáuhsàm	有心	IE: thank you for inquiring	4
yáuhsìh	有時	MA: sometimes	17,20
yáuhyuhng	有用	SV: useful, helpful	16
yéh	嘢	N: thing	5
yeuhk	藥	N: medicine	22
yeuhkhaih	若係	MA: if, in case	14
yeuhkṁhaih	若唔係	MA: otherwise	23
yeuhng	樣	M: kind, sort	14
yèuhnghóng	洋行	N: foreign firm	24
yéung	樣	N: style, appearance	13
yí	椅	N: chair	3
yih	二	NU: two	3
yih	易	P: prefixed to functive verbs, means 'easy to...'	20
yíhchìhn ...yíhchìhn	以前	MA: formerly, before, previously, ...before....; ago	18
yìhgā	而家	TW: now, at present, at this time	7
yíhgìng	已經	MA: already	12
yíhhauh ...yíhhauh	以後	MA: (t)hereafter, afterwards, from now on, after...	18
yihk, yihkdōu	亦	A: also; too, as well	8
yihngdāk	認得	V: to recognize	23

yiht	熱	SV: be hot	20
yíhwàih	以爲	CV: to think that, suppose (erroneously)	22
Yihyuht	二月	TW: February	13
yīkwaahk	抑或	MA: or (as in 'whether...or...')	17
yīn(jái)	烟	N: cigarette	23
yìngfahn (or yìnggòi)		MA: ought to, should	17
Yìnggwok	應份 英國	PW: England	14, 21
yíngóng	演講	V/N: to give a speech/ a speech	24
Yìngmàn, Yìngmán 英文		N: English (language)	8
yīsāng	醫生	N: physician	24
yisi	意思	N: meaning, idea, intention	16
yiu (or ngoi) 要		V: want	2
yiu	要	AV: want to; have to, must, need to, would like to, be going to	7
yiulèih	要來	CV: used (or needed) for	16
yú	魚	N: fish	15
yúh	雨	N: rain	14
yuhbeih	預備	V: prepare	19
yuhdóu	遇到	V: to meet with; to encounter	21
yùhgwó	如果	MA: if, in case	14
yuhk	肉	N: meat	20
-yùhn	完	P: verb suffix indicates the finishing of an action	12
yuhng	用	V/N: use	16

yuhnglèih	用來	CV: used for	16
yùhngyih (or yih)	容易	A: easy/ easily, easy to	20
yùhnleuhng	原諒	V: to excuse	24
yúhn	遠	SV: be far	21
yùhnlòih	原來	MA: so...after all...	24
yuht	月	N: month	13

SPEAK CANTONESE

INDEX OF PATTERNS & NOTES